COMPLETE YEAR 2

Weekly Learning Activities

Thinking Kids™
Carson-Dellosa Publishing LLC
Greensboro, North Carolina

Thinking Kids
An imprint of Carson-Dellosa Publishing LLC
P.O. Box 35665
Greensboro, NC 27425 USA

© 2014 Carson-Dellosa Publishing LLC. Except as permitted under the United States Copyright Act, no part of this publication may be reproduced, stored, or distributed in any form or by any means (mechanically, electronically, recording, etc.) without the prior written consent of Carson-Dellosa Publishing LLC. Thinking Kids is an imprint of Carson-Dellosa Publishing LLC.

Printed in the USA • All rights reserved.

ISBN 978-1-48380-192-6
01-153147784

Table of Contents

Table of Contents

Table of Contents

Introduction to *Complete Year: Grade 2*

The *Complete Year* series has been designed by educators to provide an entire school year's worth of practice pages, teaching suggestions, and multi-sensory activities to support your child's learning at home. Handy organizers are included to help students and parents stay on track and to let you see at a glance the important skills for each quarter and each week of the academic year.

A variety of resources are included to help you provide high-quality learning experiences during this important year of your child's development.

Suggested Calendar (Page 7)
Use this recommended timetable to plan learning activities for your child during all 36 weeks of the school year.

A Guide to School Skills and Subject Areas for Second Grade: Reading and Language Arts, Math, Science, Social Studies (Page 8)
Refer to this useful guide for information about what your child will be learning this school year, what to expect from your second grader, and how to help your child develop skills in each subject area.

Quarter Introductions (Pages 14, 108, 202, 296)
Four brief introductions outline the skills covered in practice pages for each nine-week grading period of the school year. In addition, they include a variety of ideas for multi-sensory learning activities in each subject area. These active, hands-on projects are fun for parents and children to do together and emphasize real-world applications for school skills.

Weekly Skill Summaries (Example: Page 17)
Thirty-six handy charts precede the practice pages for each week and give a snapshot of the skills covered. In addition, they provide ideas for fun, multi-sensory learning activities for each subject area.

Practice Pages (Example: Page 18)
Nine practice pages are provided each week for a total of over 300 skill-building activities to help your child succeed this year.

Quarter Check-Ups (Pages 107, 201, 295, 389)
Four informal assessment pages allow students to do a quick self-check of the important skills emphasized during the previous nine weeks. Parents can use these pages to see at a glance the skills their children have mastered.

Suggested *Complete Year* Calendar*	
First Quarter: Weeks 1–9 (First nine-week grading period of the school year, usually August–October)	During Each Nine-Week Quarter: • Read the **Quarter Introduction** to get an overview of the skills and subject areas emphasized. Choose several multi-sensory learning activities you plan to do with your child this quarter.
Second Quarter: Weeks 10–18 (Second nine-week grading period of the school year, usually October–December)	• Each week, glance at the **Weekly Skill Summary** to see targeted skills. Make a quick plan for the practice pages and multi-sensory learning activities your child will complete.
Third Quarter: Weeks 19–27 (Third nine-week grading period of the school year, usually January–March)	• Choose **Practice Pages** that emphasize skills your child needs to work on. Each page should take 10 minutes or less to complete.
Fourth Quarter: Weeks 28–36 (Fourth nine-week grading period of the school year, usually April–June)	• Ask your child to check the boxes on the **Quarter Check-Up** to show what skills he or she has mastered. Praise your child's progress and take note of what he or she still needs to work on.
* This calendar provides a schedule for using *Complete Year* during a typical nine-month academic calendar. If your child attends a year-round school or a school with a different schedule, you can easily adapt this calendar by counting the weeks your child attends school and dividing by four.	

A Guide to School Skills for Second Grade

This guide provides background information about the skills and subject areas that are important for success in second grade. Tips are provided for helping your child develop in each curricular area.

Complete Year supports skills included in the Grade 2 Common Core State Standards for English Language Arts and Mathematics, which have been adopted by most U.S. states. A complete guide to these standards may be found at www.corestandards.org.

In addition, activities in *Complete Year* support the study of science and social studies topics appropriate for second grade.

Reading and Language Arts

Reading

Teach reading with texts that fit your child's ability and interests, using a variety of books, children's magazines, Web sites, charts and graphs, and other materials. Make regular visits to your local library so that there is always something interesting to read at your home. Choose two kinds of books—books at or near your child's reading level that can be read independently, and those at a higher reading level for read-aloud time.

Even after your child becomes an independent reader, it will benefit him or her greatly when you read aloud together every day. Read a variety of books aloud, including realistic stories, fantasy stories, adventure stories, mystery stories, and nonfiction books about topics of interest. See page 394 for a list of books that will appeal to second graders.

Before reading, activate your child's prior knowledge of the book's subject. For example, discuss the stages of a butterfly's life cycle and what caterpillars eat before reading Eric Carle's *The Very Hungry Caterpillar*. During reading, stop occasionally to make predictions, discuss the meaning of new words, and discuss confusing parts. After reading, talk about what you liked and didn't like about the story.

Look for opportunities to teach the following skills as you read with your child.

- Word Recognition and Vocabulary Development
  When your child encounters a new word in reading, encourage him or her to use different strategies to find its meaning:
  - Look at the surrounding text for context clues;
  - Look at the syntax of the sentence and use the position of the new word as a clue;
  - Sound out the word phonetically;
  - Ask an adult or other knowledgeable person to provide a definition; or
  - Look up the word in a dictionary.

- Phonics
  Look for opportunities to teach the following skills in the context of words found in books: beginning, middle, and ending sounds and spellings; consonant blends and digraphs (as in **tr**ain and **sh**ip); rhyming words; and long and short vowel sounds and spellings. Keep lists of words that have different vowel sounds: **short a**, **long a**, **short e**, **long e**, etc. Encourage your child to break longer words into syllables, identifying one or more vowel letters in each syllable.

- Reading Comprehension
  In second grade, your child will use his or her ability to read longer texts to greatly expand reading comprehension, or understanding the full meaning of what he or she reads. He or she will learn to recognize cause and effect relationships in different situations, draw conclusions, and infer information that is implied but not directly stated in a text. Your child will learn to read, write, and perform a series of events in sequential order. He or she will distinguish fiction and nonfiction and fact from opinion. As your child progresses, he or she will recognize important elements of a text such as the main idea, supporting details, characters, settings, and plots.

  To aid reading comprehension, take time to talk to your child about books he or she has read. Ask questions such as "What do you think the characters meant by…" or "Did that happen before or after…." After reading a good book, your child may have interest in doing a project based on what he or she learned. Some project ideas are making time lines, making new illustrations for the story, writing an alternate ending, or writing a letter to the author.

Language Skills

Language skills are often taught in the context of reading and writing. When you read together or look at your child's written work, take the opportunity to point out individual words, sentences, and punctuation marks on the page and talk about them. This will give your child a deeper understanding of how language works. Focus on the following topics.

- Spelling
  In second grade, your child will be encouraged to move away from "invented spelling" (or attempting to spell words the way they sound) toward "conventional spelling," which follows special rules and patterns. A first grader may be praised for spelling **luv**, but second graders will begin to learn that the correct spelling is **love**. Gently encourage your child to spell words correctly and point out interesting patterns in the spellings of words.

- Vocabulary Development
  During second grade, your child will study types of words such as nouns, pronouns, verbs, adjectives, adverbs, compound words (such as **sandbox**), contractions (such as **don't**), words with prefixes and suffixes added to a root word (such as **undo** and **trying**), synonyms (such as **pretty** and **beautiful**), and antonyms (such as **noisy** and **silent**). Make sure your child can provide an example of each type of word.

- Sentences
  Your child will learn to identify the subject and predicate of a sentence and combine two short sentences into one longer sentence. He or she will review types of sentences: statements, questions, exclamations, and commands. Your son or daughter will be encouraged to write complete sentences that begin with capital letters and end with punctuation marks.

Writing

As the year progresses, your child will be able to produce a piece of writing that stays on topic, includes supporting ideas, and has a beginning, middle, and end. Your child will write stories, fact-based reports, and pieces that give an opinion. Encourage your child to write frequently at home, experimenting with different formats such as traditional letters and notes, e-mails, illustrated stories, and diaries or journals. Keep a folder of your child's writing. From time to time, encourage your child to improve an old story or look over the year's work to celebrate his or her growth as a writer.

Speaking and Listening

Good speaking and listening skills are essential to school success. By paying careful attention to what is being said, your child will not only learn more but will develop the skill of being a good conversationalist as well. Make sure to provide ample opportunities for your child to listen to songs, poetry, and stories.

Math

Math is everywhere in your child's world. Encourage your child to think about how math is used in daily activities such as helping in the kitchen, playing games, using blocks and other toys, and doing household chores. Let your child see that you use math every day, too, when you shop, pay bills, keep a calendar, or make home repairs. When helping with math, move from the concrete to the abstract. For example, help with subtraction first by modeling a problem with pennies or other small items, then by drawing pictures to show the problem, and finally by solving the problem with numbers on paper. Whenever possible, relate math concepts to your child's experiences. Focus on these second-grade math skills.

- Skip-Counting
  Help your child begin with any number and count forward and backward by ones, twos, fives, and tens. Encourage your child to count while clapping, jumping rope, or doing other rhythmic activities.

- Addition and Subtraction Without Regrouping
  Make sure your child has mastered basic single-digit addition and subtraction facts. Flash cards are a good tool for developing speed and memorization. As your child advances to two- and three-digit problems, point out that these are quick and easy to do once basic math facts are memorized.

- Place Value
  Help your child understand that the digits in numbers represent quantities of ones, tens, and hundreds. A number such as **368** has eight ones, six tens, and three hundreds. Be creative in finding ways for your child to use manipulatives to represent place value. To show a ten, your child might use a graph paper cut-out of ten squares, ten stacked interlocking blocks, or ten craft sticks bound with a rubber band. Let your child use such materials to model a variety of numbers.

A Guide to School Skills for Second Grade, cont.

- Addition and Subtraction with Regrouping
  Your child will solve problems that require him or her to "carry" a digit to the next place (when adding) or to "borrow" a digit from the next place (when subtracting). Help your child discuss each step in the process. It will help greatly if your child has a firm understanding of place value and if the manipulatives described above are used to model example problems.

- Word Problems
  Your child will use addition and subtraction to solve word problems. You can help at home by inventing word problems that relate to your child's activities and interests.

- Working with Patterns
  Encourage your child to notice patterns in the environment. Give your child number patterns such as 1, 3, 5, 7, and ask him or her to add the next number and state the rule ("add two, or odd numbers"). Emphasize that place value is based on a pattern of tens.

- Study Shapes
  In second grade, your child will recognize and draw two-dimensional shapes. He or she will partition shapes into halves and thirds to begin to explore fractions.

- Working with Time and Money
  Your child will tell time using digital and analog clocks and will solve problems that involve money amounts. These skills are ideal for practice at home. Provide pretend money to use for "buying" things at home or let your child earn a small amount of money to spend at a yard sale or discount store. Look for analog clocks in stores and restaurants and compare the times they show to the time shown on digital devices such as your phone.

- Measurement
  This year, your child will measure length using inches, feet, and yards as well as centimeters and meters. Provide a ruler and a meter stick for your child to use at home. Encourage him or her to estimate the length of objects in your home and then measure to test the prediction.

- Graphing
  Look for graphs to read with your child in nonfiction books, in print and online newspapers, and on Web sites. Point out bar graphs, line graphs, and pie graphs. Find a simple graph and ask your child to use the information shown to answer questions. It can be fun to make graphs to represent things that are important to your child. Can he or she make a graph to show the different kinds of toys in a collection?

Science

Science is the process of wondering, and a good scientist asks lots of questions. In second grade, your child will construct knowledge about science from asking questions, reading nonfiction texts, and conducting simple experiments. Science topics addressed in this book include properties of water, birds and their habitats, and rocks and geology. For more information about topics and experiments for your child, consult your local library, a science center or museum, the park system or forest service, or magazines such as *Ranger Rick* and *National Geographic Kids*.

Social Studies

Social studies involves people and their relationship to their social and physical environments. Topics addressed in this book include neighborhoods and communities, Native American history, U.S. states and presidents, world geography, and communication. Make sure your child has access to a globe or world map, videos and articles about current events, and books about history. Encourage your child to explore these resources to learn more about the world and its people.

First Quarter Introduction

The first weeks of a new school year are an exciting and eventful time for your child. As he or she becomes accustomed to new routines during the school day, take time to establish routines at home, too. Set a regular bedtime, provide a good breakfast each day, and allow time for active play. Make sure that reading is part of your child's daily routine, too. Supporting your child's learning at home is a vital part of his or her academic success. Using the weekly resources and activities in this book will help.

First Quarter Skills

Practice pages in this book for Weeks 1–9 will help your child improve the following skills.

Reading and Language Arts

- Review long and short vowel sounds and spellings
- Understand that in some words, **y** is a vowel letter
- Understand side-by-side vowels, or "vowel teams"
- Understand consonant blends and digraphs
- Spell the hard **c** heard in **cow** and the soft **c** heard in **circle**
- Spell **r**-controlled vowels
- Spell the /**oo**/ and /**ow**/ sounds

Math

- Count forward and backward from any number
- Skip-count by twos, fives, and tens
- Add single-digit, two-digit, and three-digit numbers
- Add with and without regrouping
- Use mental math strategies to add
- Review single-digit subtraction

Multi-Sensory Learning Activities

Try these fun activities for enhancing your child's learning and development during the first quarter of the school year. Be sure to choose activities that include speaking, listening, touching, and active movement.

Reading and Language Arts

Review these vowel rules with your child:

- In a single-syllable word, if a single vowel is followed by one or two consonants, the vowel is short. Examples: **fun, tent**
- In a single-syllable word with two vowels, the first vowel is long and the second vowel is silent. Examples: **coat, tile**
- In a single-syllable word in which the vowel is not followed by a consonant, the vowel is long. Examples: **so, we**

On one set of index cards, write consonant blends **sc, st, sw, sl, sp, sn, sk, sm, br, fr, tr, pr, gr, cr, dr, pl, bl, fl, cl, gl**. On another set of cards, write word parts **at, ame, eed, an, ate, ew, op, ide, ied, eep, y, oke, ay, ip**. Can your child match cards from the two sets to make words?

Explain that the letter **r** is very rude! When it appears after a vowel, it interrupts and forces the vowel to make a different sound. This can be heard in words such as **mother** and **bird**. **R** is very rude when it follows **a** in words like **far**. In these words, you can hardly hear **a** at all!

Math

The commutative property of addition states that switching the addends of an addition problem does not affect the sum. So, 3 + 4 = 4 + 3. To help your child understand this concept, place five small objects in one pile and eight small objects in another pile. Ask your child to count the total. Then, physically switch the piles. Ask your child to add them again. Ask why it was the same sum. Repeat with other numbers. Assess your child's understanding by observing whether he or she adds the numbers each time they are switched.

Use a free Web site to print graph paper with large squares. Cut out squares to make hundreds blocks, tens blocks, and ones blocks. You may wish to color-code the blocks and laminate them for durability. Your child can use them for a variety of place value activities like the ones on pages 57, 67, and 87.

First Quarter Introduction, cont.

Science

Read *Rocks: Hard, Soft, Smooth, and Rough* by Natalie M. Rosinsky. Then, begin a rock collection. Find rocks around lakes, rivers, in woods, and along roads. Think about the origins of the rocks you find. Wash and sort the rocks. Describe one rock in the collection. Can your child guess which rock you are talking about?

Social Studies

Have your child look at a map of your state and choose a town or city. Use the legend to determine its distance from your home. Research to find out the city's population, geography, and other features. Use the Internet to request information from the visitor center or chamber of commerce. Finally, plan a visit to see the city's downtown area, parks, library, or other attractions.

Seasonal Fun

Make smores in a solar oven. Prop open a pizza box with a ruler. Line the entire inside of the box with aluminum foil, shiny side out. Then, place a paper plate with several marshmallows inside the box. Cover the bottom of the box (over the marshmallows) with plastic wrap and tape in place. Set the box in the sun and wait up to an hour for the marshmallows to heat. Add graham crackers and smores for an autumn treat!

Have your child make a fall "camp" sign for his or her room. Glue twigs to a sheet of corrugated cardboard to spell your child's name. Decorate with acorn caps and leaves. Hang the sign from a piece of twine.

Week 1 Skills

Subject	Skill	Multi-Sensory Learning Activities
Reading and Language Arts	Review short and long vowel sounds.	• Complete Practice Pages 18–22. • Cut a star from construction paper and tape it to the end of a drinking straw or craft stick to make a magic wand. Write **e** on the star. Then, write three-letter words with short vowel sounds, such as **hop**, **cap**, **cub**, **dim**, **rob**, and **tub**. Let your child place the silent "magic e" at the end of each word to change it into a new word with a long vowel sound. • Choose 10 words from a favorite book and write each on an index card. Can your child sort the words into those with short and long vowel sounds?
Math	Review numbers and number words.	• Complete Practice Page 23. • Write number words such as **thirty-six** or **one hundred ninety-two**. Can your child read each number you wrote and quickly turn to that page in a chapter book?
	Count on from any number.	• Complete Practice Page 25. • While driving in the car with your child, notice numbers that tell the addresses of houses and other buildings. Choose one number and ask questions about it. What number comes before it? After it? Can your child begin with that number and count up or down?

Short Vowels

Vowels can make short or long sounds. The **short a** sounds like the **a** in **cat**. The **short e** is like the **e** in **leg**. The **short i** sounds like the **i** in **pig**. The **short o** sounds like the **o** in **box**. The **short u** sounds like the **u** in **cup**.

Look at each picture. Write the missing short vowel letter.

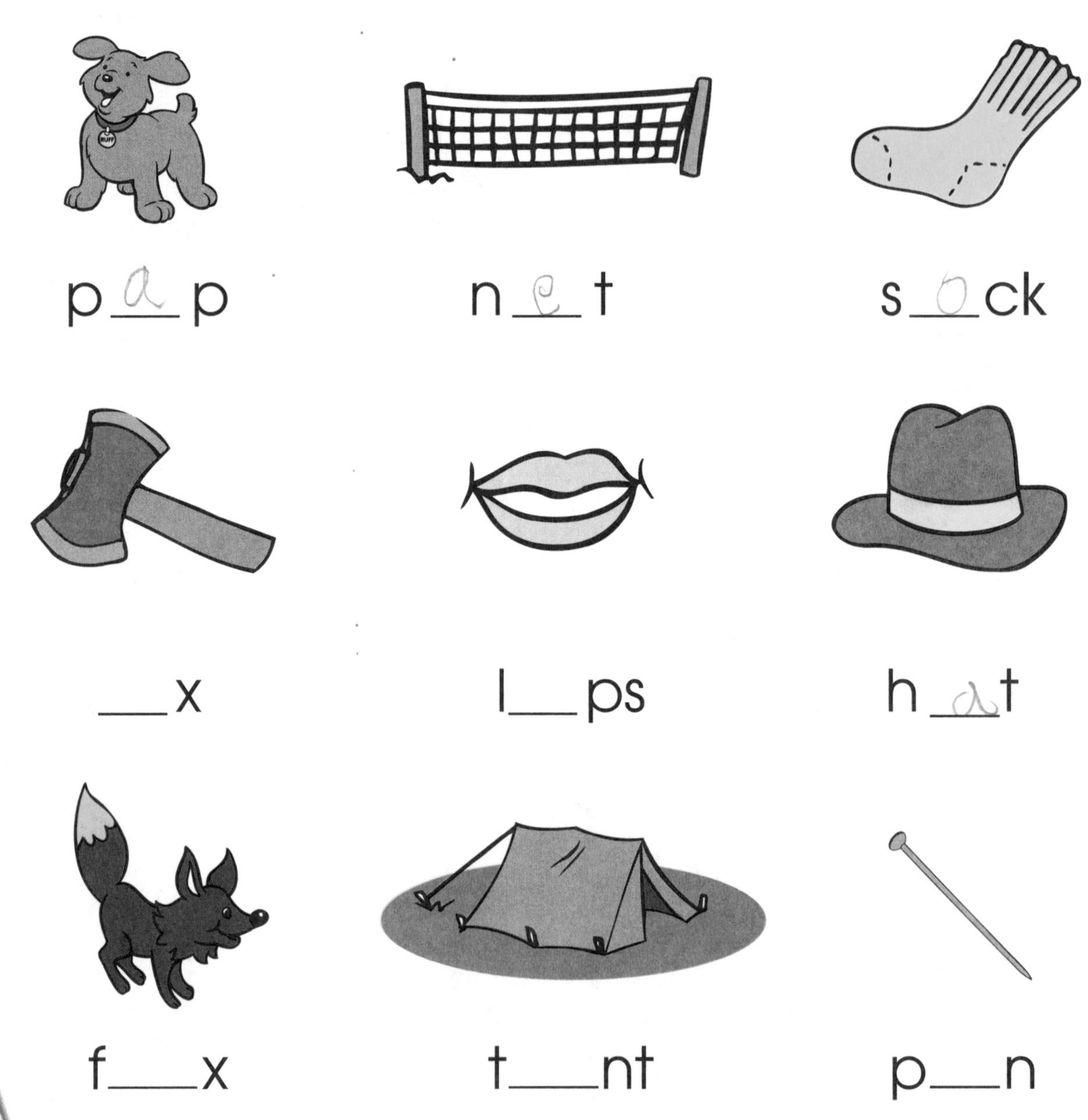

Short and Long

˘ means short vowel sound. ¯ means long vowel sound.

Color the correct pictures in each box.

ă **blue** ā **orange**	
ĕ **red** ē **yellow**	
ĭ **green** ī **purple**	 9
ŏ **yellow** ō **blue**	
ŭ **green** ū **orange**	

Phonics

In some word "families," the vowels have a long sound when you would expect them to have a short sound. For example, the **i** has a short sound in **chill**, but a long sound in **child**. The **o** has a short sound in **cost**, but a long sound in **most**.

Read the words in the word box below. Write the words that have a long vowel sound under the word **LONG**, and the words that have a short vowel sound under the word **SHORT**. (Remember, a long vowel says its name—like **a** in **ate**.)

old	odd	gosh	gold	sold	soft	toast	frost	lost	most
doll	roll	bone	done	kin	mill	mild	wild	blink	blind

LONG		SHORT	
bone	________	doll	________
________	________	________	________
________	________	________	________
________	________	________	________
________	________	________	________

Numbers and Number Words

he word **teen** means "and ten"
ınd **ty** means "tens."

xample: Sixteen means **six and ten.**
Sixty means **six tens.**

Cut out the word endings and glue them to end the correct numbers.

90	nine ☐	**13**	thir ☐
17	seven ☐	**14**	four ☐
30	thir ☐	**40**	for ☐
19	nine ☐	**20**	twen ☐
70	seven ☐	**15**	fif ☐
		16	six ☐
		60	six ☐
		18	eigh ☐
		50	fif ☐
		80	eigh ☐

ty	ty	ty
ty	ty	ty
ty	ty	teen
teen	teen	teen
teen	teen	teen

Unpack the Teddy Bears

Cut out the bears at the bottom of the page. Glue them where they belong in number order.

Week 2 Skills

Subject	Skill	Multi-Sensory Learning Activities
Reading and Language Arts	Review the **long a** and **short a** sounds.	• Complete Practice Pages 28 and 29. • Review the rules for short and long vowel sounds on page 15. Then, read "Spring" in *Frog and Toad Are Friends* by Arnold Lobel. Have your child use the rules to find words in the story that have **short a** and **long a** sounds.
	Review the **long e** and **short e** sounds.	• Complete Practice Pages 30 and 31. • Review the rules for short and long vowel sounds on page 15. Then, read "The Story" in *Frog and Toad Are Friends* by Arnold Lobel. Have your child use the rules to find words in the story that have **short e** and **long e** sounds.
	Review the **short i** sound.	• Complete Practice Page 32. • Review the rules for short and long vowel sounds on page 15. Then, read "The Lost Button" in *Frog and Toad Are Friends* by Arnold Lobel. Have your child use the rules to find words in the story that have the **short i** sound.
Math	Count forward and backward from any number.	• Complete Practice Pages 33 and 34. • Say a number followed by **backward** or **forward**. Can your child quickly supply the number before or after?
	Skip-count by twos, fives, and tens.	• Complete Practice Pages 35 and 36. • Have your child count a collection of 20 seashells, rocks, or other items. Then, ask him or her to group them so they can be counted by twos, fives, or tens.

Sail Away

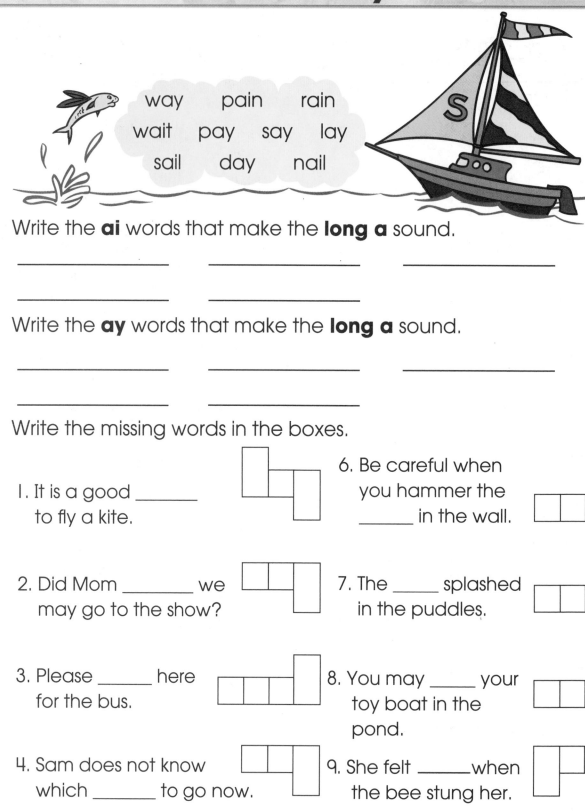

way pain rain
wait pay say lay
sail day nail

Write the **ai** words that make the **long a** sound.

________ ________ ________

________ ________

Write the **ay** words that make the **long a** sound.

________ ________ ________

________ ________

Write the missing words in the boxes.

1. It is a good ______ to fly a kite.

2. Did Mom ________ we may go to the show?

3. Please ______ here for the bus.

4. Sam does not know which _______ to go now.

5. Ray and Mable will ______ for the tickets.

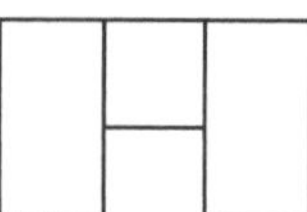

6. Be careful when you hammer the ______ in the wall.

7. The _____ splashed in the puddles.

8. You may _____ your toy boat in the pond.

9. She felt ______when the bee stung her.

10. Please __________ the blankets on the bed.

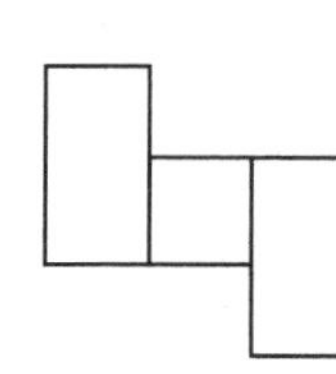

Nestling

wet fell tell
men rest well set
met best pen

Write the words that rhyme with the pictures.

____
____
____

____
____
____

10

____
____

____
____

Complete the puzzle.

Across

3. Please ______ the vase on the table.
5. Mom won a prize for baking the _____ pie.
6. Ted has a bad cold and does not feel _____.
7. We ______ Grandmother downtown.
8. Betsy wrote the letter with a ______.

Down

1. You should ______ if you are sick.
2. He tripped on a rock and ______ down.
4. Please ______ them we will be late.
6. The puppy ran through the sprinkler and got all ______ .
7. Five ______ help coach the baseball team.

It's a Dilly!

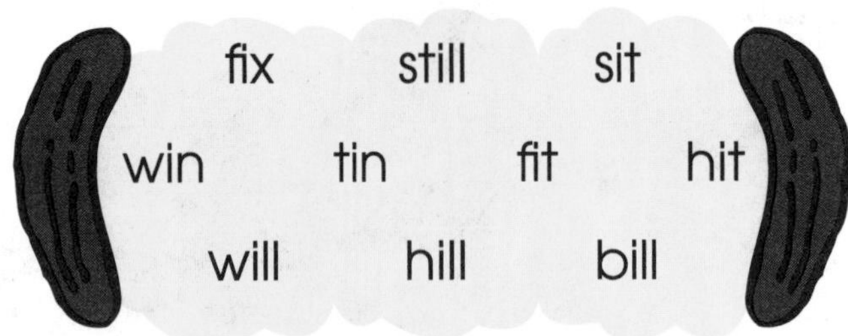

fix
still
sit
win
tin
fit
hit
will
hill
bill

Write the words that rhyme with the pictures. Circle the letters that rhyme.

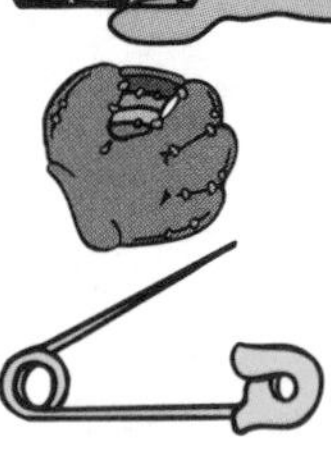

_________ _________ _________ _________

_________ _________ _________

_________ _________

Write the word that did not rhyme. _________

Write the missing words in the boxes.

1. The cat stood ____ as the dog walked by him.

2. Do the new shoes _____ you?

3. My sister helped me _____ the broken toy.

4. When _______ we go on our trip?

5. Willy wants his friend to ______ the contest.

6. We walked to the top of the _______ .

7. Minna swung the bat and _______ the ball into the field.

8. Some cans are made of _________ .

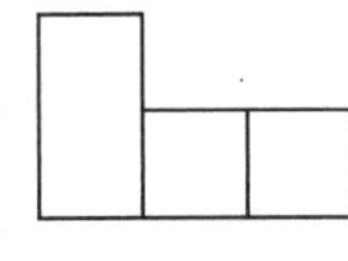

9. Mom paid the phone_______ .

10. We want to ______ next to each other.

Week 3 Skills

Subject	Skill	Multi-Sensory Learning Activities
Reading and Language Arts	Review the **long i** sound.	• Complete Practice Pages 38 and 39. • Review the rules for short and long vowel sounds on page 15. Then, read "The Lost Button" in *Frog and Toad Are Friends* by Arnold Lobel. Have your child use the rules to find words in the story that have the **long i** sound.
	Review the **short o** and **long o** sounds.	• Complete Practice Pages 40 and 41. • Review the rules for short and long vowel sounds on page 15. Then, read "A Swim" in *Frog and Toad Are Friends* by Arnold Lobel. Have your child use the rules to find words in the story that have the **short o** and **long o** sounds.
	Review the **short u** and **long u** sound.	• Complete Practice Page 42. • Review the rules for short and long vowel sounds on page 15. Then, read "The Letter" in *Frog and Toad Are Friends* by Arnold Lobel. Have your child use the rules to find words in the story that have the **short u** and **long u** sounds.
Math	Skip-count by fives and tens.	• Complete Practice Pages 43–46. • Play "Hide and Seek." Model for your child how to count to 100 by fives or tens before seeking. • Encourage your child to clap, stomp, jump rope, or do another rhythmic motion while skip-counting by fives or tens.

Lighting the Sky

sky might dry by night

sight cry light right fly

Write the **igh** words that make the **long i** sound.

_______________ _______________

_______________ _______________ _______________

Write the spelling words ending in **y** that make the **long i** sound.

_______________ _______________

_______________ _______________ _______________

Circle the misspelled word in each sentence. Then, write the word correctly on the line.

1. We will liht the campfire when it gets dark. _______________
2. Hang the wet towel on the rack so it will dri. _______________
3. Diane likes to walk bi the candy store. _______________
4. The Moon and stars can be seen on a clear nite. _______________
5. Bright flashes of lightning lit up the dark sci. _______________
6. A baby will kri when it is frightened. _______________
7. You can see a deer behind the tree on the rite. _______________
8. Wild geese fli to the river every morning. _______________
9. Mike mite catch the bus if he runs. _______________
10. Quickly, the groundhog jumped into the hole and was out of syte. _______________

Wind It Up!

Write the missing words in the boxes.

side wind mind
mile line kind bike
fine find time

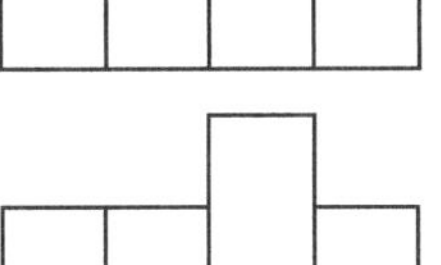

1. The ball bounced on the other ________ of the fence.

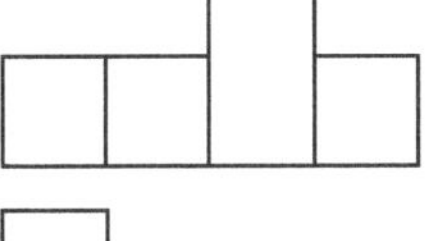

2. It is almost ________ to go to school.

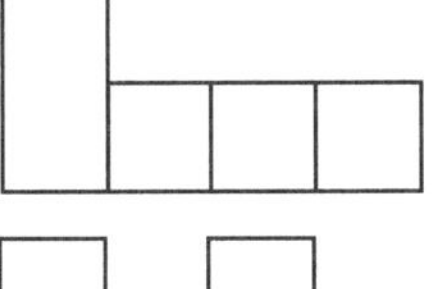

3. We have to walk one ________ to the swimming pool.

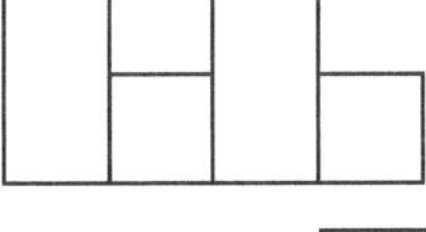

4. The men painted a ________ down the middle of the road.

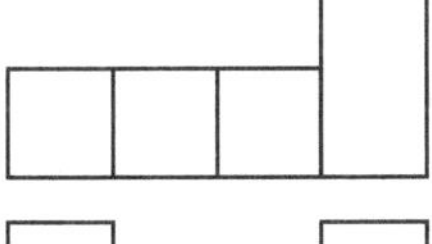

5. Do you ride your ________ to school?

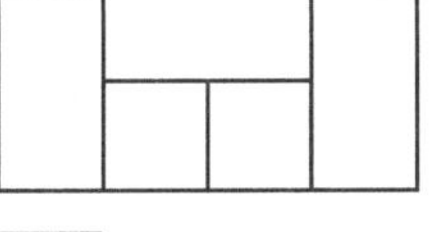

6. Always ________ your parents.

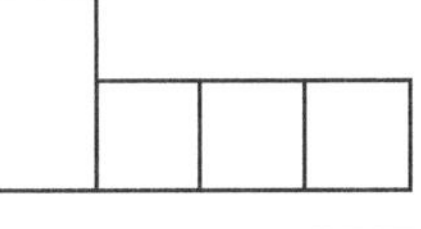

7. Bill can't ________ his other sneaker.

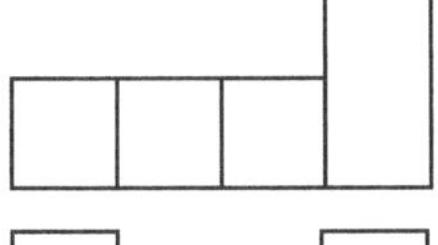

8. It is a ________ day for a picnic in the park.

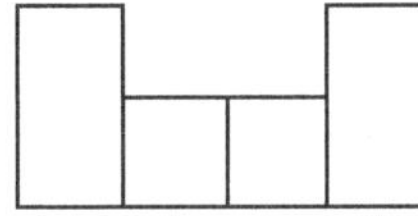

9. Mike's toy car races along the floor if you ________ it up.

10. Everyone should be ________ to his or her pet.

Sow and Grow

sow	own	hope	know	show
woke	hole	grow	joke	pole

Write the words ending with **e** that make the **long o** sound.

_______________ _______________ _______________

_______________ _______________

Write the **ow** words that make the **long o** sound.

_______________ _______________ _______________

_______________ _______________

Read each sentence. Write the missing word on the line.

1. We all laughed at the funny _______________.
2. Did you _______________ your mother your pictures?
3. The loud siren _______________ up the baby.
4. He wants to use his _______________ bike for the race tomorrow.
5. Water and sunshine will make the plants _______________.
6. A tiny gray mouse ran into the _______________ in the ground.
7. They will _______________ the corn seeds in the spring.
8. Grace helped raise the flag to the top of the _______________.
9. Does she _______________ that her report is due today?
10. Cole and Roberta _______________ that they did well on the test.

Loading Cargo

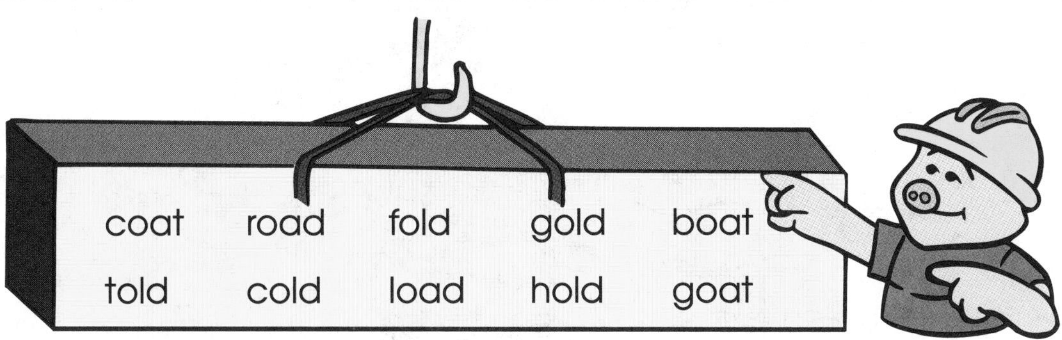

coat
road
fold
gold
boat
told
cold
load
hold
goat

Write the words with **o** followed by **ld** that make the **long o** sound.

____________ ____________ ____________

____________ ____________

Write the **oa** words that make the **long o** sound.

____________ ____________ ____________

____________ ____________

Complete the puzzle.

Across

1. An animal
3. Opposite of **hot**
6. A ship
7. To fill
8. A street

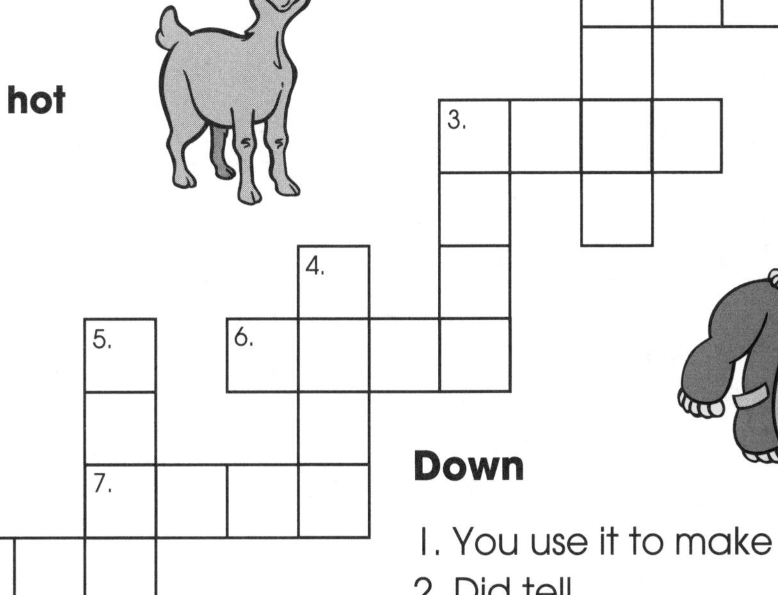

Down

1. You use it to make jewelry.
2. Did tell
3. Something to wear
4. You use your hands to do this.
5. To bend something over

Submerging Subs

Write the words that rhyme. Circle the letters in each word that make the same sound.

1. bun ______________
____
____

3. hut ______________
____
____

2. rub ______________
____

4. pup ______________

5. us ______________

Write the correct word on each line.

1. To move very fast. ______________
2. Some kids ride to school in one of these. ______________
3. It is in the sky and gives off heat and light. ______________
4. A party can be this. ______________
5. You do this with a knife. ______________
6. You drink out of this. ______________
7. A boat that goes under the water. ______________
8. You can eat this for a snack. ______________
9. One kitten is sleeping, the other is playing. ______________
10. You take a bath in this. ______________

Counting by Fives

Count by fives to draw the path to the playground

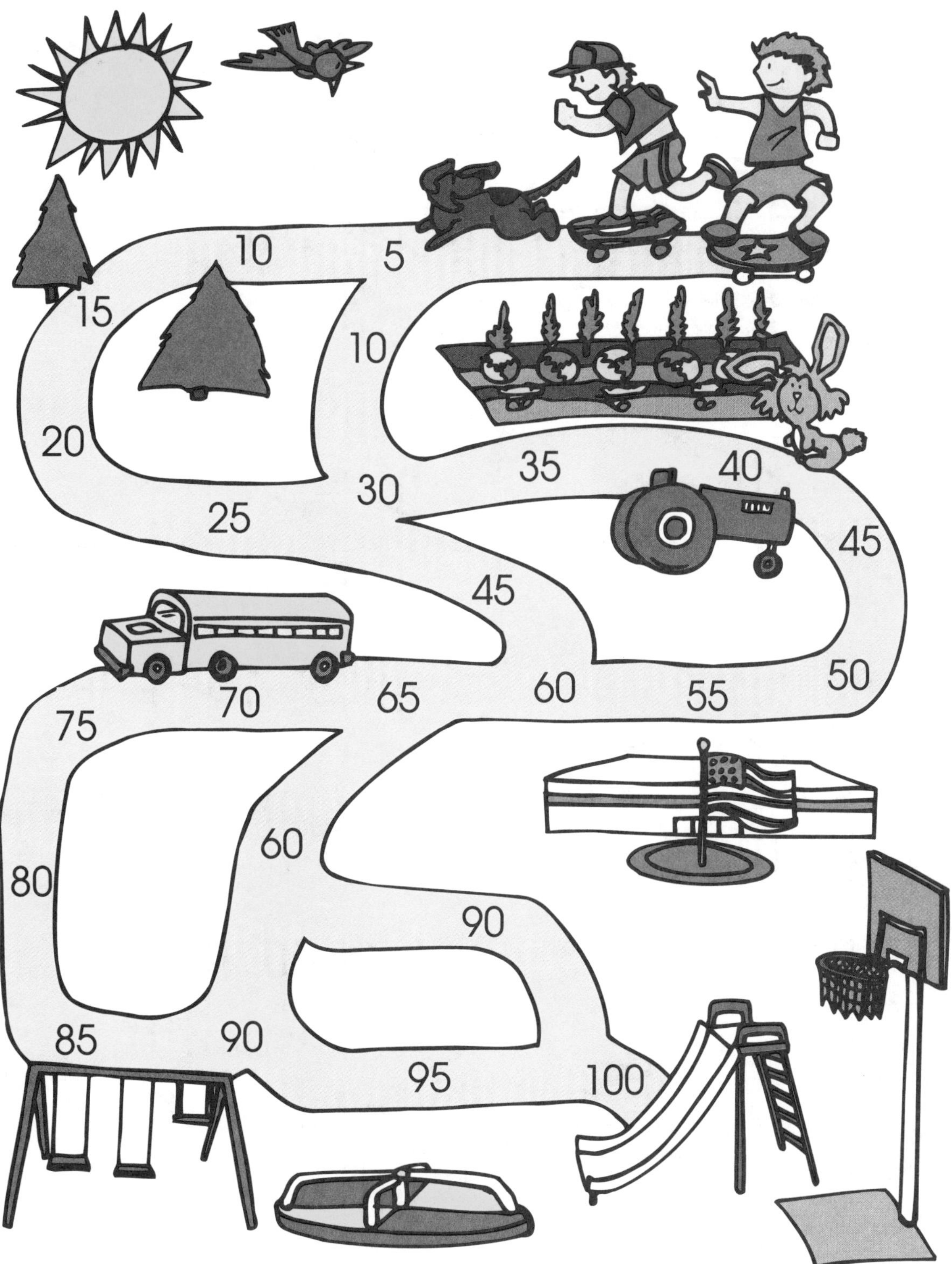

Counting by Fives

Use tally marks to count to fives. Write the number next to the tallies.

Example: A tally mark stands for one = l. Five tally marks look like this = 𝍸

Counting by Tens

Count by tens to draw the path the boy takes to the store.

Counting by Tens

Use the groups of 10s to count to 100.

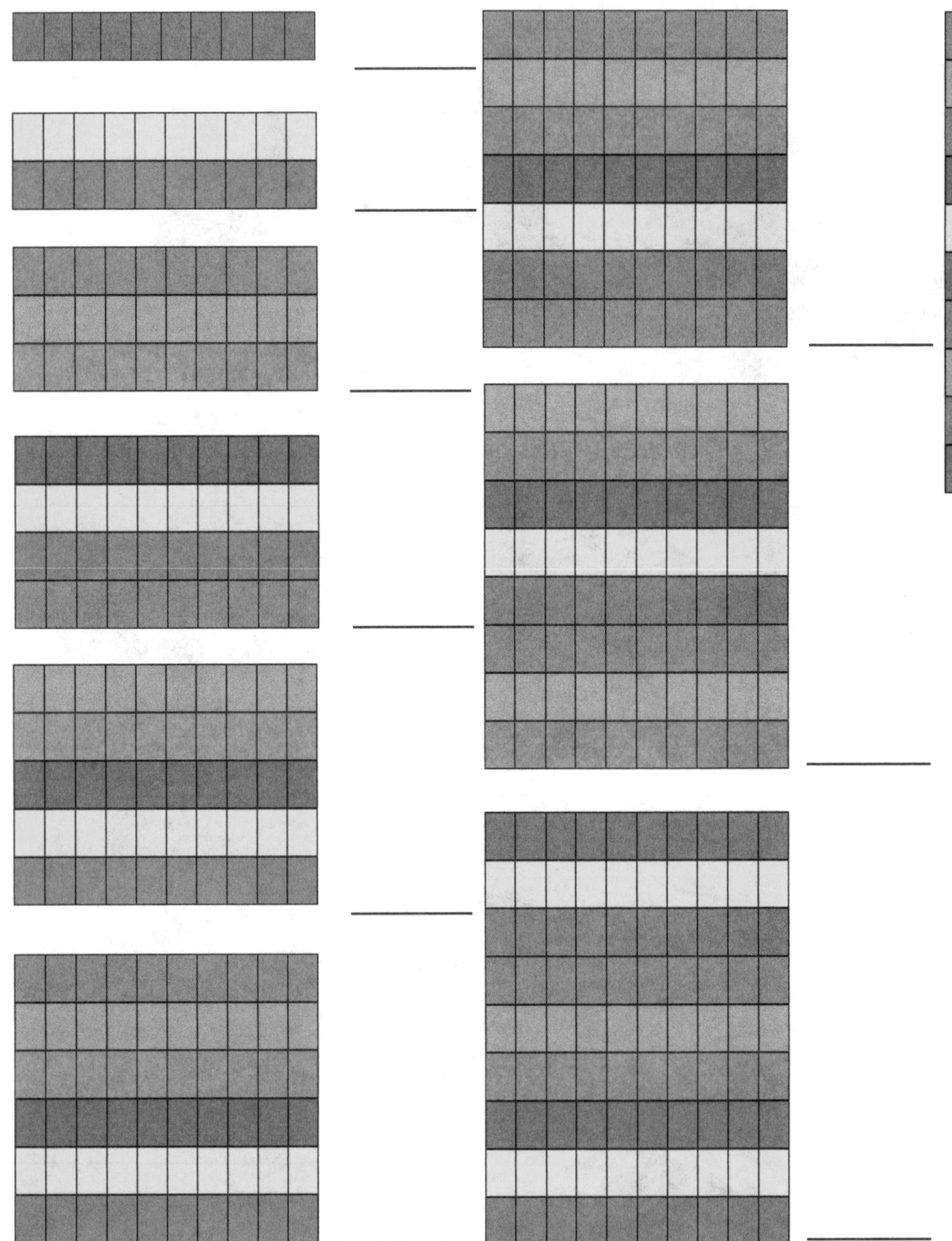

Week 4 Skills

Subject	Skill	Multi-Sensory Learning Activities
Reading and Language Arts	Understand that in some words, the letter **y** has a vowel sound.	• Complete Practice Pages 48–52. • Read *Lyle, Lyle, Crocodile* by Bernard Waber. Point out the **long i** sound **y** makes in Lyle's name. Ask your child to write a new adventure for Lyle that includes a shy bunny, a lazy kitty, or a funny party. Point to several words and ask what sound **y** makes in them. • Write these words at the top of three columns: **yell**, **cry**, and **happy**. Then, ask your child to write these words in the columns according to the sound **y** makes: **pony**, **by**, **my**, **yarn**, **year**, **baby**.
Math	Review single-digit addition.	• Complete Practice Pages 53–56. • Purchase or create a set of flash cards for single-digit addition facts such as **8 + 7** and **3 + 9**. Show each card to your child. If the problem is answered correctly within three seconds, then he or she knows the fact. If it takes longer, set the card aside to be practiced later. Spend a few minutes practicing addition facts each day this week.
Bonus: Science		• Encourage your child to build a boat from a sheet of aluminum foil and float it in a dishpan of water. How many pennies will the boat hold before it sinks? Can the boat be redesigned to hold more pennies?

A Fork in the Road

Write the words below on the correct "road."

sky jelly try kitty fly my
fry cry funny dry penny
candy by sleepy happy lazy baby
sly fuzzy shy many why

Y sounds like **long e**.

Y sounds like **long i**.

Y as a Vowel

Color the spaces:
purple – y sounds like **i**.
yellow – y sounds like **e**.

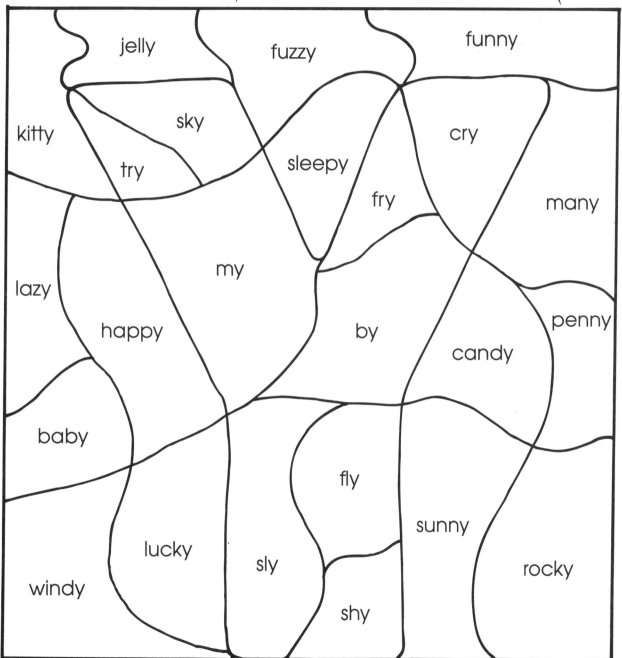

jelly
fuzzy
funny
kitty
sky
try
sleepy
cry
fry
many
lazy
my
happy
by
penny
candy
baby
fly
sunny
lucky
sly
rocky
windy
shy

Y as a Vowel

When **y** comes at the end of a word, it is a vowel. When **y** is the only vowel at the end of a one-syllable word, it has the sound of a **long i** (like in **my**). When **y** is the only vowel at the end of a word with more than one syllable, it has the sound of a **long e** (like in **baby**).

Look at the words in the word box. If the word has the sound of a **long i**, write it under the word **my**. If the word has the sound of a **long e**, write it under the word **baby**. Write the word from the word box that answers each riddle.

happy	penny	fry	try	sleepy	dry
bunny	why	windy	sky	party	fly

my ______ ______ ______ ______ ______ ______

baby ______ ______ ______ ______ ______ ______

1. It takes five of these to make a nickel. ______
2. This is what you call a baby rabbit. ______
3. It is often blue and you can see it if you look up. ______
4. You might have one of these on your birthday. ______
5. It is the opposite of wet. ______
6. You might use this word to ask a question. ______

Y as a Vowel

Read the rhyming story. Choose the words from the box to fill in the blanks.

Larry	Mary
money	funny
honey	bunny

__________ and __________ are friends. Larry is

selling __________ . Mary needs __________ to

buy the honey. "I want to feed it to my __________," said

Mary. Larry laughed and said, "That is __________ . Everyone

knows that bunnies do not eat honey."

Y as a Vowel

Read the rhyming story. Choose the words from the box to fill in the blanks.

try	my	Why	cry	shy	fly

Sam is very ____________________. Ann asks, "Would you like to

____________________ my kite?" Sam starts to ____________________ .

Ann asks, " ____________________ are you crying?"

Sam says, "I am afraid to ____________________ ."

"Oh, ____________________! You are a very good kite flyer," cries Ann.

Addition

Complete the facts to 10.

3	9	6	4	8
+1	+1	+3	+2	+2

7	6	5	2	1
+3	+2	+5	+4	+6

4	1	2	4	2	3	6	5	8	1
+5	+4	+8	+1	+2	+4	+1	+1	+1	+7

5	7	6	5	3	1	2	4	1	2
+4	+1	+4	+2	+7	+2	+6	+3	+9	+1

5	7	3	1	3	4	3	2	5	2
+3	+2	+4	+3	+7	+4	+5	+7	+2	+3

3	4	3	4	3
+5	+3	+6	+5	+2

4	1	2	4	1
+6	+8	+7	+6	+1

The Numbers Game

Roll dice to find two addends. Write them on the first two lines. Then, add to find the sum.

1. ______ + ______ = ______

2. ______ + ______ = ______

3. ______ + ______ = ______

4. ______ + ______ = ______

5. ______ + ______ = ______

6. ______ + ______ = ______

7. ______ + ______ = ______

8. ______ + ______ = ______

9. ______ + ______ = ______

10. ______ + ______ = ______

Ride the Rapids

Write each problem on the life jacket with the correct answer.

8 + 5	8 + 6	9 + 8	9 + 6	9 + 4
6 + 6	9 + 7	7 + 5	8 + 4	4 + 9
7 + 8	7 + 9	9 + 5	6 + 7	5 + 9
6 + 9	7 + 6	8 + 9	8 + 8	
9 + 3	9 + 9	5 + 8	3 + 9	
6 + 8	5 + 7	8 + 7	7 + 7	

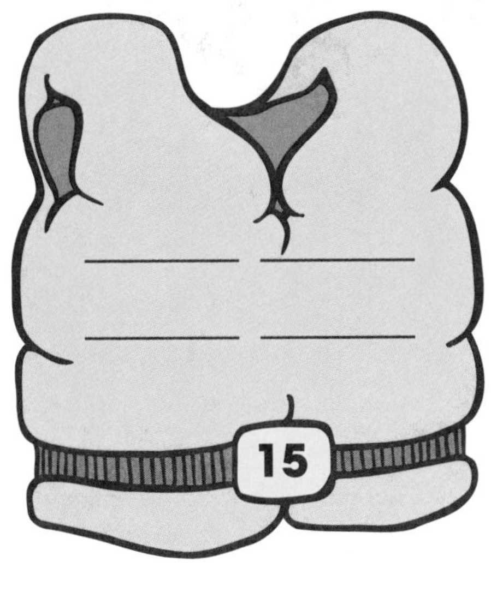

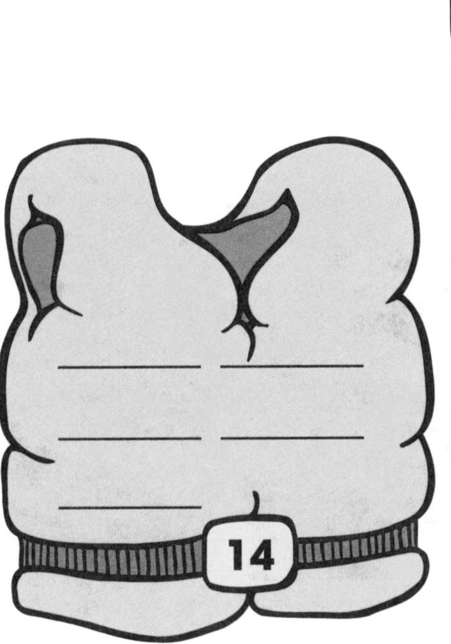

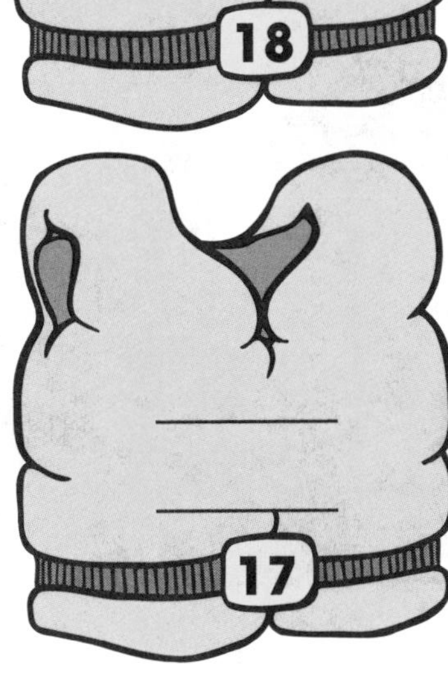

Addition

Complete the facts to 18.

2	6	4	5	8
+9	+6	+9	+4	+7

5	7	3	9	7
+9	+7	+5	+9	+9

9	6	8	9	9	4	8	9	4	4
+8	+5	+5	+6	+4	+4	+6	+7	+8	+7

4	5	4	9	7	6	7	3	6	2
+6	+3	+5	+9	+3	+6	+8	+8	+3	+6

8	4	6	3	7	3	8	5	3	6
+3	+4	+7	+2	+5	+4	+8	+2	+9	+8

Week 5 Skills

Subject	Skill	Multi-Sensory Learning Activities
Reading and Language Arts	Identify words that have side-by-side vowel letters or "vowel teams."	• Complete Practice Pages 58–62. • Read *Cloudy With a Chance of Meatballs* by Judi Barrett. Look for words with vowel teams. Do they have short or long vowel sounds? • Write words that contain vowel teams such as **tail**, **boat**, **eat**, **rain**, **meat**, **tied**, **jail**, **road**, **team**, **oat**, and **pie**. Have your child underline the vowel he or she hears in each word and draw an **X** over the silent vowel. Ask your child to use his or her own words to state the rule for pronouncing these words.
Math	Review single-digit addition.	• Complete Practice Page 63. • Use the addition flash cards from Week 4. Have your child group the cards according to categories that you propose, such as facts that add up to 12, facts with odd sums, or facts with even sums.
	Add three numbers.	• Complete Practice Pages 64 and 65. • Name a number greater than three. Can your child quickly give three numbers that have that sum?
	Add two-digit numbers without regrouping.	• Complete Practice Page 66. • Ask your child to choose several problems from page 66 to model with ten-blocks and one-blocks. See directions for creating these on page 15. Alternately, have your child model problems using stacks of ten interlocking blocks and single interlocking blocks.

Double Vowel Words

Usually when two vowels appear together, the first one says its name and the second one is silent.

Example: bean

Unscramble the double vowel words below. Write the correct word on the line.

 **ocat** ____________

 **etar** ____________

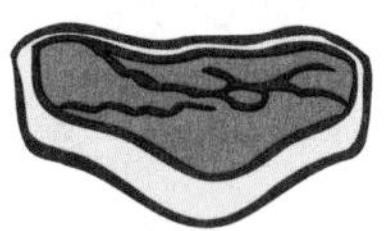 **mtea** ____________

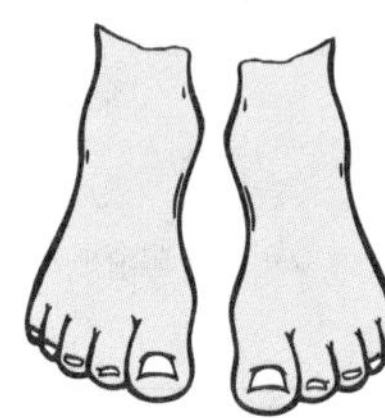 **eetf** ____________

 **teas** ____________

 **otab** ____________

 **ogat** ____________

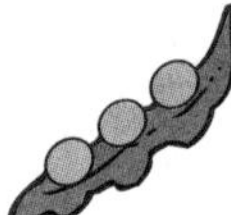 **spea** ____________

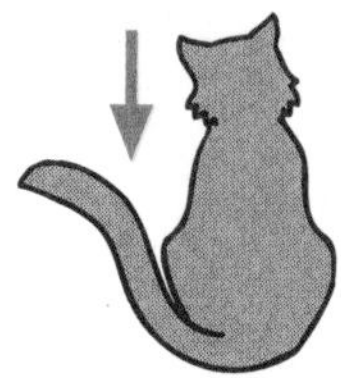 **atli** ____________

 **apil** ____________

Vowel Teams

The vowel teams **ou** and **ow** can have the same sound. You can hear it in the words **clown** and **cloud**. The vowel teams **au** and **aw** have the same sound. You hear it in the words **because** and **law**.

Look at the pictures. Write the correct vowel team to complete the words. The first one is done for you. You may need to use a dictionary to help you with the correct spelling.

Vowel Teams

The vowel team **ea** can have a **short e** sound like in **head**, or a **long e** sound like in **bead**. An **ea** followed by an **r** makes a sound like the one in **ear** or like the one in **heard**.

Read the story. Listen for the sound **ea** makes in the bold words.

Have you ever **read** a book or **heard** a story about a **bear**? You might have **learned** that bears sleep through the winter. Some bears may sleep the whole **season**. Sometimes they look almost **dead**! But they are very much alive. As the cold winter passes and the spring **weather** comes **near**, they wake up. After such a nice rest, they must be **ready** to **eat** a **really** big **meal**!

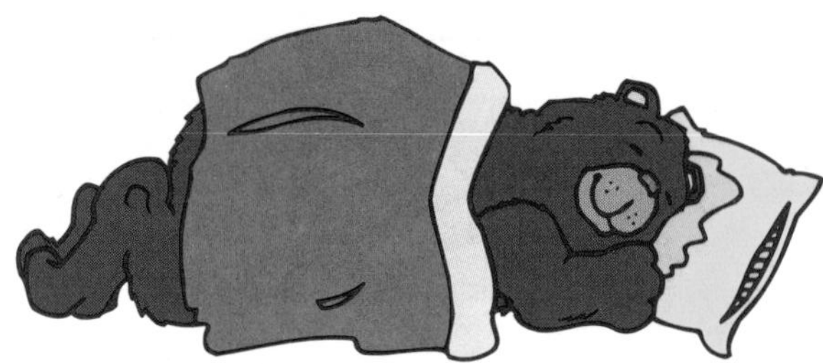

words with **long ea**	words with **short ea**	**ea** followed by **r**
____________	____________	____________
____________	____________	____________
____________	____________	____________
____________	____________	____________

Vowel Teams

The vowel team **ie** makes the **long e** sound like in **believe**. The team **ei** also makes the **long e** sound like in **either**. But **ei** can also make a **long a** sound like in **eight**.

Circle the **ei** words with the **long a** sound.

neighbor	veil
receive	reindeer
reign	ceiling

The teams **eigh** and **ey** also make the **long a** sound.

Finish the sentences with words from the word box.

chief	sleigh	obey	weigh	thief	field	ceiling

1. Eight reindeer pull Santa's ______________________________ .
2. Rules are for us to ______________________________ .
3. The bird got out of its cage and flew up to the ______________ .
4. The leader of an Indian tribe is the ____________________ .
5. How much do you ______________________________ ?
6. They caught the ____________________ who took my bike.
7. Corn grows in a ______________________________ .

Vowel Teams: oi, oy, ou, ow

Look at the first picture in each row. Circle the pictures that have the same sound.

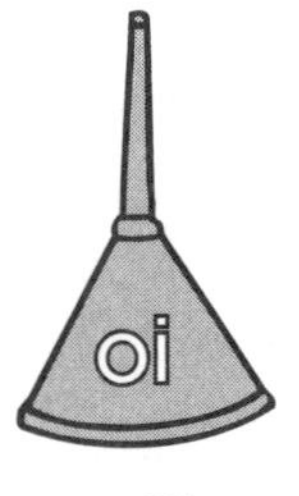

oil

toy

couch

howl

Addition

Complete the facts to 18.

3	7	9	5	7
+3	+4	+6	+6	+4

9	4	4	5	2
+3	+6	+8	+5	+4

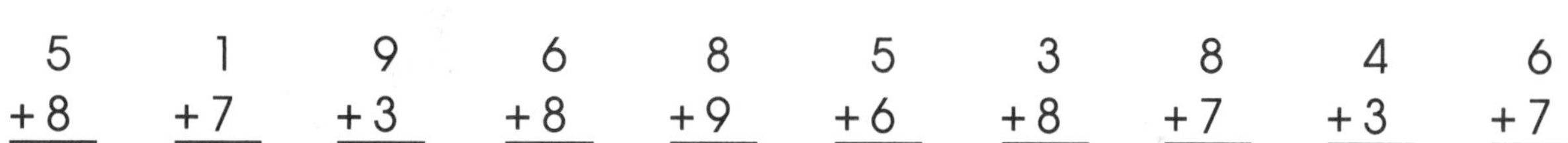

5	1	9	6	8	5	3	8	4	6
+8	+7	+3	+8	+9	+6	+8	+7	+3	+7

5	7	9	3	2	7	4	3	9	3
+9	+3	+4	+6	+8	+6	+5	+9	+7	+4

8	3	5	9	8	8	6	9	7	8
+6	+5	+7	+9	+6	+5	+7	+8	+9	+4

Adding Strategies

When adding three numbers, add two numbers first, then add the third to that sum. To decide which two numbers to add first, try one of these strategies.

Look for doubles.

8	**4** ⟩ **8**	**2** ⟩
3 ⟩ **6**	**4**	**9** ⟩ **4**
+ 3	**+ 5**	**+ 2** ⟩
14	13	13

Look for a ten.

7 ⟩ **10**	**8**	**1** ⟩
3	**4** ⟩ **10**	**5** ⟩ **10**
+ 4	**+ 6**	**+ 9** ⟩
14	18	15

Solve. Look for a 10 or doubles.

5	2	7	3	6
5	6	1	7	2
+ 4	+ 8	+ 7	+ 4	+ 6

7	7	6	5
6	8	7	5
+ 6	+ 3	+ 4	+ 3

Adding 3 or More Numbers

Add all the numbers to find the sum. Draw pictures to help or break up the problem into two smaller problems.

Example:

$$\begin{array}{r} 1 \\ 2 \\ +3 \\ \hline 6 \end{array}$$

$$\begin{array}{r} 2 \\ +5 \\ 2 \\ +4 \\ \hline \end{array} \quad \begin{array}{r} 7 \\ +6 \\ \hline 13 \end{array}$$

$$\begin{array}{r} 3 \\ 6 \\ +2 \\ \hline \end{array} \qquad \begin{array}{r} 8 \\ 5 \\ +4 \\ \hline \end{array} \qquad \begin{array}{r} 3 \\ 1 \\ +5 \\ \hline \end{array} \qquad \begin{array}{r} 8 \\ 2 \\ +9 \\ \hline \end{array}$$

$$\begin{array}{r} 2 \\ 8 \\ 4 \\ +3 \\ \hline \end{array} \qquad \begin{array}{r} 3 \\ 6 \\ 5 \\ +2 \\ \hline \end{array} \qquad \begin{array}{r} 4 \\ 1 \\ 2 \\ +5 \\ \hline \end{array} \qquad \begin{array}{r} 6 \\ 7 \\ 3 \\ +1 \\ \hline \end{array}$$

2-Digit Addition

Study the example. Follow the steps to add.

Example: 33 +41

Step 1: Add the one.

tens	ones
3	3
+4	1
	4

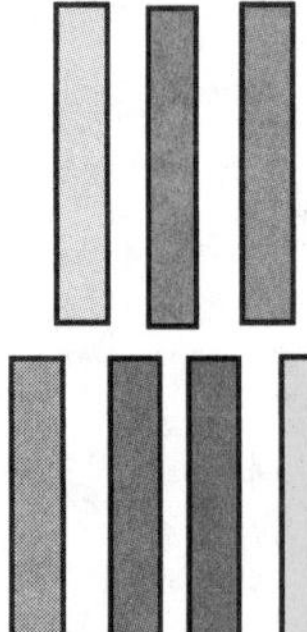

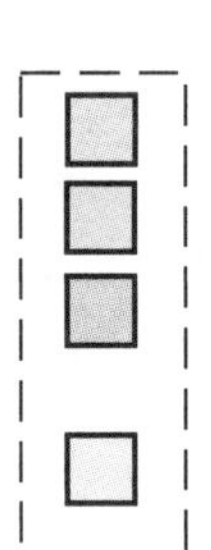

Step 2: Add the tens.

tens	ones
3	3
+4	1
7	4

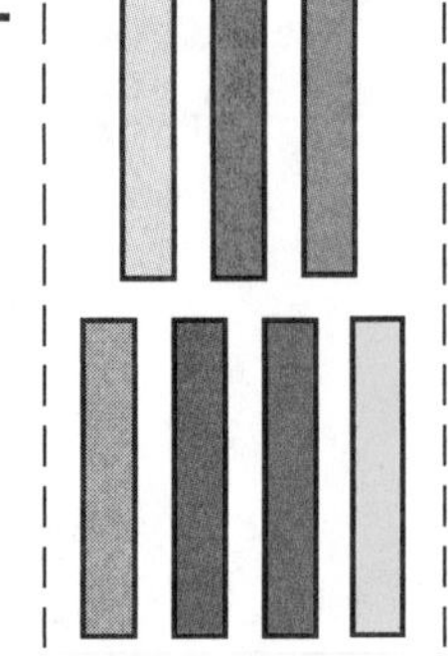

tens	ones
4	2
+ 2	4
6	6

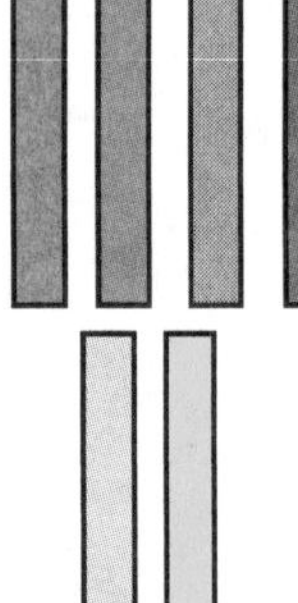

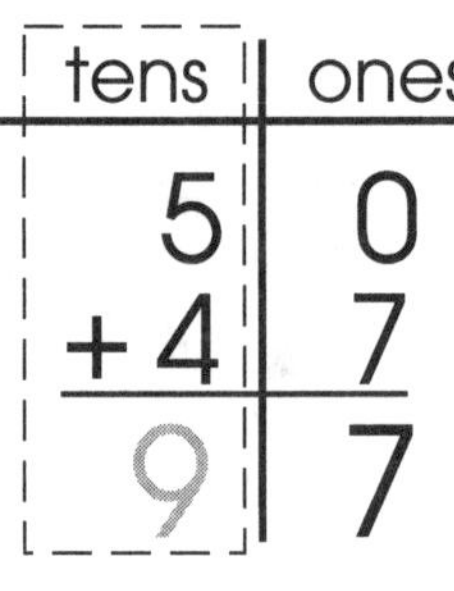

tens	ones
5	0
+ 4	7
9	7

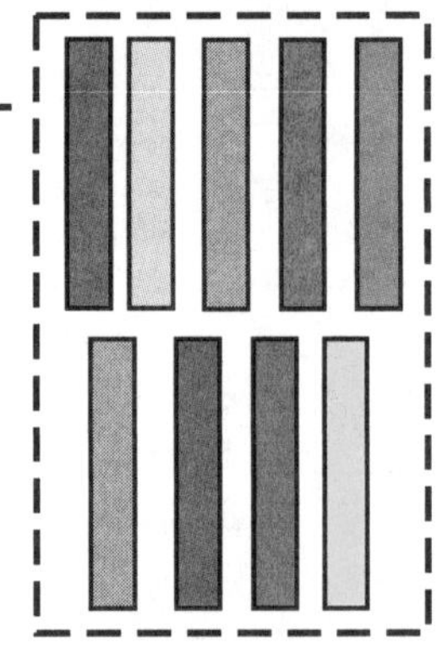

24	15	38	11	37	72	33	10
+62	+23	+61	+26	+42	+11	+51	+30

25	62	32	25	82	91	16	55
+42	+14	+44	+13	+ 6	+ 5	+71	+ 3

Week 6 Skills

Subject	Skill	Multi-Sensory Learning Activities
Reading and Language Arts	Identify words with consonant blends.	• Complete Practice Pages 68–72. • Read *Frederick* by Leo Lionni. Look for words that contain consonant blends. Make a list. • Look for tongue twisters that contain consonant blends to read and enjoy together. Here is one: Swan swam over the pond,/Swim swam swim!/Swan swam back again,/Well swum, swan!
Math	Add two-digit numbers without regrouping.	• Complete Practice Page 73. • Create ten-blocks and one-blocks using the directions on page 15. Have your child glue several onto construction paper to make a picture. What number does the picture represent?
	Add two-digit numbers with regrouping.	• Complete Practice Page 74–76. • Model a problem such as **24 + 47** with pennies and dimes. Draw lines to divide a sheet of paper into two rows and two columns. In the first row, place two dimes in the first column and four pennies in the second column. In the second row, place four dimes in the first column and seven pennies in the second column. Show how to add 4 + 7 in the ones column, swapping out (or "regrouping") 10 pennies for one dime to be moved over top of the tens column.

Consonant Blends

Consonant blends are two or three consonant letters in a word whose sounds combine, or blend. **Examples: br, fr, gr, pr, tr**

Look at each picture. Say its name. Write the blend you hear at the beginning of each word.

______

______

______

______

______

______

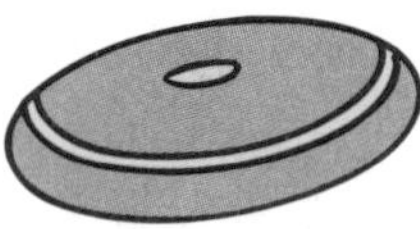

______

______

______

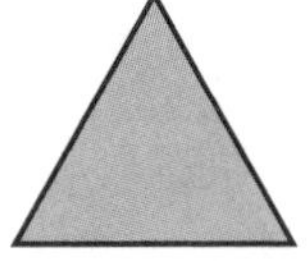

______

______

______

Blends: fl, br, pl, sk, sn

Blends are two consonants put together to form a single sound.

Look at the pictures and say their names. Write the letters for the beginning sound in each word.

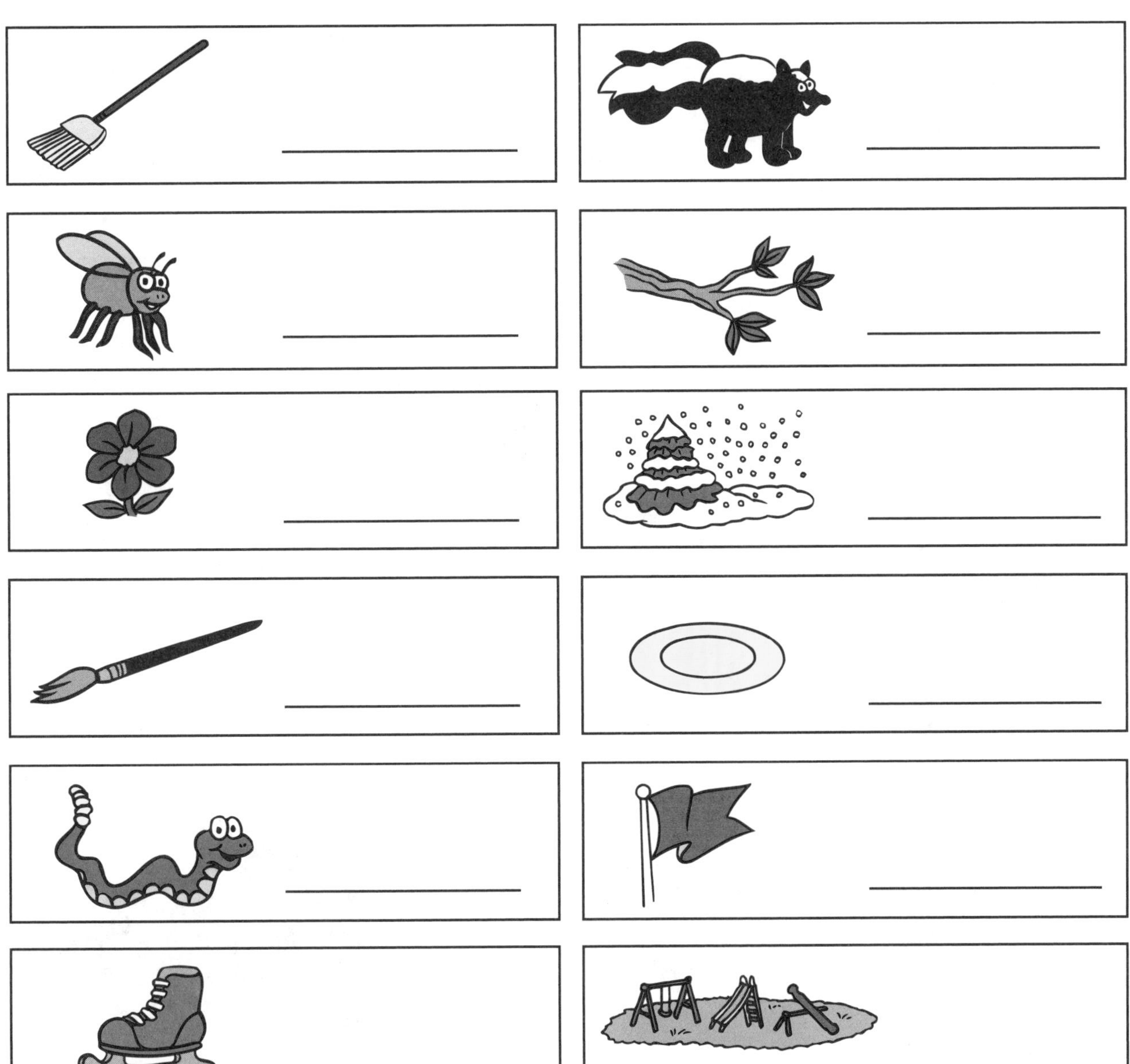

Blends: bl, sl, cr, cl

Look at the pictures and say their names. Write the letters for the beginning sound in each word.

______ own

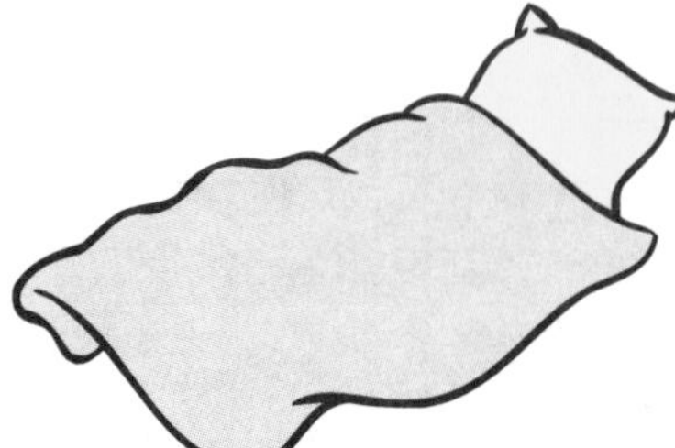

______ anket

______ ayon

______ ock

______ ide

______ oud

______ ed

______ ab

______ ocodile

Consonant Blends

Write a word from the word box to answer each riddle.

clock	glass	blow	climb	slipper
sleep	gloves	clap	blocks	flashlight

1. You need me when the lights go out. **What am I?** ____________
2. People use me to tell the time. **What am I?** ____________
3. You put me on your hands in the winter to keep them warm. **What am I?** ____________
4. Cinderella lost one like me at midnight. **What am I?** ____________
5. This is what you do with your hands when you are pleased. **What is it?** ____________
6. You can do this with a whistle or with bubble gum. **What is it?** ____________
7. These are what you might use to build a castle when you are playing. **What are they?** ____________
8. You do this to get to the top of a hill. **What is it?** ____________
9. This is what you use to drink water or milk. **What is it?** ____________
10. You do this at night with your eyes closed. **What is it?** ____________

Consonant Teams

Read the words in the box. Write a word from the word box to finish each sentence. Circle the consonant team in each word.
Hint: There are three letters in each team!

splash	screen	spray	street	scream
screw	shrub	split	strong	string

1. Another word for a bush is a ________________.
2. I tied a ________________ to my tooth to help pull it out.
3. I have many friends who live on my________________.
4. We always________________when we ride the roller coaster.
5. A ________________helps keep bugs out of the house.
6. It is fun to________________in the water.
7. My father uses an ax to ________________ the firewood.
8. We will need a________________ to fix the chair.
9. You must be very ________________ to lift this heavy box.
10. The firemen________________ the fire with water.

2-Digit Addition

Add the total points scored in each game. Remember to add ones first and tens second.

Example:

Total 39

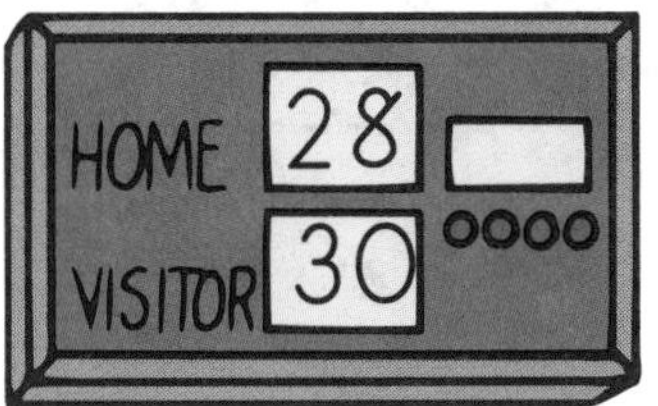

Total ________

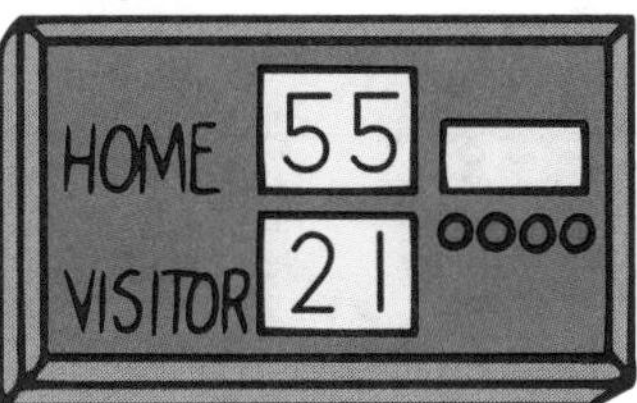

Total ________

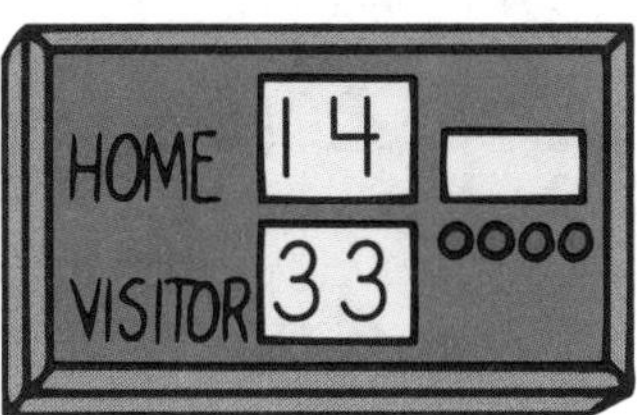

Total ________

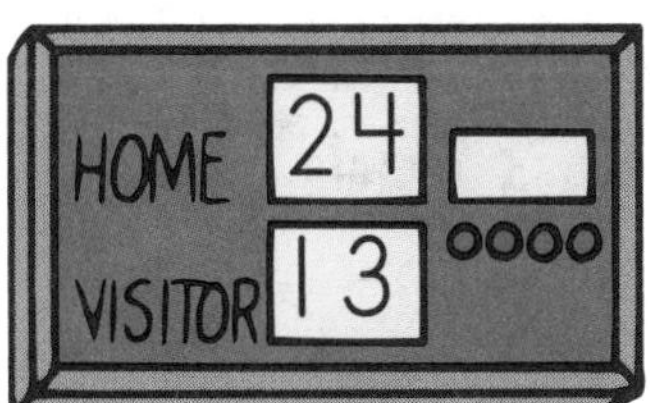

Total ________

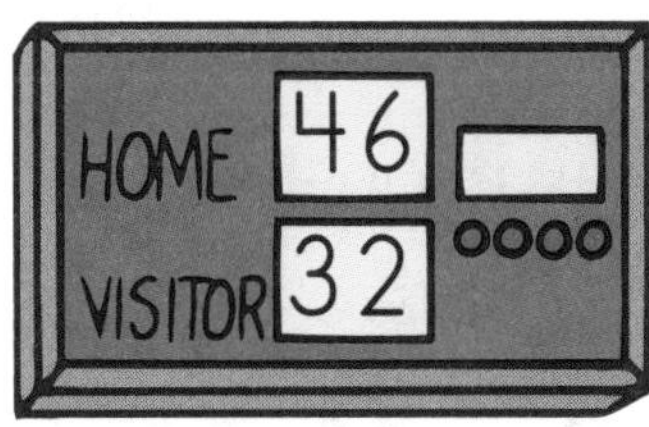

Total ________

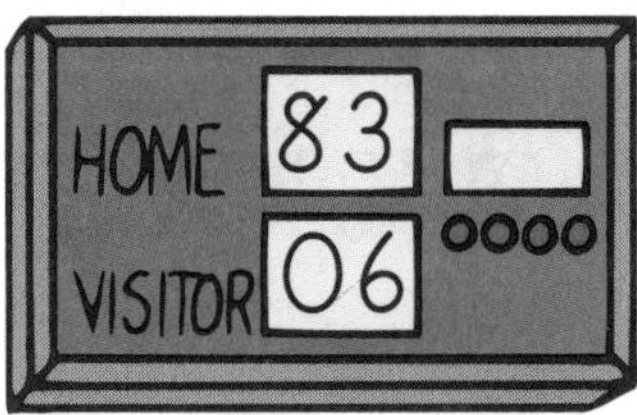

Total ________

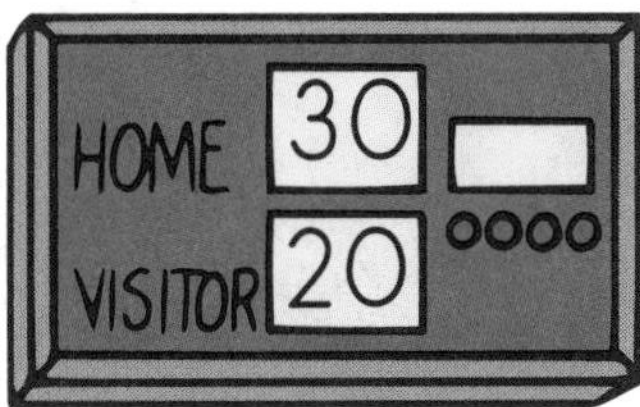

Total ________

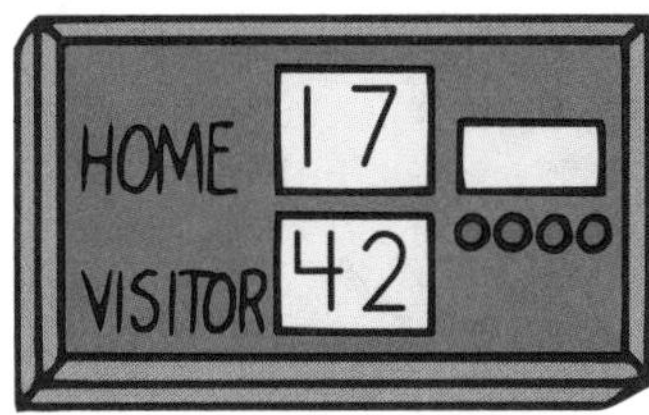

Total ________

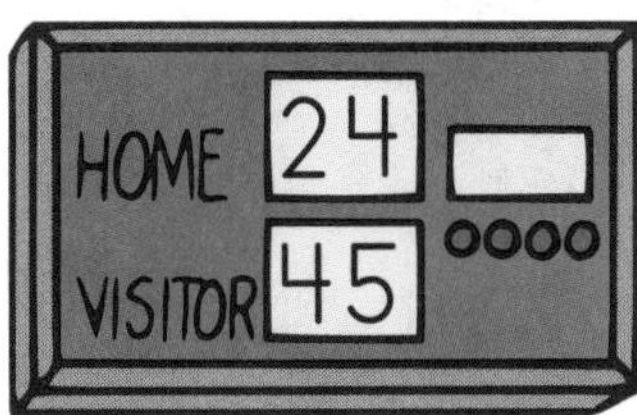

Total ________

2-Digit Addition: Regrouping

Addition is "putting together" or adding two or more numbers to find the sum. Regrouping is using ten ones to form one ten, ten tens to form one 100, fifteen ones to form one ten and five ones and so on.

Study the examples. Follow the steps to add.

Example:

```
  14
+  8
```

Step 1: Add the ones. **Step 2:** Regroup the tens. **Step 3:** Add the tens.

tens	ones
1	4
+	8
	12

tens	ones
1	
1	4
+	8
	2

tens	ones
1	
1	4
+	8
2	2

tens	ones
1	
1	6
+3	7
5	3

tens	ones
1	
3	8
+5	3
9	1

tens	ones
1	
2	4
+4	7
7	1

28	32	54	19	44	25	29	79
+17	+38	+25	+55	+48	+64	+33	+15

2-Digit Addition: Regrouping

Add the total points scored in each game. Remember to add ones first, regroup, and then add the tens.

Example:

Total 85

HOME 33
VISITOR 57

Total ________

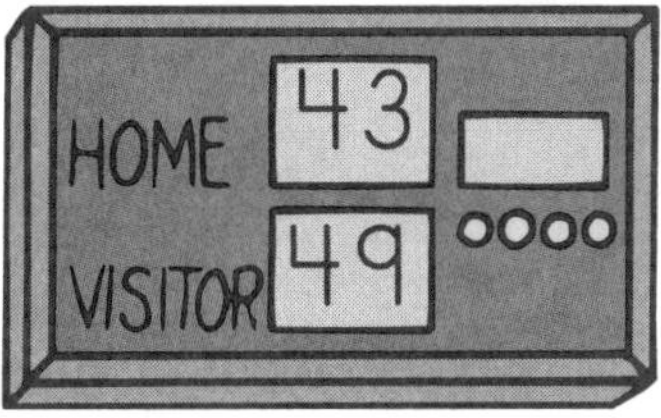

Total ________

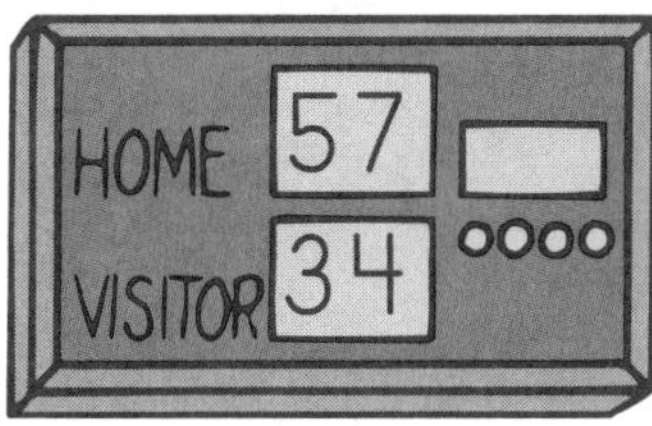

Total ________

Total ________

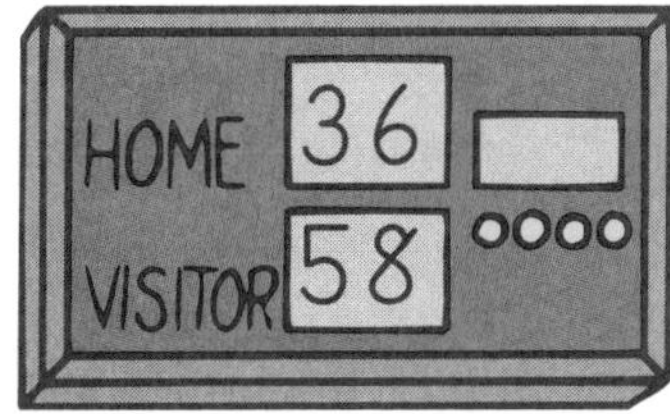

Total ________

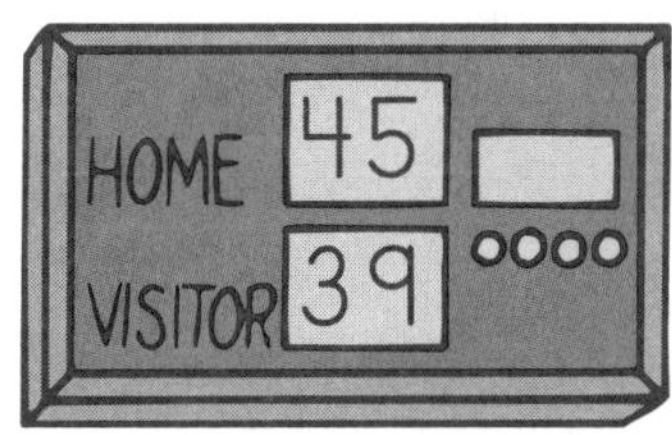

Total ________

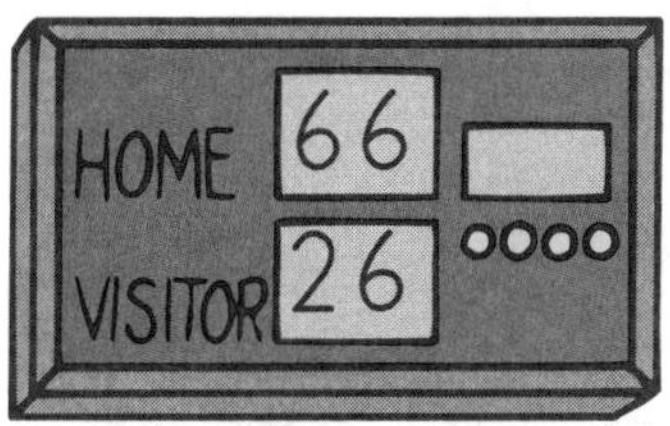

Total ________

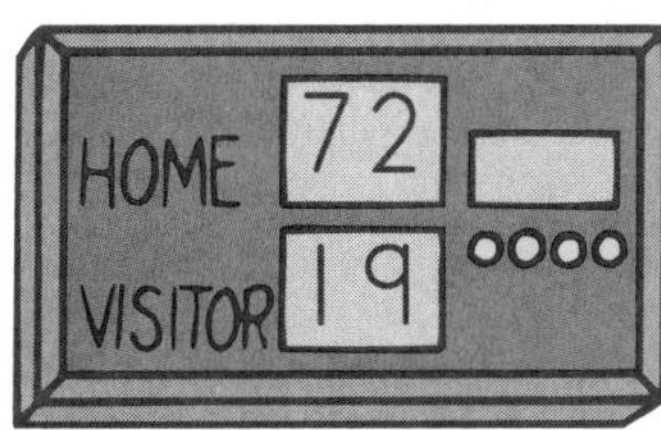

Total ________

HOME 54
VISITOR 26

Total ________

Keep On Truckin'

Write each sum. Connect the sums of 83 to make a road for the truck.

			17 +66	48 +26	42 +19
28 +38	64 +19	26 +57	58 +25	17 +75	65 +29
37 +39	48 +35	58 +37	65 +16	38 +25	39 +59
59 +27	55 +28	39 +44			

Week 7 Skills

Subject	Skill	Multi-Sensory Learning Activities
Reading and Language Arts	Spell beginning and ending consonant blends.	• Complete Practice Pages 78–81. • Write some riddles for words that contain consonant blends and digraphs. Examples: I rhyme with **tag**. I hang on a pole. (**flag**) I rhyme with **keep**. I am covered in soft wool. (**sheep**) Can your child guess and write each word?
Math	Add two-digit numbers with regrouping.	• Complete Practice Pages 82–86. • When you help your child with addition problems that require regrouping, be careful not to say "carry a one" or "carry a two," etc. to describe the process of writing a digit over the tens place. Instead, say, "carry one ten" or "carry two tens," etc. This will reinforce for your child that the digit represents a number of tens to be added to the tens column.
Bonus: Social Studies		• Encourage your child to choose a Native American tribe to research. In what part of the country did the people live originally? Where do tribe members live now? What types of traditional houses did they build? Have your child use natural materials to construct a model of a traditional dwelling.

Shoe Sale Rush

what why rush when shoe
ship where cash sheep while

Write the words that begin like **shark**.

___________ ___________ ___________

Write the words that begin like **whistle**.

___________ ___________ ___________ ___________ ___________

Write the words that end like **brush**.

___________ ___________

Write the correct word on the line.

1. Money ___________
2. To hurry ___________
3. A word used to tell about two things happening at the same time ___________
4. It asks for a reason. ___________
5. A large boat ___________
6. It asks about a thing. ___________
7. It asks about a place. ___________
8. A farm animal ___________
9. It asks about a time. ___________
10. You wear it on your foot. ___________

Inching Along

Write the words that begin like **cheese**.

_______________ _______________

Write the words that begin like **thumb**.

_______________ _______________ _______________

Write the words that end like **branch**.

_______________ _______________ _______________

Write the words that end like **teeth**.

_______________ _______________

Circle the misspelled word. Then, write the word correctly on the line.

1. Which team do you thick will win the game? _______________
2. The dentist filled the cavity in her toth. _______________
3. We will boff ride on the train. _______________
4. A baby kangaroo is about 1 itch long when it is born. _______________
5. There is an apple for eack person. _______________
6. Theo had to chanj his clothes after he fell in the mud. _______________
7. What is that furry ting under the table? _______________
8. A star soccer player will teech us how to kick the ball. _______________
9. She wrote a letter to tank her grandmother for the gift. _______________
10. Mom helped the lost cilde find his mother. _______________

Fluttering Flags

floor	glue	blink	play	glad
flag	club	plant	blow	clean

Write the spelling words that begin with the sound you hear at the beginni
of the pictures.

Complete the puzzle.

Across

2. Opposite of **work**
3. To open and close your eyes quickly
4. Part of a room
5. Opposite of **dirty**
6. Paste

Down

1. Happy
2. To put seeds in the ground
3. The wind can do this
4. A banner
5. A heavy stick

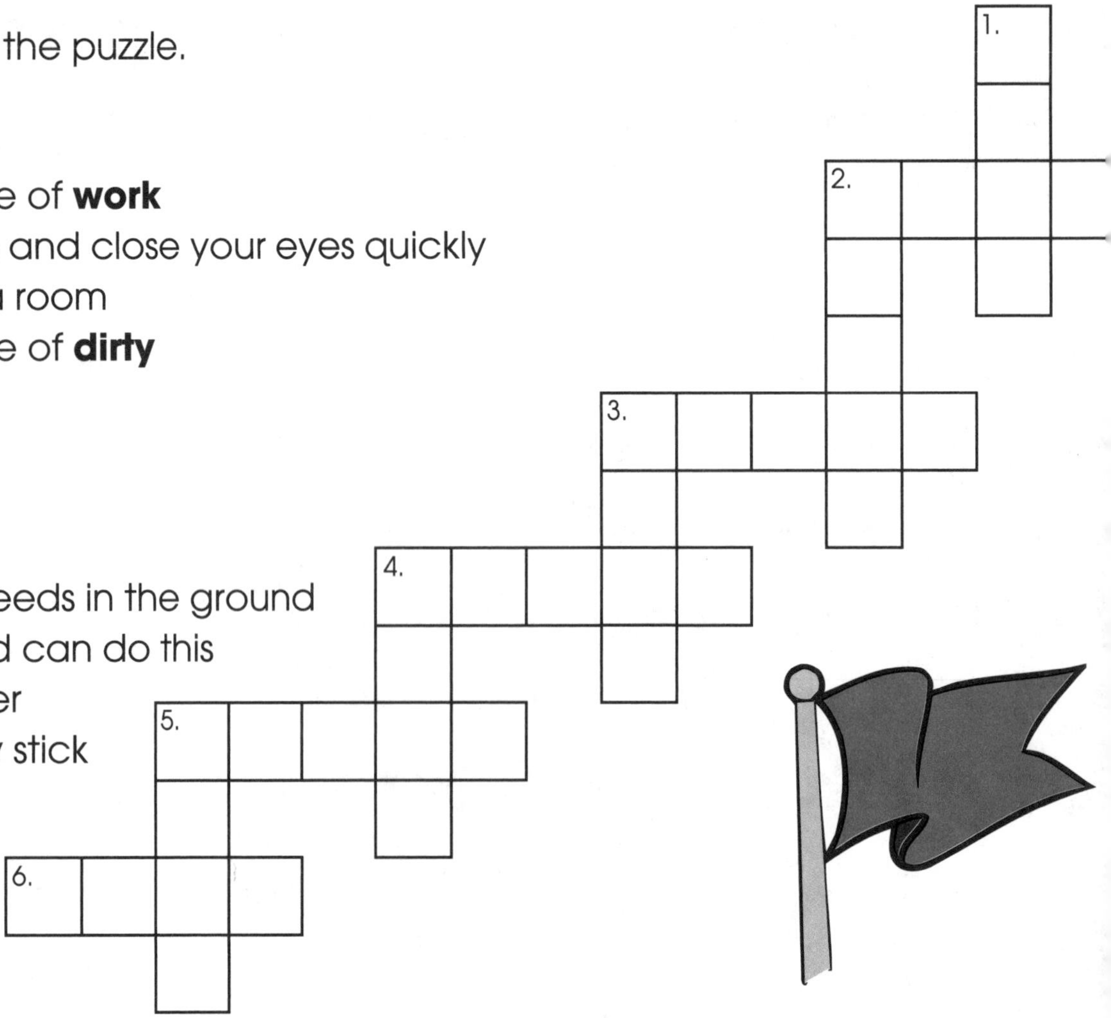

Smile, Please!

sleep small speak snap slow

smart spin smile spell snow

Write the words that begin with the sound you hear at the beginning of the pictures.

____

____

____

____

____

____

____

____

____

____

Write the missing word on the line.

1. Can you ____________ all the words correctly?
2. The clown has a big ____________ painted on his face.
3. A baby needs lots of ____________ .
4. Steve likes sledding on the fresh white ____________ .
5. A ____________ white bunny hid behind the bush.
6. Studying and learning will help make you ____________ .
7. Bike wheels ____________ when you pedal.
8. Do you know how to ____________ your fingers?
9. Cars must ____________ down near a school.
10. Please ____________ louder, so that everyone can hear you.

Just Like Magic

Add.

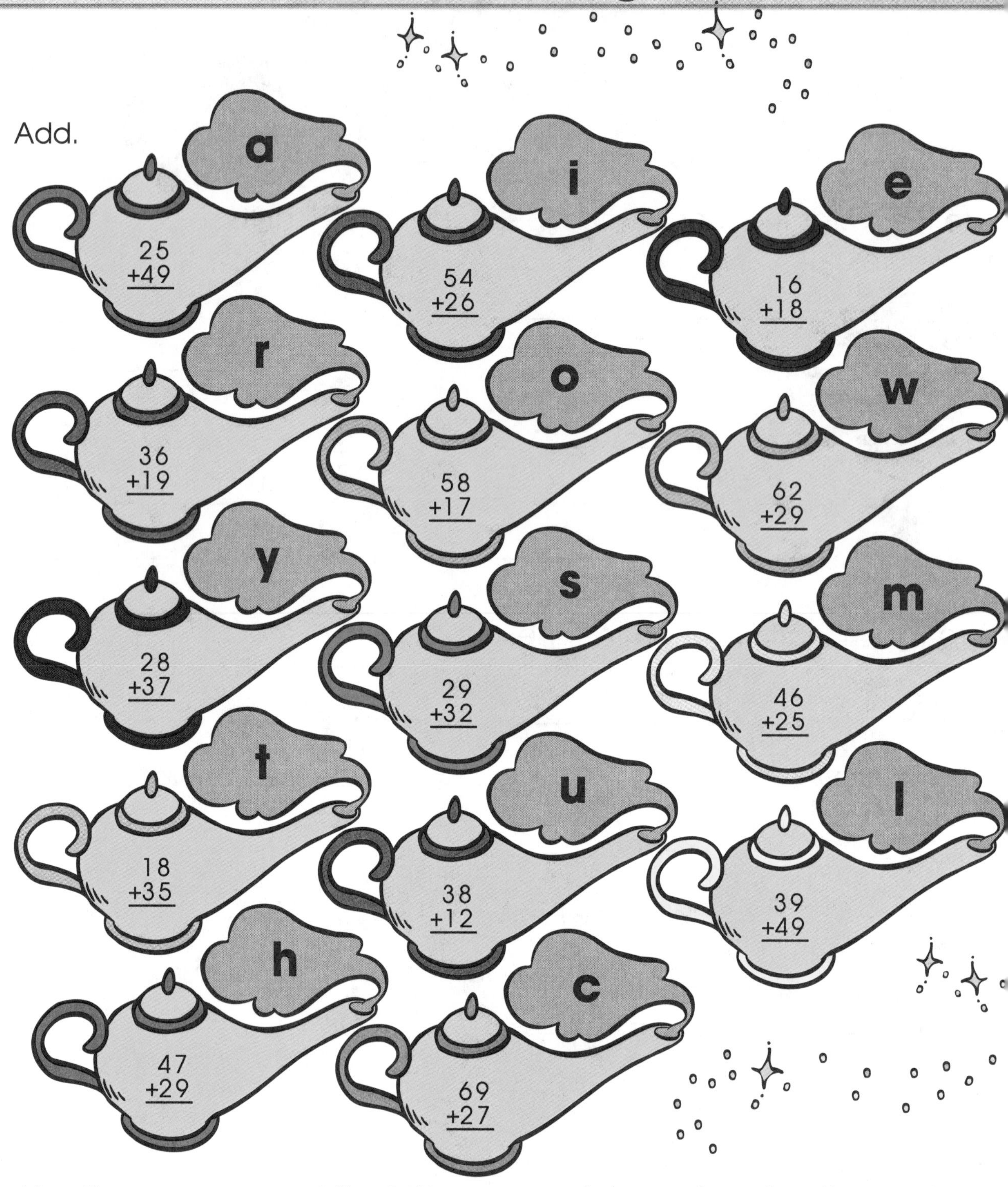

Use the answers and the letter on each lamp to solve the code.

___ ___ ___   ___ ___ ___   ___ ___ ___ ___

71 74 65   74 88 88   65 75 50 55

___ ___ ___ ___ ___ ___   ___ ___ ___ ___   ___ ___ ___ ___ !

91 80 61 76 34 61   96 75 71 34   53 55 50 34

Nutty Addition

am Squirrel and his friend Wendy were gathering acorns. When hey gather 10 acorns, they put them in a bucket. The picture hows how many acorns Sam and Wendy each gathered. Vrite the number that tells how many.

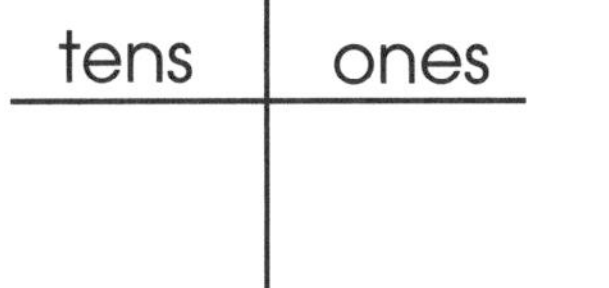

tens	ones

______

tens	ones

______

How many acorns did Sam and Wendy gather in all?

. Put numbers on tens and ones table.

tens	ones
3	6
+ 2	7

2. Add ones first.

tens	ones
1	
3	6
+ 2	7
	3

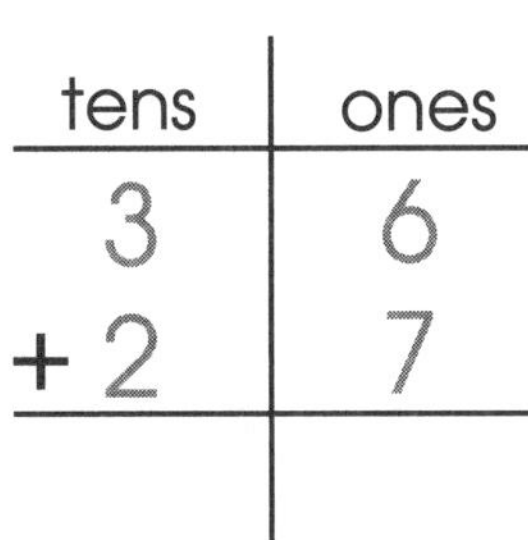

3. Add tens.

tens	ones
1	
3	6
+ 2	7
6	3

Sam and Wendy gathered 63 in all.

Add and regroup as needed.

tens	ones
3	8
+ 4	6

tens	ones
5	4
+ 2	7

tens	ones
4	9
+ 1	3

tens	ones
2	6
+ 1	7

Circus Fun

Add. Remember to add the ones first.

tens	ones
2	5
+ 1	4

tens	ones
5	3
+ 3	2

tens	ones
7	1
+ 2	8

tens	ones
4	4
+ 3	2

tens	ones
5	1
+ 3	7

tens	ones
2	6
+ 5	2

tens	ones
2	6
+ 4	2

tens	ones
3	7
+ 5	1

tens	ones
1	9
+ 3	0

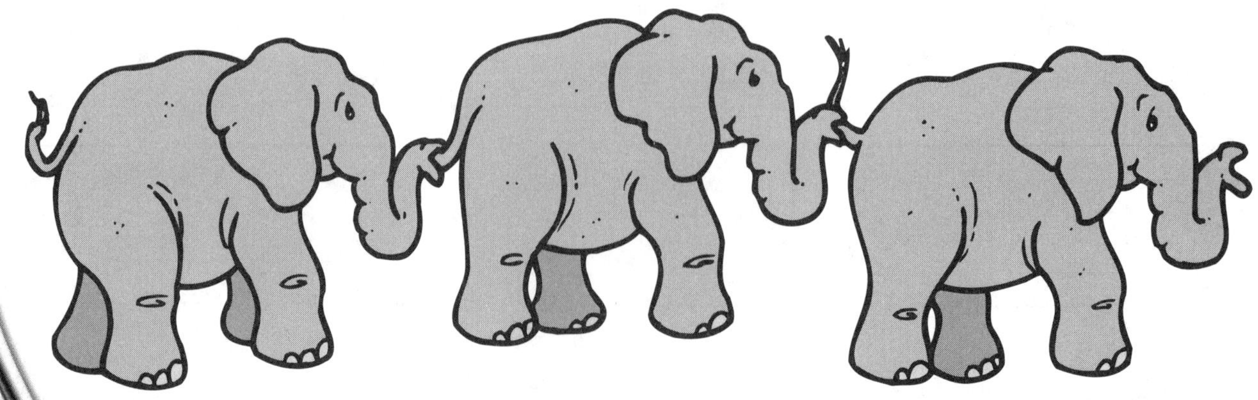

Addition

Add.

Example:

Add the ones.

$$\begin{array}{r} 26 \\ +21 \\ \hline 7 \end{array}$$

Add the tens.

$$\begin{array}{r} 26 \\ +21 \\ \hline 47 \end{array}$$

$$\begin{array}{r} 18 \\ +11 \\ \hline \end{array} \qquad \begin{array}{r} 24 \\ +35 \\ \hline \end{array} \qquad \begin{array}{r} 38 \\ +21 \\ \hline \end{array} \qquad \begin{array}{r} 49 \\ +50 \\ \hline \end{array} \qquad \begin{array}{r} 52 \\ +33 \\ \hline \end{array}$$

$$\begin{array}{r} 75 \\ +12 \\ \hline \end{array} \qquad \begin{array}{r} 83 \\ +16 \\ \hline \end{array} \qquad \begin{array}{r} 67 \\ +32 \\ \hline \end{array} \qquad \begin{array}{r} 44 \\ +25 \\ \hline \end{array} \qquad \begin{array}{r} 28 \\ +41 \\ \hline \end{array}$$

68 + 20 = _____ 54 + 25 = _____ 71 + 17 = _____

The Lions scored 42 points. The Clippers scored 21 points.

How many points were scored in all? __________

Addition: Regrouping

Addition means "putting together" or adding two or more numbers to find the sum. For example, 3 + 5 + 8. To **regroup** is to use ten ones to form one ten, ten tens to form one 100, and so on.

Add using regrouping.

Example:

Add the ones.	Add the tens with regrouping.
88 +21 9	88 +21 109

37 +72	56 +67	51 +88	37 +55	70 +68
93 +54	47 +82	81 +77	23 +92	36 +71

92 + 13 = _____   73 + 83 = _____   54 + 61 = _____

The Blues scored 63 points. The Reds scored 44 points. How many points were scored in all?

____

Week 8 Skills

Subject	Skill	Multi-Sensory Learning Activities
Reading and Language Arts	Spell beginning and ending consonant blends.	• Complete Practice Page 88. • Say a word with a consonant blend or digraph, such as **wash**. How many more words can you and your child think of that contain the same consonant team?
	Spell the hard **c** sound heard in **cow** and the soft **c** sound heard in **circle**.	• Complete Practice Pages 89–91. • Review these rules with your child. The /**k**/ sound is spelled **c** in blends and when followed by **a**, **o**, and **u**. It is spelled **k** when followed by **i** and **e**. The /**s**/ sound is spelled **c** when followed by **i** or **e**. It is spelled **s** in blends and when followed by **a**, **o**, and **u**.
Math	Add three-digit numbers with regrouping.	• Complete Practice Pages 92–94. • Ask your child to choose several problems from page 93 to model with hundred-blocks, ten-blocks, and one-blocks. See directions for creating these on page 15.
	Use mental math skills to add.	• Complete Practice Page 95. • Ask your child to point to numbers in the problems on page 95 that contain zero ones or zero tens.
	Review single-digit subtraction.	• Complete Practice Page 96. • Purchase or create flash cards for single-digit subtraction facts such as **10 - 3** and **8 - 5**. Show each card to your child. If the problem is answered correctly within three seconds, then he or she knows the fact. If it takes longer, set the card aside to be practiced later. Spend a few minutes practicing subtraction facts each day this week.

Bumper Cars

jump pond kind hand land stamp bump send camp ramp

Write the words that end with the same consonants as **sand**.

______ ______ ______ ______ ______

Write the words that end with the same consonants as **stump**.

______ ______ ______ ______ ______

Write the words on the lines. Then, use the numbered letters to solve the code.

1. To run into — __ __ __ __ (2nd letter: 1)
2. Not mean — __ __ __ __ (1st letter: 2, 2nd letter: 3)
3. To live in a tent in the woods — __ __ __ __ (2nd letter: 4)
4. A small lake — __ __ __ __ (2nd letter: 5)
5. A walkway that slopes — __ __ __ __ (1st letter: 6)
6. To leap — __ __ __ __ (4th letter: 7)
7. The ground — __ __ __ __ (1st letter: 8)
8. A part of your body — __ __ __ __ (1st letter: 9, 4th letter: 10)
9. To make or order someone to leave — __ __ __ __ (2nd letter: 11, 3rd letter: 12)
10. You need this to mail a letter — __ __ __ __ __ (2nd letter: 13)

Y __ __   __ __ __ __ __ __ __
(Y) 5 1   9 4 12 10 8 11 10

__ __   __ __ __ __   __   __ __ __!
3 13   8 3 2 11   4   7 6 5

Phonics

There are several consonants that make the **k** sound: **c** when followed by **a**, **o** or **u** as in **cow** or **cup**; the letter **k** as in **milk**; the letters **ch** as in **Christmas** and **ck** as in **black**.

Read the following words. Circle the letters that make the **k** sound. The first one is done for you.

a(ch)e	school	market	comb
camera	deck	darkness	Christmas
necklace	doctor	stomach	crack
nickel	skin	thick	escape

Use your own words to finish the following sentences. Use words with the **k** sound.

1. If I had a nickel, I would ______________________________.

2. My doctor is very ______________________________.

3. We bought ripe, juicy tomatoes at the ______________________________.

4. If I had a camera now, I would take a picture of ______________________________.

5. When my stomach aches, ______________________________.

Backpacking

kite	sick	key	pick	king
back	call	cake	duck	candy

Write the words beginning with **c** that make the **k** sound.

_______________ _______________ _______________

Write the words beginning with **k** that make the **k** sound.

_______________ _______________ _______________

Write the words ending with **ck** that make the **k** sound.

_______________ _______________ _______________ _______________

Write the missing words in the boxes.

1. Which ________ will open the lock?

2. The front and ______ of the folder look the same.

3. A mother ______ waddled to the pond.

4. Many people are needed to ______ the ripe apples.

5. The wind blew the ________ high into the sky.

6. Kate had to stay home because she was ________.

7. The ________ and queen live in a castle.

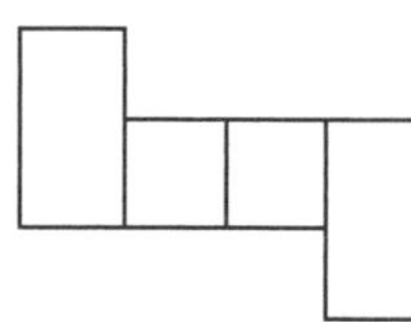

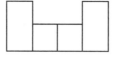

8. Buck gave his mom a box of chocolate ______.

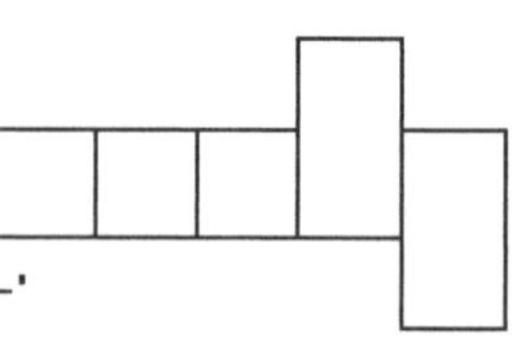

9. Let's ______ our friends and invite them to a party.

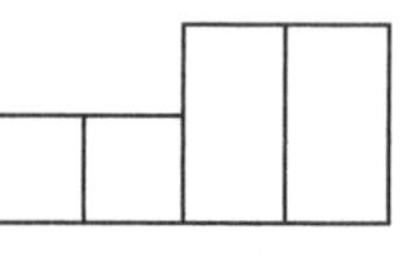

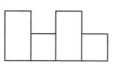

10. There are eight candles on her birthday _________ .

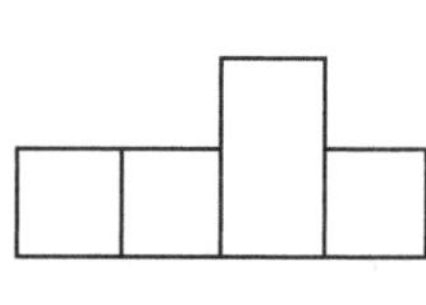

Hard and Soft c and g

Circle as many words in each word search as you can find. List them in the correct column. **Hint**: the words going up and down have the hard sound, and the words going across and backwards are soft.

g

Hard ⇩								Soft ⇨
	t	s	g	e	m	n	r	
________	e	l	t	n	e	g	p	________
________	g	n	s	g	e	r	m	________
________	i	t	o	a	h	o	f	________
________	r	i	h	p	r	a	o	________
________	l	e	g	i	a	n	t	________

Two words in the **c** word find go diagonally. They have both a hard and a soft **c** sound.

c

Hard ⇩								Soft ⇨
	c	e	n	t	e	r	c	
________	a	i	c	r	a	i	a	________
________	s	x	r	a	r	g	r	________
________	t	n	e	c	l	f	p	________
________	p	y	u	a	l	n	e	
________	a	s	r	n	s	e	t	
________	c	i	t	y	o	m	u	

Both Hard and Soft

________ ________

3-Digit Addition: Regrouping

Study the examples. Follow the steps to add.

Example:

Step 1: Add the ones

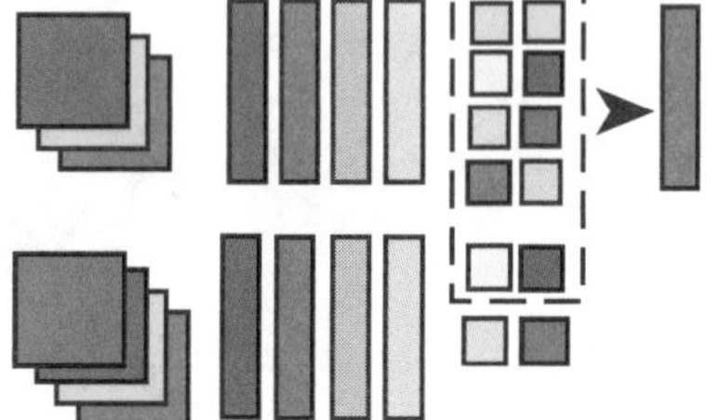

Do you regroup? Yes

Step 2: Add the tens

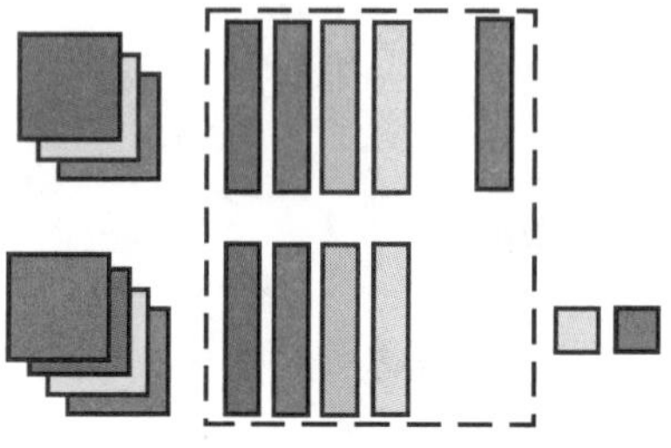

Do you regroup? No

Step 3: Add the hundreds

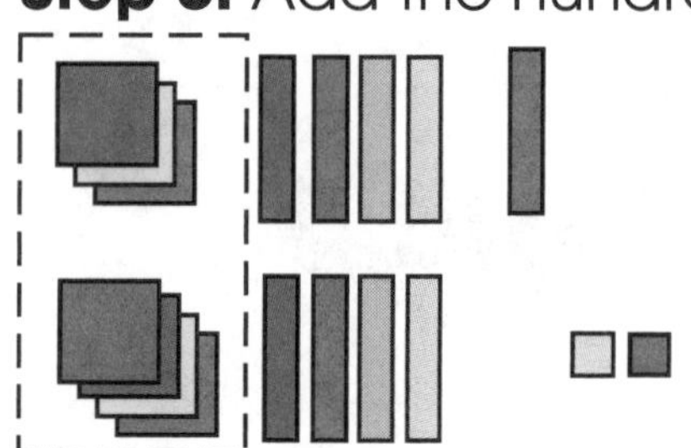

hundreds	tens	ones
	1	
3	4	8
+4	4	4
		2

hundreds	tens	ones
	1	
3	4	8
+4	4	4
	9	2

hundreds	tens	ones
	1	
3	4	8
+4	4	4
7	9	2

hundreds	tens	ones
	1	
2	1	4
+2	3	8
4	5	2

hundreds	tens	ones
	1	
3	6	8
+2	1	3
___	8	1

hundreds	tens	ones
	1	
1	1	9
+5	6	5
___	___	4

418	471	334	659	736	426	567	327
+323	+319	+528	+127	+145	+165	+228	+354

3-Digit Addition: Regrouping

Study the examples. Follow the steps to add. Regroup when needed.

Step 1: Add the ones.

Step 2: Add the tens.

Step 3: Add the hundreds.

hundreds	tens	ones
1	1	
3	4	8
+4	5	4
8	0	2

348	172	575	623	369	733
+214	+418	+329	+268	+533	+229

411	423	639	624	272	393
+299	+169	+177	+368	+469	+418

Addition: Regrouping

Study the examples. Add using regrouping.

Examples:

Add the ones. Regroup		Add the tens. Regroup		Add the hundreds.
1 156 +267 3	6 +7 13	1 5 +6 12	11 156 +267 23	1 156 +267 423

29 46 +12	81 78 +33	52 67 +23	49 37 +19	162 +349
273 +198	655 +297	783 +148	385 +169	428 +122

Sally went bowling. She had scores of 115, 129, and 103. What was her total score for three games? ______

Addition: Mental Math

Try to do theses addition problems in your head without using paper and pencil.

7 +4	6 +3	8 +1	10 + 2	2 +9	6 +6
10 +20	40 +20	80 +100	60 +30	50 +70	100 + 40
350 +150	300 +500	400 +800	450 + 10	680 +100	900 + 70
1,000 + 200	4,000 400 + 30	300 200 + 80	8,000 500 + 60	9,800 + 150	7,000 300 + 30

Subtraction

Complete the facts to 10.

10	7	6	4	9
− 5	− 2	− 3	− 3	− 1

3	8	10	7	8
− 2	− 6	− 7	− 1	− 5

10	7	2	6	8	9	8	9	7	5
− 1	− 4	− 1	− 4	− 4	− 5	− 1	− 2	− 6	− 3

10	8	9	5	10	7	4	6	9	4
− 3	− 7	− 6	− 4	− 6	− 3	− 2	− 2	− 7	− 1

10	5	9	9	8	7	6	5	8	7
− 8	− 1	− 5	− 3	− 5	− 3	− 4	− 2	− 2	− 4

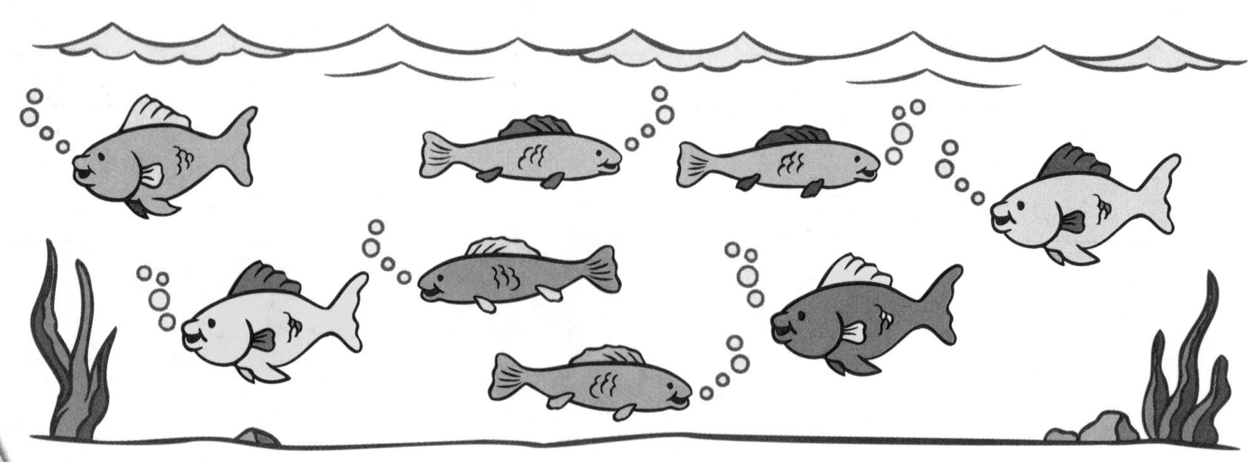

Week 9 Skills

Subject	Skill	Multi-Sensory Learning Activities
Reading and Language Arts	Spell the /**oo**/ and /**ow**/ sounds in words.	• Complete Practice Pages 98–100. • Vowel sounds in words like **foot**, **push**, **mouse**, and **town** can be tricky to spell. Have your child use a highlighter pen to mark the letters that spell the vowel sounds in words he or she wrote on pages 98–100.
	Spell words with **r**-controlled vowels.	• Complete Practice Pages 101 and 102. • Review the story of "rude **r**" (page 15). Then, read *Gregory, the Terrible Eater* by Mitchell Sharmat. Look for words with **r**-controlled vowels.
Math	Review single-digit subtraction.	• Complete Practice Pages 103–106. • After your child completes page 103, ask him or her to supply a related addition problem for each solved problem. For **11 – 9 = 2**, a related problem is **2 + 9 = 11**. Choose several problems and challenge your child to write complete fact families for them. For the problem above, the complete fact family includes these facts: **2 + 9 = 11**, **9 + 2 = 11**, **11 – 9 = 2**, **11 – 2 = 9**. • Place 10 pennies on a table. Use your hand to cover some of the pennies. Can your child quickly tell you how many pennies are hidden by counting the number of visible pennies?

Baking Cookies

wood book push

put took pull foot

cook look full

Write the words with double **o** that make the sound you hear in the middle of **hook**.

______ ______ ______

______ ______ ______

Write the words with **u** that make the sound you hear in the middle of **foot**.

______ ______

______ ______

Write the correct word on each line.

1. You do this with your eyes. ______
2. Opposite of **empty** ______
3. You burn this in a fireplace. ______
4. A part of your body ______
5. Something to read ______
6. Opposite of **push** ______
7. Did take ______
8. To set something down ______
9. To fix food for a meal ______
10. Opposite of **pull** ______

Clowning Around

clown
our down
count how town
house about now out

Write the **ou** words that make the vowel sound you hear in **mouse**.

_______________ _______________ _______________

_______________ _______________

Write the **ow** words that make the vowel sound you hear in **cow**.

_______________ _______________ _______________

_______________ _______________

Write the missing words in the boxes.

. Sally lives in the ______ on the corner.

2. Do you know ______ to make a robot?

3. Please take the towels ______ of the dryer.

4. We must leave for the airport ______ !

5. It is ______ time for the race to start.

6. They rode the elevator ______ to the bottom floor.

7. This is ______ new four-wheel drive truck.

8. The big funny ______ rode a tiny bike.

9. Can you ______ to 100?

10. The farmer took his fresh fruit to ______.

Super Cool!

food	huge	room	soon	zoo
school	use	cute	rude	moon

Write the double **o** words that make the **oo** sound.

Write the words ending with **e** that make the **oo** sound.

Complete the puzzle.

Across

2. Rhymes with **choose**
4. A place where you learn
6. Opposite of **polite**
7. A place to see many different animals
9. It shines in the sky at night

Down

1. Pretty
3. In a short time
5. Very, very big
6. Part of a house
8. You eat this

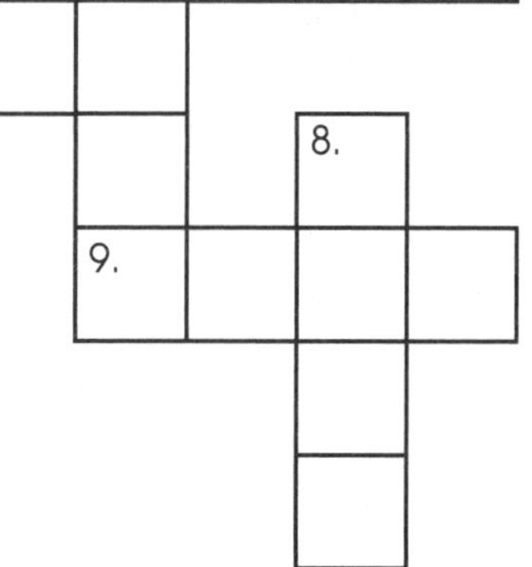

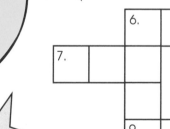

Stir Up a Dessert

stir girl verb

skirt herd her clerk

first bird jerk

Write the words with **er** that make the sound you hear in the middle of **fern**.

_______________ _______________ _______________

_______________ _______________

Write the words with **ir** that make the sound you hear in the middle of **shirt**. _______________ _______________ _______________

_______________ _______________

Write the missing words in the boxes.

1. Our class will sing the ________ song in the program.
2. The cowboys will drive the cattle _______ to the range.
3. Sara wore her new _________ to the party.
4. A tiny _________ chirped when it hatched from its egg.
5. A part of speech that describes an action is called a _________.
6. Trudy met ________ grandmother at the train station.
7. You must ________ the cake batter before you put it in the pan.
8. The car started to _______ as it ran out of gas.
9. Mother paid the ______ for my new shirt.
10. That _______ lives next door to me.

Horsing Around

story	park	corn	part	north
horse	far	farm	hard	start

Write the words with the same vowel sound as in **horn**. Then, circle the letters that make that sound.

______ ______ ______ ______

Write the words with the same vowel sound as in **jar**. Then, circle the letters that make that sound.

______ ______ ______

______ ______ ______

Complete the puzzle.

Across

1. Opposite of **near**
2. A place to play
3. Opposite of **stop**
4. A yellow vegetable
7. An animal you can ride

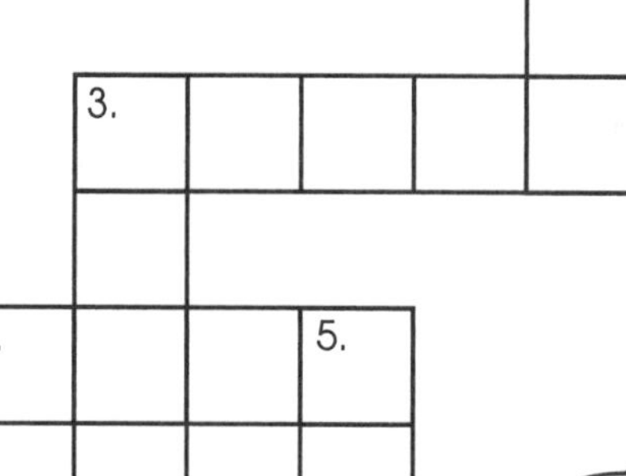

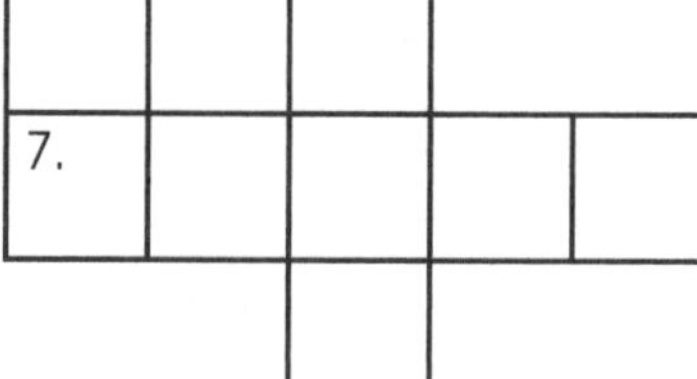

Down

1. A place to raise animals and crops
2. A piece of something
3. Something you can read or write
5. Opposite of **south**
8. Opposite of **soft**

Subtraction

Complete the facts to 18.

11	12	13	9	15
− 9	− 6	− 9	− 4	− 7

14	14	8	11	14
− 9	− 7	− 5	− 2	− 9

17	11	13	15	13	8	14	16	12	11
− 1	− 5	− 5	− 6	− 4	− 4	− 6	− 7	− 8	− 7

10	8	9	18	10	14	15	11	9	8
− 6	− 3	− 5	− 9	− 3	− 8	− 8	− 8	− 3	− 6

11	14	13	5	12	7	16	7	12	11
− 3	− 4	− 7	− 2	− 5	− 4	− 8	− 2	− 9	− 6

Connect the Facts

Subtract. Write the answer.

Missing Subtrahends and Minuends

Fill in the missing part of the subtraction problems.

10 – ◯ = 3 ◯ – 7 = 3 ◯ – 4 = 3 10 – ◯ = 2

Fill in the missing numbers in the problems below.

10 – ___ = 3	___ – 7 = 4	3 – ___ = 1
9 – ___ = 6	7 – ___ = 5	___ – 6 = 2
___ – 2 = 2	___ – 5 = 4	8 – ___ = 3
6 – ___ = 2	7 – ___ = 6	___ – 8 = 2
10 – ___ = 4	___ – 6 = 3	___ – 2 = 7

Fill in the missing numbers in the problems below.

5 – ☐ = 2	8 – ☐ = 4	9 – ☐ = 6	☐ – 3 = 6	☐ – 8 = 1	☐ – 4 = 5	6 – ☐ = 3
☐ – 3 = 5	7 – ☐ = 1	☐ – 4 = 6	9 – ☐ = 4	☐ – 2 = 1	☐ – 7 = 3	4 – ☐ = 2

Subtraction

Complete the facts to 18.

6 − 3	11 − 4	15 − 6	11 − 6	11 − 4					
12 − 3	10 − 6	12 − 4	10 − 5	6 − 4					
13 − 5	8 − 7	12 − 3	14 − 8	17 − 9	11 − 6	11 − 8	15 − 7	7 − 3	13 − 7
14 − 9	10 − 3	13 − 4	9 − 6	10 − 8	13 − 6	9 − 6	12 − 9	16 − 7	7 − 4
14 − 6	8 − 5	12 − 7	18 − 9	14 − 6	13 − 8	13 − 6	17 − 8	16 − 9	12 − 4

First Quarter Check-Up

Reading and Language Arts

- ❑ I can spell long vowel sounds and short vowel sounds.
- ❑ I know that, in some words, **y** is a vowel.
- ❑ I can read words with vowel pairs or vowel "teams."
- ❑ I can read words with consonant blends and digraphs.
- ❑ I can spell the hard and soft sounds of **c**.
- ❑ I can spell words with **r**-controlled vowels.
- ❑ I can spell words with the /**oo**/ and /**ow**/ sounds.

Math

- ❑ I can count forward and backward from any number.
- ❑ I can skip-count by twos, fives, and tens.
- ❑ I know the sums of single-digit numbers (addition facts).
- ❑ I can add two- and three-digit numbers without regrouping.
- ❑ I can add two- and three-digit numbers with regrouping.
- ❑ I can use mental math skills to add.
- ❑ I know the differences of single-digit numbers (subtraction facts).

Final Project

Do a different exercise each day for one week. Try jumping jacks, push-ups, squats, and leg-lifts. On a sheet of paper, write each date, the name of the exercise, and how many times you did it. Then, add the numbers to find the total number of exercises you did. Make a sign that says "I Did It!" and shows the total number surrounded by the names of the exercises. Make sure the vowel sound is spelled correctly in each word.

Second Quarter Introduction

During the second quarter of the school year, many children are settled into routines at home and at school. Make sure your family's routines include time for playing, eating and talking together, and reading aloud. Supporting your child's learning and development will build his or her confidence in all areas.

Second Quarter Skills

Practice pages in this book for Weeks 10–18 will help your child improve the following skills.

Reading and Language Arts

- Understand that nouns name people, places, and things
- Understand that proper nouns name specific people, places, and things and begin with a capital letter
- Understand that pronouns take the place of nouns
- Understand how to make nouns plural
- Understand action verbs, helping verbs, and linking verbs
- Understand that verbs take different forms and that subjects and verbs must agree
- Understand that adjectives are describing words

Math

- Subtract single-digit, two-digit, and three-digit numbers
- Subtract with and without regrouping
- Use mental math strategies to subtract
- Review addition and subtraction facts
- Use addition and subtraction to solve word problems
- Work with picture and number patterns

Multi-Sensory Learning Activities

Try these fun activities for enhancing your child's learning and development during the second quarter of the school year. Be sure to choose activities that include speaking, listening, touching, and active movement.

Reading and Language Arts

Make a three-column chart on the inside of a manila file folder. Label the columns **Noun**, **Verb**, and **Adjective**. Write different words such as **blue**, **rabbit**, **go**, **six**, **girl**, **clap**, **happy**, **school**, **fork**, **soft**, **are**, and **walk** on self-sticking notes and ask your child to sort them into the columns.

Ask your child to draw a self-portrait on a large sheet of drawing paper. Underneath, help your child write his or her first and last names, birthdate, and address. Remind your child to begin each proper noun with a capital letter.

To form the past tense of a regular verb, add **ed** (example: **talk/talked**). The past tense of irregular words is spelled differently. (example: **draw/drew**). Linking verbs show no action, but link the subject with a description. They are always in some form of the verb **to be** (example: The dog **is** funny). A helping verb comes before the main verb in a sentence (example: We **must** go soon). When you read together, ask your child to point to the verb in a sentence, tell which kind of verb it is, and tell whether it is in the present or past tense.

Math

Say or write word problems for your child that include a missing number. For example, ask, "I had __ books. I read 4 books. I have 2 left to read. What number is missing?" or "I had 10 grapes. I ate ___ grapes. I had 7 left. What number is missing?"

Use card stock to make triangle cards like the one shown at right. On each card, use one color to write addends in two corners. Use another color to write the sum in the third corner. To practice, hide one corner. Your child must supply the missing number. If the two visible numbers are the same color, add them. If the numbers are different colors, subtract.

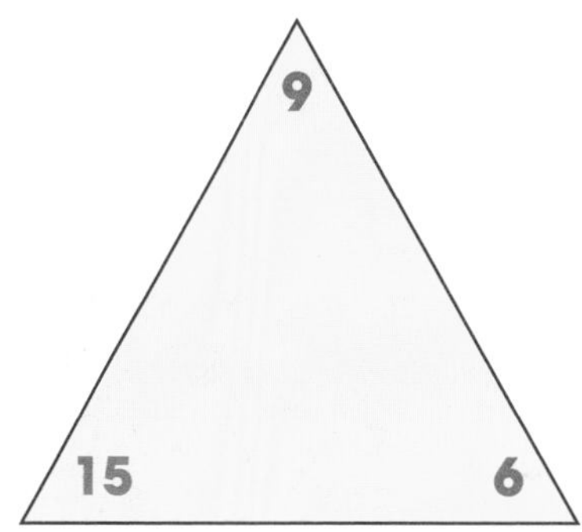

Give your child plenty of opportunities to recognize shape, picture, and number patterns. Begin with concrete materials such as blocks or coins and move to number patterns on paper. Numbers written in the base-ten system have repetition from 0–9 in the tens and ones places. Seeing this pattern will give your child confidence with numbers 1–100 and help him or her understand place value.

Second Quarter Introduction, cont.

Science

The water in the ocean contains salt from dissolved rock. Create salt water by dissolving one teaspoon of salt in one cup of water. Prepare a second cup with the same amount of fresh water. Drop a light object, such as a slice of carrot, in both cups. If the carrot is just the right size, it will float in the salt water and sink in the fresh water. It is easier to float in salt water than in freshwater because salt water is denser.

Social Studies

Help your child name 50 U.S. states. Print a blank map of the U.S. from the Internet. Name a state and help your child color it and label it. Make sure to begin its name with a capital letter. Help your child draw a compass rose on the map showing North, South, East, and West. Then, name several states and ask your child to use the compass rose to tell in what part of the country it is found.

Seasonal Fun

Purchase a poinsettia and display it out of the reach of younger children and pets. Encourage your child to think of 10 adjectives to describe the plant. Read *The Legend of the Poinsettia* by Tomie dePaola. Then, use red tissue paper, green pipe cleaners, and glitter glue to create holiday poinsettia ornaments.

Make a menorah by lining up eight square-sided candleholders made from clear glass. Cut squares of tissue paper in different colors. Use watered-down white glue and a paintbrush to attach the tissue to the sides of the candleholders and to coat all surfaces. Let dry and insert tea lights for a colorful holiday display.

Week 10 Skills

Subject	Skill	Multi-Sensory Learning Activities
Reading and Language Arts	Use common nouns (or words that name people, places, and things).	• Complete Practice Pages 112–115. • Read a fairy tale. Ask your child to find 15 nouns in the story. He or she should write the words in three columns labeled **People**, **Places**, and **Things**.
Math	Review single-digit subtraction.	• Complete Practice Page 116. • Have your child trace his or her hand 10 times on drawing paper. Write a number **1–10** on the palm of each hand. Then, on each finger, have your child write a subtraction problem whose difference equals the number shown on the palm. A hand with **4** on the palm could have these problems on the fingers: **9 – 5**, **5 – 1**, **4 – 0**, **10 – 6**, **7 – 3**.
	Subtract two-digit numbers without regrouping.	• Complete Practice Page 117. • Have your child model one problem from page 117 with ten-blocks and one-blocks. See directions for creating these on page 15. If this is difficult, your child probably needs more practice with single-digit subtraction facts.
	Subtract two-digit numbers with regrouping.	• Complete Practice Pages 118–120. • Choose one problem from page 118 to walk though carefully with your child using ten- and one-blocks from the previous activity. Make sure your child understands that 10 ones are regrouped as 1 ten to solve the problem.

Singular Nouns

A **singular noun** names one person, place or thing.

Example: My **mother** unlocked the old **trunk** in the **attic**.

If the noun is singular, draw a line from it to the trunk. If the noun is not singular, draw an **X** on the word.

teddy bear	hammer	picture	sweater
bonnet	letters	seashells	fiddle
kite	ring	feather	books
postcard	crayon	doll	dishes
blocks	hats	bicycle	blanket

Common Nouns

A **common noun** names a person, place or thing.

Example: The **boy** had several **chores** to do.

Fill in the circle below each common noun.

1. First, the boy had to feed his puppy.
2. He got fresh water for his pet.
3. Next, the boy poured some dry food into a bowl.
4. He set the dish on the floor in the kitchen.
5. Then, he called his dog to come to dinner.
6. The boy and his dad worked in the garden.
7. The father turned the dirt with a shovel.
8. The boy carefully dropped seeds into little holes.
9. Soon, tiny plants would sprout from the soil.
10. Sunshine and showers would help the radishes grow.

Nouns

Nouns are words that tell the names of people, places or things.

Read the words below. Then, write them in the correct column.

goat	Mrs. Jackson	girl
beach	tree	song
mouth	park	Jean Rivers
finger	flower	New York
Kevin Jones	Elm City	Frank Gates
Main Street	theater	skates
River Park	father	boy

Person

Place

Thing

Common Nouns

Common nouns are nouns that name any member of a group of people, places or things, rather than specific people, places or things.

Read the sentences below and write the common noun found in each sentence.

Example: socks My socks do not match.

1. ______________ The bird could not fly.
2. ______________ Ben likes to eat jelly beans.
3. ______________ I am going to meet my mother.
4. ______________ We will go swimming in the lake tomorrow.
5. ______________ I hope the flowers will grow quickly.
6. ______________ We colored eggs together.
7. ______________ It is easy to ride a bicycle.
8. ______________ My cousin is very tall.
9. ______________ Ted and Jane went fishing in their boat.
10. ______________ They won a prize yesterday.
11. ______________ She fell down and twisted her ankle.
12. ______________ My brother was born today.
13. ______________ She went down the slide.
14. ______________ Ray went to the doctor today.

Subtraction

Subtraction is "taking away" or subtracting one number from another to find the difference.

Subtract.

Example:

4
−3
1

5	6	4	3	2	1
−3	−1	−3	−1	−0	−1

9	7	10	14	15	12
−2	−4	− 5	− 6	− 9	− 3

18	13	14	11	17	16
− 8	− 5	− 7	− 4	− 9	− 8

2-Digit Subtraction

Study the example. Follow the steps to subtract.

Example:

$$\begin{array}{r} 28 \\ -14 \\ \hline \end{array}$$

Step 1: Subtract the ones

tens	ones
2	8
-1	4
	4

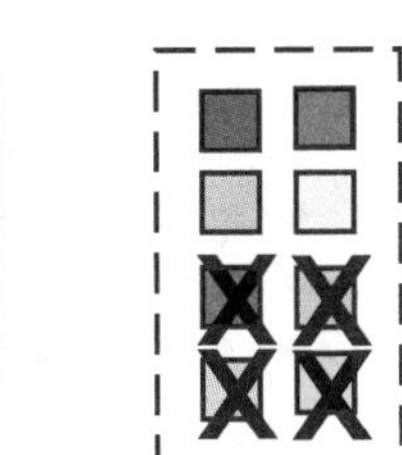

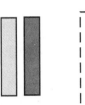

Step 2: Subtract the tens

tens	ones
2	8
-1	4
1	4

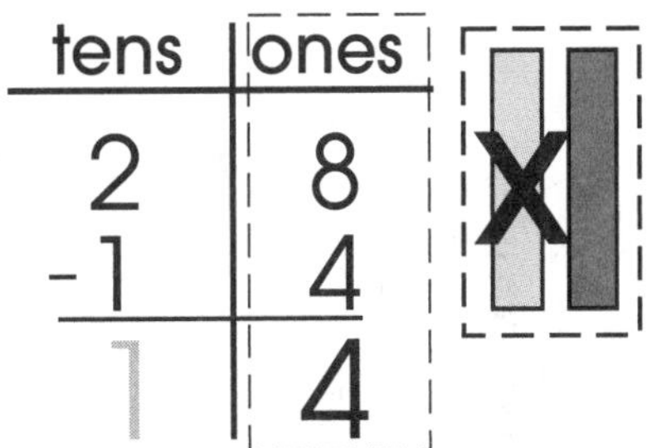

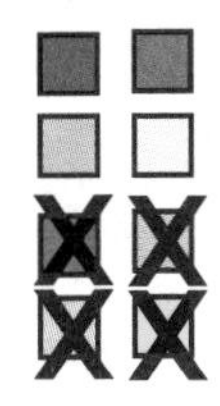

tens	ones
2	4
-1	2
1	2

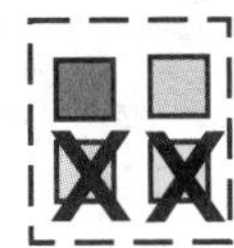

tens	ones
3	8
-1	5
2	3

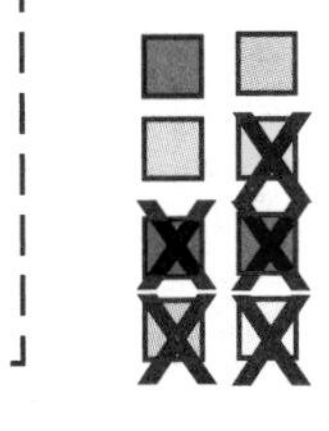

24	61	77	85	57	87	59	96
− 12	− 30	− 44	− 24	− 23	− 33	− 34	− 16

29	74	46	69	95	33	78	22
− 15	− 51	− 32	− 35	− 32	− 33	− 26	− 11

2-Digit Subtraction: Regrouping

Subtraction is "taking away" or subtracting one number from another to find the difference. **Regrouping** is using one ten to form ten ones, one 100 to form ten tens and so on.

Study the examples. Follow the steps to subtract.

Example:

$$\begin{array}{r} 37 \\ -19 \\ \hline \end{array}$$

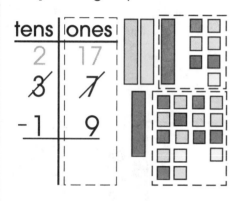

Step 1: Regroup.

tens	ones
2	17
~~3~~	~~7~~
-1	9

Step 2: Subtract the ones.

tens	ones
2	17
~~3~~	~~7~~
-1	9
	8

Step 3: Subtract the tens.

tens	ones
2	17
~~3~~	~~7~~
-1	9
1	8

tens	ones
0	12
~~1~~	~~2~~
-	9
	3

tens	ones
2	14
~~3~~	~~4~~
-1	6
1	8

tens	ones
3	15
~~4~~	~~5~~
-2	9
1	6

$$\begin{array}{r} 28 \\ -19 \\ \hline \end{array} \quad \begin{array}{r} 46 \\ -18 \\ \hline \end{array} \quad \begin{array}{r} 12 \\ -8 \\ \hline \end{array} \quad \begin{array}{r} 30 \\ -12 \\ \hline \end{array} \quad \begin{array}{r} 52 \\ -25 \\ \hline \end{array} \quad \begin{array}{r} 47 \\ -35 \\ \hline \end{array} \quad \begin{array}{r} 21 \\ -13 \\ \hline \end{array} \quad \begin{array}{r} 45 \\ -25 \\ \hline \end{array}$$

2-Digit Subtraction: Regrouping

Study the steps for subtracting. Solve the problems using the steps.

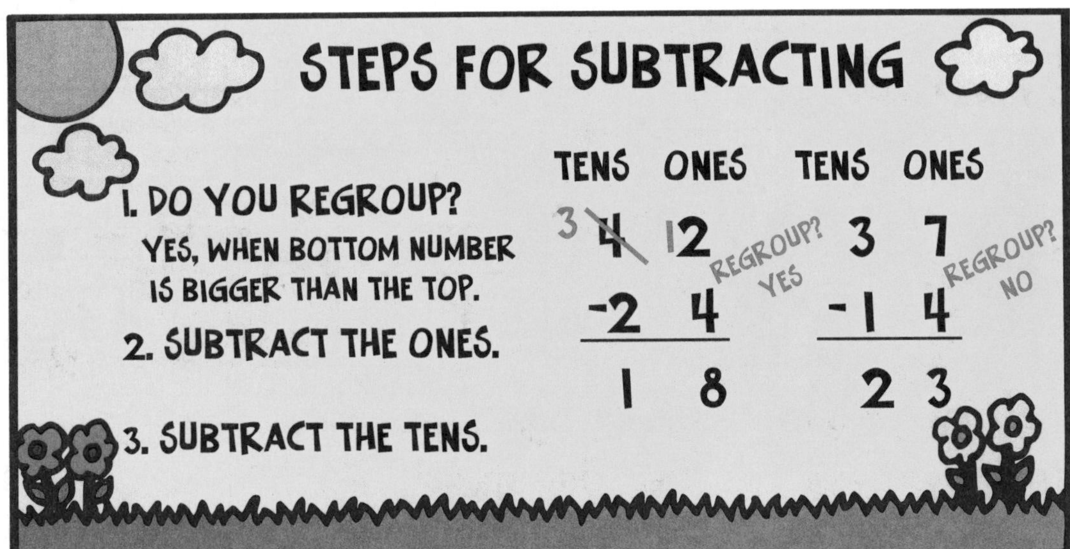

tens	ones
4	7
- 2	8

tens	ones
6	4
- 3	4

tens	ones
5	3
- 3	9

$$\begin{array}{r} 56 \\ -27 \\ \hline \end{array} \quad \begin{array}{r} 83 \\ -47 \\ \hline \end{array} \quad \begin{array}{r} 43 \\ -39 \\ \hline \end{array} \quad \begin{array}{r} 75 \\ -53 \\ \hline \end{array} \quad \begin{array}{r} 91 \\ -18 \\ \hline \end{array}$$

$$\begin{array}{r} 73 \\ -66 \\ \hline \end{array} \quad \begin{array}{r} 35 \\ -14 \\ \hline \end{array} \quad \begin{array}{r} 67 \\ -58 \\ \hline \end{array} \quad \begin{array}{r} 26 \\ -7 \\ \hline \end{array} \quad \begin{array}{r} 68 \\ -45 \\ \hline \end{array}$$

Airport Action

To find out if the answer to a subtraction problem is correct, add the answer to the number taken away. If the sum is the same as the first number in the subtraction problem, then the answer is correct.

Example 1

$$\begin{array}{r} \overset{3\ 13}{\cancel{4}\cancel{3}} \\ -\ 27 \\ \hline 16 \end{array} \qquad \begin{array}{r} \overset{1}{16} \\ +\ 27 \\ \hline 43 \end{array}$$

Since the sum is the same as the first number in the subtraction problem, the answer must be correct.

Example 2

$$\begin{array}{r} \overset{6\ 11}{\cancel{7}\cancel{1}} \\ -\ 28 \\ \hline 43 \end{array} \qquad \begin{array}{r} \overset{1}{43} \\ +\ 28 \\ \hline 71 \end{array}$$

Check the subtraction by adding.

$$\begin{array}{r} 52 \\ -\ 37 \\ \hline 25 \end{array} \qquad \begin{array}{r} \\ +\ \_\_\_ \\ \hline \end{array}$$

Is the subtraction problem correct? ________

How do you know?

Subtract. Then, add to check.

$$\begin{array}{r} 52 \\ -\ 37 \\ \hline \end{array} \qquad \begin{array}{r} \\ +\ \_\_\_ \\ \hline \end{array} \qquad\qquad \begin{array}{r} 80 \\ -\ 26 \\ \hline \end{array} \qquad \begin{array}{r} \\ +\ \_\_\_ \\ \hline \end{array} \qquad\qquad \begin{array}{r} 64 \\ -\ 48 \\ \hline \end{array} \qquad \begin{array}{r} \\ +\ \_\_\_ \\ \hline \end{array}$$

Week 11 Skills

Subject	Skill	Multi-Sensory Learning Activities
Reading and Language Arts	Use proper nouns (or words that name specific people, places, and things).	• Complete Practice Pages 122–125. • Read *Q Is for Duck: An Alphabet Guessing Game* by Mary Elting and Michael Folsom. Have your child point to the noun on each page that names an animal. Explain that these are common nouns. Then, encourage your child to create names for each animal, such as Delaney Duck, and write them on a sheet of paper, making sure to begin each with a capital letter. Explain that these are examples of proper nouns that name specific people, places, and things.
Math	Subtract two-digit numbers with and without regrouping.	• Complete Practice Pages 126–130. • Spend time with your child making sure he or she understands how to regroup to solve subtraction problems. Use ten-blocks and one-blocks (see page 15) to model a number such as **52**. Then, have your child roll a die and subtract the number rolled from 52. Will regrouping be needed? Use the blocks to model the problem before writing it on paper. Continue to roll the die and subtract numbers until you approach 0.

Proper Nouns

Proper nouns are names of specific people, places or things. Proper nouns begin with a capital letter.

Read the sentences below and circle the proper nouns found in each sentence.

Example: Aunt Frances gave me a puppy for my birthday.

1. We lived on Jackson Street before we moved to our new house.
2. Angela's birthday party is tomorrow night.
3. We drove through Cheyenne, Wyoming on our way home.
4. Dr. Charles always gives me a treat for not crying.
5. George Washington was our first president.
6. Our class took a field trip to the Johnson Flower Farm.
7. Uncle Jack lives in New York City.
8. Amy and Elizabeth are best friends.
9. We buy doughnuts at the Grayson Bakery.
10. My favorite movie is *E.T.*
11. We flew to Miami, Florida in a plane.
12. We go to Riverfront Stadium to watch the baseball games.
13. Mr. Fields is a wonderful music teacher.
14. My best friend is Tom Dunlap.

Proper Nouns

Rewrite each sentence, capitalizing the proper nouns.

1. mike's birthday is in september.

2. aunt katie lives in detroit, michigan.

3. In july, we went to canada.

4. kathy jones moved to utah in january.

5. My favorite holiday is valentine's day in february.

6. On friday, mr. polzin gave the smith family a tour.

7. saturday, uncle cliff and I will go to the mall of america in minnesota.

Proper Nouns

Write about you! Write a proper noun for each category below. Capitalize the first letter of each proper noun.

1. Your first name: ____________________
2. Your last name: ____________________
3. Your street: ____________________
4. Your city: ____________________
5. Your state: ____________________
6. Your school: ____________________
7. Your best friend's name: ____________________
8. Your teacher: ____________________
9. Your favorite book character: ____________________
10. Your favorite vacation place: ____________________

Proper Nouns

A **proper noun** names a specific or certain person, place or thing. A proper noun always begins with a capital letter.

Example: Becky flew to **St. Louis** in a **Boeing 747**.

Put a ✓ in front of each proper noun.

_________ 1. uncle

_________ 2. Aunt Retta

_________ 3. Forest Park

_________ 4. Gateway Arch

_________ 5. Missouri

_________ 6. school

_________ 7. Miss Hunter

_________ 8. Northwest Plaza

_________ 9. New York Science Center

_________ 10. Ms. Small

_________ 11. Doctor Chang

_________ 12. Union Station

_________ 13. Henry Shaw

_________ 14. museum

_________ 15. librarian

_________ 16. shopping mall

Underline the proper nouns.

1. Becky went to visit Uncle Harry.
2. He took her to see the Cardinals play baseball.
3. The game was at Busch Stadium.
4. The St. Louis Cardinals played the Chicago Cubs.
5. Tony Thompson hit a home run.

Subtraction on the Beach

Subtract. Regroup as needed. Color the spaces with differences of:

10–19 **red** 20–29 **blue** 30–39 **green**

40–49 **yellow** 50–59 **brown** 60–69 **orange**

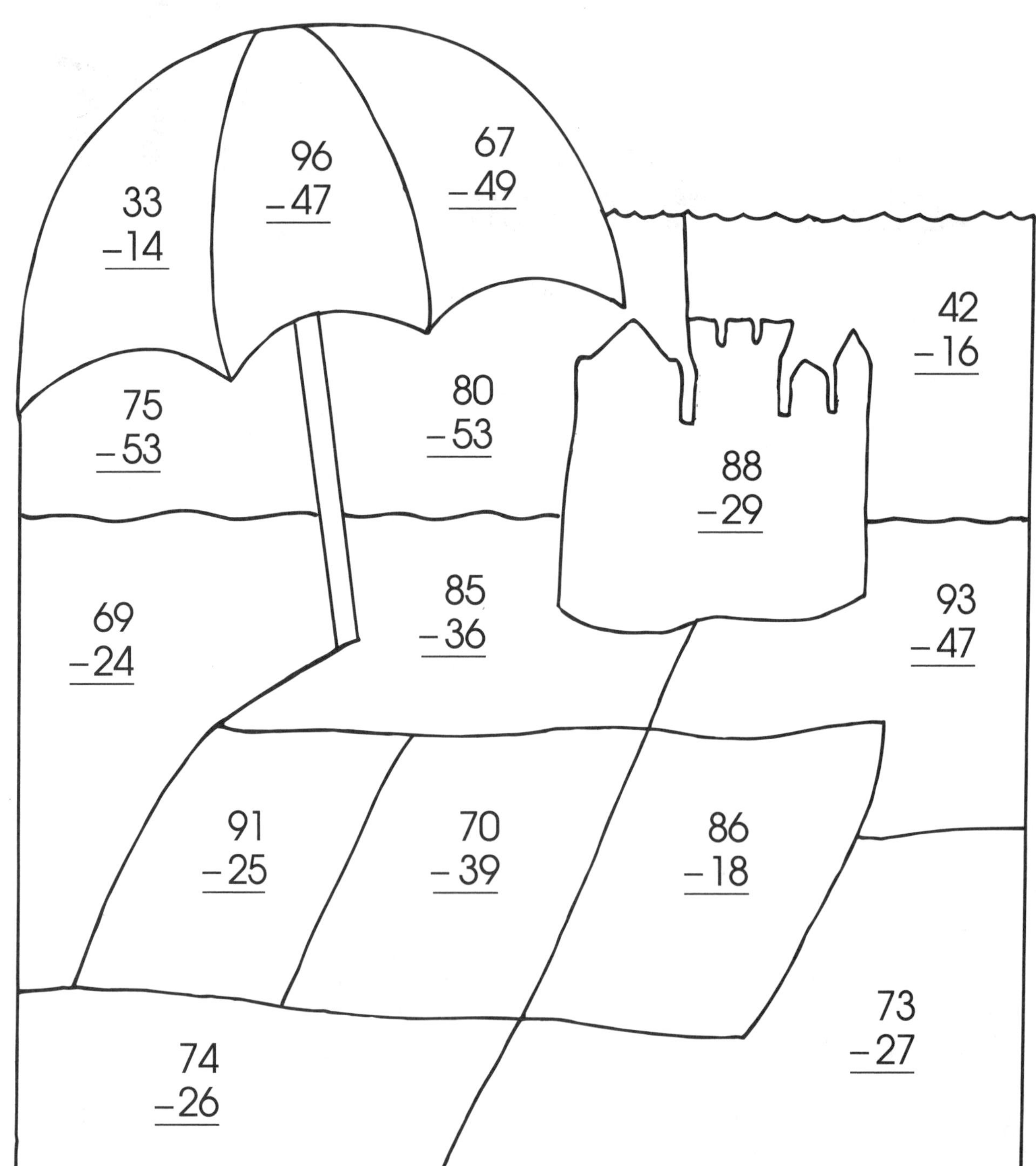

Subtraction with Regrouping

Find the difference.

1.

Tens	Ones
4	14
~~5~~	~~4~~
− 1	7
3	7

2.

Tens	Ones
3	3
− 1	5

3.

Tens	Ones
6	1
− 3	3

4.

Tens	Ones
2	7
− 1	6

5.

Tens	Ones
4	2
− 2	4

6.

Tens	Ones
5	2
− 2	6

7.

Tens	Ones
9	4
− 4	8

8.

Tens	Ones
7	7
− 3	4

9.

Tens	Ones
6	5
− 2	6

Just Like Magic... Again

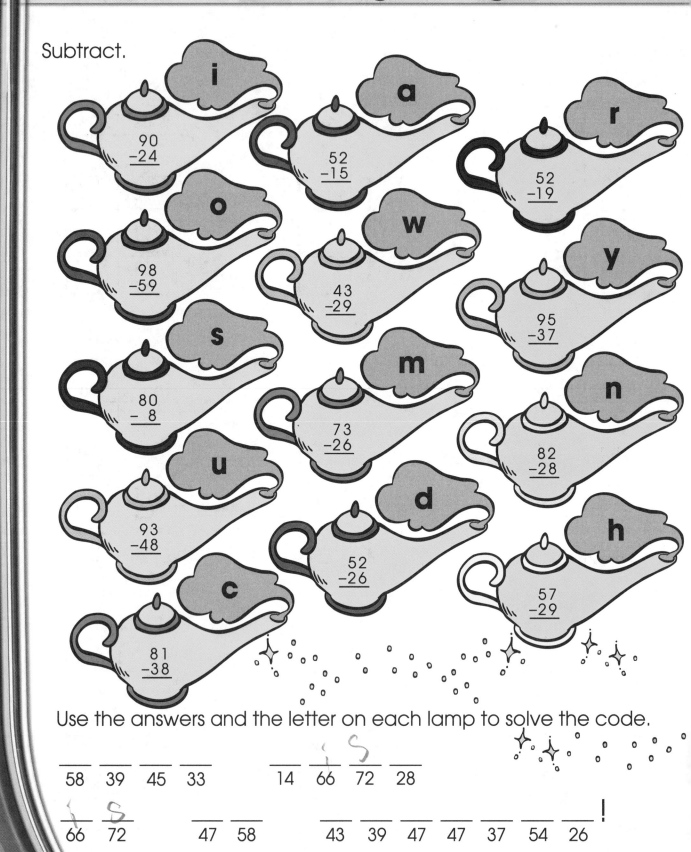

Subtract.

Use the answers and the letter on each lamp to solve the code.

___ ___ ___ ___   ___ ___ ___ ___
58 39 45 33   14 66 72 28

___ ___   ___ ___   ___ ___ ___ ___ ___ ___ ___ !
66 72   47 58   43 39 47 47 37 54 26

Subtraction

Subtraction means "taking away" or subtracting one number from another to find the difference. For example, 10 – 3 = 7.

Subtract.

Example: Subtract the ones. Subtract the tens.

$$\begin{array}{r} 39 \\ -24 \\ \hline 5 \end{array} \qquad \begin{array}{r} 39 \\ -24 \\ \hline 15 \end{array}$$

$$\begin{array}{r} 48 \\ -35 \\ \hline \end{array} \qquad \begin{array}{r} 95 \\ -22 \\ \hline \end{array} \qquad \begin{array}{r} 87 \\ -16 \\ \hline \end{array} \qquad \begin{array}{r} 55 \\ -43 \\ \hline \end{array}$$

$$\begin{array}{r} 37 \\ -14 \\ \hline \end{array} \qquad \begin{array}{r} 69 \\ -57 \\ \hline \end{array} \qquad \begin{array}{r} 44 \\ -23 \\ \hline \end{array} \qquad \begin{array}{r} 99 \\ -78 \\ \hline \end{array}$$

66 – 44 = _____ 57 – 33 = _____

The yellow car traveled 87 miles per hour. The orange car traveled 66 miles per hour. How much faster was the yellow car traveling? __________

Subtraction: Regrouping

Subtraction means "taking away" or subtracting one number from another to find the difference. For example, 10 – 3 = 7. To **regroup** is to use one ten to form ten ones, one 100 to form ten tens and so on.

Study the example. Subtract using regrouping.

Example:

$$\begin{array}{rcrcr} 32 & = & 2\text{ tens} & + & 12\text{ ones} \\ -13 & = & 1\text{ ten} & + & 3\text{ ones} \\ \hline 19 & = & 1\text{ ten} & + & 9\text{ ones} \end{array}$$

$$\begin{array}{r} 33 \\ -28 \\ \hline \end{array} \qquad \begin{array}{r} 86 \\ -59 \\ \hline \end{array} \qquad \begin{array}{r} 92 \\ -37 \\ \hline \end{array} \qquad \begin{array}{r} 71 \\ -48 \\ \hline \end{array}$$

$$\begin{array}{r} 63 \\ -47 \\ \hline \end{array} \qquad \begin{array}{r} 45 \\ -18 \\ \hline \end{array} \qquad \begin{array}{r} 31 \\ -22 \\ \hline \end{array} \qquad \begin{array}{r} 55 \\ -39 \\ \hline \end{array}$$

82 – 69 = _____

73 – 36 = _____

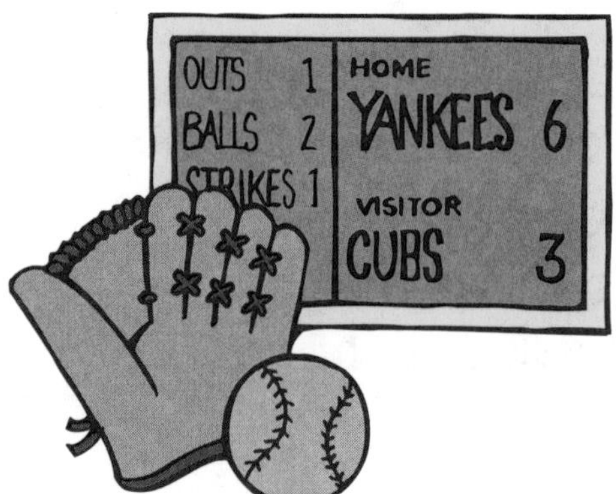

The Yankees won 85 games.
The Cubs won 69 games.
How many more games did the Yankees win? __________

Week 12 Skills

Subject	Skill	Multi-Sensory Learning Activities
Reading and Language Arts	Use pronouns (or words that take the place of nouns).	• Complete Practice Pages 132–136. • Brainstorm different pronouns such as **I**, **you**, **he**, **she**, **it**, **we**, **you**, and **they**. Then, recite sentences using different pronouns. Examples: I am going to a party. You are going to a party. He is going to a party. We are going to a party. • Have your child write two sentences about a friend. In the second sentence, use a pronoun in place of the friend's name. Explain that the pronoun refers to the friend's name.
Math	Subtract three-digit numbers with regrouping.	• Complete Practice Pages 137–140. • Make sure your child understands that three-digit numbers have digits in the hundreds place, tens place, and ones place. Write several subtraction problems with three-digit numbers. Ask your child to inspect them and decide whether regrouping will be needed to solve each one. Then, choose one problem to model with hundreds-blocks, tens-blocks, and ones-blocks (see page 15) before solving it on paper.

Pronouns

Rewrite each sentence. Replace the underlined words with the correct pronoun.

<u>Tommy</u> packed sandwiches and apples.

____

Tommy hiked along <u>the trail</u>.

____

<u>Ed and Larry</u> caught up with Tommy.

____

<u>Rita</u> met the boys at the trail's end.

____

Tommy sent <u>Bill</u> one of his photos later.

____

<u>The boys</u> ate their lunches under a tree.

____

After lunch, <u>Rita</u> gave the boys a cookie.

____

Subject Pronouns

I, **you**, **he**, **she**, **it**, **we** and **they** are subject pronouns. They take the place of nouns or noun phrases in the subject part of the sentence.

Example: Cinderella is my favorite fairy tale character.
She is my favorite fairy tale character.

Write the pronoun that takes the place of the underlined words.

1. A prince was looking for a wife.

   ______________ was looking for a wife.

2. A big ball was held at the palace.

   ______________ was held at the palace.

3. Cinderella's stepmother wouldn't let her go.

   ______________ wouldn't let her go.

4. Cinderella was left at home to work.

   ______________ was left at home to work.

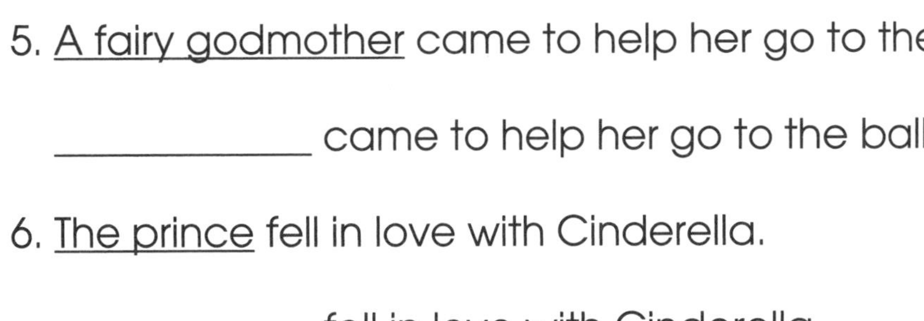

5. A fairy godmother came to help her go to the ball.

   ______________ came to help her go to the ball.

6. The prince fell in love with Cinderella.

   ______________ fell in love with Cinderella.

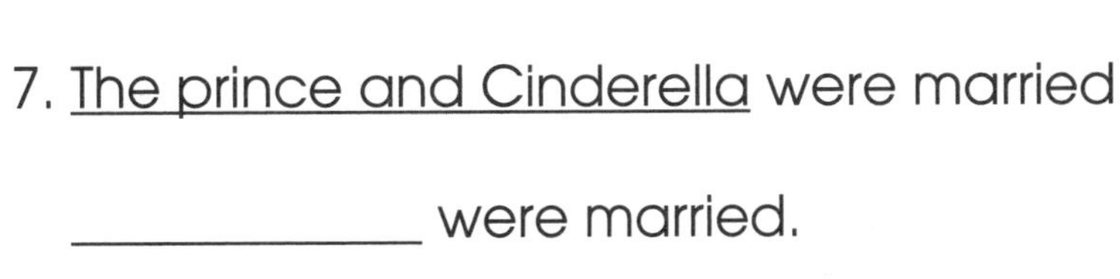

7. The prince and Cinderella were married.

   ______________ were married.

Object Pronouns

An **object pronoun** replaces a noun or noun phrase in the predicate part of a sentence. **Me**, **you**, **him**, **her**, **it**, **us** and **them** are object pronouns.

Example: Tommy packed **his backpack**.
Tommy packed **it**.

Rewrite each sentence. Replace the underlined words with the correct object pronoun.

1. Tommy packed <u>sandwiches and apples</u>.

____

2. He saw <u>the trail</u>.

____

3. Tommy heard <u>the birds</u>.

____

4. Tommy called <u>Ed and Larry</u>.

____

5. Rita met <u>Tommy</u> at the trail's end.

____

6. Tommy gave <u>Rita</u> one of his sandwiches.

____

7. They ate <u>their lunches</u> under a tree.

____

Picking Pronouns

The words **he, she, it** and **they** can be used in place of a noun.

Write the correct pronoun in each blank.

He **She** **It** **They**

1. John won first place.

_____________ got a blue ribbon.

2. Janet and Gail rode on a bus.

_____________ went to visit their grandmother.

3. Sarah had a birthday party.

_____________ invited six friends to the party.

4. The kitten likes to play.

_____________ likes to tug on shoelaces.

5. Ed is seven years old.

_____________ is in the second grade.

Pronouns

Pronouns are words that are used in place of nouns.

Examples: he, she, it, they, him, them, her, him

Read each sentence. Write the pronoun that takes the place of each noun.

Example:
The **monkey** dropped the banana.  ________

1. **Dad** washed the car last night. ________
2. **Mary and David** took a walk in the park. ________
3. **Peggy** spent the night at her grandmother's house. ________
4. The baseball **players** lost their game. ________
5. **Mike Van Meter** is a great soccer player. ________
6. The **parrot** can say five different words. ________
7. **Megan** wrote a story in class today. ________
8. They gave a party for **Teresa**. ________
9. Everyone in the class was happy for **Ted**. ________
10. The children petted the **giraffe**. ________
11. Linda put the **kittens** near the warm stove. ________
12. **Gina** made a chocolate cake for my birthday. ________
13. **Pete and Matt** played baseball on the same team. ________
14. Give the books to **Herbie**. ________

3-Digit Subtraction: Regrouping

Study the example. Follow the steps to subtract.

Step 1: Regroup ones.
Step 2: Subtract ones.
Step 3: Subtract tens.
Step 4: Subtract hundreds.

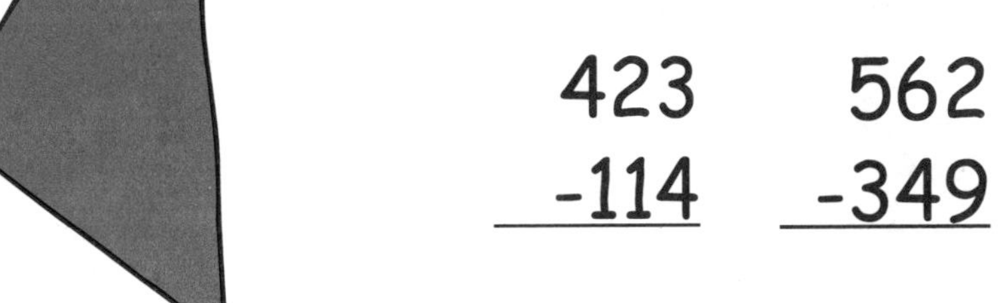

Example:

hundreds	tens	ones
	5	12
4	~~6~~	~~2~~
-2	5	3
2	0	9

$$\begin{array}{r} 423 \\ -114 \\ \hline \end{array} \qquad \begin{array}{r} 562 \\ -349 \\ \hline \end{array}$$

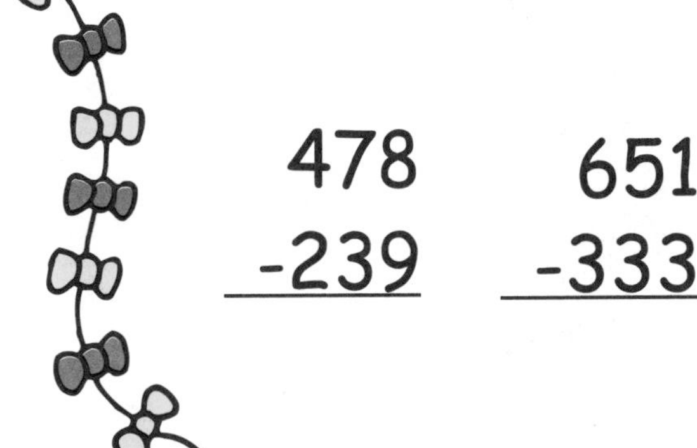

$$\begin{array}{r} 478 \\ -239 \\ \hline \end{array} \qquad \begin{array}{r} 651 \\ -333 \\ \hline \end{array}$$

Draw a line to the correct answer. Color the kites.

$$\begin{array}{r} 347 \\ -218 \\ \hline \end{array} \quad \begin{array}{r} 144 \\ -135 \\ \hline \end{array} \quad \begin{array}{r} 963 \\ -748 \\ \hline \end{array} \quad \begin{array}{r} 762 \\ -553 \\ \hline \end{array} \quad \begin{array}{r} 287 \\ -179 \\ \hline \end{array} \quad \begin{array}{r} 427 \\ -398 \\ \hline \end{array}$$

215 209 129

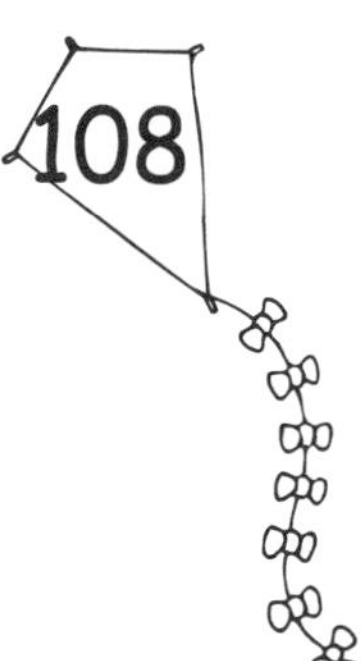

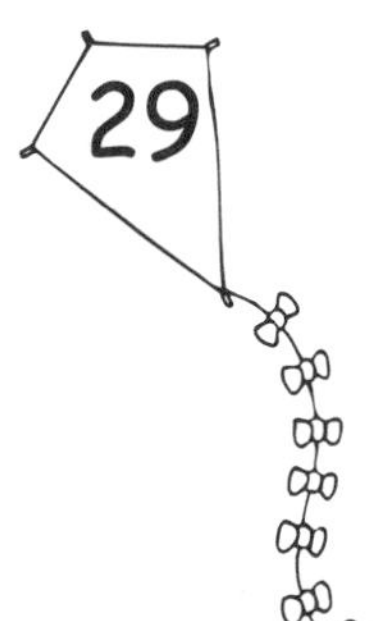

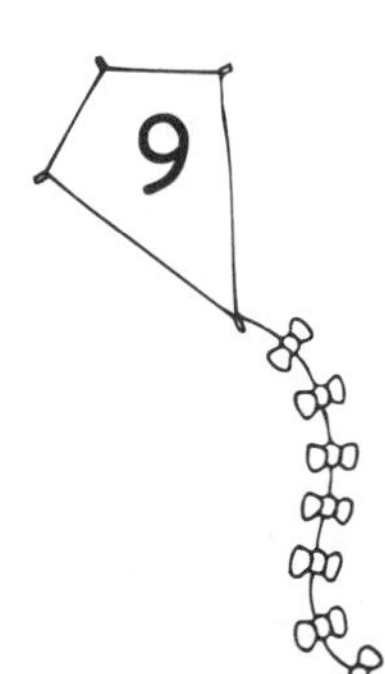

3-Digit Subtraction: Regrouping

Subtract. Circle the **7**s that appear in the tens place.

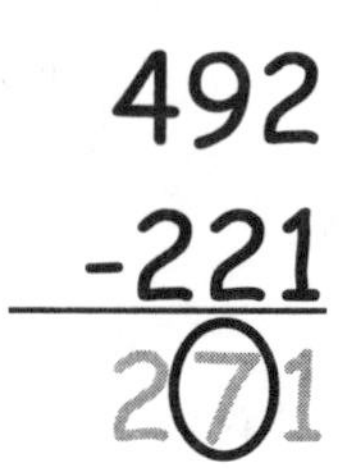

492	184
-221	-129
271	55

358	765	584	693	921
-238	-326	-435	-314	-362

128	744	835	248	635
-109	-674	-217	-199	-428

Subtraction: Regrouping

Regrouping for subtraction is the opposite of regrouping for addition. Study the example. Subtract using regrouping. Then, use the code to color the flowers.

Example:

```
 647
-453
 194
```

Steps:

1. Subtract ones.
2. Subtract tens. Five tens cannot be subtracted from 4 tens.
3. Regroup tens by regrouping 6 hundreds (5 hundreds + 10 tens).
4. Add the 10 tens to the four tens.
5. Subtract 5 tens from 14 tens.
6. Subtract the hundreds.

If the answer has:
1 ones, color it red;
8 ones, color it pink;
5 ones, color it yellow.

Subtraction: Regrouping

Study the example. Follow the steps. Subtract using regrouping.

Example:

```
  634
 -455
  179
```

Steps:

1. Subtract ones. You cannot subtract five ones from 4 ones.
2. Regroup ones by regrouping 3 tens to 2 tens + 10 ones.
3. Subtract 5 ones from 14 ones.
4. Regroup tens by regrouping hundreds (5 hundreds + 10 tens).
5. Subtract 5 tens from 12 tens.
6. Subtract hundreds.

635 −169	553 −174	832 −563	944 −578
423 −268	941 −872	733 −498	266 −197
387 −198	594 −385	960 −759	887 −598

Sue goes to school 185 days a year. Yoko goes to school 313 days a year. How many more days of school does Yoko attend each year? ____________

Week 13 Skills

Subject	Skill	Multi-Sensory Learning Activities
Reading and Language Arts	Use pronouns (or words that take the place of nouns).	• Complete Practice Pages 142 and 143. • Print a short story from a free Web site. Ask your child to circle each pronoun and draw an arrow from it back to the noun to which it refers.
	Use possessive pronouns to show ownership.	• Complete Practice Page 144. • Encourage your child to use possessive pronouns to describe things around your home (his coat, her shoes, their toys, our room).
	Make nouns plural.	• Complete Practice Pages 145 and 146. • Make one set of cards with labeled pictures of single objects (example: chair) and one set with labeled pictures of plural objects (example: chairs). Shuffle the cards and use them to play "Memory."
Math	Subtract three-digit numbers with regrouping.	• Complete Practice Page 147. • Ask your child to solve one problem from page 147 on an easel or large sheet of paper taped to the wall. Video your child explaining the problem. Share the video with a younger sibling, cousin, or friend.
	Use mental math skills to subtract.	• Complete Practice Page 148. • Have your child solve a problem from page 148 mentally and with a calculator. Which was faster? Why?
	Practice addition and subtraction facts.	• Complete Practice Pages 149 and 150. • Mix decks of flash cards for addition and subtraction. How many in a row can your child solve correctly?

Pronouns

Singular Pronouns			
I	me	my	mine
you	your	yours	
he	she	it	her
hers	his	its	him

Plural Pronouns			
we	us	our	ours
you	your	yours	
they	them	their	theirs

Underline the pronouns in each sentence.

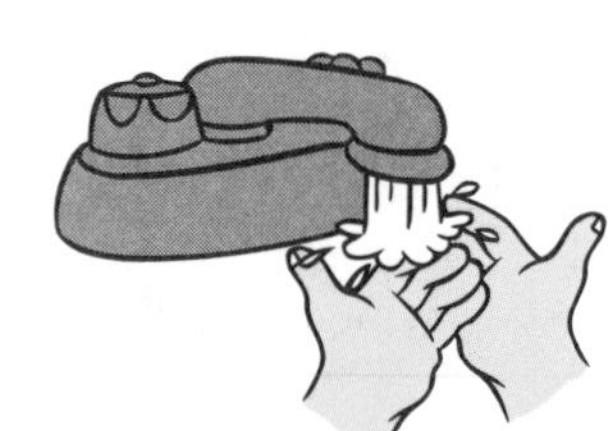

1. Mom told us to wash our hands.
2. Did you go to the store?
3. We should buy him a present.

4. I called you about their party.
5. Our house had damage on its roof.

6. They want to give you a prize at our party.
7. My cat ate her sandwich.
8. Your coat looks like his coat.

Pronouns

We use the pronouns **I** and **we** when talking about the person or people doing the action.

Example: I can roller skate. **We** can roller skate.

We use **me** and **us** when talking about something that is happening to a person or people.

Example: They gave **me** the roller skates.
They gave **us** the roller skates.

Circle the correct pronoun and write it in the blank.

Example:

___We___ are going to the picnic together. **(We), Us**

1. ________ am finished with my science project. **I, Me**
2. Eric passed the football to ________. **me, I**
3. They ate dinner with ________ last night. **we, us**
4. ________ like spinach better than ice cream. **I, Me**
5. Mom came in the room to tell ________ good night. **me, I**
6. ________ had a pizza party in our backyard. **Us, We**
7. They told ________ the good news. **us, we**
8. Tom and ________ went to the store. **me, I**
9. She is taking ________ with her to the movies. **I, me**
10. Katie and ________ are good friends. **I, me**

Possessive Pronouns

Possessive pronouns show ownership.
Example: his hat, **her** shoes, **our** dog
We can use these pronouns before a noun:
my, our, you, his, her, its, their

Example: That is **my** bike.

We can use these pronouns on their own:
mine, yours, ours, his, hers, theirs, its

Example: That is **mine**.

Write each sentence again, using a pronoun instead of the words in bold letters. Be sure to use capitals and periods.

Example:

My **dog's** bowl is brown. **Its** bowl is brown.

1. That is **Lisa's** book. ______________________________

2. This is **my pencil**. ______________________________

3. This hat is **your hat**. ______________________________

4. Fifi is **Kevin's** cat. ______________________________

5. That beautiful house is **our home**.

____

6. **The gerbil's** cage is too small.

____

Plural Nouns

A **plural noun** names more than one person, place or thing.

Example: Some **dinosaurs** ate **plants** in **swamps**.

Underline each plural noun.

1. Large animals lived millions of years ago.
2. Dinosaurs roamed many parts of the Earth.
3. Scientists look for fossils.
4. The bones can tell a scientist many things.
5. These bones help tell what the creatures were like.
6. Some had curved claws and whip-like tails.
7. Others had beaks and plates of armor.
8. Some dinosaurs lived on the plains, and others lived in forests.
9. You can see the skeletons of dinosaurs at some museums.
10. We often read about these animals in books.

Plural Nouns

A **plural** is more than one person, place or thing. We usually add an **s** to show that a noun names more than one. If a noun ends in **x**, **ch**, **sh** or **s**, we add an **es** to the word.

Example: **pizza** 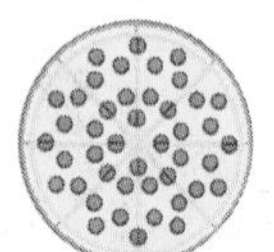 **pizzas** 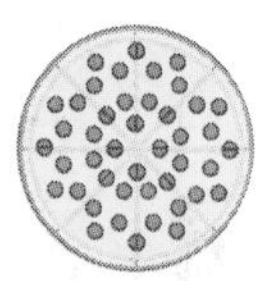 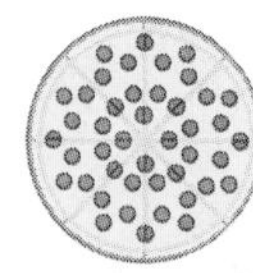 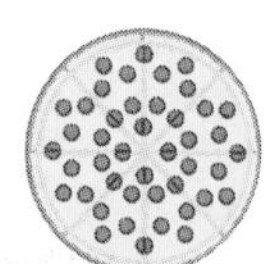

Write the plural of the words below.

Example: dog + s = dogs

cat ______________________

boot ______________________

house ______________________

Example: peach + es = peaches

lunch ______________________

bunch ______________________

punch ______________________

Example: ax + es = axes

fox ______________________

tax ______________________

box ______________________

Example: glass + es = glasses

mess ______________________

guess ______________________

class ______________________

Example: dish + es = dishes

bush ______________________

ash ______________________

brush ______________________

walrus 

walruses 

Subtraction: Regrouping

Study the example. Follow the steps. Subtract using regrouping. If you have to regroup to subtract ones and there are no tens, you must regroup twice.

Example:

$$\begin{array}{r} 300 \\ -182 \\ \hline 118 \end{array}$$

Steps:

1. Subtract ones. You cannot subtract 2 ones from 0 ones.
2. Regroup. No tens. Regroup hundreds (2 hundreds + 10 tens).
3. Regroup tens (9 tens + 10 ones).
4. Subtract 2 ones from ten ones.
5. Subtract 8 tens from 9 tens.
6. Subtract 1 hundred from 2 hundreds.

$$\begin{array}{r} 602 \\ -423 \\ \hline \end{array} \quad \begin{array}{r} 306 \\ -128 \\ \hline \end{array} \quad \begin{array}{r} 600 \\ -263 \\ \hline \end{array} \quad \begin{array}{r} 807 \\ -499 \\ \hline \end{array} \quad \begin{array}{r} 703 \\ -328 \\ \hline \end{array}$$

$$\begin{array}{r} 800 \\ -557 \\ \hline \end{array} \quad \begin{array}{r} 206 \\ -137 \\ \hline \end{array} \quad \begin{array}{r} 400 \\ -224 \\ \hline \end{array} \quad \begin{array}{r} 508 \\ -379 \\ \hline \end{array} \quad \begin{array}{r} 909 \\ -769 \\ \hline \end{array}$$

$$\begin{array}{r} 207 \\ -138 \\ \hline \end{array} \quad \begin{array}{r} 604 \\ -397 \\ \hline \end{array} \quad \begin{array}{r} 308 \\ -199 \\ \hline \end{array} \quad \begin{array}{r} 700 \\ -531 \\ \hline \end{array} \quad \begin{array}{r} 900 \\ -278 \\ \hline \end{array}$$

Subtraction: Mental Math

Try to do these subtraction problems in your head without using paper and pencil.

9 - 3	12 - 6	7 - 6	5 -1	15 - 5	2 - 0
40 -20	90 - 80	100 - 50	20 -20	60 -10	70 - 40
450 -250	500 - 300	250 - 20	690 -100	320 - 20	900 - 600
1,000 - 400	8,000 - 500	7,000 - 900	4,000 -2,000	9,500 - 4,000	5,000 -2,000

Addition and Subtraction

Complete the facts to 10.

10	7	4	6	9
− 6	+ 3	− 2	− 2	− 7

4	10	5	6	3
+ 1	− 8	− 1	+ 4	− 2

5	7	6	5	3
+ 4	− 1	− 3	+ 2	+ 7

9	2	4	1	2	8	2	10	4	7
− 2	+ 6	+ 3	+ 9	− 1	− 6	+ 1	− 3	+ 2	+ 2

9	3	2	6	5	5	8	5	3	8
− 4	+ 5	+ 8	− 3	+ 5	− 3	+ 2	− 4	+ 7	− 1

Addition and Subtraction

Complete the facts to 10.

7	9	2	10	5
+ 2	− 3	+ 5	− 7	− 1

7	4	6	8	1
− 3	+ 3	+ 3	− 3	+ 6

7	9	10	3	4
− 6	− 8	− 2	+ 5	+ 6

10	2	5	3	9	6	4	8	7	8
− 2	+ 5	+ 3	+ 3	− 6	− 3	+ 5	− 5	− 5	+ 1

6	10	8	7	6	3	4	9	4	5
− 2	− 9	− 2	+ 1	+ 2	− 1	+ 2	− 7	− 2	+ 2

Week 14 Skills

Subject	Skill	Multi-Sensory Learning Activities
Reading and Language Arts	Work with irregular plurals.	• Complete Practice Pages 152–156. • Quickly name singular nouns, such as **tree** and **friend**, and ask your child to supply the plural form. See if you can trick your child by giving the singular forms **tooth**, **child**, **foot**, **mouse**, **woman**, or **man**. Reinforce that these words have special plural forms.
Math	Practice addition and subtraction facts.	• Complete Practice Pages 157–160. • Finding the missing addend in an addition problem will help your child understand the relationship between addition and subtraction. Take the face cards out of a deck of cards. Then, hold up one card, using your finger to cover one or more of the symbols. Ask your child to count the remaining symbols and tell how many you are hiding.
Bonus: Science		• Play with static electricity. Have your child cut out bug, fish, or snake shapes from tissue paper. Rub a plastic ruler over a piece of silk or wool in one direction. Pass the ruler over the shapes and observe the effects.

Plural Nouns

Write the plural of each noun to complete the sentences below. Remember to change the **y** to **ie** before you add **s**!

1. I am going to two birthday ______________________ this week.
(party)

2. Sandy picked some ______________________ for Mom's pie.
(cherry)

3. At the store, we saw lots of ______________________.
(bunny)

4. My change at the candy store was three ______________________.
(penny)

5. All the ______________________ baked cookies for the bake sale.
(lady)

6. Thanksgiving is a special time for ______________________ to gather together.
(family)

7. Boston and New York are very large ______________________.
(city)

Plural Nouns

To write the plural forms of words ending in **y**, we change the **y** to **ie** and add **s**.

Example: pony ponies

Write the plural of each noun on the lines below.

berry ____________________

cherry ____________________

bunny ____________________

penny ____________________

family ____________________

candy ____________________

party ____________________

Now, write a story using some of the words that end in **y**. Remember to use capital letters and periods.

Plural Nouns

Some words have special plural forms.

Example: leaf leaves

tooth	teeth
child	children
foot	feet
mouse	mice
woman	women
man	men

Some of the words in the box are special plurals. Complete each sentence with a plural from the box. Then, write the letters from the boxes in the blanks below to solve the puzzle.

1. I lost my two front ___ ___ ___ [___] ___ !

2. My sister has two pet ___ ___ ___ [___].

3. Her favorite book is Little ___ ___ ___ [___] ___.

4. The circus clown had big ___ ___ ___ [___].

5. The teacher played a game with the ___ [___] ___ ___ ___ ___ ___ ___.

Take good care of this pearly plural!

___ ___ ___ ___ ___.
1 2 3 4 5

Plural Nouns

Plural nouns name more than one person, place or thing.

Read the words in the box. Write the words in the correct column.

children	girl	mice	kittens	cake
feet	glass	book	horse	teeth

Plural Pronouns

The **singular form** of a word shows one person, place or thing. Write the singular form of each noun on the lines below.

cherries ____________________

lunches ____________________

countries ____________________

leaves ____________________

churches ____________________

arms ____________________

boxes ____________________

men ____________________

wheels ____________________

pictures ____________________

cities ____________________

places ____________________

ostriches ____________________

glasses ____________________

Something's Missing

In the forest, 10 animals have a picnic. Skunk brings 8 sandwiches. How many sandwiches should Raccoon bring so that each animal can have one?

$$8 + \ ? = 10$$

What number added to 8 equals 10?
To find the missing addend, find the difference of 10 and 8.
That is, subtract the given addend (8) from the sum (10).

$$10 - 8 = 2$$

Since 10 – 8 = 2, then 8 + 2 = 10.
Raccoon should bring 2 sandwiches.

Find the missing addends.

___ + 6 = 9 ___ + 7 = 9

9 + ___ = 10 5 + ___ = 10

___ + 5 = 8 3 + ___ = 10

A Hidden Message

Add or subtract. Use the code to find out your new motto!

Code:

9	18	6	15	13	12	16	11	8	7	14	17
H	Y	D	E	V	T	S	O	A	M	N	I

9 +8

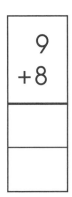

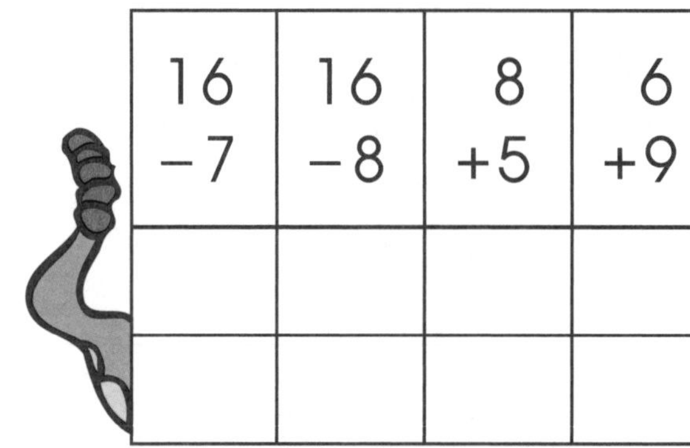

16 −7	16 −8	8 +5	6 +9

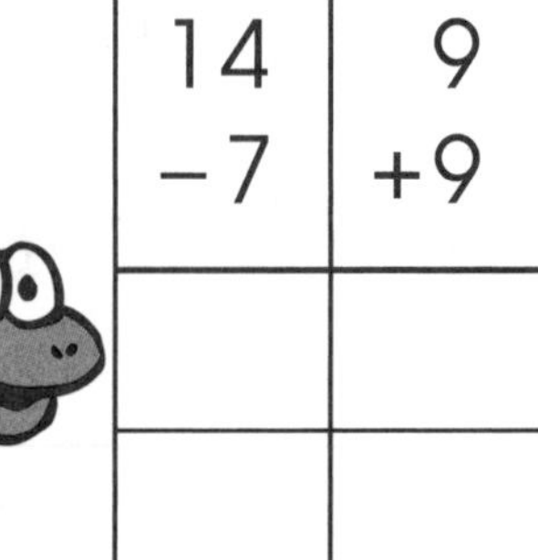

14 −7	9 +9

17 −8	15 −7	9 +5	13 −7	8 +8

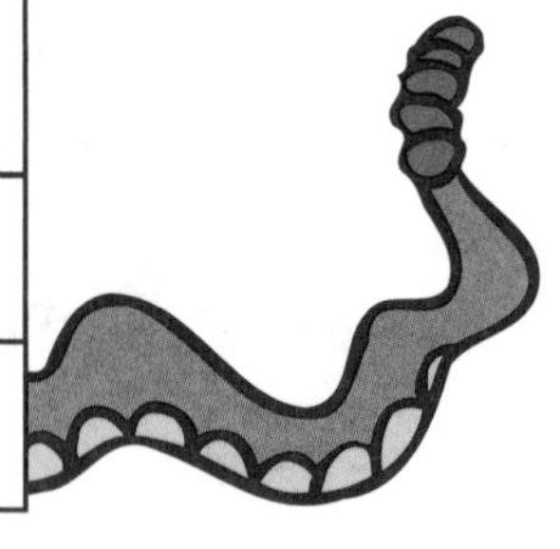

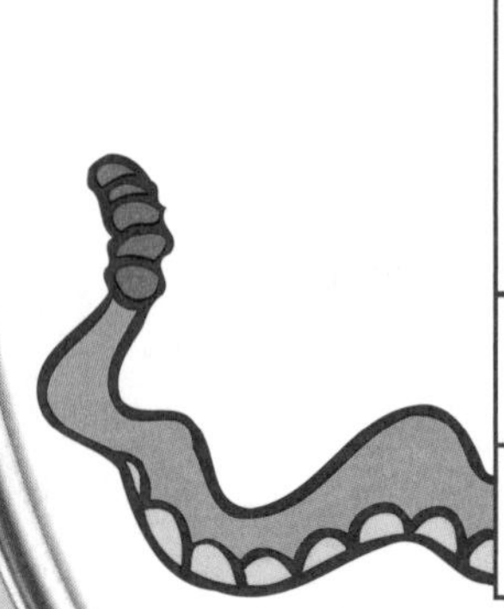

4 +7	6 +8

12 −5	17 −9	6 +6	15 −6

Missing Numbers

Fill in the missing addend.

9 + ◯ = 17 ◯ + 5 = 12 8 + ◯ = 14 5 + ◯ = 11

7 + ◯ = 13 8 + ◯ = 16 ◯ + 6 = 12 ◯ + 9 = 18

Fill in the missing subtrahends.

12 – ___ = 3 11 – ___ = 4

14 – ___ = 6 17 – ___ = 5

17 – ___ = 8 15 – ___ = 10

16 – ___ = 9 15 – ___ = 6

18 – ___ = 9 15 – ___ = 9

Fill in the missing subtrahends and minuends.

15	18	12	□	□
– □	– □	– □	– 7	– 8
9	9	6	6	3

□	15	□	13	□
– 8	– □	– 4	– □	– 9
5	8	6	4	6

All Aboard

Add or subtract. Match the related facts.

5 + 9	14	6 + 9 =	______
8 + 7 =	______	14 − 9 =	5
15 − 9 =	______	15 − 7 =	______
17 − 8 =	______	14 − 7 =	______
7 + 7	______	9 + 8 =	______

Add or subtract. Color spaces brown with answers greater than 12. Color the rest green.

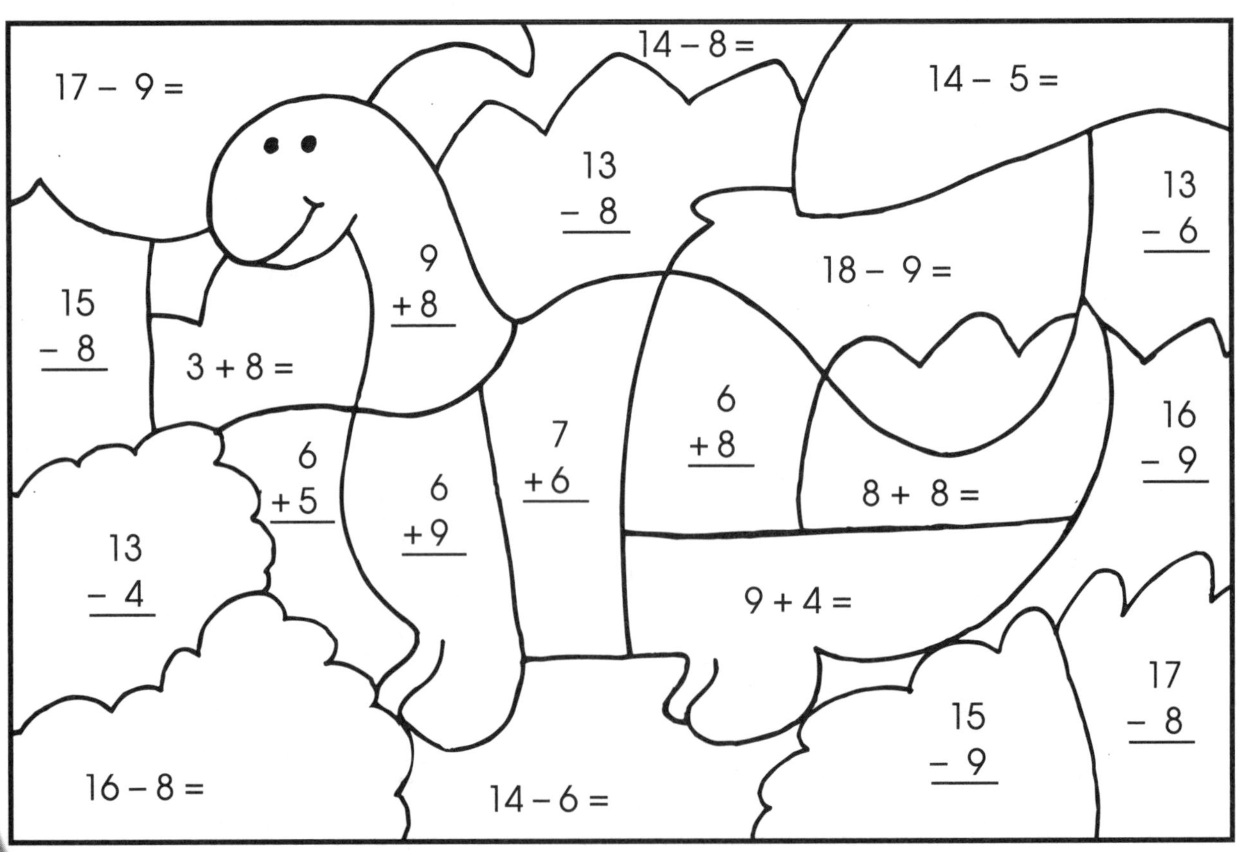

Week 15 Skills

Subject	Skill	Multi-Sensory Learning Activities
Reading and Language Arts	Use verbs, including helping verbs and linking verbs.	• Complete Practice Pages 162–166. • Read *Tacky the Penguin* by Helen Lester. Ask your child to point out the verbs that describe Tacky's actions. Then, write five sentences that tell what Tacky and the other penguins do. • Explain that although every sentence must contain a verb, not every verb describes an action. Talk about helping verbs and linking verbs such as **was** and **were** and look for examples in *Tacky the Penguin*.
Math	Practice addition and subtraction with and without regrouping.	• Complete Practice Pages 167–170. • Roll two dice and have your child do the same. Write each number rolled as one digit of a two-digit number. The person who writes that larger number chooses whether players must add the two numbers together or subtract the smaller number from the larger one. Compare your answers and talk about whether regrouping was required. Then, roll again.
Bonus: Social Studies		• Study a globe or world map with your child, tracing the outline of each continent with a finger. Then, encourage your child to tear a sheet of construction paper to form the approximate outline of each continent. Glue all the continents in their correct positions on a sheet of blue paper.

Action Verbs

A **verb** is a word that can show action.

Example: I **jump**. He **kicks**. He **walked**.

Underline the verb in each sentence. Write it on the line.

1. Our school plays games on Field Day. ____________
2. Juan runs 50 yards. ____________
3. Carmen hops in a sack race. ____________
4. Paula tosses a ball through a hoop. ____________
5. One girl carries a jellybean on a spoon. ____________
6. Lola bounces the ball. ____________
7. Some boys chase after balloons. ____________
8. Mark chooses me for his team. ____________
9. The children cheer for the winners. ____________
10. Everyone enjoys Field Day. ____________

Verbs

A **verb** is the action word in a sentence, the word that tells what something does or that something exists.
Examples: run, jump, skip.

Draw a box around the verb in each sentence below.

1. Spiders spin webs of silk.
2. A spider waits in the center of the web for its meals.
3. A spider sinks its sharp fangs into insects.
4. Spiders eat many insects.
5. Spiders make their nests with silk.
6. Female spiders wrap silk around their eggs to protect them.

Choose the correct verb from the box and write it in the sentences below.

hides	swims	eats	grabs	hurt

1. A crab spider ______________ deep inside a flower where it cannot be seen.
2. The crab spider ___________ insects when they land on the flower.
3. The wolf spider is good because it _______________ wasps.
4. The water spider _______________ under water.
5. Most spiders will not _______________ people.

Verbs

When a verb tells what one person or thing is doing now, it usually ends in **s**. **Example:** She **sings**.

When a verb is used with **you**, **I** or **we**, we do not add an **s**.

Example: I **sing**.

Write the correct verb in each sentence.

Example:

I ___write___ a newspaper about our street. **writes, write**

1. My sister __________ me sometimes. **helps, help**
2. She __________ the pictures. **draw, draws**
3. We __________ them together. **delivers, delive**
4. I __________ the news about all the people. **tell, tells**
5. Mr. Macon __________ the most beautiful flowers. **grow, grows**
6. Mrs. Jones __________ to her plants. **talks, talk**
7. Kevin Turner __________ his dog loose everyday. **lets, let**
8. Little Mikey Smith __________ lost once a week. **get, gets**
9. You may __________ I live on an interesting street. **thinks, think**
10. We __________ it's the best street in town. **say, says**

Helping Verbs

A **helping verb** is a word used with an action verb.

Examples: might, **shall** and **are**

Write a helping verb from the box with each action verb.

can	could	must	might
may	would	should	will
shall	did	does	do
had	have	has	am
are	were	is	
be	being	been	

Example:

Tomorrow, I __might__ play soccer.

1. Mom ______________ buy my new soccer shoes tonight.

2. Yesterday, my old soccer shoes ______________ ripped by the cat.

3. I ______________ going to ask my brother to go to the game.

4. He usually ______________ not like soccer.

5. But, he ______________ go with me because I am his sister.

6. He ______________ promised to watch the entire soccer game.

7. He has ______________ helping me with my homework.

8. I ______________ spell a lot better because of his help.

9. Maybe I ______________ finish the semester at the top of my class.

Linking Verbs

A **linking verb** does not show action. Instead, it links the subject with a word in the predicate. **Am, is, are, was** and **were** are **linking verbs**.

Example: Many people **are** collectors.
(**Are** connects **people** and **collectors**.)
The collection **was** large.
(**Was** connects **collection** and **large**.)

Underline the linking verb in each sentence.

1. I am happy.
2. Toy collecting is a nice hobby.
3. Mom and Dad are helpful.
4. The rabbit is beautiful.
5. Itsy and Bitsy are stuffed mice.
6. Monday was special.
7. I was excited.
8. The class was impressed.
9. The elephants were gray
10. My friends were a good audience.

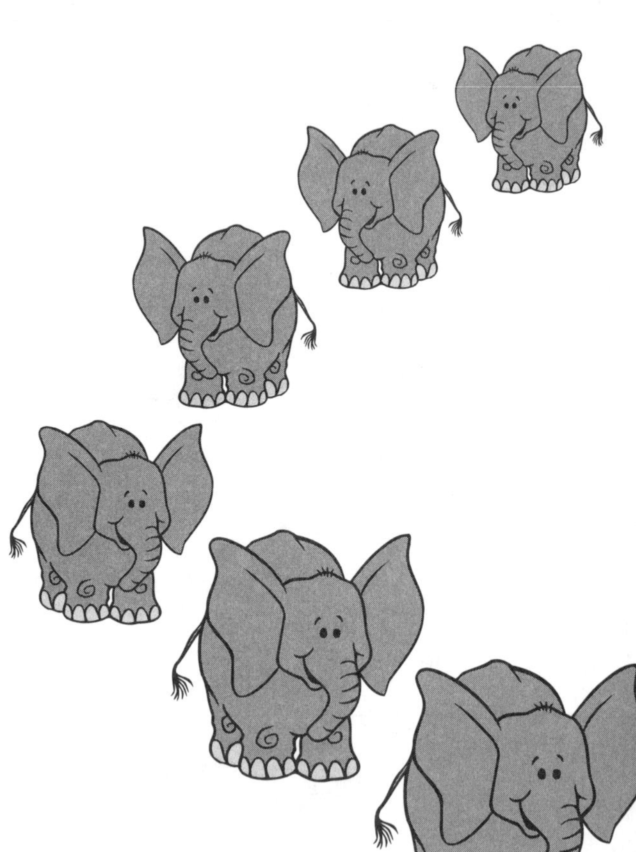

Week 16 Skills

Subject	Skill	Multi-Sensory Learning Activities
Reading and Language Arts	Use irregular verbs.	• Complete Practice Pages 172–176. • Open a manila file folder and use a marker to divide the right side into two columns labeled **Present Tense** and **Past Tense**. On the left side, write these subjects in a column: **I**, **He/She**, **You**, **We/They**. Keep a supply of self-stick notes in the folder. Occasionally, ask your child to work with a verb found in a book he or she is reading. On the self-stick notes, write forms of the verb to match each subject on the left side of the folder and each tense on the right side of the folder. Stick the notes in the appropriate column.
Math	Practice addition and subtraction with and without regrouping.	• Complete Practice Pages 177–180. • Help your child practice addition and subtraction by making fact family houses. Draw a house with a triangular roof and four windows. On each corner of the roof, write one number from the fact family (example: **15**, **7**, **8**). Ask your child to write one related addition or subtraction fact in each window (examples: 7 + 8, 8 + 7, 15 – 8, 15 – 7).

Is, Are and Am

Is, **are** and **am** are special action words that tell us something is happening now.

Use **am** with **I**. **Example: I am**.
Use **is** to tell about one person or thing. **Example: He is**.
Use **are** to tell about more than one. **Example: We are**.
Use **are** with **you**. **Example: You are**.

Write **is, are** or **am** in the sentences below.

1. My friends ____________________ helping me build a tree house.

2. It ____________________ in my backyard.

3. We ____________________ using hammers, wood and nails.

4. It ____________________ a very hard job.

5. I ____________________ lucky to have good friends.

Was and Were

Was and **were** tell us about something that already happened.

Use **was** to tell about one person or thing. **Example**: I **was**, he **was**. Use **were** to tell about more than one person or thing or when using the word **you**. **Example**: We **were**, you **were**.

Write **was** or **were** in each sentence.

1. Lily ____________________ eight years old on her birthday.

2. Tim and Steve ____________________ happy to be at the party.

3. Megan ____________________ too shy to sing "Happy Birthday."

4. Ben ____________________ sorry he dropped his cake.

5. All of the children ____________________ happy to be invited.

Go, Going and Went

We use **go** or **going** to tell about now or later. Sometimes we use going with the words **am** or **are**. We use **went** to tell about something that already happened.

Write **go**, **going** or **went** in the sentences below.

1. Today, I will ________________ to the store.

2. Yesterday, we ________________ shopping.

3. I am ________________ to take Muffy to the vet.

4. Jan and Steve ________________ to the party.

5. They are ________________ to have a good day.

Have, Has and Had

We use **have** and **has** to tell about now. We use **had** to tell about something that already happened.

Write **has, have** or **had** in the sentences below.

1. We ________________ three cats at home.

2. Ginger ________________ brown fur.

3. Bucky and Charlie ________________ gray fur.

4. My friend Tom ________________ one cat, but he died.

5. Tom ________________ a new cat now.

See, Saw and Sees

We use **see** or **sees** to tell about now. We use **saw** to tell about something that already happened.

Write **see**, **sees** or **saw** in the sentences below.

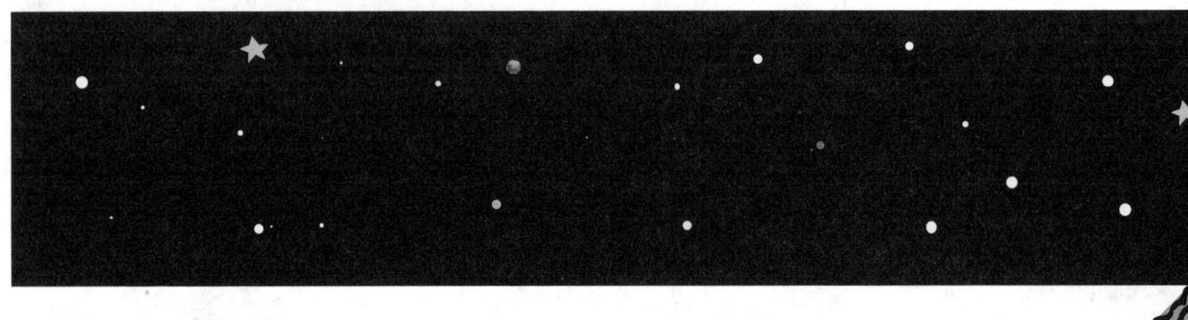

1. Last night, we ________________ the stars.

2. John can ________________ the stars from his window.

3. He ________________ them every night.

4. Last week, he ________________ the Big Dipper.

5. Can you ________________ it in the night sky, too?

6. If you ________________ it, you would remember it!

7. John ________________ it often now.

8. How often do you ________________ it?

2-Digit Addition and Subtraction

Add or subtract using regrouping

23 +48	84 -56	69 +29	41 -17
52 -28	73 +18	84 -27	57 -39
33 -15	64 +17	37 +58	36 -19
65 -28	48 -30	33 +18	25 +35

Review

Counting

Write the number that is:

next	one less	one greater
68, 69, ____	____ , 57	12, ____
786, 787, ____	____ , 650	843, ____

Place Value: Tens and Ones

Draw a line to the correct number.

4 tens + 7 ones	20
2 tens + 0 ones	51
7 tens + 3 ones	47
5 tens + 1 one	73

Addition and Subtraction

Add or subtract.

$$\begin{array}{r}15\\+\ 5\\\hline\end{array}\qquad\begin{array}{r}14\\-\ 4\\\hline\end{array}\qquad\begin{array}{r}7\\+3\\\hline\end{array}\qquad\begin{array}{r}8\\-6\\\hline\end{array}\qquad\begin{array}{r}10\\+7\\\hline\end{array}\qquad\begin{array}{r}14\\-\ 5\\\hline\end{array}$$

Review

2-Digit Addition and Subtraction

Add or subtract.

66	38	87	52	40
− 37	+ 18	− 69	− 15	+ 17

84	65	99	61	56
+ 17	+ 14	− 48	− 36	+ 46

Place Value: Hundreds and Thousands

Draw a line to the correct number.

4 hundreds + 3 tens + 2 ones	7,201
6 hundreds + 7 tens + 6 ones	290
5 thousands + 3 hundreds + 7 tens + 2 ones	432
2 hundreds + 9 tens + 0 ones	676
7 thousands + 2 hundreds + 0 tens + 1 one	5,372

3-Digit Addition and Subtraction

Add or subtract, remembering to regroup, if needed.

458	793	822	528	697	569
− 248	− 414	− 460	+ 319	+ 108	+ 288

Training With Facts

Use the numbers on each train to write the fact families.

___ + ___ = ___

___ + ___ = ___

___ − ___ = ___

___ − ___ = ___

___ + ___ = ___

___ + ___ = ___

___ − ___ = ___

___ − ___ = ___

___ + ___ = ___

___ + ___ = ___

___ − ___ = ___

___ − ___ = ___

___ + ___ = ___

___ + ___ = ___

___ − ___ = ___

___ − ___ = ___

Week 17 Skills

Subject	Skill	Multi-Sensory Learning Activities
Reading and Language Arts	Use irregular verbs.	• Complete Practice Pages 182–184. • Send a text or e-mail message to your child that contains errors in subject-verb agreement. Choose an irregular verb such as **eat**, **give**, or **have** and write an incorrect message such as, "Can you brought me a towel?" Let your child correct the message and send it back.
	Use adjectives.	• Complete Practice Pages 185 and 186. • Challenge your child to brainstorm a list of adjectives that describe a treasured stuffed animal, a memorable place, a favorite movie, or something else that is special to him or her. When your child begins to run out of ideas, suggest thinking of words that describe color, shape, pattern, texture, temperature, smells, tastes, sounds, etc. You may wish to make a list of the words.
Math	Use addition and subtraction to solve word problems.	• Complete Practice Pages 187–190. • Create word problems for your child that relate to his or her interests and activities. For example, ask, "If there are 19 players on one soccer team and 17 players on another team, how many players are there in all?"

Eat, Eats and Ate

We use **eat** or **eats** to tell about now. We use **ate** to tell about what already happened.

Write **eat, eats** or **ate** in the sentences below.

1. We like to ______________ in the lunchroom.

2. Today, my teacher will ____________ in a different room.

3. She _______________with the other teachers.

4. Yesterday, we ______________ pizza, pears and peas.

5. Today, we will ______________ turkey and potatoes.

Leave, Leaves and Left

We use **leave** and **leaves** to tell about now. We use **left** to tell about what already happened.

Write **leave**, **leaves** or **left** in the sentences below.

1. Last winter, we __________ seeds in the bird feeder everyday.

2. My mother likes to __________ food out for the squirrels.

3. When it rains, she __________ bread for the birds.

4. Yesterday, she __________ popcorn for the birds.

Irregular Verbs

Verbs that do not add **ed** to show what happened in the past are called **irregular verbs**.

Example: Present **Past**

Present	Past
run, runs	ran
fall, falls	fell

Jim **ran** past our house yesterday.
He fell over a wagon on the sidewalk.

Fill in the verbs that tell what happened in the past in the chart. The first one is done for you.

Present	Past
hear, hears	heard
draw, draws	
do, does	
give, gives	
sell, sells	
come, comes	
fly, flies	
build, builds	
know, knows	
bring, brings	

Adjectives

An **adjective** is a word that describes a noun. It tells **how many**, **what kind** or **which one**.

Example: Yolanda has a **tasty** lunch.

Color each space that has an adjective. Do not color the other spaces.

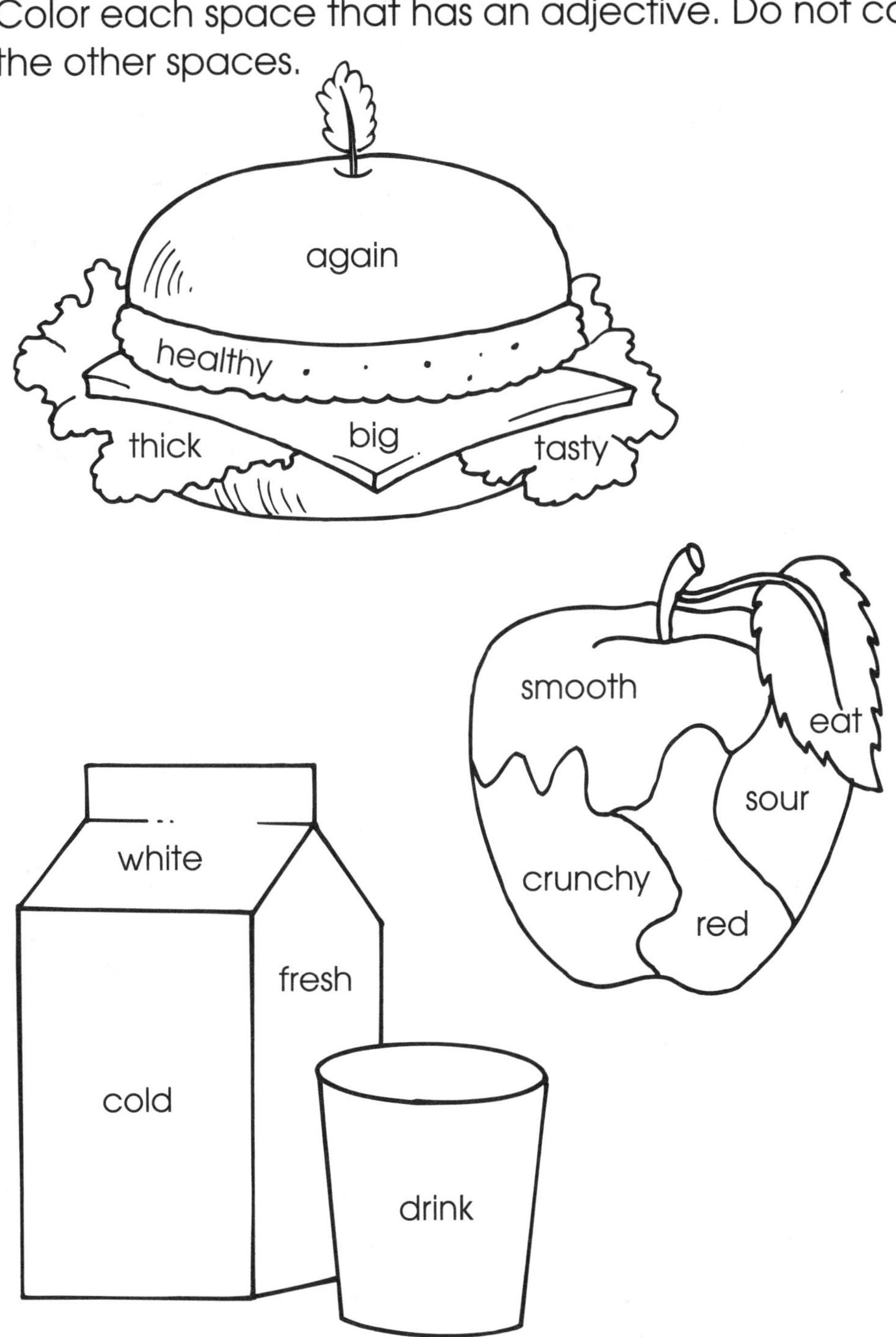

Add the Adjectives

Write a describing word on each line. Draw a picture to match each sentence.

high mountain

The ________ flag waved over the ________ building.

A ________ lion searched for food in the ________ jungle.

We saw ________ fish in the ________ aquarium.

Her ________ car was parked by the ________ van.

The ________ dog barked and chased the ________ truck.

The ________ building was filled with ________ packages.

Problems! Problems! Problems!

Read and solve these problems.

1. Craig went to the pond. He kept a tally of the animals he saw there. Which kind of animal did he see most often? ___________ Which kind of animal did he see least often? _______________

   Frog 卌 Duck III Bug 卌 卌 II Bird 卌 II Lizard II Fish 卌 III

2. Ellen went to the library. She checked out five books on zoo animals, three books on fish, eight books on airplanes and two books on dogs. How many animal books did Ellen check out? __________ How many books did she check out altogether? __________ If she returns the books on dogs and airplanes, how many books will she have then? ________

3. Complete this sequence of numbers: 14, 24, 34, _______ , _______ , 64

Problems! Problems! Problems!

Read and solve these problems.

1. Debbie and Missy have 12 pieces of candy. If they share equally, how many pieces of candy should each girl get? __________ Suppose they decide to share equally the 12 pieces of candy with Kimberly, too. Now, how many pieces of candy will each girl get?__________

2. Mike has 40 cents. Lynette has 23 cents. How much more money does Lynette need to have as much money as Mike? __________ If she had the same amount as Mike, how much money would they have altogether? __________ Does Mike have enough money to purchase a ball for 50¢? __________

3. Use a number line. Start at zero. Count up 12, back three, up two, back eight, up four. What number are you on now? __________

Problem-Solving

Tell whether you should add or subtract. "In all" is a clue to add. "Left" is a clue to subtract. Draw pictures to help you.

Example: Jane's dog has 5 bones. He ate 3 bones. How many bones are left?

subtract

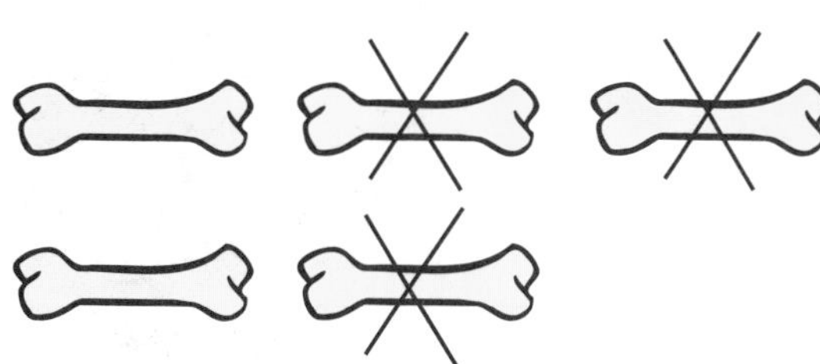

5
[-] 3
2 bones

Lucky the cat had 5 mice. She got 4 more for her birthday. How many mice did she have in all?

____

[ ] ______

______ mice

Sam bought 6 fish. She gave 2 fish to a friend. How many fish does she have left?

____

[ ] ______

______ fish

Problem-Solving: Addition, Subtraction

Tell if you add or subtract.
Then, write the answer.

There were 12 frogs sitting on a log by a pond, but 3 frogs hopped away. How many frogs are left?

____________ ________ frogs

A tree had 7 squirrels playing in it. Then, 8 more came along. How many squirrels are there in all?

____________ ________ squirrels

There were 27 birds living in the trees around the pond, but 9 flew away. How many birds are left?

____________ ________ birds

Week 18 Skills

Subject	Skill	Multi-Sensory Learning Activities
Reading and Language Arts	Use adjectives.	• Complete Practice Pages 192–196. • Cut from a magazine or print out from the Internet four similar pictures (for example, four cars, four flowers, or four dogs). Describe one picture and ask your child to choose it from the group. For example, say, "Find the car with four doors," or "Find the car with round headlights." Explain that describing words such as **four** and **round** are adjectives. • Begin with a simple sentence such as, "I see a tree outside." How many adjectives and other words can you and your child add to the sentence to make it more interesting and detailed?
Math	Solve number and picture patterns.	• Complete practice pages 197–200. • Go on a walk around your home looking for patterns in wallpaper, floor tiles, blankets, dishes, etc. Challenge your child to describe each pattern you find. • Ask your child to look at the chart of numbers to 100 on page 393. Then, give clues to one number and ask your child to point to it on the chart. For example, say, "I'm thinking of a number between 50 and 59. You can count by fives to get to this number." (Answer: 55)

Adjectives

Adjectives are words that tell more about nouns, such as a **happy** child, a **cold** day or a **hard** problem. Adjectives can tell how many (**one** airplane) or which one (**those** shoes).

The nouns are in bold letters. Circle the adjectives that describe the nouns.

Example: Some people have (unusual) **pets**.

1. Some people keep wild **animals**, like lions and bears.
2. These **pets** need special care.
3. These **animals** want to be free when they get older.

4. Even small **animals** can be difficult if they are wild.
5. Raccoons and squirrels are not tame **pets**.
6. Never touch a wild **animal** that may be sick.

Complete the story below by writing in your own adjectives. Use your imagination.

My Cat

My cat is a very _____________ animal. She has _____________

and _____________ fur. Her favorite toy is a _____________ ball.

She has _____________ claws. She has a _____________ tail.

She has a _____________ face and _____________ whiskers.

I think she is the _____________ cat in the world!

Adjectives

Read the story below and underline the adjectives that are used in the story.

The Best Soup I Ever Had

I woke up one cold winter morning and decided to make a delicious pot of hot vegetable soup. The first vegetables I put in the big gray pot were some sweet white onions. Then I added orange carrots and dark green broccoli. The broccoli looked just like little, tiny trees. Fresh, juicy tomatoes and crisp potatoes were added next. I cooked it for a long, long time. This soup turned out to be the best soup I ever had.

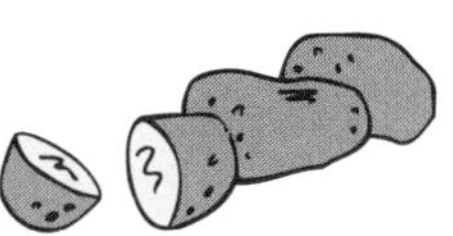

Write two adjectives to describe each of the words below

cucumber ____________________ peas ____________________

____________________ ____________________

spinach ____________________ corn ____________________

____________________ ____________________

Now, rewrite two of the sentences from the story. Substitute your own adjectives for the words you underlined to make your own soup.

____

____

____

Using Exact Adjectives

Use an **adjective** that best describes the noun or pronoun. Be specific

Example: David had a nice birthday.
David had a **fun** birthday.

Rewrite each sentence, replacing **nice** or **good** with a better adjective from the box or one of your own.

sturdy	new	great	chocolate	delicious	special

1. David bought a nice pair of in-line skates.

____

2. He received a nice helmet.

____

3. He got nice knee pads.

____

4. Father baked a good cake.

____

5. David made a good wish.

____

6. Mom served good ice cream.

____

Our House

Choose two words from the box that describe each character. Then, complete each sentence to tell why you chose those words.

understanding	spoiled	responsible	lazy	helpful	upset	happy
busy	caring	kind	mean	confused	unhappy	patient	nice

The girl is ______________ and ______________

because she ______________________________

____

____

____

Mother is ______________ and ______________

because she ______________________________

____

____

____

Father is ______________ and ______________

because he ______________________________

____

____

____

Better Sentences

Describing words like adjectives can make a better sentence. Write a word on each line to make the sentences more interesting. Draw a picture of your sentence.

1. The skater won a medal.

   The ______________ skater won a ______________ medal.

2. The jewels were in the safe.

   The ______________ jewels were in the ______________ safe.

3. The airplane flew through the storm.

   The ______________ airplane flew through the______________storm

4. A fireman rushed into the house.

   A ______________ fireman rushed into the ______________ house.

5. The detective hid behind the tree.

   The ______________ detective hid behind the ______________ tree

1.	2.

3.	4.	5.

Patterns

Write or draw what comes next in the pattern.

Example: 1, 2, 3, 4, 5

1.       ________

2. A, 1, B, 2, C ________

3. 2, 4, 6, 8, ________

4. A, C, E, G, ________

5. 5, 10, 15, 20, ________

Finding Patterns: Numbers

Mia likes to count by twos, threes, fours, fives, tens and hundreds.

Complete the number patterns.

1. 5, ____, ____, 20, ____, ____, 35, ____, ____, 50

2. 100, ____, ____, 400, ____, ____, ____, 800, ____

3. ____, 4, 6, ____, ____, 12, ____, 16, ____, ____

4. 10, ____, ____, 40, ____, ____, 70, ____, 90

5. 4, ____, 12, ____, ____, 24, ____, 32, ____, 40

6. ____, 6, 9, ____, ____, 18, ____, 24, ____, 30

Make up two of your own number patterns.

____, ____, ____, ____, ____, ____, ____, ____

____, ____, ____, ____, ____, ____, ____, ____

Finding Patterns: Shapes

Complete each row by drawing the correct shape.

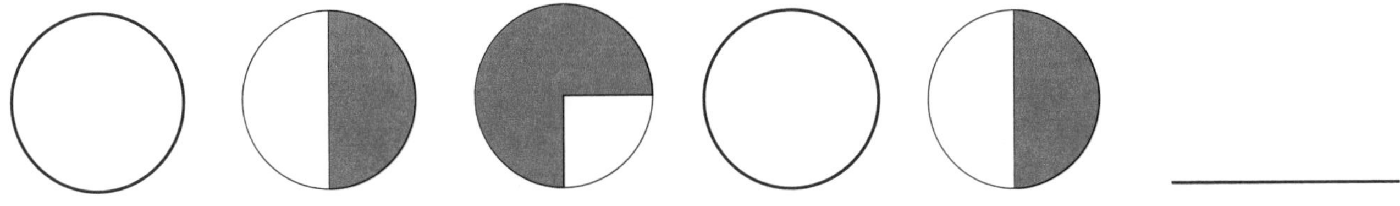

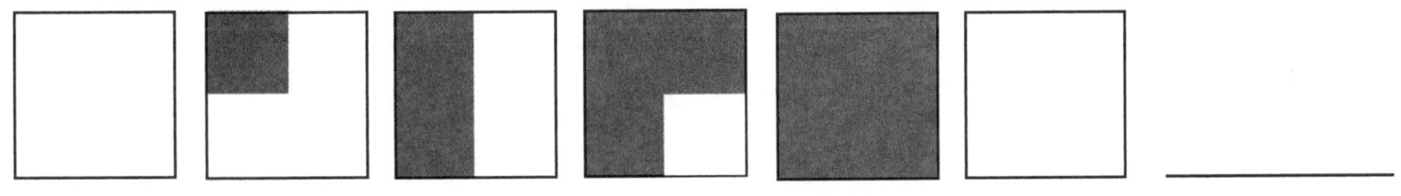

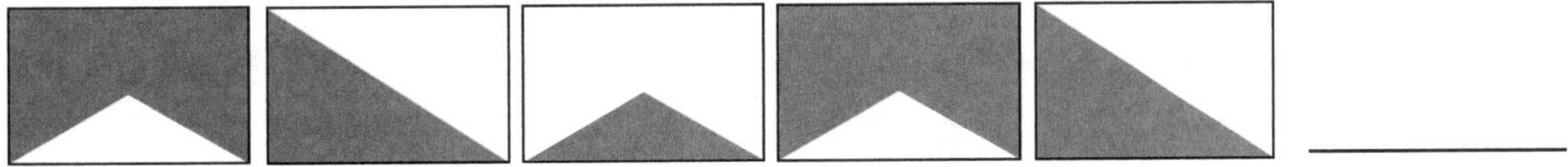

Patterns

Write the one that would come next in each pattern.

0 2 0 4 0 6 ________

1 3 5 7 9 11 ________

5 10 20 40 80 ________

 ________

 ________

 ________

1 A 2 B 3 C ________

A B C 1 2 3 A ________

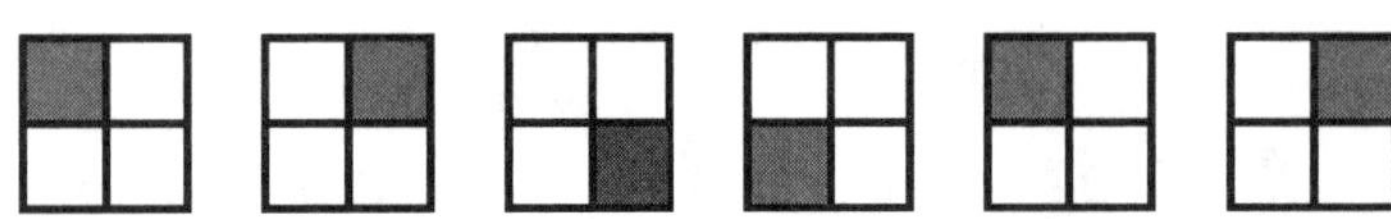 ________

Second Quarter Check-Up

Reading and Language Arts

- ☐ I understand that nouns name people, places, and things.
- ☐ I begin proper nouns with capital letters.
- ☐ I can use pronouns to take the place of nouns.
- ☐ I can make nouns plural.
- ☐ I use action verbs, helping verbs, and linking verbs correctly.
- ☐ I write sentences in which the subject and verb agree.
- ☐ I can use adjectives to describe people, places, and things.

Math

- ☐ I can subtract single-digit, two-digit, and three-digit numbers.
- ☐ I can subtract when regrouping is required.
- ☐ I can use mental math to subtract.
- ☐ I can use addition and subtraction to solve word problems.
- ☐ I recognize picture and number patterns.

Final Project

Read the nursery rhyme "Sing a Song of Sixpence." Then, write four addition or subtraction word problems based on the poem. Read your sentences carefully to make sure you are using nouns, verbs, pronouns, adjectives, and plurals correctly. Type the poem along with your problems to make a worksheet on the computer. Print the worksheet and share it with a sibling or friend, or ask your teacher if you can pass out copies to your class at school.

Third Quarter Introduction

In the weeks after the winter or mid-year break, students are often ready to tackle new learning challenges. In many classrooms, brand-new concepts and skills are introduced during third quarter that may be difficult for your child. You can help at home by encouraging your child and providing positive learning support using resources found in *Complete Year*.

Third Quarter Skills
Practice pages in this book for Weeks 19–27 will help your child improve the following skills.

Reading and Language Arts

- Understand adverbs, or words that describe verbs
- Understand and identify compound words
- Understand contractions, or a shortened form of two words
- Identify prefixes, or word parts added to the beginning of words to change the meaning
- Identify suffixes, or word parts added to the ending of words to change the meaning
- Work with one-, two-, and three-syllable words
- Understand and identify synonyms as words that have similar meanings
- Understand and identify antonyms as words that have opposite meanings
- Understand capitalization of proper nouns
- Identify articles **a**, **an**, and **the**

Math

- Work with ordinal numbers **first** through **sixteenth**
- Understand place value up to six digits
- Understand greater than and less than
- Work with two- and three-dimensional shapes
- Understand time intervals, such as seconds, minutes, hours, days, weeks, and years
- Tell time to the nearest five-minute intervals
- Solve time word problems
- Identify and count pennies, nickels, dimes, quarters, and dollar bills
- Write money as a decimal
- Add money

Multi-Sensory Learning Activities

Try these fun activities for enhancing your child's learning and development during the third quarter of the school year. Be sure to choose activities that include speaking, listening, touching, and active movement.

Reading and Language Arts

Write one contraction on each of 15 index cards. Write the words that make up the contractions on separate index cards. Mix up the cards and place them facedown in an array. Play a game of "Memory" where you take turns turning over two cards, attempting to match the contraction and its components.

Write a sentence, leaving out the verb. Draw a line to show where the word is missing, and write the root word of the missing word in parentheses at the end of the sentence. Have your child write the word in the blank, adding the appropriate suffix.

Have your child think about and explain the difference in meaning between the following two sentences: "I chased after a cat. I chased after the cat." Ask your child to describe situations in which he or she would use both sentences.

Math

Write the numerals **1–16** on index cards, one number per card. Mix them up and have your child put them in order. Have your child name each numeral. Tell your child that each of these cards has a place in order. For example, point to **1** and say "first," point to **2** and say "second," etc. Ask your child to write the ordinal number below the numeral on each card.

Make several flash cards to practice greater than and less than. On two index cards, write **<** and **>**. On several other cards, write a one- or two-digit number, one number per card. Then, have your child randomly choose two numbers, placing the correct < or > card between them.

Set up a real or imaginary budget with your child. Include money earned by your child and money spent. Have your child keep track of how much money he or she has at all times.

Third Quarter Introduction, cont.

Science

Show pictures of some birds of prey. Birds of prey include owls, hawks, vultures, eagles, kites, and falcons. Ask your child to choose one type of bird and do some additional research on that bird. Ask your child to find the answers to questions like these: How much do these birds weigh? What do they eat? How do they protect themselves?

Fill one small paper cup with water and one with juice. Put ice pop sticks in the cups. Put the cups into the freezer, and take them out every 15 minutes. Ask your child to describe what he or she sees as the liquid freezes, including differences between the water and the juice.

Social Studies

With your child, read and discuss *Arthur Meets the President* by Marc Brown. Then, write an essay about "How I Can Help Make America Great." Send the essay to the President in care of The White House, 1600 Pennsylvania Ave., Washington, D.C. 20500.

Read *This Is the Way We Go to School: A Book About Children Around the World* by Edith Baer with your child. Compare and discuss the different neighborhoods: city, urban, rural, downtown, suburb, village, and town. Then, read the fable *The Town Mouse and the Country Mouse.* Have your child imagine and describe how each mouse would fare in your neighborhood.

Seasonal Fun

With a paintbrush, help your child paint his or her feet to make a penguin footprint. Paint the middle area of the bottom of your child's foot white, then paint his or her toes and around the edges of the foot with black paint to make the outer part of the penguin's body. Then, have your child press his or her foot onto a piece of construction paper. Next, have your child paint his or her thumbs with the black paint, and press them on either side of the penguin to create arms. Once the paint is dry, use a black marker to draw in the penguin's eyes. Cut a small triangle out of orange construction paper and glue it in place for the penguin's beak.

Week 19 Skills

Subject	Skill	Multi-Sensory Learning Activities
Reading and Language Arts	Review nouns, verbs, and adjectives.	• Complete Practice Pages 206–209. • Divide a large piece of paper into three columns. At the top of the columns, write the headings **noun**, **verb**, and **adjective**. Then, write several nouns, verbs, and adjectives on small cards, one word per card. Have your child place the cards in the correct columns.
	Understand adverbs, or words that describe verbs.	• Complete Practice Page 210. • Have your child add adverbs to tongue twisters. For example, say, "Sally saw seven silly slippery silver seals swimming slowly." • Review adverbs. Choose an action that your child can perform, such as **run** or **jump**. Have your child act out different adverbs with that action, such as **run quickly**, **run outside**, or **run noisily**.
Math	Work with ordinal numbers **first** through **sixteenth**.	• Complete Practice Pages 211–214. • Make a mini book with your child about something that comes in a certain order, such as days of the week, the ingredients in a recipe, or events in a story. On each page, have your child write an ordinal number and one part of the series. For example, on Page 1, your child may write, "The first day of the week is Monday."

Is It a World Record?

Write the correct word on the line.

big — 1. Emmett made a __________________ snowball.

bigger — 2. Sara helped him make it even __________________.

biggest — 3. The town made the ____________ snowball on reco

fast — 1. The snowball started to roll very __________________.

faster — 2. It was the __________________ rolling snowball anyor had ever seen.

fastest — 3. It rolled __________________ than they could run.

white — 1. After it snowed all night, the town was the __________________ it had ever been.

whiter — 2. Mr. Wetzel's face turned __________________ when h saw the snowball rolling toward his candy store.

whitest — 3. As the snowball rolled closer, Mr. Wetzel's face became even __________________.

Adjectives

Adjectives are used to describe nouns.

Look at the pictures. Complete each chart.

Example:

Noun	What Color?	What Size?	What Number?
flower	red	small	two

Noun	What Color?	What Size?	What Number?

Noun	What Color?	What Size?	What Number?

Noun	What Color?	What Size?	What Number?

Down to Basics

In each sentence, circle the nouns, draw an **X** above the verbs and draw two lines under all adjectives.

1. The children saw a black cloud in the sky.
2. Rain fell from the enormous black cloud.
3. Lightning flashed and thunder crashed.
4. The rain made puddles on the ground.
5. Moving cars splashed water.
6. The children raced into the house.

7. Ten boys and six girls belong to the Wildcat team.
8. The Wildcats played the Greyhounds from Central City.
9. The Wildcats won the big game.
10. The coach said, "The Wildcats made two more goals than our team.

11. The circus came to town on Thursday.
12. On Friday, the circus had a parade.
13. The silly monkeys rode in a cage and did tricks.
14. The huge elephants pulled heavy wagons.
15. People laughed at the funny clowns.

Adjectives

Underline the nouns in each sentence below. Then, draw an arrow from each adjective to the noun it describes.

Example:

A platypus is a furry animal that lives in Australia.

1. This animal likes to swim.

2. The nose looks like a duck's bill.
3. It has a broad tail like a beaver.
4. Platypuses are great swimmers.
5. They have webbed feet which help them swim.
6. Their flat tails also help them move through the water.
7. The platypus is an unusual mammal because it lays eggs.
8. The eggs look like reptile eggs.
9. Platypuses can lay three eggs at a time.
10. These babies do not leave their mothers for one year.
11. This animal spends most of its time hunting near streams.

Adverbs

An **adverb** describes a verb. It tells how, when or where an action takes place.

Example:

The space shuttle blasted off **yesterday**. (when)
It rose **quickly** into the sky. (how)
We watched **outdoors**. (where)

Write **how, when** or **where** to explain what each adverb tells.

1. I run **today**. ____________
2. I run **outside**. ____________
3. I run **tomorrow**. ____________
4. I run **around**. ____________
5. I run **nearby**. ____________
6. I run **sometimes**. ____________
7. I run **there**. ____________
8. I run **far**. ____________
9. I run **happily**. ____________
10. I run **weekly**. ____________
11. I run **swiftly**. ____________
12. I run **first**. ____________
13. I run **next**. ____________
14. I run **gracefully**. ____________

Circle the adverb in each pair of words. Remember, an adverb describes an action.

1. soon, supper
2. neatly, nine
3. proudly, prove
4. help, easily
5. warmly, wonder
6. quilt, quickly
7. finally, feather
8. quietly, quacks
9. sail, safely

Ordinal Numbers

Ordinal numbers are used to indicate order in a series, such as **first, second** or **third**.

Draw a line to the picture that corresponds to the ordinal number in the left column.

eighth

third

sixth

ninth

seventh

second

fourth

first

fifth

tenth

Ordinal Numbers

Ordinal numbers indicate order in a series, such as **first**, **second** or **thi**

Follow the instructions to color the train cars. The first car is the engine

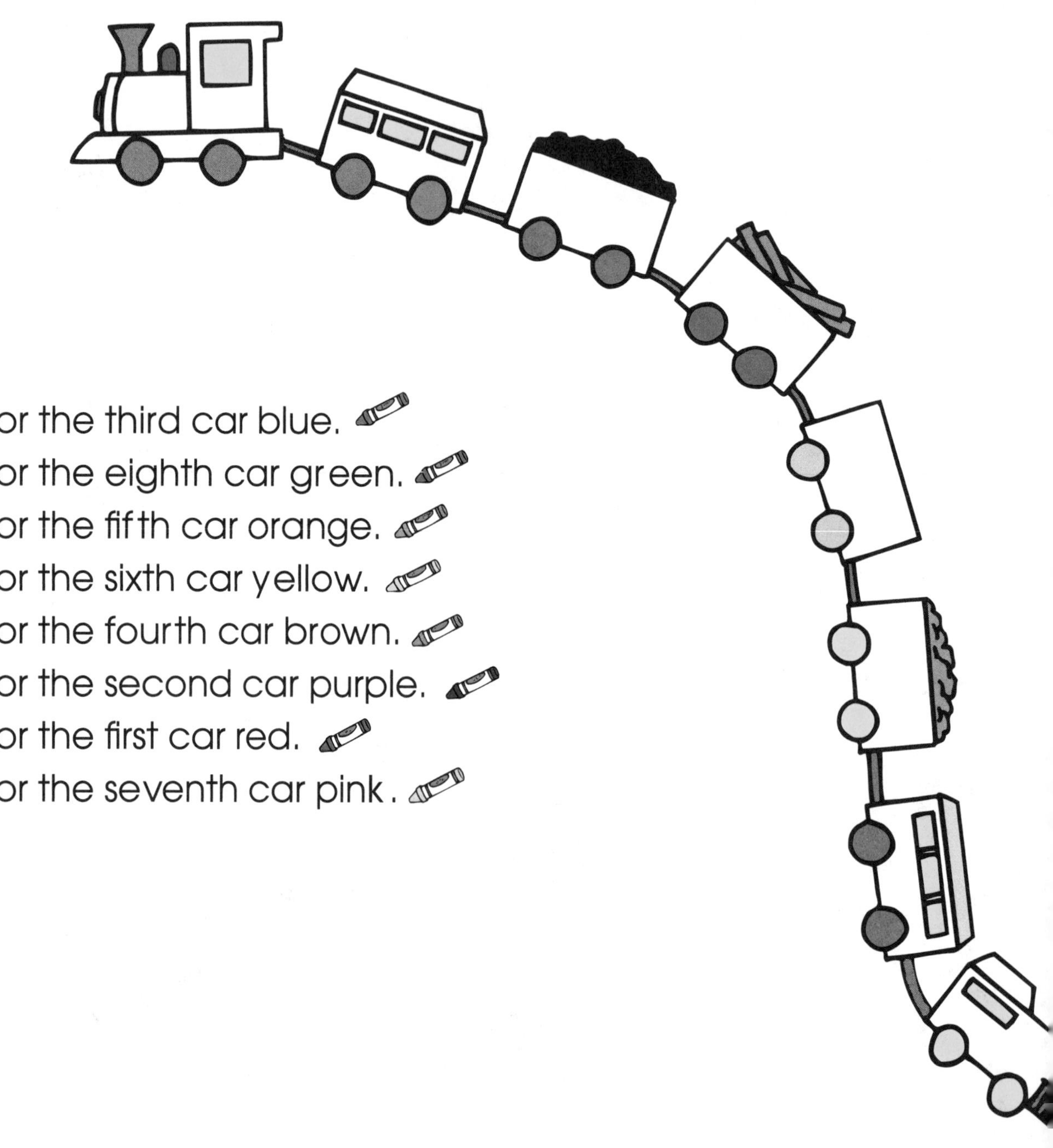

Color the third car blue.
Color the eighth car green.
Color the fifth car orange.
Color the sixth car yellow.
Color the fourth car brown.
Color the second car purple.
Color the first car red.
Color the seventh car pink.

Ordinal Numbers

Follow the instructions.

Draw glasses on the second one.

Put a hat on the fourth one.

Color blonde hair on the third one.

Draw a tie on the first one.

Draw ears on the fifth one.

Draw black hair on the seventh one.

Put a bow on the head of the sixth one.

My First Treat Will Be...

Circle the ordinal number word for each treat.

1 2 3 4

16 15 14

third, sixteenth, fifth

5

fifteenth, fourth, first

twelfth, second, seventh

third, eleventh, fifteenth

6

eighth, first, tenth

sixteenth, thirteenth, third

7

ninth, second, thirteenth

sixth, seventh, ninth

13

12 11 10 9 8

Week 20 Skills

Subject	Skill	Multi-Sensory Learning Activities
Reading and Language Arts	Understand and identify compound words.	• Complete Practice Pages 216–219. • With your child, read *The Mysterious Tadpole* by Steven Kellogg. Have your child find and list the compound words in the book. • Have your child form compound words from clues. For example, tell your child, "The time you go to bed is your … ." Your child would then supply the correct compound word, **bedtime**.
Math	Understand place value up to six digits.	• Complete Practice Pages 221–224. • Use dried beans, raisins, dried macaroni, or other small objects to group into sets of 10. Put each group of 10 in a small cup. Then, move the groups around to show 10, 20, 30, 40, 50, 60, 70, 80, 90, and 100. Add single pieces to display numbers with 1–9 in the ones place. • Look in newspapers, magazines, and catalogs or on bottles, boxes, and license plates for numbers from **10** to **999**. Make a list of these numbers and tell how many hundreds, tens, and ones are in each number.

Compound Words

Compound words are formed by putting together two smaller words.

Help the cook brew her stew. Mix words from the first column with words from the second column to make new words.

Write your new words on the lines at the bottom.

grand	brows
snow	light
eye	stairs
down	string
rose	book
shoe	mother
note	ball
moon	bud

1. ____________________
2. ____________________
3. ____________________
4. ____________________
5. ____________________
6. ____________________
7. ____________________
8. ____________________

Compound Words

Compound words are two words that are put together to make one new word.

Read the sentences. Fill in the blank with a compound word from the box.

raincoat	bedroom	lunchbox	hallway	sandbox

1. A box with sand is a

_______________________________.

2. The way through a hall is a

_______________________________.

3. A box for lunch is a

_______________________________.

4. A coat for the rain is a

_______________________________.

5. A room with a bed is a

_______________________________.

Compound Words

Draw a line under the compound word in each sentence. On the line, write the two words that make up the compound word.

1. A firetruck came to help put out the fire.

____

2. I will be nine years old on my next birthday.

____

3. We built a treehouse at the back.

____

4. Dad put a scarecrow in his garden.

____

5. It is fun to make footprints in the snow.

____

6. I like to read the comics in the newspaper.

____

7. Cowboys ride horses and use lassos.

____

Compound Words

Cut out the words below. Glue them together in the box to make compound words.

Can you think of any more compound words?

sun	air	mail	ball
box	room	water	guard
foot	bath	class	flower
plane	room	melon	body

Tens and Ones

Write the number indicated by tally marks.

 ______ 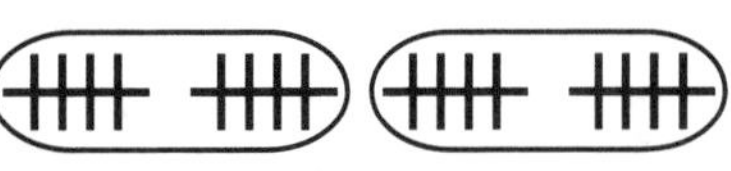 ______

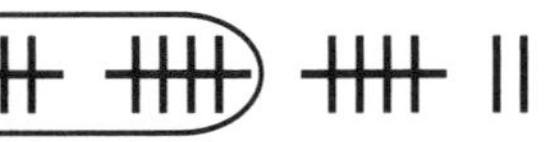 ______  ______

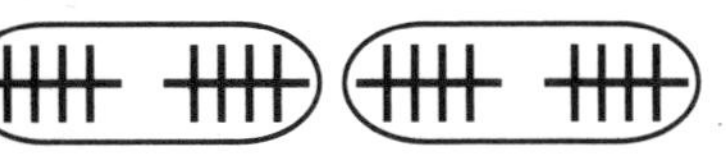 ______  ______

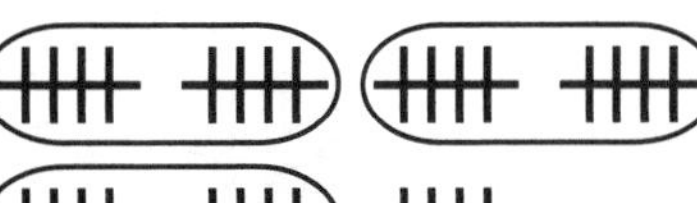 ______  ______

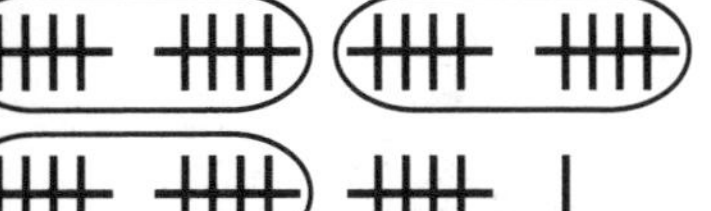 ______ 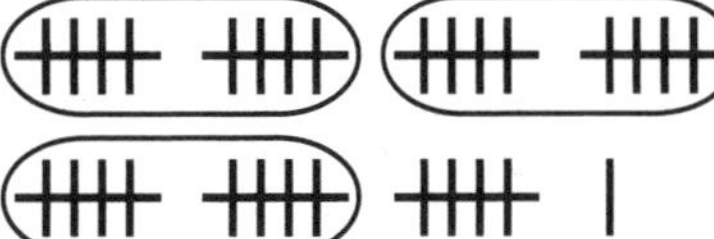 ______

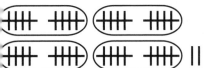

Using tally marks, draw the numbers named.

35

41

15

22

45 

7 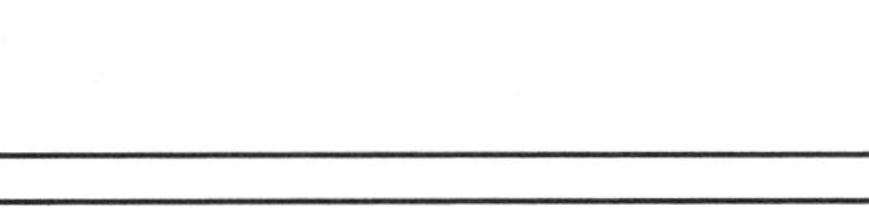

11 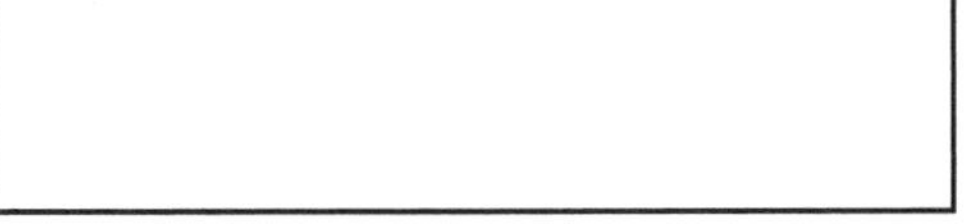

29 

30 

26 

18 

10

Place Value: Hundreds

Write the numbers for hundreds, tens and ones. Then, add.

Example:

What Big Numbers!

Write each number. The first one has been done for you.

Hundreds	Tens	Ones

1 hundreds
3 tens
2 ones = 132

Hundreds	Tens	Ones

___ hundreds
___ tens
___ ones = _______

Hundreds	Tens	Ones

___ hundreds
___ tens
___ ones = _______

Hundreds	Tens	Ones

___ hundreds
___ tens
___ ones = _______

Hundreds	Tens	Ones

___ hundreds
___ tens
___ ones = _______

Hundreds	Tens	Ones

___ hundreds
___ tens
___ ones = _______

Hundreds	Tens	Ones

___ hundreds
___ tens
___ ones = _______

Hundreds	Tens	Ones

___ hundreds
___ tens
___ ones = _______

Place Value

The place value of a digit, or numeral, is shown by where it is in the number. For example, in the number **1,234**, **1** has the place value of thousands, **2** is hundreds, **3** is tens and **4** is ones.

Hundred Thousands	Ten Thousands	Thousands	Hundreds	Tens	Ones
9	4	3	8	5	2

Match the numbers in Column A with the words in Column B.

A	B
62,453	two hundred thousand
7,641	three thousand
486,113	four hundred thousand
11,277	eight hundreds
813,463	seven tens
594,483	five ones
254,089	six hundreds
79,841	nine ten thousands
27,115	five tens

Week 21 Skills

Subject	Skill	Multi-Sensory Learning Activities
Reading and Language Arts	Review compound words.	• Complete Practice Pages 226–230. • Write several compound words on a piece of paper, like **raincoat**, **doghouse**, **football**, and **inside**. Have your child read each word and draw a line between the two words that make up each compound word. • Play a game of "Memory" with your child. Make at least 10 pairs of flash cards, writing one half of a compound word on each card. Flip the cards upside down in a grid pattern and take turns choosing two cards. If a compound word is made from the two cards, the player keeps those cards and gets to go again. If a compound word is not made, flip the cards back upside down and the other player gets to go. The player with the most cards after all matches have been made wins the game.
Math	Review place value.	• Complete Practice Pages 231–234. • Create place value art. Using strips of ten squares and single squares, have your child create a picture by gluing the parts onto construction paper. Below the picture, write the number it portrays.

Word Magic

Maggie Magician announced, "One plus one equals one!" The audience giggled. So Maggie put two words into a hat and waved her magic wand. When she reached into the hat, Maggie pulled out one word and a picture. "See," said Maggie, "I was right!"

Use the box to help write a compound word for each picture below.

ball	door	rain	star	shirt	bell	fish	shoe	book	foot	basket
bow	lace	box	stool	light	sun	cup	mail	tail	cake	worm

____

____

____

____

____

____

____

____

____

____

____

Mixing a Compound

sometimes downtown girlfriend
everybody maybe myself lunchbox
baseball outside today

Write the correct compound word on the line. Then, use the numbered letters to solve the code.

1. Opposite of **inside** ___ ___ ___ ___ ___ ___ ___ (1 under letter 2)
2. Another word for **me** ___ ___ ___ ___ ___ ___ (2 under letter 2, 3 under letter 6)
3. A girl who is a friend ___ ___ ___ ___ ___ ___ ___ ___ ___ ___ (4 under letter 1, 5 under letter 7)
4. Not yesterday or tomorrow, but . . . ___ ___ ___ ___ ___ (6 under letter 3)
5. All of the people ___ ___ ___ ___ ___ ___ ___ ___ ___ (7 under letter 4, 8 under letter 7)
6. A sport ___ ___ ___ ___ ___ ___ ___ ___ (9 under letter 8)
7. The main part of a town ___ ___ ___ ___ ___ ___ ___ ___ (10 under letter 3, 11 under letter 8)
8. Not always, just . . . ___ ___ ___ ___ ___ ___ ___ ___ ___ (12 under letter 1, 13 under letter 5)
9. A box for carrying your lunch ___ ___ ___ ___ ___ ___ ___ ___ (14 under letter 5)
10. Perhaps or might ___ ___ ___ ___ ___ (15 under letter 5)

___ ___ ___ ___ ___ ___ ___ ___ ___ ! ___ ___ ___
10 8 11 6 15 7 3 1 9 ! 2 8 1

___ ___ ___ ___ ___ ___ ___ ___
3 8 1 11 6 13 14 15

___ ___ ___ ___ ___ ___ ___ ___ ___ ___ ___ ___ ___ !
7 5 4 14 13 12 8 9 1 13 5 8 11 !

Compound Your Effort

Find the word in the word box that goes with the words numbered below to make a compound word. Cross it out. Then, write the compound word on the line.

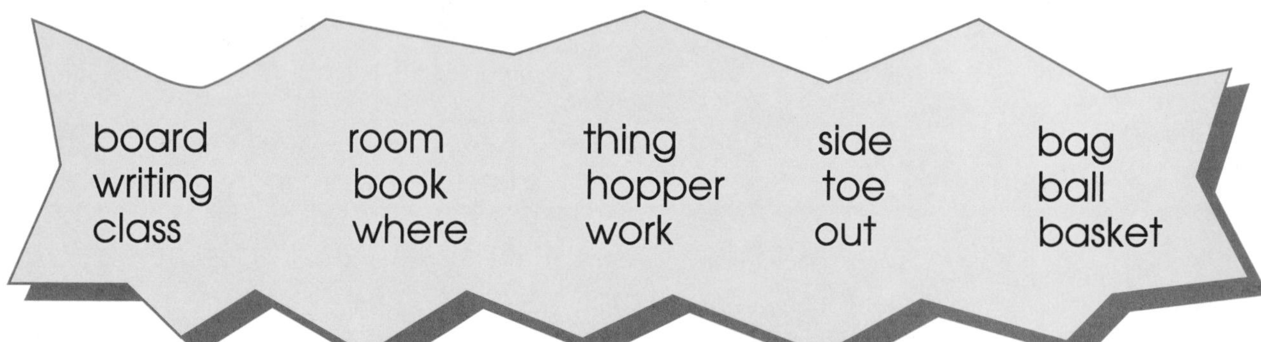

1. coat ____________________
2. snow ____________________
3. home ____________________
4. waste ____________________
5. tip ____________________
6. chalk ____________________
7. note ____________________
8. grass ____________________
9. school ____________________
10. with ____________________

Look at the words in the word box that you did not use. Use those words to make your own compound words.

1. ____________________
2. ____________________
3. ____________________
4. ____________________
5. ____________________

Compound Words

A **compound word** is two small words put together to make one new word. Compound words are usually divided into syllables between the two words.

Read the words. Then, divide them into syllables. The first one is done for you.

1. playground play ground
2. sailboat ____________
3. doghouse ____________
4. dishpan ____________
5. pigpen ____________
6. outdoors ____________
7. beehive ____________
8. airplane ____________
9. cardboard ____________
10. nickname ____________
11. hilltop ____________
12. broomstick ____________
13. sunburn ____________
14. oatmeal ____________
15. campfire ____________
16. somewhere ____________
17. starfish ____________
18. birthday ____________
19. sidewalk ____________
20. seashore ____________

Compound Words

Read the compound words in the word box. Then, use them to answe the questions. The first one is done for you.

sailboat	blueberry	bookcase	tablecloth	beehive
dishpan	pigpen	classroom	playground	bedtime
broomstick	treetop	fireplace	newspaper	sunburn

Which compound word means . . .

1. a case for books? bookcase
2. a berry that is blue? ______

3. a hive for bees? ______
4. a place for fires? ______
5. a pen for pigs? ______
6. a room for a class? ______

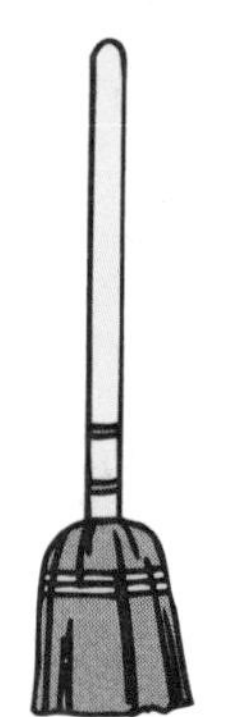

7. a pan for dishes? ______
8. a boat to sail? ______
9. a paper for news? ______
10. a burn from the sun? ______
11. the top of a tree? ______
12. a stick for a broom? ______

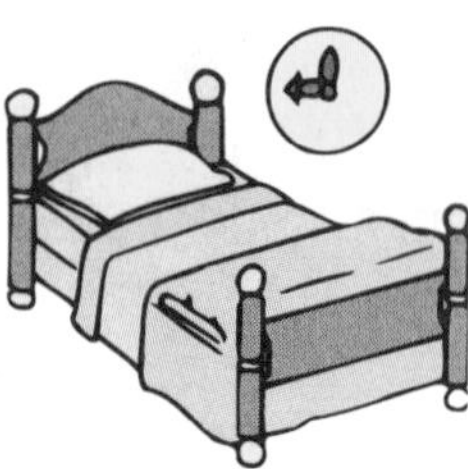

13. the time to go to bed? ______
14. a cloth for the table? ______
15. ground to play on? ______

Review: Place Value

The place value of each digit, or numeral, is shown by where it is in the number. For example, in the number **123**, **1** has the place value of hundreds, **2** is tens, and **3** is ones.

Count the groups of crayons and add.

Example:

				Hundreds	Tens	Ones
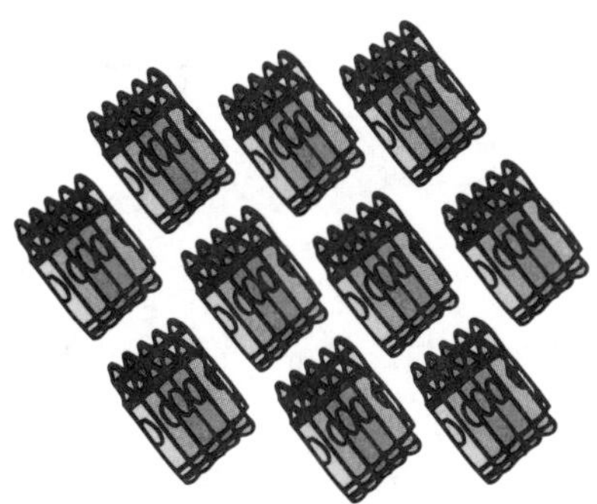	+	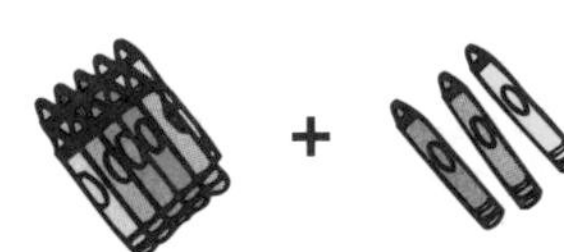	=	1	1	3
I Hundred	+	I Ten + 3 Ones				
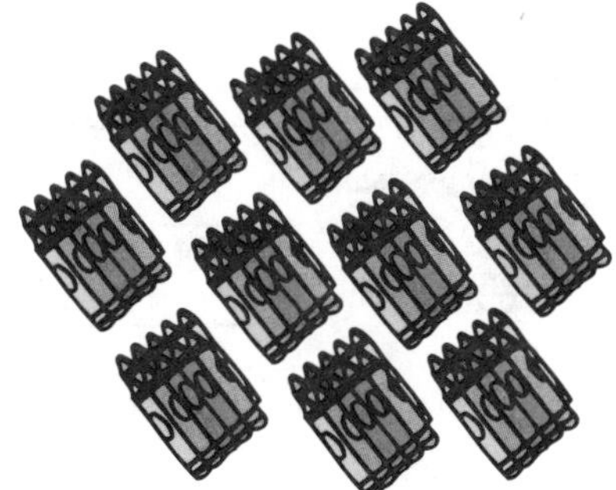	+	+	=	____	____	____
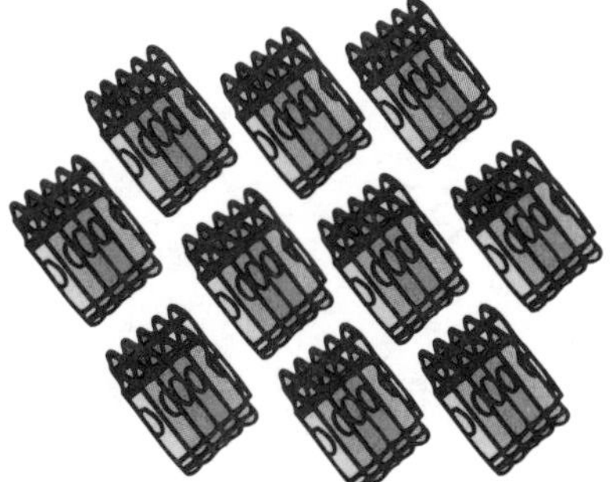	+ 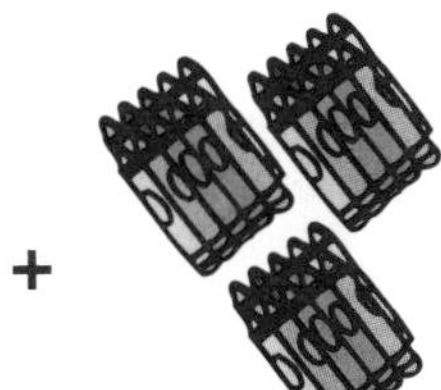	+ 	=	____	____	____

Place Value: Ones, Tens

The place value of a digit or numeral is shown by where it is in the number. For example, in the number **23**, **2** has the place value of tens and **3** is ones.

Add the tens and ones and write your answers in the blanks.

Example:

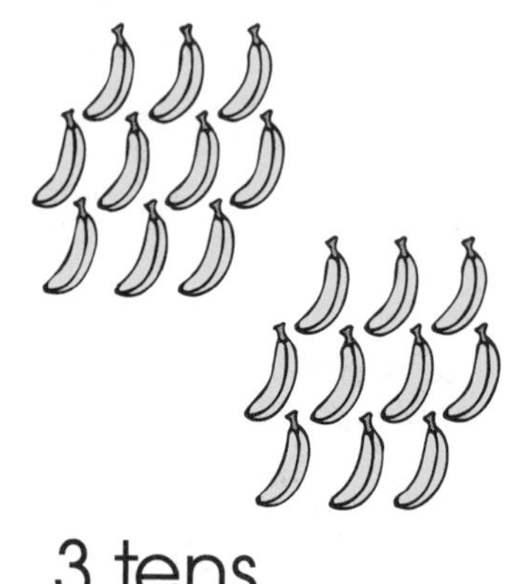

\+  = 33

3 tens + 3 ones = 33

	tens ones		tens ones
7 tens + 5 ones =	______	4 tens + 0 ones =	______
2 tens + 3 ones =	______	8 tens + 1 one =	______
5 tens + 2 ones =	______	1 ten + 1 one =	______
5 tens + 4 ones =	______	6 tens + 3 ones =	______
9 tens + 5 ones =	______		

Draw a line to the correct number.

6 tens + 7 ones	73
4 tens + 2 ones	67
8 tens + 0 ones	51
7 tens + 3 ones	80
5 tens + 1 one	42

Place Value: Ones, Tens

Write the numbers for the tens and ones. Then, add.

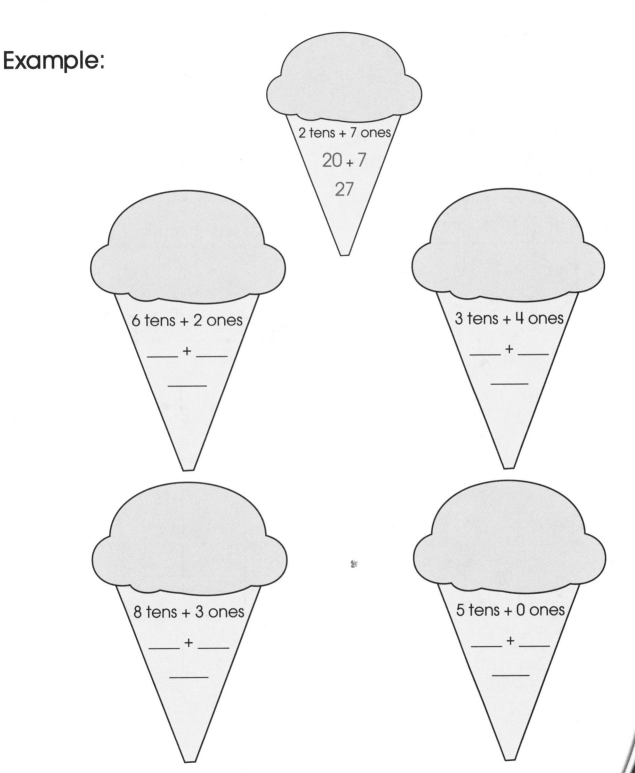

Example:

2 tens + 7 ones

20 + 7

27

6 tens + 2 ones

____ + ____

_____

3 tens + 4 ones

____ + ____

_____

8 tens + 3 ones

____ + ____

_____

5 tens + 0 ones

____ + ____

_____

Place Value: Hundreds

The place value of a digit or numeral is shown by where it is in the number. For example, in the number **123**, **1** has the place value of hundreds, **2** is tens and **3** is ones.

Study the examples. Then, write the missing numbers in the blanks.

Examples:

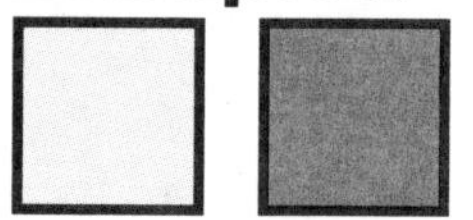 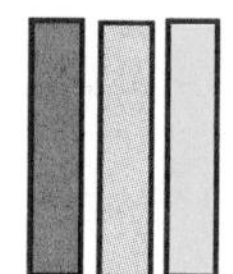 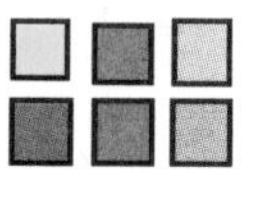

2 hundreds + 3 tens + 6 ones =

hundreds	tens	ones	
2	3	6	= 236

 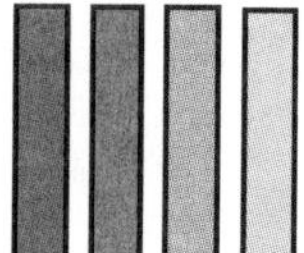 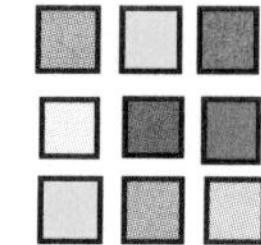

1 hundred + 4 tens + 9 ones =

hundreds	tens	ones	
1	4	9	= 149

	hundreds	tens	ones	total
3 hundreds + 4 tens + 8 ones =	3	4	8	= ______
_ hundreds + _ ten + _ ones =	2	1	7	= ______
_ hundreds + _ tens + _ ones =	6	3	5	= ______
_ hundreds + _ tens + _ ones =	4	7	9	= ______
_ hundreds + _ tens + _ ones =	2	9	4	= ______
_ hundreds + 5 tens + 6 ones =	4	____	____	= ______
3 hundreds + 1 ten + 3 ones =	____	____	____	= ______
3 hundreds + _ tens + 7 ones =	____	5	____	= ______
6 hundreds + 2 tens + _ ones =	____	____	8	= ______

Week 22 Skills

Subject	Skill	Multi-Sensory Learning Activities
Reading and Language Arts	Understand contractions, or a shortened form of two words.	• Complete Practice Pages 236–241. • Write several sentences containing contractions for your child to read. Ask your child to name each contraction, as well as the two words the contraction represents.
Math	Understand greater than and less than.	• Complete Practice Pages 242–244. • Show two pictures of like objects in differing amounts, such as three cats and six cats or ten squares and twelve squares. Have your child write the number of objects on each picture, compare, and tell which number is greater (or less). • Show your child a baseball. Ask your child to describe its size. He or she may do that by comparing it to other objects. Teach your child to use the words **greater** and **less** (in size).
Bonus: Science		• Read *Birds, Nests & Eggs* by Mel Boring. Then, discuss birds that are symbols, such as the eagle for strength, the dove for peace, and the owl for wisdom. Have your child select a new bird to be a symbol. Have him or her describe for what it is a symbol and why he or she chose that bird. Have your child draw a picture of the bird.

Contractions

Contractions are a short way to write two words, such as **isn't**, **I've** a **weren't**. **Example: it is = it's**

Draw a line from each word pair to its contraction.

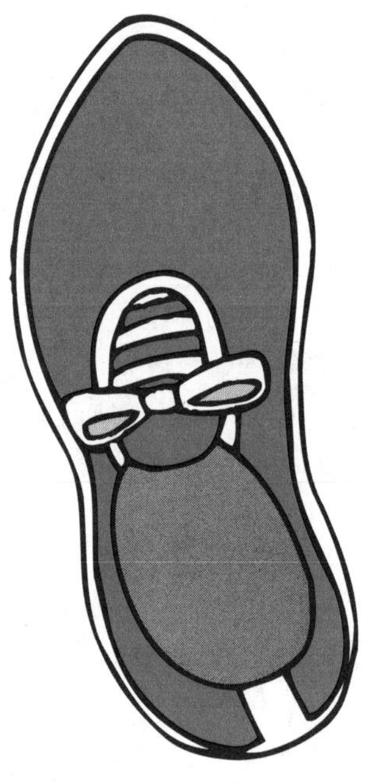

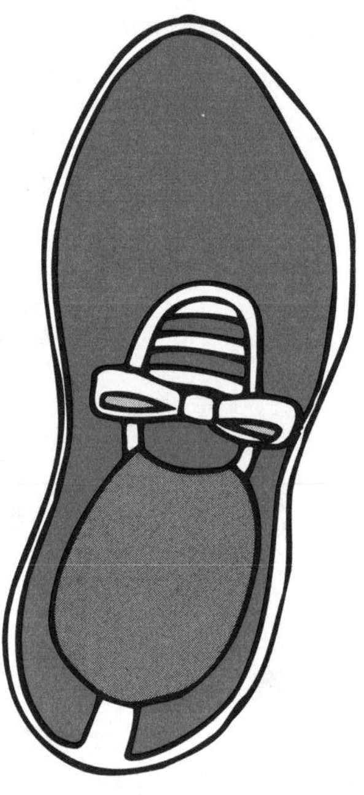

I am	she's
it is	they're
you are	we're
we are	he's
they are	I'm
she is	it's
he is	you're

Contractions

Circle the contraction that would replace the underlined words.

Example: were not = **weren't**

1. The boy <u>was not</u> sad.
   wasn't weren't

2. We <u>were not</u> working.
   wasn't weren't

3. Jen and Caleb <u>have not</u> eaten lunch yet.
   haven't hasn't

4. The mouse <u>has not</u> been here.
   haven't hasn't

Contractions

Match the words with their contractions.

would not	I've
was not	he'll
he will	wouldn't
could not	wasn't
I have	couldn't

Make the words at the end of each line into contractions to complete the sentences.

1. He ________________ know the answer. **did not**

2. ________________ a long way home. **It is**

3. ________________ my house. **Here is**

4. ________________ not going to school today. **We are**

5. ________________ take the bus home tomorrow. **They will**

Contractions

Cut out the heart halves and put them together to show what two words make the contraction. Glue them over the contraction.

Contractions

A **contraction** is a word made up of two words joined together with one or more letters left out. An **apostrophe** is used in place of the missing letters.

Examples: I am—**I'm**
do not—**don't**
that is—**that's**

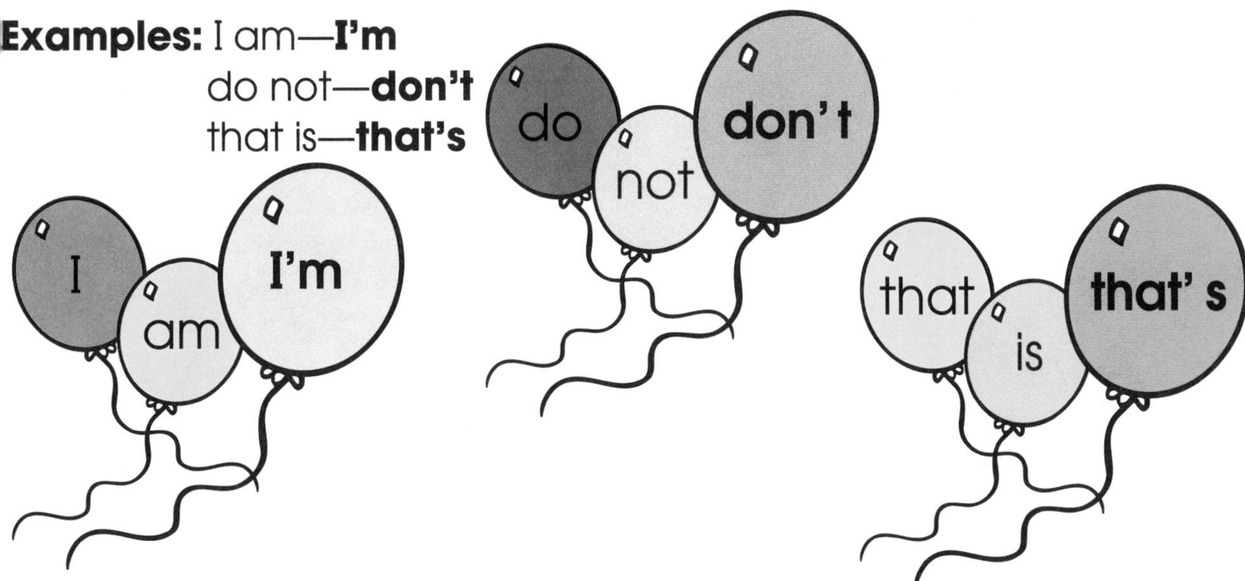

Draw a line to match each contraction to the words from which it was made. The first one is done for you.

1. he's	we are	6. they'll	are not
2. we're	cannot	7. aren't	they will
3. can't	he is	8. I've	you have
4. I'll	she is	9. you've	will not
5. she's	I will	10. won't	I have

Write the contraction for each pair of words.

1. you are ____________________
2. does not ____________________
3. do not ____________________
4. would not ____________________
5. she is ____________________
6. we have ____________________
7. has not ____________________
8. did not ____________________

"Mouth" Math

Write **<** or **>** in each circle. Make sure the "mouth" is open toward the greater number!

36		49	35		53
20		18	74		21
53		76	68		80
29		26	45		19
90		89	70		67

Number Lines

Write the circled numbers in the correct order on the lines.

A.

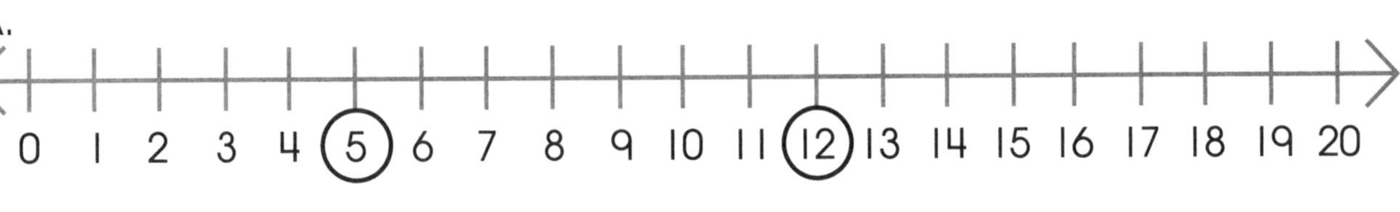

_____ > _____

B.

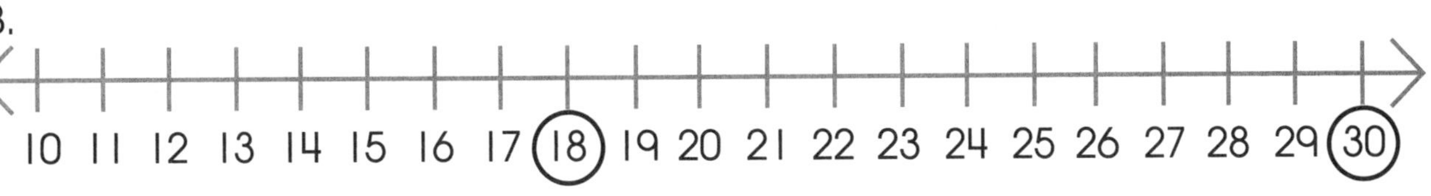

_____ < _____

C.

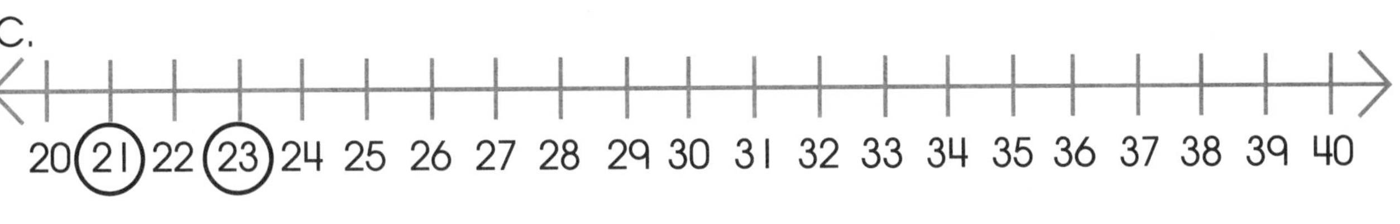

_____ > _____

D.

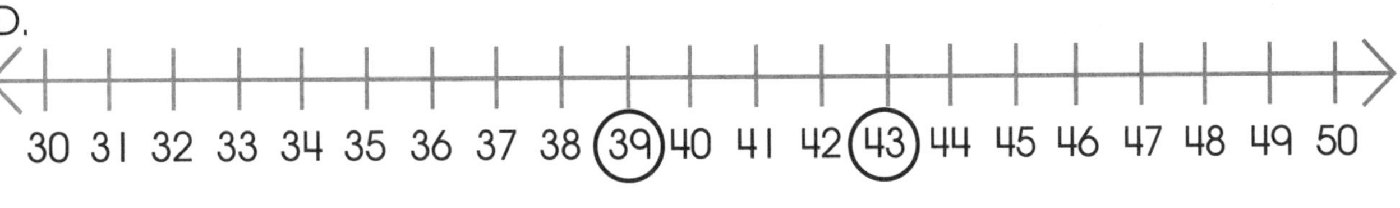

_____ < _____

E.

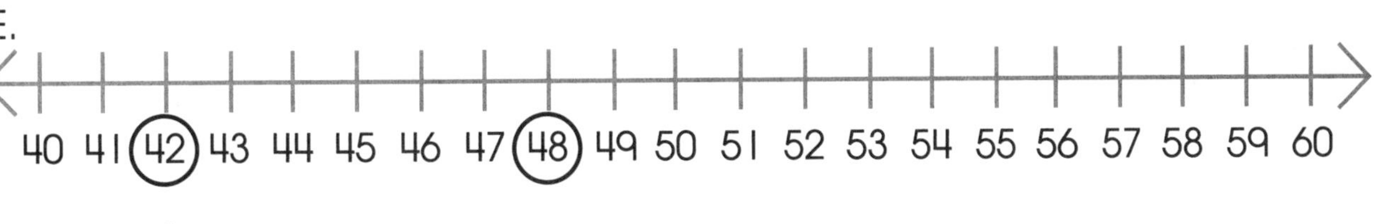

_____ > _____

F.

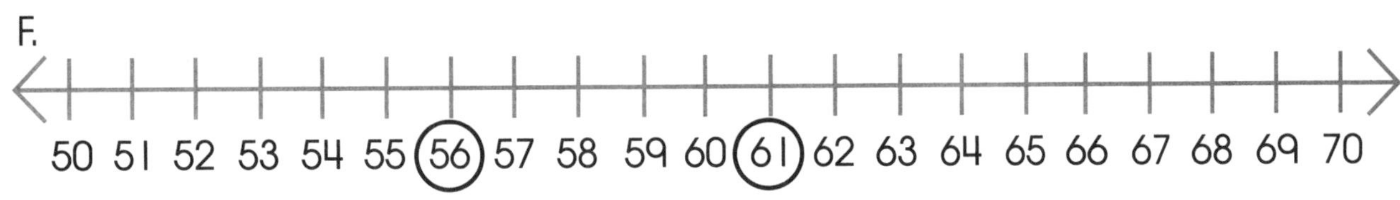

_____ < _____

Less Than, Greater Than

The open mouth points to the larger number. The small point goes to the smaller number. Draw the symbol **<** or **>** to the correct number.

Example: 5  3

This means that 5 is greater than 3, and 3 is less than 5.

12 ◯ 2

16 ◯ 6

16 ◯ 15

1 ◯ 2

7 ◯ 1

19 ◯ 5

9 ◯ 6

11 ◯ 13

Week 23 Skills

Subject	Skill	Multi-Sensory Learning Activities
Reading and Language Arts	Identify prefixes, or word parts added to the beginning of words to change the meaning.	• Complete Practice Pages 246–249. • Put several pennies on the table. Have your child count them. Write **count** on a piece of paper. Put a couple more pennies on the table and ask your child to recount the pennies. Write **recount**. Then, have your child underline the root word and circle the prefix. Introduce other words with the **re** prefix, such as **reread**, **return**, and **refreeze**. Have your child draw a line under each root word, circle the prefix, and use each word in a sentence.
	Identify suffixes, or word parts added to the ending of words to change the meaning.	• Complete Practice Page 250. • Have your child make a list of words that end in **er**. Prompt him or her to think of the jobs and actions of people. For example, someone who paints is a painter.
Math	Work with two- and three-dimensional shapes.	• Complete Practice Pages 251–253. • On index cards, write the names of two- and three-dimensional shapes and draw a matching shape card for each. Have your child match the shapes with the names.

Prefixes

Change the meaning of the sentences by adding the prefixes to the **bold** words.

The boy was **lucky** because he guessed the answer **correctly**.

The boy was (un) ____________________ because he guessed the

answer (in) ____________________________.

When Mary **behaved**, she felt **happy**.

When Mary (mis) ____,

she felt (un) ____.

Mike wore his jacket **buttoned** because the dance was **formal**.

Mike wore his jacket (un) _____________________ because the dance

was (in) ____.

Tim **understood** because he was **familiar** with the book.

Tim (mis) ____________________________ because he was

(un) ___________________________ with the book.

Prefixes

Read the story. Change the story by removing the prefix **re** from the **bold** words. Write the new words in the new story.

Repete is a **rewriter** who has to **redo** every story. He has to **rethink** up the ideas. He has to **rewrite** the sentences. He has to **redraw** the pictures. He even has to **retype** the pages. Who will **repay** **Repete** for all the work he **redoes**?

________________ is a ________________ who has to ________________ every story. He has to ________________ up the ideas. He has to ________________ the sentences.

He has to ________________ the pictures.

He even has to ________________ the pages.

Who will ________________ ________________ for all the work he ________________?

Prefixes

Read each sentence. Look at the words in **bold**. Circle the prefix and write the root word on the line.

1. The **preview** of the movie was funny. __________
2. We always drink **nonfat** milk. __________
3. We will have to **reschedule** the trip. __________
4. Are you tired of **reruns** on television? __________
5. I have **outgrown** my new shoes already. __________
6. You must have **misplaced** the papers. __________
7. Police **enforce** the laws of the city. __________
8. I **disliked** that book. __________
9. The boy **distrusted** the big dog. __________
10. Try to **enjoy** yourself at the party. __________
11. Please try to keep the cat **inside** the house. __________
12. That song is total **nonsense**! __________
13. We will **replace** any parts that we lost. __________
14. Can you help me **unzip** this jacket? __________
15. Let's **rework** today's arithmetic problems. __________

Prefixes

Prefixes are special word parts added to the beginnings of words. Prefixes change the meaning of words.

Prefix	Meaning	Example
un	not	**un**happy
re	again	**re**do
pre	before	**pre**view
mis	wrong	**mis**understanding
dis	opposite	**dis**obey

Circle the word that begins with a prefix. Then, write the prefix and the root word.

1. The dog was unfriendly. ________ + ____________
2. The movie preview was interesting. ________ + ____________
3. The referee called an unfair penalty. ________ + ____________
4. Please do not misbehave. ________ + ____________
5. My parents disapprove of that show. ________ + ____________
6. I had to redo the assignment. ________ + ____________

Suffixes

Suffixes are word parts added to the ends of words. Suffixes change the meaning of words.

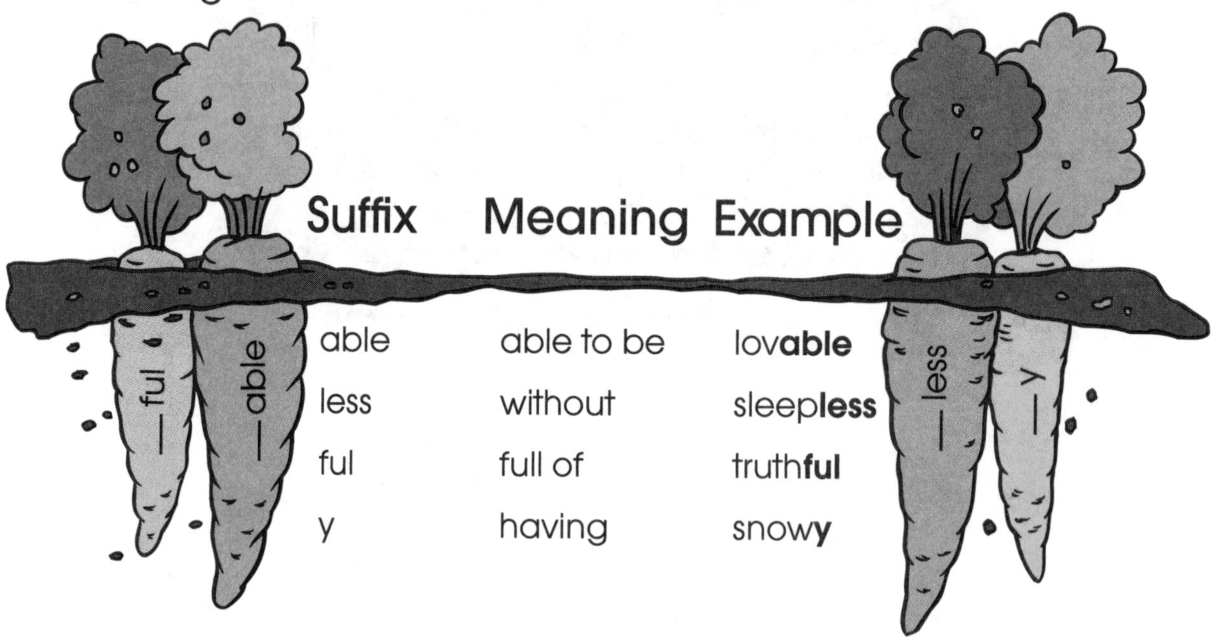

Suffix	Meaning	Example
able	able to be	lov**able**
less	without	sleep**less**
ful	full of	truth**ful**
y	having	snow**y**

Circle the suffix in each word below.

Example: fluff(y)

rainy	thoughtful	likeable
blameless	enjoyable	helpful
peaceful	careless	silky

Write a word for each meaning.

full of hope ________________ having rain ________________

without hope ________________ able to break ________________

without power ________________ full of cheer ________________

How Many?

Find the shapes and color them using the code.

▲	red	●	blue	◇	yellow
⬬	green	■	orange	▬	black

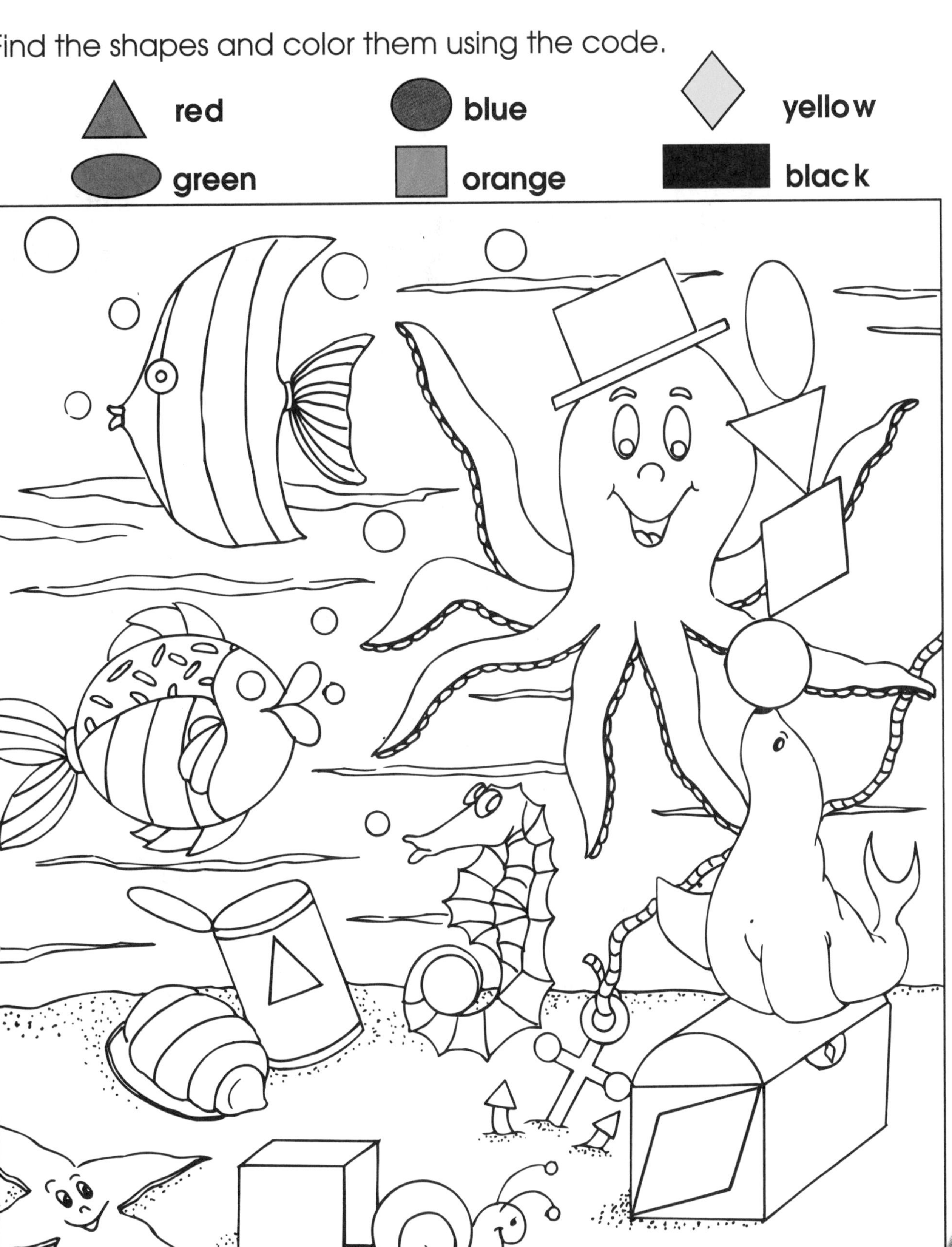

Geometry

Geometry is the branch of mathematics that has to do with points, lines and shapes.

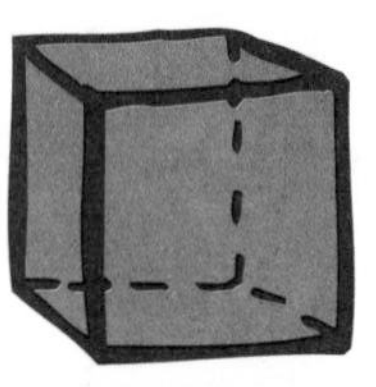

cube

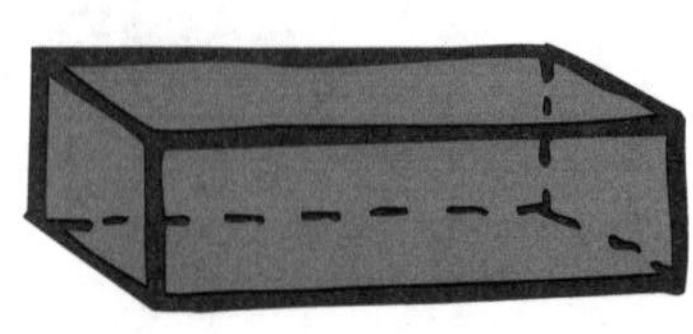

rectangular prism

cone

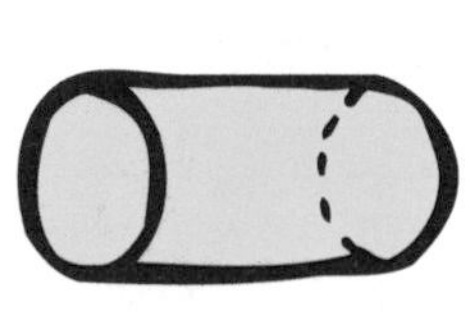

cylinder

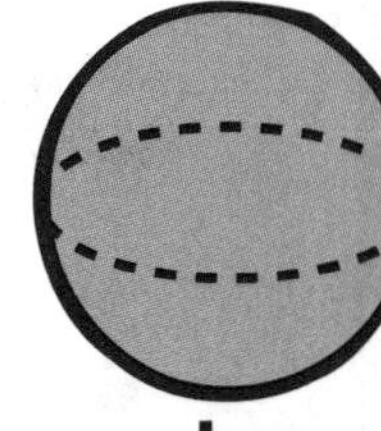

sphere

Use the code to color the picture.

Color:
cubes — blue
rectangular prisms — red
cones — green
cylinders — yellow
spheres — orange

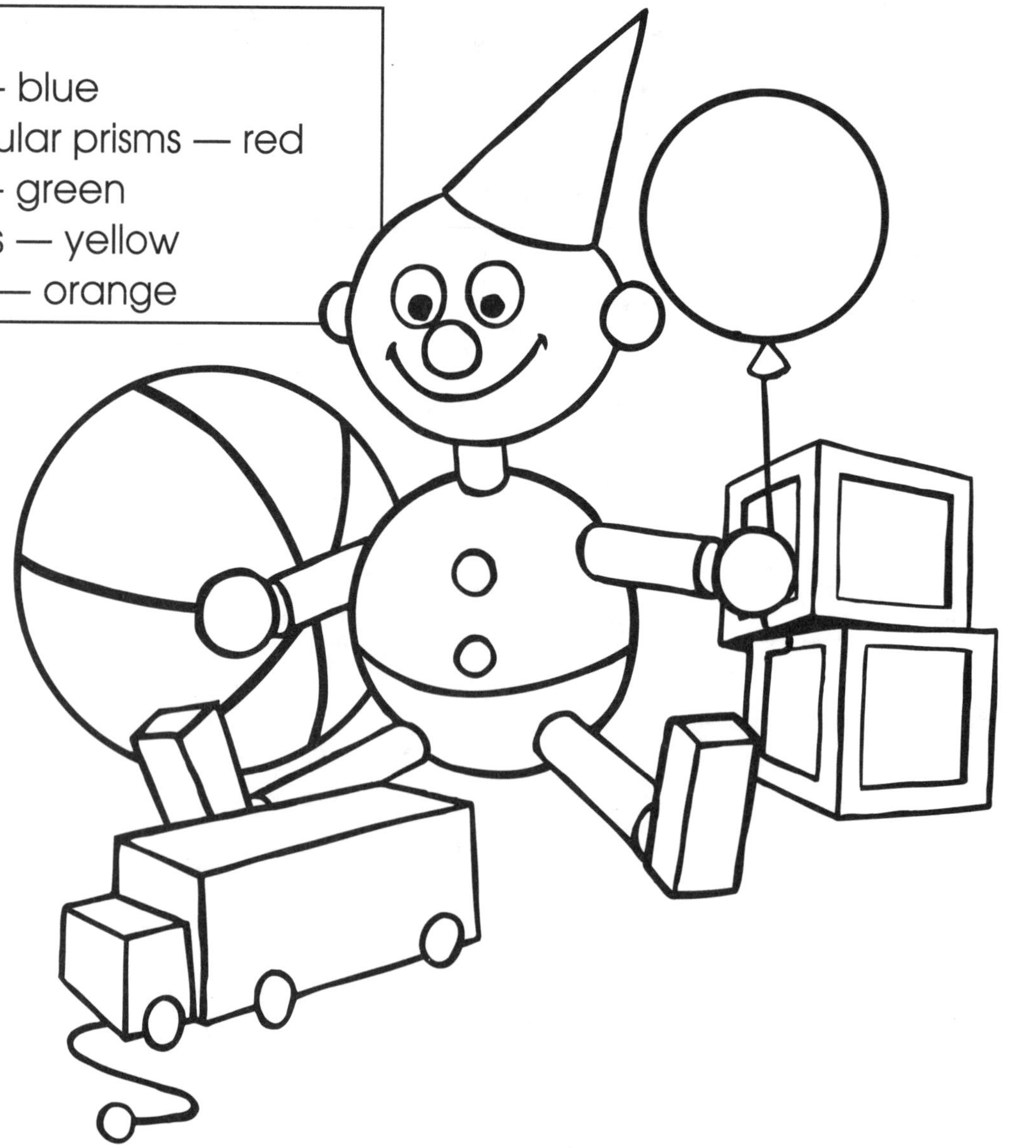

Tangram

Cut out the tangram below. Use the shapes to make a cat, a chicken, a boat and a large triangle.

Week 24 Skills

Subject	Skill	Multi-Sensory Learning Activities
Reading and Language Arts	Work with one-, two-, and three-syllable words.	• Complete Practice Pages 256–260. • Make a list of two-syllable words on a piece of paper. At this time, use only easily divided words such as those with two consonants in the middle and compound words. Have your child draw a line between the two syllables.
Math	Understand time intervals, such as seconds, minutes, hours, days, weeks, and years.	• Complete Practice Page 261. • Look at a calendar with your child and review the day and date. Look ahead on the calendar for family events, birthdays, or holidays. Discuss how much time will pass before these events occur.
	Tell time to the nearest five minutes.	• Complete Practice Page 262–264. • Have your child look at the clock and tell what time it is. Then, ask your child to tell what the time will be five minutes from now.
Bonus: Social Studies		• On a map, help your child locate the four state capitals named after presidents (Madison, WI; Jefferson City, MO; Lincoln, NE; and Jackson, MS). Then, look at your own state map. Are there any cities or towns named after presidents? Are there any streets in your city named to honor a president?

Syllables

Write **1** or **2** on the line to tell how many syllables are in each word. If the word has two syllables, draw a line between the syllables.

Example: sup|per

dog	__________	timber	__________
bedroom	__________	cat	__________
slipper	__________	street	__________
tree	__________	chalk	__________
batter	__________	blanket	__________
chair	__________	marker	__________
fish	__________	brush	__________
master	__________	rabbit	__________

Syllables

When a double consonant is used in the middle of a word, the word can usually be divided between the consonants.

Look at the words in the word box. Divide each word into two syllables. Leave space between each syllable. One is done for you.

butter	puppy	kitten	yellow
dinner	chatter	ladder	happy
pillow	letter	mitten	summer

but ter ________ ________

________ ________ ________

________ ________ ________

________ ________ ________

Many words are divided between two consonants that are not alike.

Look at the words in the word box. Divide each word into two syllables. One is done for you.

window	doctor	number	carpet
mister	winter	pencil	candle
barber	sister	picture	under

win dow ________ ________

________ ________ ________

________ ________ ________

________ ________ ________

Syllables

One way to help you read a word you don't know is to divide it into parts called **syllables**. Every syllable has a vowel sound.

Say the words. Write the number of syllables. The first one is done for you.

bird	1	rabbit	________
apple	________	elephant	________
balloon	________	family	________
basketball	________	fence	________
breakfast	________	ladder	________
block	________	open	________
candy	________	puddle	________
popcorn	________	Saturday	________
yellow	________	wind	________
understand	________	butterfly	________

Syllables

Dividing a word into syllables can help you read a new word. You also might divide syllables when you are writing if you run out of space on a line. Many words contain two consonants that are next to each other. A word can usually be divided between the consonants.

Divide each word into two syllables. The first one is done for you.

kitten kit ten

lumber ______________________

batter ______________________

winter ______________________

funny ______________________

harder ______________________

dirty ______________________

sister ______________________

little ______________________

dinner ______________________

Syllables

Words are made up of parts called **syllables**. Each syllable has a vowel sound. One way to count syllables is to clap as you say the word.

Example:		
cat	1 clap	1 syllable
table	2 claps	2 syllables
butterfly	3 claps	3 syllables

"Clap out" the words below. Write how many syllables each word has.

movie______________	dog______________
piano______________	basket______________
tree______________	swimmer______________
bicycle______________	rainbow______________
sun______________	paper______________
cabinet______________	picture______________
football______________	run______________
television______________	enter______________

It's About Time!

Trace each mouse with red if it has a time word.

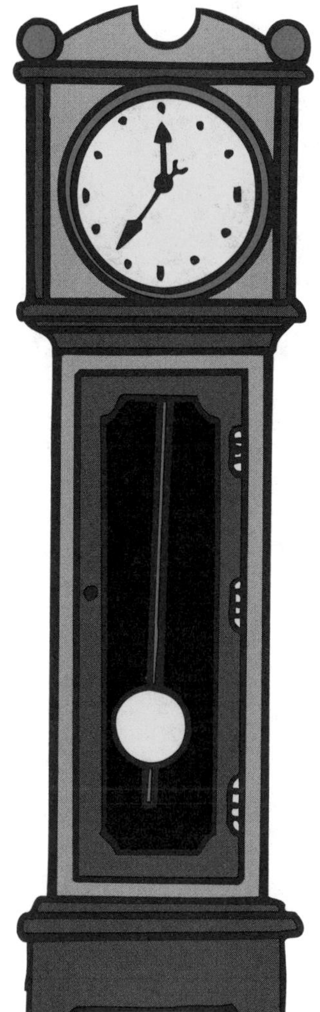

Circle the correct answer.

1. There are 60 seconds in a	minute. year.
2. There are 60 minutes in an	second. hour.
3. There are 24 hours in a	minute. day.
4. There are 365 days in a	year. week.
5. There are 7 days in a	week. hour.
6. There are 12 months in a	year. week.

Turtle Time

Write the time each clock shows.

Time: Hour, Half-Hour

An **hour** is sixty minutes. The short hand of a clock tells the hour. It is written **0:00**, such as **5:00**. A **half-hour** is thirty minutes. When the long hand of the clock is pointing to the six, the time is on the half-hour. It is written **:30**, such as **5:30**.

Study the examples. Tell what time it is on each clock.

Example:

9:00

The minute hand is on the 12. The hour hand is on the 9. It is 9 o'clock.

4:30

The minute hand is on the 6. The hour hand is *between* the 4 and 5. It is 4:30.

Time: Hour, Half-Hour

Draw lines between the clocks that show the same time.

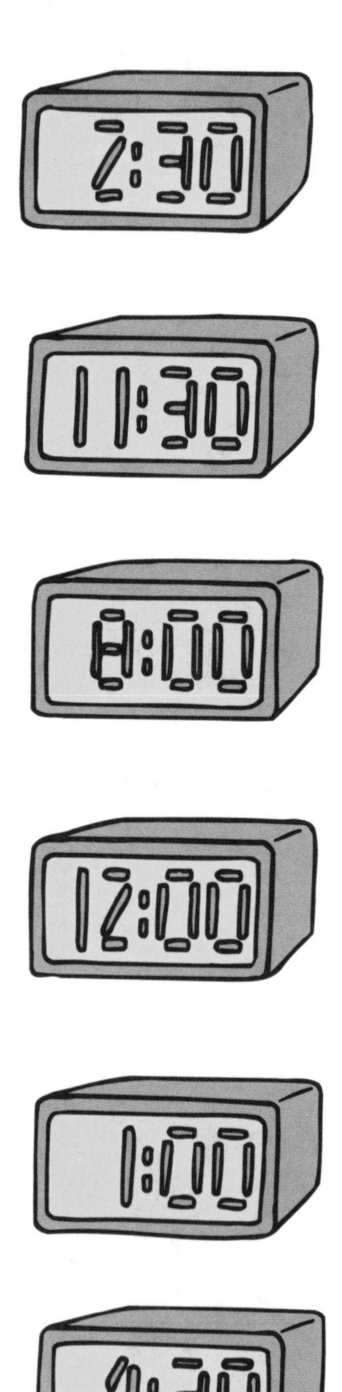

Week 25 Skills

Subject	Skill	Multi-Sensory Learning Activities
Reading and Language Arts	Understand and identify synonyms as words that have similar meanings.	• Complete Practice Pages 266–269. • Create a list of 10 words and have your child find the words in a thesaurus, then write a synonym for each word.
Math	Review time to five-minute intervals.	• Complete Practice Pages 270–272. • Help your child make a clock face using a large paper plate or pizza wheel. Put the numbers **1–12** around the clock. Then, begin at 12 and put 60 marks around the outside for minutes—every fifth being darker. Make the hands out of construction paper and attach with a paper fastener. Number by fives going around the clock. On the clock, have your child practice showing times that you call out.
	Solve time word problems.	• Complete Practice Page 273. • Create real-life word problems about time. For example, say, "You ate breakfast this morning at 7:45. It took you 20 minutes to eat. At what time did you finish eating breakfast?"
	Identify and count pennies and nickels.	• Complete Practice Page 274. • In an envelope, put an index card and some pennies and nickels. Tell your child to count the change and use the index card to design a postage stamp worth that amount of money.

Synonyms

Words that mean the same or nearly the same are called **synonyms**.

Read the sentence that tells about the picture. Draw a circle around the word that means the same as the **bold** word.

 The child is **unhappy**. sad hungry	 The flowers are **lovely**. pretty green
 The baby was very **tired**. sleepy hurt	 The **funny** clown made us laugh. silly glad
 The ladybug is so **tiny**. small red	 We saw a **scary** tiger. frightening ugly

Flower Fun

Write the words from the box that are **synonyms** for the words in the flower pots.

pick	start	easy	sky
kind	rain	afraid	fall
close	hard	scream	awake
put	whisper	dirt	tired

yell ______________

begin ______________

scared ______________

drop ______________

nice ______________

sleepy ______________

soil ______________

near ______________

place ______________

difficult ______________

Synonyms

Read each sentence. Choose a word from the box that has the same meaning as the **bold** word. Write the synonym on the line next to the sentence. The first one has been done for you.

skinniest	biggest	jacket	little	quickly	woods	joyful
grin	alike	trip	rabbit	fix	autumn	infant

1. The deer ran through the **forest**. woods
2. White mice are very **small** pets. ____________
3. Goldfish move **fast** in the water. ____________
4. The twins look exactly the **same**. ____________
5. Trees lose their leaves in the **fall**. ____________
6. The blue whale is the **largest** animal on Earth. ____________
7. We will go to the ocean on our next **vacation**. ____________
8. The **bunny** hopped through the tall grass. ____________
9. The **baby** was crying because it was hungry. ____________
10. Put on your **coat** before you go outside. ____________
11. Does that clown have a big **smile** on his face? ____________
12. That is the **thinnest** man I have ever seen. ____________
13. I will **repair** my bicycle as soon as I get home. ____________
14. The children made **happy** sounds when they won. ____________

Synonyms

Match the pairs of synonyms.

delight •	• discover
speak •	• tidy
lovely •	• start
find •	• talk
nearly •	• beautiful
neat •	• almost
big •	• joy
sad •	• unhappy
begin •	• large

Read each sentence. Write the synonym pairs from each sentence in the boxes.

1. That unusual clock is a rare antique.

2. I am glad you are so happy!

3. Becky felt unhappy when she heard the sad news.

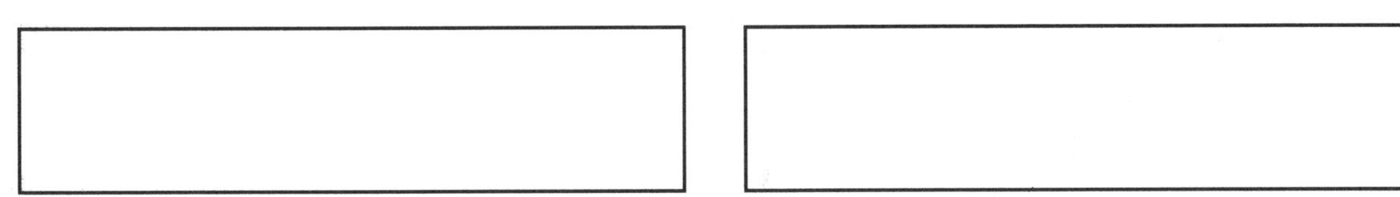

Time: Counting by 5s

Fill in the numbers on the clock face. Count by fives around the clock.

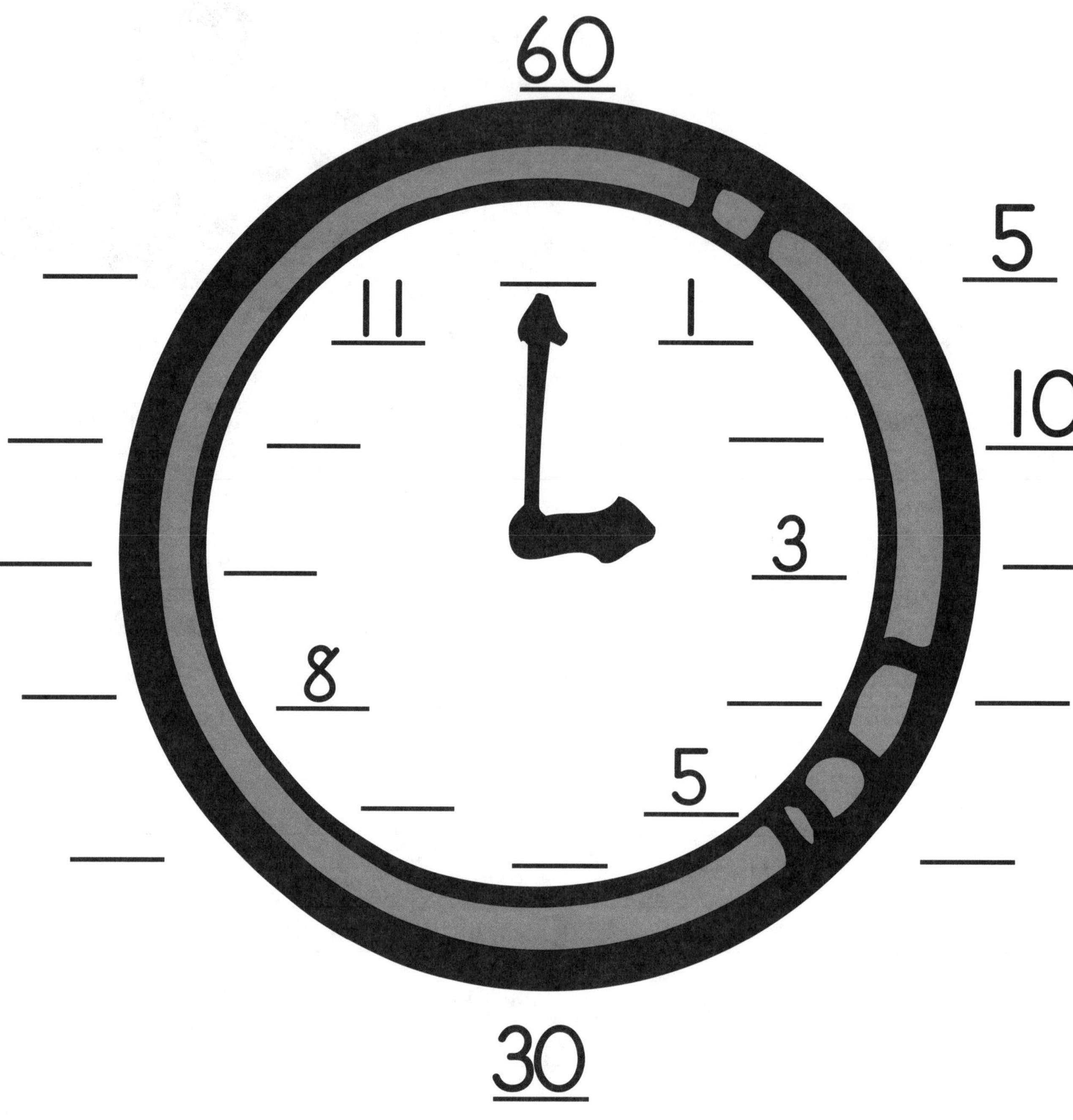

There are 60 minutes in one hour.

Time: Quarter-Hours

Time can also be shown as fractions. 30 minutes = $\frac{1}{2}$ hour.

Shade the fraction of each clock and tell how many minutes you have shaded.

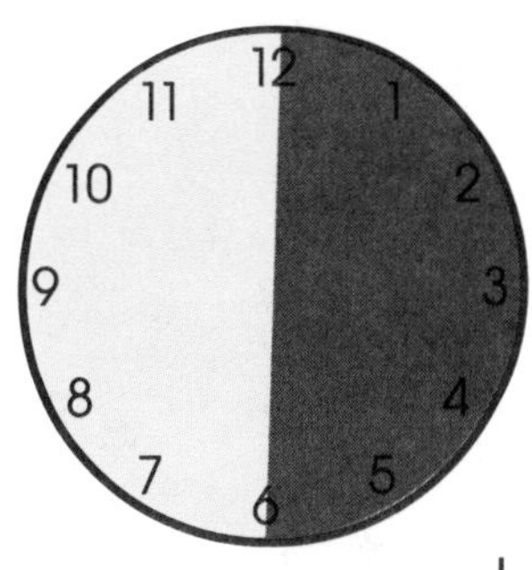

$\frac{1}{2}$ hour

30 minutes

$\frac{1}{4}$ hour

______ minutes

$\frac{2}{4}$ hour

______ minutes

$\frac{3}{4}$ hour

______ minutes

$\frac{1}{2}$ hour

______ minutes

Time: Counting by 5s

The **minute hand** of a clock takes five minutes to move from one number to the next. Start at the 12 and count by fives to tell how many minutes it is past the hour.

Study the examples. Tell what time is on each clock.

Examples:

9:10

8:25

______

______

______

______

______

______

______

______

______

Problem-Solving: Time

Solve each problem.

Tracy wakes up at 7:00. She has 30 minutes before her bus comes. What time does her bus come?

____ : ______

Vera walks her dog for 15 minutes after supper. She finishes supper at 6:30. When does she get home from walking her dog?

____ : ______

Chip practices the piano for 30 minutes when he gets home from school. He gets home at 3:30. When does he stop practicing?

____ : ______

Tanya starts mowing the grass at 4:30. She finishes at 5:00. For how many minutes does she mow the lawn?

_____ minutes

Don does his homework for 45 minutes. He starts his work at 7:15. When does he stop working?

____ : ______

Money: Penny, Nickel

Penny 1¢ Nickel 5¢

Count the coins and write the amount

Example:

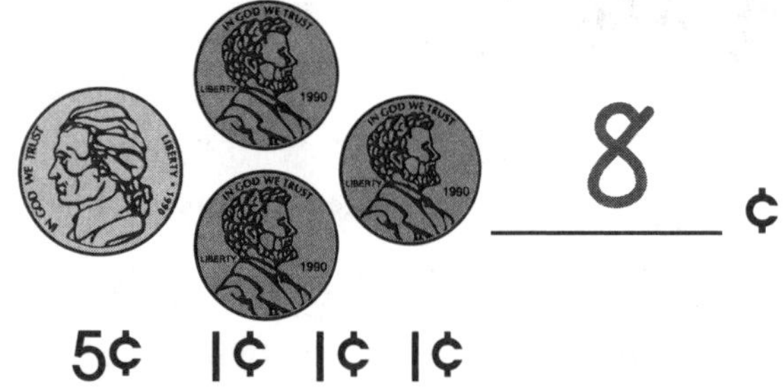

8 ¢

5¢ 1¢ 1¢ 1¢

_______ ¢

_______ ¢

_______ ¢

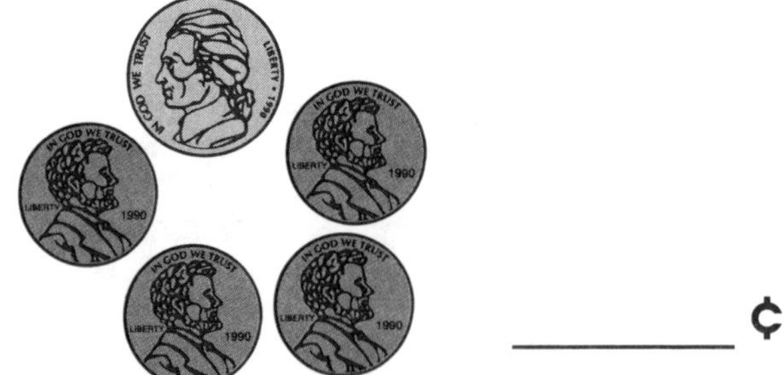

_______ ¢

Week 26 Skills

Subject	Skill	Multi-Sensory Learning Activities
Reading and Language Arts	Understand and identify antonyms as words that have opposite meanings.	• Complete Practice Pages 276–280. • Have your child brainstorm and write a list of antonyms. Then, write each word on a different index card. Shuffle the cards and give each player five cards. Place the remaining cards facedown. Turn over the top card. The player with the matching antonym card takes the card and places the pair in front of him- or herself. The next card is turned up and the game continues. If no player has a match, the next card is turned over. The player that matches all of his or her antonym pairs first wins the game.
Math	Identify and count pennies, nickels, dimes, and quarters.	• Complete Practice Pages 281–283. • Challenge your child to think of all the coin combinations that total 25¢. • Give your child a pile of pennies, nickels, dimes, and quarters. Have him or her count change orally. Encourage your child to count the larger coins first.
	Write money amounts as a decimal.	• Complete Practice Page 284. • Write $.07 on a piece of paper and have your child read the amount. Then, display a group of coins totaling less than $1. Have your child write the value correctly as a decimal.

Who's Afraid?

Help Frog and Toad escape from the snake. Read the two words in each space. If the words are antonyms, color the space green. Do no[t] color the other spaces.

Toad's House

Antonyms

An **antonym** is a word that means the opposite of another word.

Examples:

child  adult

hot  cold

Match the words that have opposite meanings. Draw a line between each pair of antonyms.

thaw	**same**
huge	**sad**
crying	**friend**
happy	**open**
enemy	**freeze**
asleep	**thin**
closed	**hide**
fat	**tiny**
seek	**awake**
different	**laughing**

Antonyms

Complete each sentence with an antonym pair from page 277. Som
pairs will not be used.

Example: Usually we wear <u>different</u> clothes, but today we are dressed the <u>same</u>.

1. A ________________ is allowed in the museum if he or she is with an ________________.

2. Mom was ________________ it rained since her garden was very dry, but I was ________________ because I had to stay inside.

3. The ________________ crowd of people tried to fit into the ________________ room.

4. The ________________ baby was soon ________________ and playing in the crib.

5. We'll ________________ the meat for now, and Dad will ________________ it when we need it.

6. The windows were wide ________________, but the door was ________________.

Now, write your own sentence using one of the antonym pairs.

____

____

____

Antonyms

Antonyms are words that are opposites.

Example:

 **hairy**

 **bald**

Choose a word from the box to complete each sentence below.

open	right	light	full	late	below
hard	clean	slow	quiet	old	nice

Example:

My car was **dirty**, but now it's **clean**.

1. Sometimes my cat is naughty, and sometimes she's ____________.
2. The sign said, "Closed," but the door was ____________.
3. Is the glass half empty or half ____________?
4. I bought new shoes, but I like my ____________ ones better.
5. Skating is easy for me, but ____________ for my brother.
6. The sky is dark at night and ____________ during the day.
7. I like a noisy house, but my mother likes a ____________ one.
8. My friend says I'm wrong, but I say I'm ____________.
9. Jason is a fast runner, but Adam is a ____________ runner.
10. We were supposed to be early, but we were ____________.

Antonyms

Write the antonym pairs from each sentence in the boxes.

Example: Many things are bought and sold at the market.

bought	sold

1. I thought I lost my dog, but someone found him.

2. The teacher will ask questions for the students to answer.

3. Airplanes arrive and depart from the airport.

4. The water in the pool was cold compared to the warm water in the whirlpool.

5. The tortoise was slow, but the hare was fast.

Money: Penny, Nickel, Dime

Penny **1¢** Nickel **5¢** Dime **10¢**

Count the coins and write the amount.

16 ¢

_____ ¢

_____ ¢

_____ ¢

_____ ¢

Money: Penny, Nickel, Dime

Draw a line to match the amounts of money.

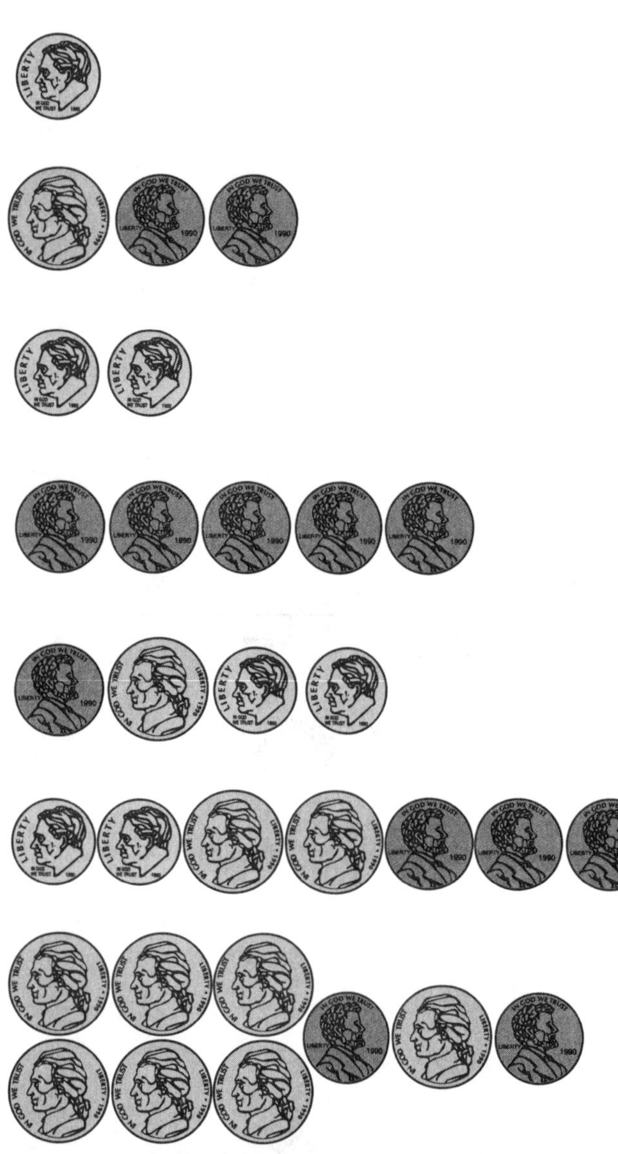

Money: Quarter

A **quarter** is worth 25¢.

Count the coins and write the amounts.

 ______ ¢

   ______ ¢

  ______ ¢

   ______ ¢

   ______ ¢

   ______ ¢

   ______ ¢

  ______ ¢

Money: Decimals

A **decimal** is a number with one or more places to the right of a decimal point, such as **6.5** or **2.25**. Money amounts are written with two places to the right of the decimal point.

25¢ 10¢ 5¢ 1¢
$.25 $.10 $.05 $.01

Count the coins and circle the amount shown.

Example:

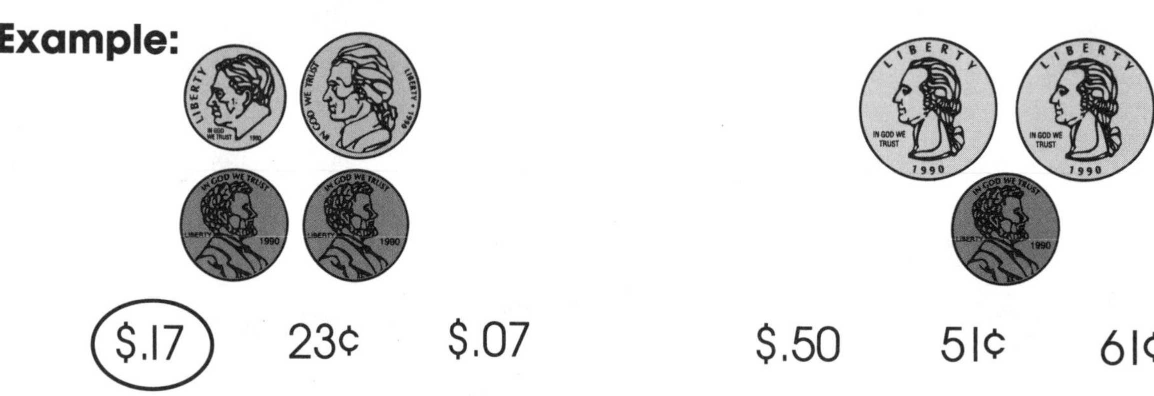

($.17) 23¢ $.07

$.50 51¢ 61¢

$.28 36¢ 42¢

37¢ 43¢ $.47

Week 27 Skills

Subject	Skill	Multi-Sensory Learning Activities
Reading and Language Arts	Understand capitalization of proper nouns.	• Complete Practice Pages 286–289. • Brainstorm with your child categories of words that are capitalized regularly. Include the first word in a sentence, names, titles, holidays, days of the week, months, and streets. Under each category established above, write several specific examples of capitalized words.
	Identify articles **a**, **an**, and **the**.	• Complete Practice Page 290. • Write a list of nouns for your child, such as **ant**, **balloon**, **cat**, **egg**, and **house**. Ask your child to write the appropriate article before each one and use each word in a sentence.
Math	Identify and count dollar bills.	• Complete Practice Page 291. • Show your child how the dollar bill is equivalent to 100 cents. Have your child count out 100 pennies. Then, have your child make 100 cents using different combinations of coins.
	Add money.	• Complete Practice Pages 292–294. • Prepare a play store with real objects or magazine pictures. Put a price tag on each object. Provide your child with real money to "buy" single objects. Then, have your child choose two or three products, add the cost, and "purchase" the objects.

Capitalization

Proper nouns are the names of specific people, places and pets. Proper nouns begin with a capital letter.

Write the proper nouns on the lines below. Use capital letters at the beginning of each word.

logan, utah

mike smith

___

lynn cramer

buster

___

fluffy

chicago, illinois

___

Capitalization

Write capital letters where they should appear in the sentences below.

Example: joe can play in january.
Joe can play in January.

1. we celebrate thanksgiving on the fourth thursday in november.

2. in june, michelle and mark will go camping every friday.

3. on mondays in october, i will take piano lessons.

Punctuation Magic

Write the sentences correctly. Be sure to use capital letters, periods and question marks.

1. mrs paris talked to richard, alex, matthew and emily about the trip to new york city

2. the children read a story about a king who was greedy

3. everyone but richard drew a picture about the story

4. why was drake sick

5. mrs gates asked matthew to take homework to drake

6. did richard's wish come true

A Sensational Scent

Circle the letters that should be capital letters. Then, write them in the matching numbered blanks below to answer the question.

1. eddie, Homer's friend, lives on elm Street.
2. Homer's aunt lives in kansas City, kansas.
3. are you sure Aunt aggie is coming?
4. old Rip Van Winkle came to town.
5. The doughnuts were made by homer Price.
6. Miss terwillinger and Uncle telly saved yarn.
7. *Homer Price* was written by robert McCloskey.
8. Uncle ulysses owned a lunch room.
9. The super-Duper was a comic book hero.
10. Doc pelly lived in Homer's town.
11. money was stolen by the robbers.
12. now you have the answer to the question.

Who is hiding in the suitcase?

__ __ __ __ __   __ __ __   __ __ __   __ __ __ __ __

3 7 4 11 3   6 5 1   10 1 6   9 2 8 12 2

Articles

A, **an** and **the** are special adjectives called **articles**. Use **a** before singular nouns that start with a consonant sound. Use **an** before singular nouns that begin with a vowel sound or a silent **h**. Use **the** before singular or plural nouns.

Examples: a city, **an** apartment, **an** hour, **the** cab, **the** building

Write **a** or **an** in the blank.

1. My apartment is in __________ skyscraper.
2. I ride __________ elevator to the fifty-seventh floor.
3. I don't have __________ yard to play in, so I go to the park.
4. We played there for __________ hour.
5. The park has a big lake and __________ zoo.
6. I can see __________ elephant every day if I want.
7. The zoo also has __________ ostrich.
8. There is __________ aquarium at the park, too.

Underline the articles in the sentences.

9. The monkey chattered at the crowd.
10. The little boy waved to the monkey.

Money: Dollar

One dollar equals 100 cents. It is written $1.00.

Count the money and write the amounts.

$__.___

$__.___

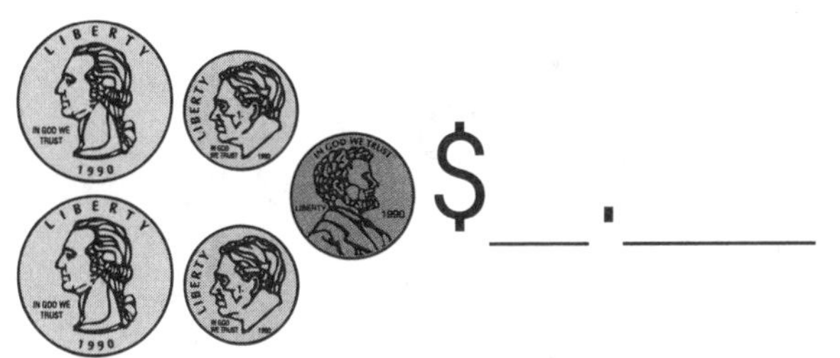

$__.___

$__.___

$__.___

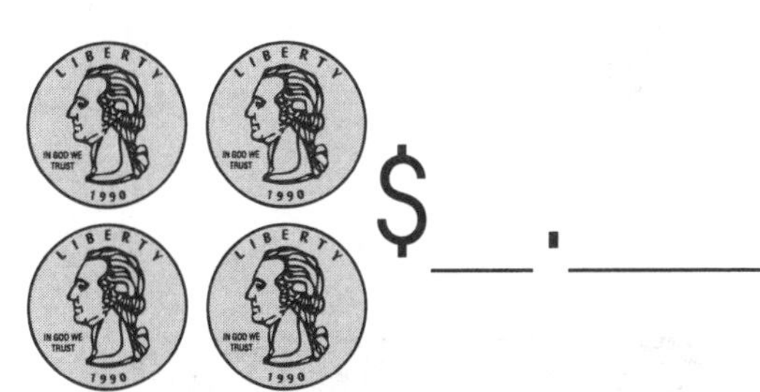

$__.___

$__.___

$__.___

Adding Money

Write the amount of money using decimals. Then, add to find the total amount.

Example: 

$ 1 . 00
 . 05
\+ . 02

$ 1 . 07

$ __ . ____
$ __ . ____
$ __ . ____
+$ __ . ____

__ . ____

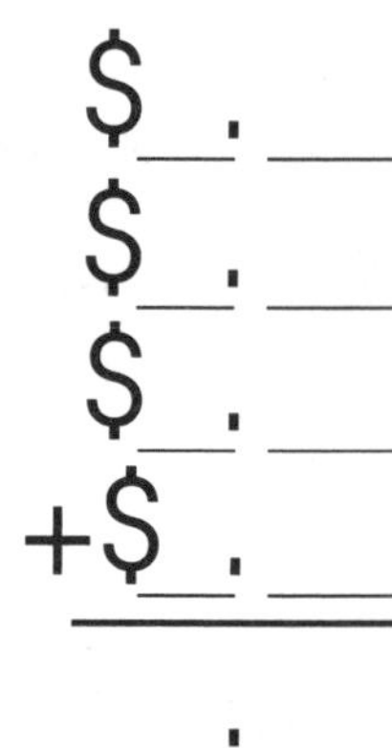

$ __ . ____
$ __ . ____
$ __ . ____
+$ __ . ____

__ . ____

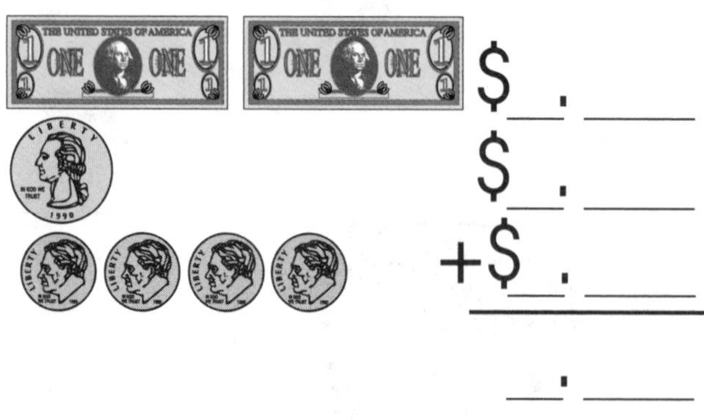

$ __ . ____
$ __ . ____
+$ __ . ____

__ . ____

$ __ . ____
$ __ . ____
$ __ . ____
+$ __ . ____

__ . ____

Money: Practice

Draw a line from each food item to the correct amount of money.

Review

Add the money and write the total.

______ ¢

______ ¢

$ ___.______

______ ¢

$ ___.______

Third Quarter Check-Up

Reading and Language Arts

- ❑ I understand adverbs, or words that describe verbs.
- ❑ I understand and can identify compound words.
- ❑ I understand contractions, or a shortened form of two words.
- ❑ I can identify prefixes, or word parts added to the beginning of words to change the meaning.
- ❑ I can identify suffixes, or word parts added to the ending of words to change the meaning.
- ❑ I can work with one-, two-, and three-syllable words.
- ❑ I understand and can identify synonyms as words that have similar meanings.
- ❑ I understand and can identify antonyms as words that have opposite meanings.
- ❑ I understand capitalization of proper nouns.
- ❑ I can identify articles **a**, **an**, and **the**.

Math

- ❑ I can work with ordinal numbers **first** through **sixteenth**.
- ❑ I understand place value up to six digits.
- ❑ I understand greater than and less than.
- ❑ I can work with two- and three-dimensional shapes.
- ❑ I understand time intervals, such as seconds, minutes, hours, days, weeks, and years.
- ❑ I can tell time to the nearest five minutes.
- ❑ I can solve time word problems.
- ❑ I can identify and count pennies, nickels, dimes, quarters, and dollar bills.
- ❑ I can write money amounts as a decimal.
- ❑ I can add money.

Final Project

Find a comic strip in your local newspaper and cut the strip into individual squares. Then, put the comic back in order and say which box is first, second, and third. Finally, look at the words in the dialogue. Can you name any synonyms or antonyms for these words? Rewrite the comic strip using your synonyms and antonyms.

Fourth Quarter Introduction

As the school year nears its end, many students are feeling confident about the new skills they have learned as second graders. This may be evident in their increasing ability to write sentences fluently and their mastery of addition and subtraction. As the days get warmer and children play outside in the evenings, don't forget to maintain school day routines and to continue supporting your child's academic growth at home.

Fourth Quarter Skills

Practice pages in this book for Weeks 28–36 will help your child improve the following skills.

Reading and Language Arts

- Add an apostrophe to show ownership in possessive nouns
- Identify statements, questions, commands, and exclamations
- Combine two sentences into one
- Choose words to complete sentences
- Understand different characters' points of view
- Understand and identify the subject and predicate of a sentence
- Understand compound subjects and compound predicates
- Practice dictionary skills
- Sequence and follow directions
- Answer questions about texts to demonstrate reading comprehension

Math

- Work with wholes, halves, thirds, and fourths
- Solve word problems involving fractions
- Measure in inches and centimeters
- Understand liquid measurements
- Create graphs and use them to determine information

Multi-Sensory Learning Activities

Try these fun activities for enhancing your child's learning and development during the fourth quarter of the school year. Be sure to choose activities that include speaking, listening, touching, and active movement.

Reading and Language Arts

Write a list of instructions in command form. Read the instructions with your child and discuss what makes these sentences commands rather than statements. Then, have your child write a list of instructions in command form. The instructions can be for cleaning a room, playing a game, following a recipe, or another procedure.

Have your child identify questions and statements read aloud. On one index card, draw a large question mark. On another, draw a large period. Read statements and questions aloud and have your child hold up the appropriate end punctuation for each sentence.

Read *The Day Jimmy's Boa Ate the Wash* by Trinka Hakes Noble. Note that the whole story is told as a conversation between two people. Discuss ideas for a story your child can tell in the same manner. Have him or her write an adventure story from the point of view of one character. Have him or her write it so that character tells the story to someone who was not there and has many questions.

Math

Make a worksheet listing objects in your child's bedroom. Have your child measure each object and record its length in inches and centimeters.

Provide several containers and a "liquid" substance for your child to explore. Rice, sand, water, and flour can each be poured easily from one container to another. Label a teaspoon, tablespoon, cup, pint, quart, and gallon container. Allow your child to pour the substance back and forth among the containers repeatedly. After quite a bit of exploration, ask your child to find out how many of each smaller container fill each larger container.

Go on a shape search. Look for geometric shapes within pictures, in man-made objects, and in nature. Have your child draw a picture of something from your shape search and color the shapes in the picture.

Make a tactile graph from actual objects organized in equally spaced columns. Choose a collection of small objects, such as marbles or buttons. Have your child sort the collection into groups and name each group. Then, write the group names at the bottom of a grid drawn on a large sheet of paper (with individual boxes large enough to hold a piece of the collection). Above each name, have your child line up the group, one object per box. Discuss the graph and answer questions about the information it shows.

Fourth Quarter Introduction, cont.

Science

Put drops of water and other liquids, such as syrup or juice, on wax paper. Bump the wax paper lightly so each liquid moves slightly. Have your child observe and compare how each drop reacts.

Gather many common objects for this exploration. Provide a dishpan with water. Your child will test the objects for buoyancy. He or she should sort the objects into two piles: things that might float and things that might sink. Have your child try each object one by one. Were his or her predictions correct?

Social Studies

Read *Where Do I Live?* by Neil Chesanow and talk about where you live. As you read the book, keep a written account of the geographic words and their meanings that are highlighted in the book, such as **room**, **home**, **land**, **street**, **neighborhood**, **continent**, **world**, **galaxy**, and **universe**.

Read *This Is Our Earth* by Laura Lee Benson. Discuss and list Earth's physical features described in the book. Learn the "This Is Our Earth" song at the end of the book.

Seasonal Fun

Conduct an experiment to show where wind comes from. Have your child draw a spiral shape on a piece of paper and cut it out. Help him or her poke a hole in the center of the spiral with a thumbtack. Then, push one end of thread into the hole, tie it, and attach the other end to the center of a clothes hanger. Ask your child to hold the hanging spiral several inches above a heat source and watch what happens. Did the spiral move? Explain that the warm air moves upward, pushing the bottom of the spiral and making it spin, which is the same motion that causes wind. Warm air rises and air pressure under it reduces and cools air nearby to take its place.

Week 28 Skills

Subject	Skill	Multi-Sensory Learning Activities
Reading and Language Arts	Add an apostrophe to show ownership in possessive nouns.	• Complete Practice Pages 300–304. • On a piece of paper, write, "the branch belonging to the tree." Ask your child to write a shorter version using a possessive. Then, repeat with other phrases that show ownership. After he or she has written the possessive, have him or her use it in a sentence.
Math	Review money addition.	• Complete Practice Pages 305–308. • Take turns rolling a die. Each dot on the die equals one cent. After each turn, draw the number of cents that you roll. Then, circle the coins that you can trade for a larger coin. For example, after two rolls, you may have eight cents, so you can circle five pennies to trade for a nickel. The first player who reaches a dollar and can trade in his or her coins for a dollar bill is the winner.
Bonus: Social Studies		• Read *Count Your Way Through Mexico* by Jim Haskins and *Colors of Mexico* by Lynn Ainsworth Olawsky. Begin writing a list of Spanish words and their English meanings.

Ownership

We add **'s** to nouns (people, places or things) to tell who or what owns something.

Read the sentences. Fill in the blanks to show ownership.

Example: The doll belongs to **Sara**.
It is **Sara's** doll.

1. Sparky has a red collar.

__________________________ collar is red.

2. Jimmy has a blue coat.

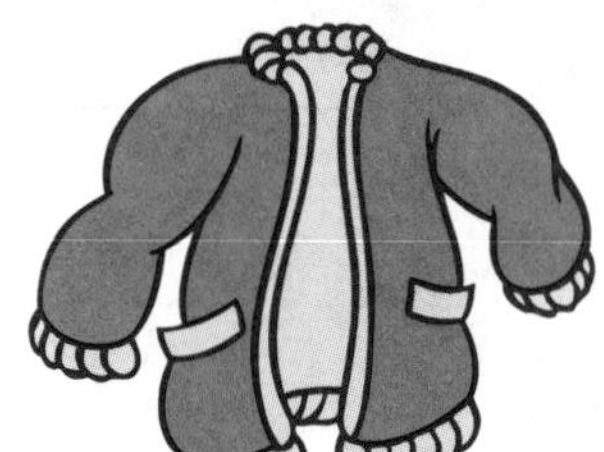

__________________________ coat is blue.

3. The tail of the cat is short.

The ______________________ tail is short.

4. The name of my mother is Karen.

My ________________________ name is Karen.

Ownership

Read the sentences. Circle the correct word and write it in the sentences below.

1. The _______________ lunchbox is broken. boys boy's
2. The _______________ played in the cage. gerbil's gerbils
3. _______________ hair is brown. Anns Ann's
4. The _______________ ran in the field. horse's horses
5. My _______________ coat is torn. sister's sisters
6. The _______________ fur is brown. cats cat's
7. Three _______________ flew past our window. birds bird's
8. The _______________ paws are muddy. dogs dog's
9. The _______________ neck is long. giraffes giraffe's
10. The _______________ are big and powerful. lion's lions

Add an Apostrophe

Add **'s** to a noun to show who or what **owns** something.

Circle the correct word under each picture.

The ___________ nose is big.

clown clowns clown's

This is ___________ coat.

Bettys Betty's Betty

I know ___________ brother.

Burt's Burt Burts

The ___________ hat is pretty.

girl girl girl's

That is the ___________ ball.

kitten's kitten kittens

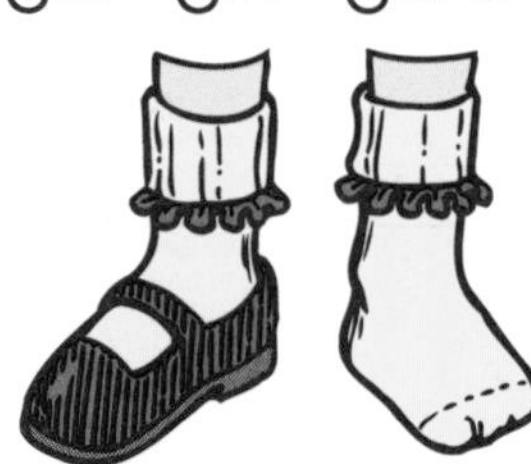

My ___________ shoe is missing.

sisters sister sister's

The ___________ coach is Mr. Hall.

team team's team

The ___________ cover is torn.

book's books book

Possessive Nouns

Possessive nouns tell who or what is the owner of something. With singular nouns, we use an apostrophe **before** the **s**. With plural nouns, we use an apostrophe **after** the **s**.

Example:

Singular: one elephant
The **elephant's** dance was wonderful.
Plural: more than one elephant
The **elephants'** dance was wonderful.

Put the apostrophe in the correct place in each bold word. Then, write the word in the blank.

1. The **lions** cage was big. ______________________
2. The **bears** costumes were purple. ______________________
3. One **boys** laughter was very loud. ______________________
4. The **trainers** dogs were dancing about. ______________________
5. The **mans** popcorn was tasty and good. ______________________
6. **Marks** cotton candy was delicious. ______________________
7. A little **girls** balloon burst in the air. ______________________
8. The big **clowns** tricks were very funny. ______________________
9. **Lauras** sister clapped for the clowns. ______________________
10. The **womans** money was lost in the crowd. ______________________
11. **Kellys** mother picked her up early. ______________________

Possessive Nouns

Circle the correct possessive noun in each sentence and write it in the blank.

Example: One ___girl's___ mother is a teacher.
girl's girls'

1. The ________________ tail is long.
cat's cats'

2. One ________________ baseball bat is aluminum.
boy's boys'

3. The ________________ aprons are white.
waitresses' waitress's

4. My ____________________________ apple pie is the best!
grandmother's grandmothers'

5. My five ________________ uniforms are dirty.
brother's brothers'

6. The ________________ doll is pretty.
child's childs'

7. These ________________ collars are different colors.
dog's dogs'

8. The ________________ tail is short.
cow's cows'

Earnings Add Up!

Wash dishes **$1.50**

Feed cat **$.95**

Mow lawn **$3.50**

Mop floors **$1.25**

Pick tomatoes **$2.75**

Wash windows **$2.85**

Use the pictures above to help you find out how much you can earn by doing each set of jobs. Write the total amount for each set.

1. pick tomatoes ____________
2. wash windows ____________
3. mow the lawn ____________

1. wash windows ____________
2. mop floors ____________
3. mow the lawn ____________

1. feed the cat ____________
2. pick tomatoes ____________
3. wash dishes ____________

1. pick tomatoes ____________
2. wash windows ____________
3. feed the cat ____________

So Many Choices!

You want to buy 3 different items in the hobby store. You have $16.00. Write all the different combinations of items you can buy using the entire $16.00.

1. ______	1. ______	1. ______	1. ______
2. ______	2. ______	2. ______	2. ______
3. ______	3. ______	3. ______	3. ______

1. ______	1. ______	1. ______	1. ______
2. ______	2. ______	2. ______	2. ______
3. ______	3. ______	3. ______	3. ______

Here's Your Order

Count the money on each tray. Write the name of the food that costs that amount.

hamburger.. **$2.45**	hot dog......... **$1.77**	sandwich.... **$1.55**
milk ....**$.64**	soda pop...... **$1.26**	milkshake.... **$1.89**
cake............ **$2.85**	pie................. **$2.25**	sundae.......... **$.95**

____

____

____

____

____

____

Problem-Solving: Money

Read each problem. Use the pictures to help you solve the problems.

Ben bought a ball. He had 11¢ left.
How much money did he have at the start? _______ ¢

Tara has 75¢. She buys a car.
How much money does she have left? _______ ¢

Leah wants to buy a doll and a ball. She has 80¢.
How much more money does she need? _______ ¢

Jacob has 95¢. He buys the car and the ball.
How much more money does he need to buy a doll for his sister? _______ ¢

Kim paid three quarters, one dime and three pennies for a hat. How much did it cost? _______ ¢

Week 29 Skills

Subject	Skill	Multi-Sensory Learning Activities
Reading and Language Arts	Identify statements, questions, commands, and exclamations.	• Complete Practice Pages 310 and 311. • Choose two photos from a photo album. Then, ask your child to write a statement, a question, a command, and an exclamation about each photo.
	Combine two sentences into one.	• Complete Practice Page 312. • Write "It snowed all day yesterday. It snowed all day today." Ask your child to make one sentence from the two without changing the meaning. Provide examples for combining other sentences.
	Choose words to complete sentences.	• Complete Practice Pages 313 and 314. • Write five incomplete sentences. Ask your child to fill in any missing words to complete the sentences.
Math	Work with halves, thirds, and fourths.	• Complete Practice Pages 315–317. • Divide a banana into thirds, an apple into fourths, and a cookie or cracker into halves. Then, cut something into three uneven parts and discuss why the parts cannot be called **thirds**.
	Solve word problems involving fractions.	• Complete Practice Page 318. • With your child, read and discuss the use of fractions in *The Doorbell Rang* by Pat Hutchins. Then, bake a dozen cookies together and divide them into as many equal groups as you can.

Four Kinds of Sentences

A **statement** tells something. A **question** asks something. An **exclamation** shows surprise or strong feeling. A **command** tells someone to do something.

Example: The shuttle is ready for takeoff. (statement)
Are all systems go? (question)
What a sight! (exclamation)
Take a picture of this. (command)

Use the code to color the spaces.

Code
statement—**yellow**
question—**red**
exclamation—**blue**
command—**gray**

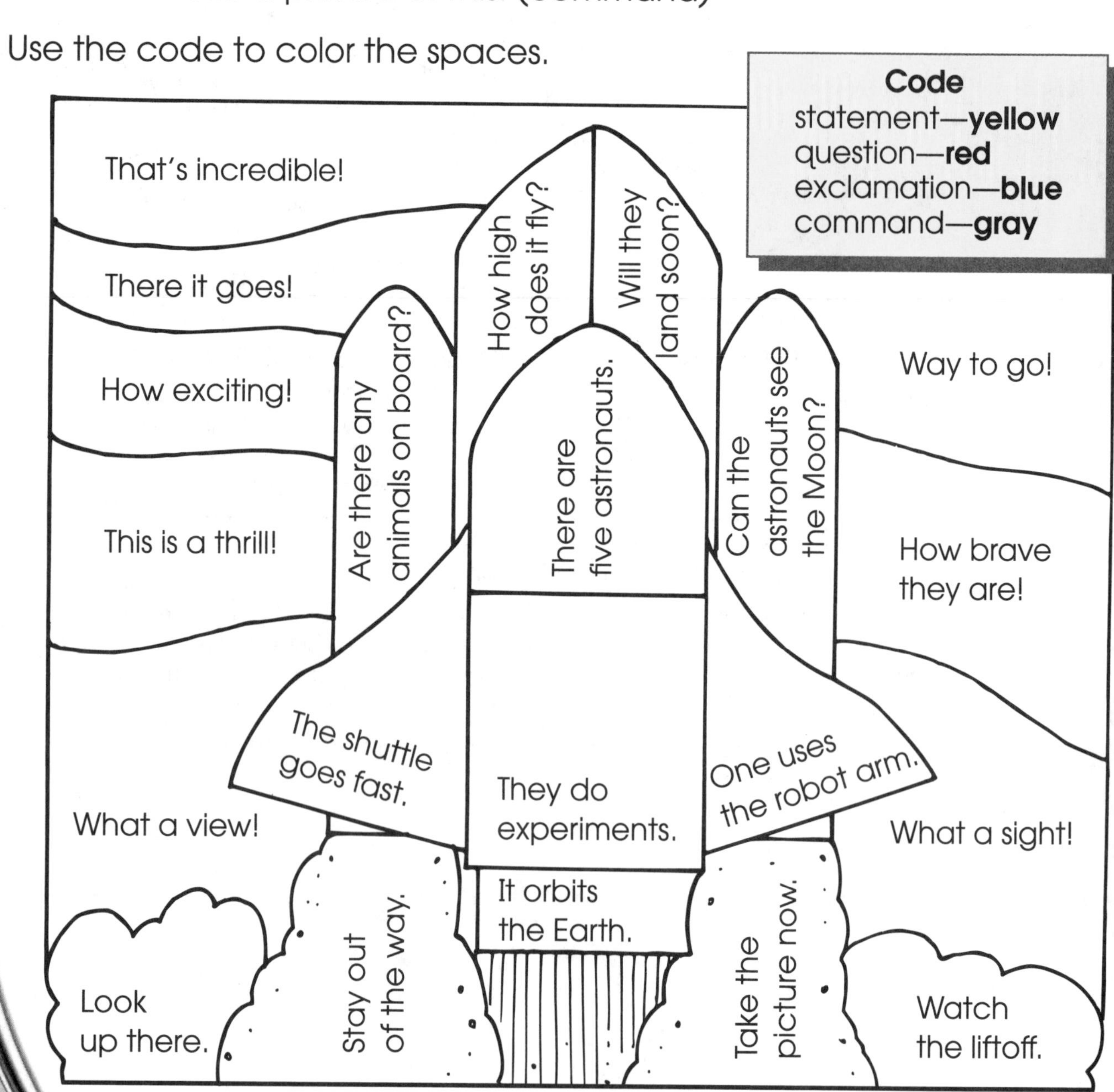
That's incredible!
There it goes!
How exciting!
This is a thrill!
Are there any animals on board?
How high does it fly?
Will they land soon?
There are five astronauts.
Can the astronauts see the Moon?
Way to go!
How brave they are!
The shuttle goes fast.
They do experiments.
One uses the robot arm.
What a view!
What a sight!
It orbits the Earth.
Stay out of the way.
Take the picture now.
Look up there.
Watch the liftoff.

Sentences

Underline the sentence that is written correctly in each group.

1. Do Penguins live in antarctica?
   do penguins live in Antartica.
   Do penguins live in Antarctica?

2. penguins cannot fly?
   Penguins cannot fly.
   penguins cannot fly.

Write **S** for **statement**, **Q** for **question**, **E** for **exclamation** or **C** for **command** on the line.

________ 1. Two different kinds of penguins live in Antarctica.

________ 2. Do emperor penguins have black and white bodies?

________ 3. Look at their webbed feet.

________ 4. They're amazing!

Underline the **subject** of the sentence with one line. Underline the **predicate** with two lines.

1. Penguins eat fish, squid and shrimp.

2. Leopard seals and killer whales hunt penguins.

3. A female penguin lays one egg.

Sentence Combining

Two sentences can become one sentence. Write two sentences as one sentence.

The bird lives in a nest.

The bird lives in the tree.

The music teacher is wearing a blue dress.

The music teacher is wearing white pearls.

I will meet you at the park.

I will meet you by the balloon stand.

My first name is Brian.

My last name is Williams.

Playing in the Summer Sun

Circle the missing word. Then, write it on the line.

It is ____________________.

rain   raining

He can ____________________ the boat.

row   rowing

The kite is ____________________.

fly   flying

He is ____________________.

swing   swinging

He is ____________________.

pick   picking

Completing Sentences

Read each sentence. Write a word or words to tell **who** or **when** on each line.

1. Mary's little ____________ is starting her first day at school ________________.

2. Aunt __________ is moving to Florida ____________.

3. It was almost ____________ when ____________ arrived at the party.

4. Mr. ___________ wants to meet with the soccer team next ______________.

5. We have an appointment at ___________ to have our teeth checked by Dr. ____________.

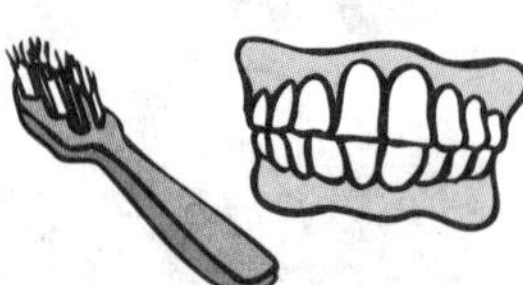

6. _____________ and _______________ are going to the movies _________ instead of ___________.

Fractions: Half, Third, Fourth

. **fraction** is a number that names part of a whole, such as $\frac{1}{2}$ or $\frac{1}{3}$.

tudy the examples. Color the correct fraction of each shape.

xamples:

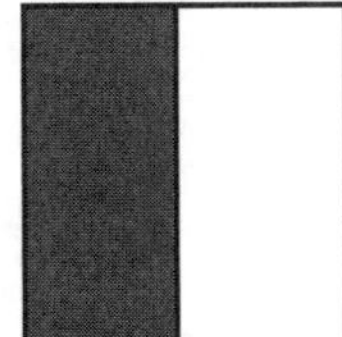

shaded part 1
equal parts 2
$\frac{1}{2}$ (one-half) shaded

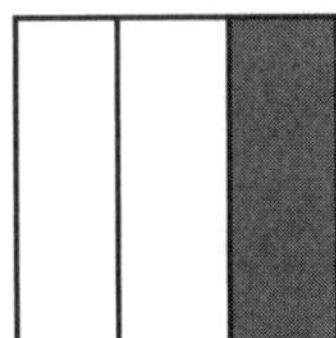

shaded part 1
equal parts 3
$\frac{1}{3}$ (one-third) shaded

shaded part 1
equal parts 4
$\frac{1}{4}$ (one-fourth) shaded

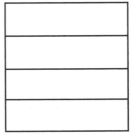

Color: $\frac{1}{3}$ red	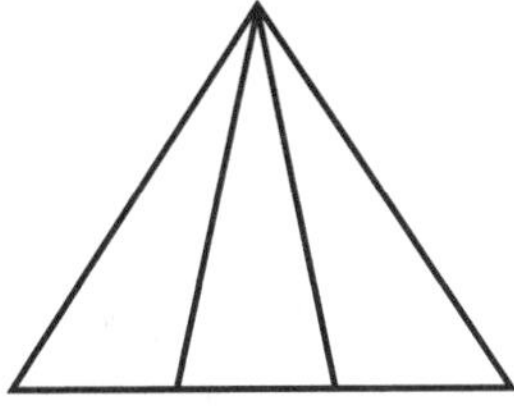 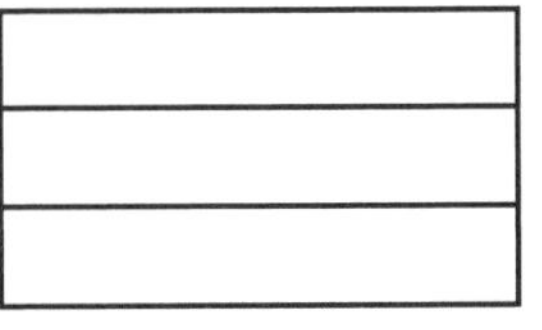 
Color: $\frac{1}{4}$ blue	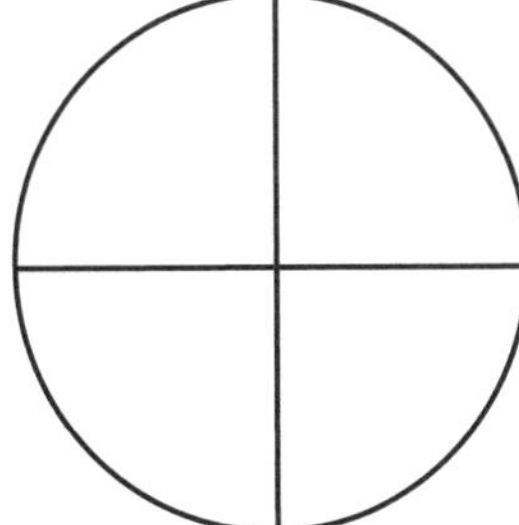 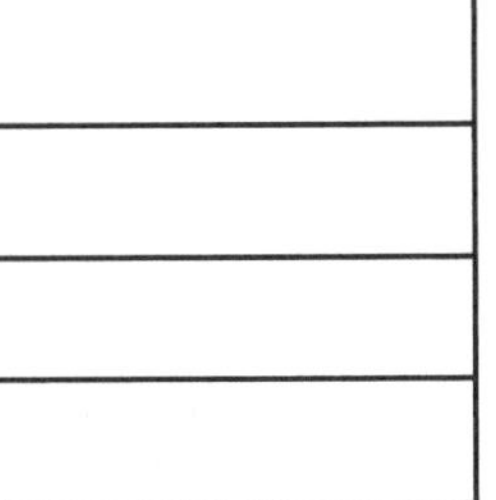 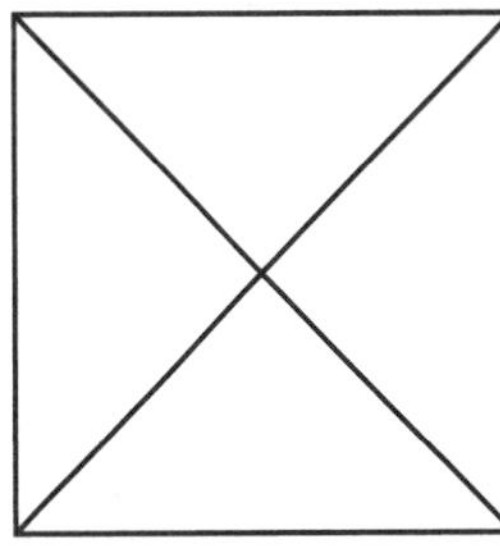
Color: $\frac{1}{2}$ orange	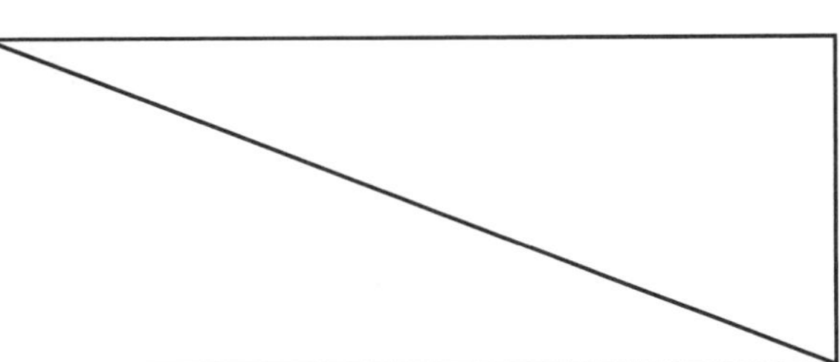 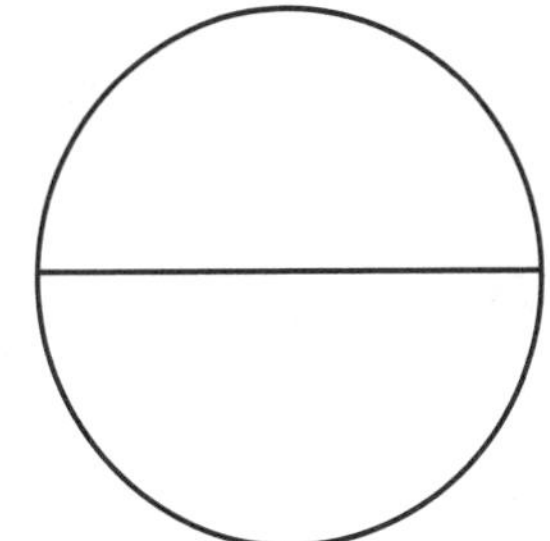

Fractions: Half, Third, Fourth

Study the examples. Circle the fraction that shows the shaded part. Then, circle the fraction that shows the white part.

Examples:

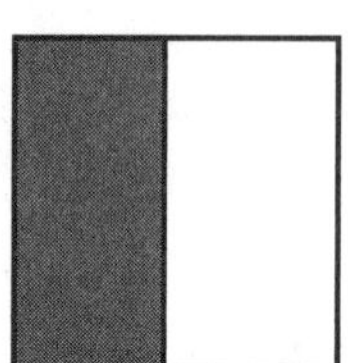

shaded $\frac{1}{4}$ $\frac{1}{3}$ $\frac{1}{2}$ **white** $\frac{1}{2}$ $\frac{1}{3}$ $\frac{1}{4}$

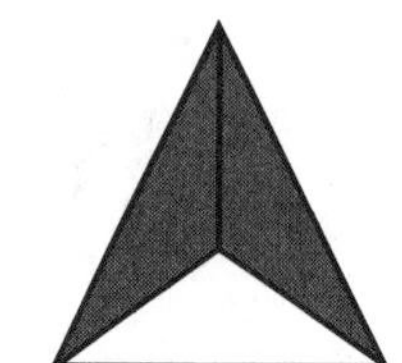

shaded $\frac{1}{2}$ $\frac{2}{3}$ $\frac{3}{4}$ **white** $\frac{2}{3}$ $\frac{1}{2}$ $\frac{1}{3}$

shaded $\frac{1}{4}$ $\frac{1}{2}$ $\frac{3}{4}$ **white** $\frac{1}{4}$ $\frac{2}{3}$ $\frac{1}{2}$

shaded $\frac{1}{4}$ $\frac{1}{3}$ $\frac{1}{2}$ **white** $\frac{2}{4}$ $\frac{2}{3}$ $\frac{2}{2}$

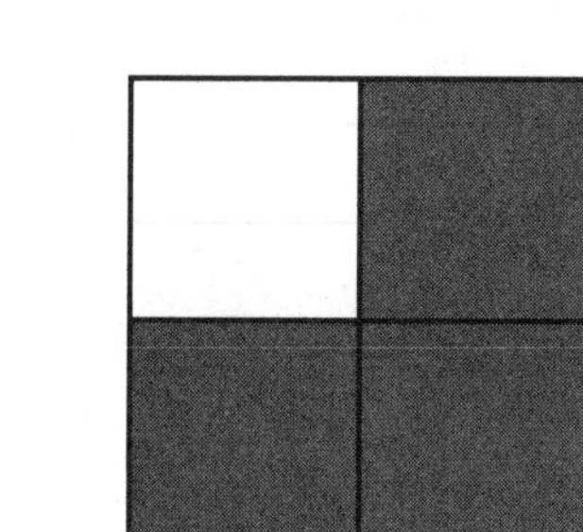

shaded $\frac{3}{4}$ $\frac{1}{3}$ $\frac{3}{2}$ **white** $\frac{1}{2}$ $\frac{1}{4}$ $\frac{1}{3}$

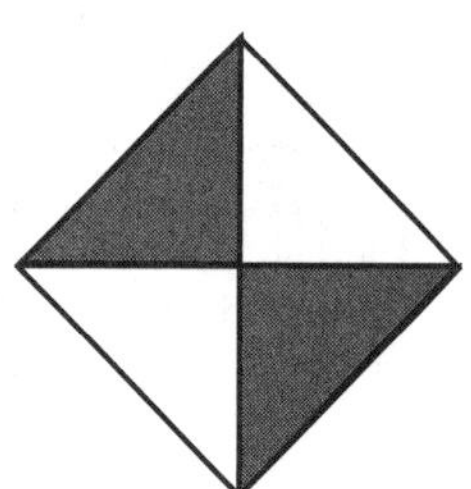

shaded $\frac{2}{3}$ $\frac{2}{4}$ $\frac{2}{2}$ **white** $\frac{1}{3}$ $\frac{2}{4}$ $\frac{2}{2}$

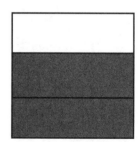

shaded $\frac{2}{4}$ $\frac{2}{3}$ $\frac{2}{2}$ **white** $\frac{1}{2}$ $\frac{1}{4}$ $\frac{1}{3}$

Fractions: Half, Third, Fourth

Draw a line from the fraction to the correct shape.

$\frac{1}{4}$ shaded

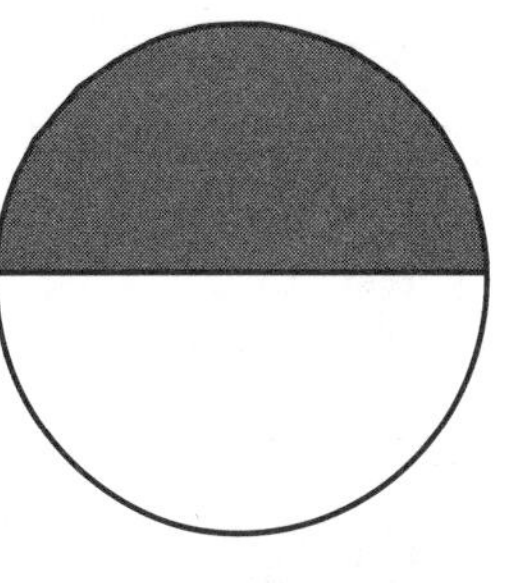

$\frac{2}{4}$ shaded

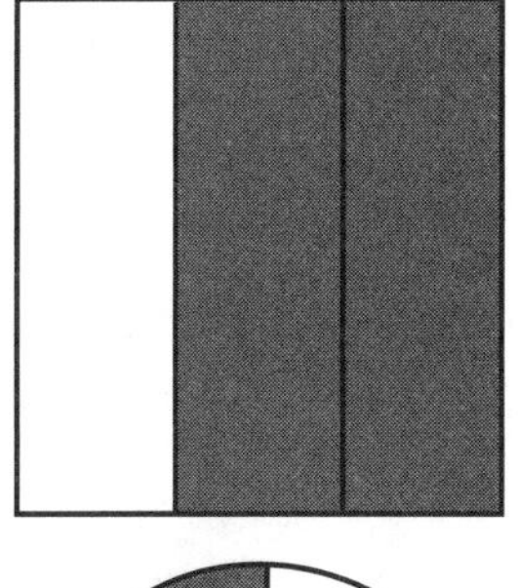

$\frac{1}{2}$ shaded

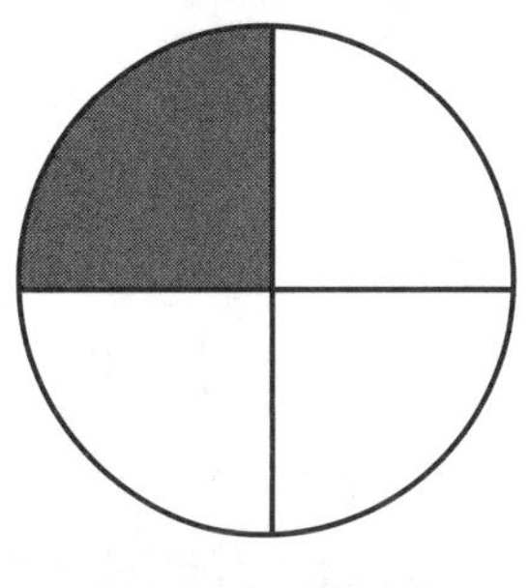

$\frac{1}{3}$ shaded

$\frac{2}{3}$ shaded

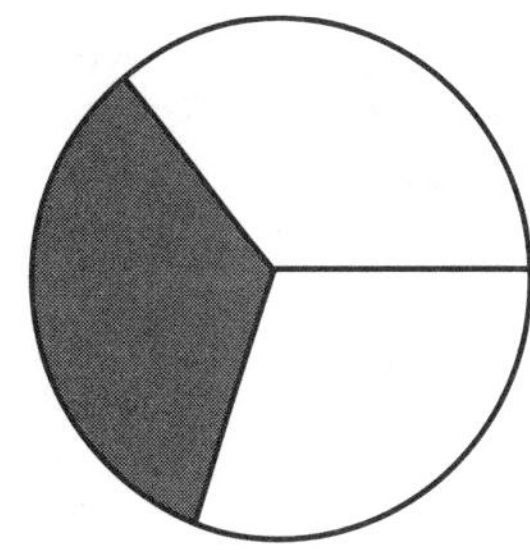

Problem Solving: Fractions

A **fraction** is a number that names part of a whole, such as $\frac{1}{2}$ or $\frac{1}{3}$. Read each problem. Use the pictures to help you solve the problem. Write the fraction that answers the question.

Simon and Jessie shared a pizza. Together they ate $\frac{3}{4}$ of the pizza. How much of the pizza is left? _____

Sylvia baked a cherry pie. She gave $\frac{1}{3}$ to her grandmother and $\frac{1}{3}$ to a friend. How much of the pie did she keep? _____

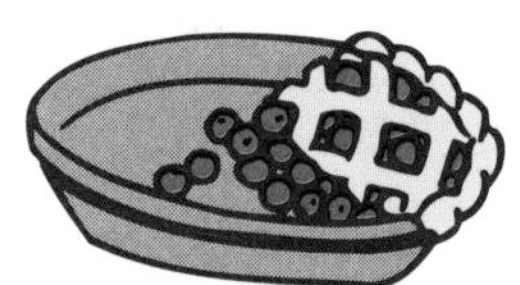

Timmy erased $\frac{1}{2}$ of the blackboard before the bell rang for recess. How much of the blackboard does he have left to erase? _____

Read the problem. Draw your own picture to help you solve the problem. Write the fraction that answers the question.

Sarah mowed $\frac{1}{4}$ of the yard before lunch. How much does she have left to mow? _____

Week 30 Skills

Subject	Skill	Multi-Sensory Learning Activities
Reading and Language Arts	Review statements and questions.	• Complete Practice Pages 320–324. • Learn a story well enough to tell it from memory. After telling it, ask your child to recall some of the events from the story. Write the events as statements. • Write several statements on a piece of paper. Ask your child to change the word order to turn the statements into questions.
Math	Review wholes, halves, thirds, and fourths.	• Complete Practice Pages 325–328. • Invite your child to help you in the kitchen, especially when you are measuring. Talk about cups, $\frac{1}{2}$ teaspoon, $\frac{1}{3}$ cup, $\frac{1}{4}$ teaspoon, and so on.
Bonus: Science		• Gather a dozen rocks of different colors, shapes, textures, and sizes. Draw a large Venn diagram (two large circles that overlap in the middle) on a sheet of paper. Write an adjective above each circle and have your child sort the rocks into the diagram. For example, if the categories were **shiny** and **pink**, your child would place pink rocks in one circle, shiny rocks in the other circle, and any rocks that are both shiny and pink into the overlapping area. Choose different adjectives and sort the rocks again.

Summer Camp

A **statement** is a telling sentence. It begins with a capital letter and ends with a period. Write each statement correctly on the lines.

1. everyone goes to breakfast at 6:30 each morning

____

2. only three people can ride in one canoe

____

3. each person must help clean the cabins

____

4. older campers should help younger campers

____

5. all lights are out by 9:00 each night

____

6. everyone should write home at least once a week

____

Statements

Statements are sentences that tell us something. They begin with a capital letter and end with a period.

Write the sentences on the lines below. Begin each sentence with a capital letter and end it with a period.

1. we like to ride our bikes

____

2. we go down the hill very fast

____

3. we keep our bikes shiny and clean

____

4. we know how to change the tires

____

Questions

A **question** is an asking sentence. It begins with a capital letter and ends with a question mark.

Write each question correctly on the line.

1. is our class going to the science museum

____

2. will we get to spend the whole day there

____

3. will a guide take us through the museum

____

4. do you think we will see dinosaur bones

____

5. is it true that the museum has a mummy

____

6. can we take lots of pictures at the museum

____

7. will you spend the whole day at the museum

____

More Questions

Write five questions about the picture.

Questions

Questions are sentences that ask something. They begin with a capital letter and end with a question mark.

Write the questions on the lines below. Begin each sentence with a capital letter and end it with a question mark.

1. will you be my friend

____

2. what is your name

____

3. are you eight years old

____

4. do you like rainbows

____

Fractions: Whole and Half

A fraction is a number that names part of a whole, such as $\frac{1}{2}$ or $\frac{3}{4}$.

Color half of each object.

Example:

Whole apple

Half an apple

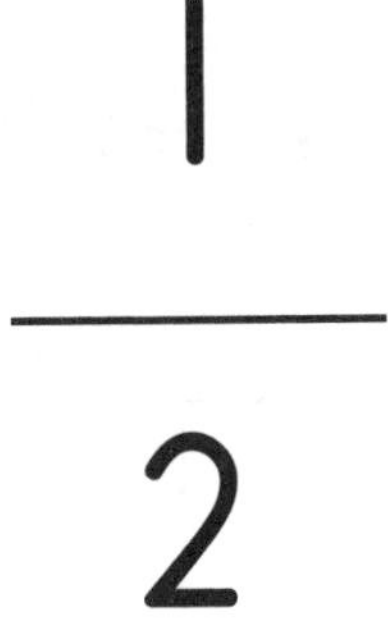

Fractions: Halves

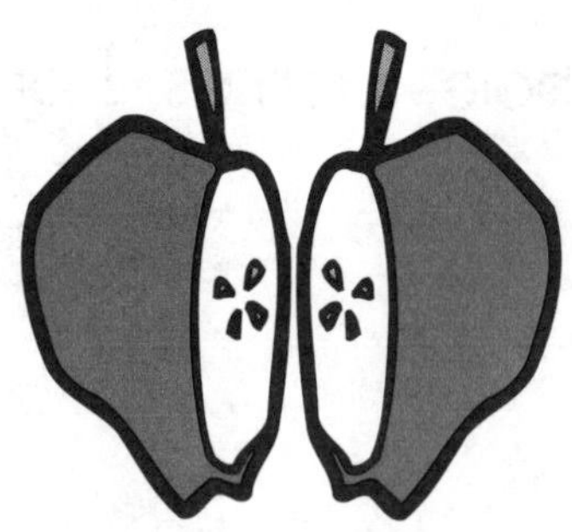

$\frac{1}{2}$ — 1: Part shaded or divided; 2: Number of equal parts

Color only the shapes that show halves.

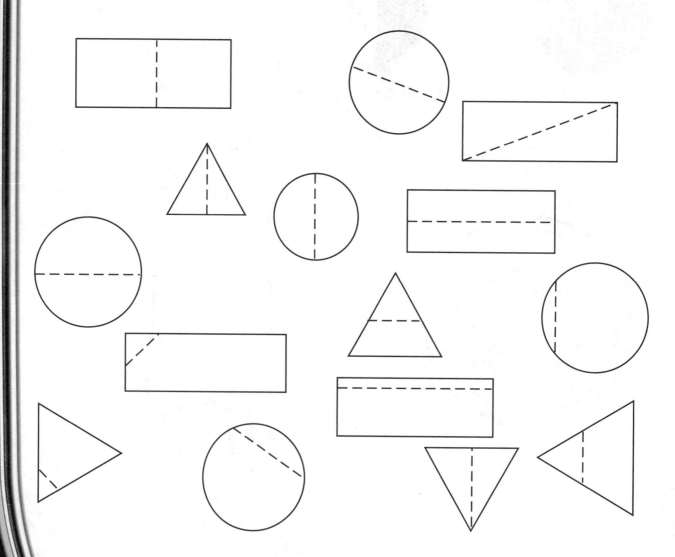

Fractions: Thirds

Circle the objects that have three equal parts.

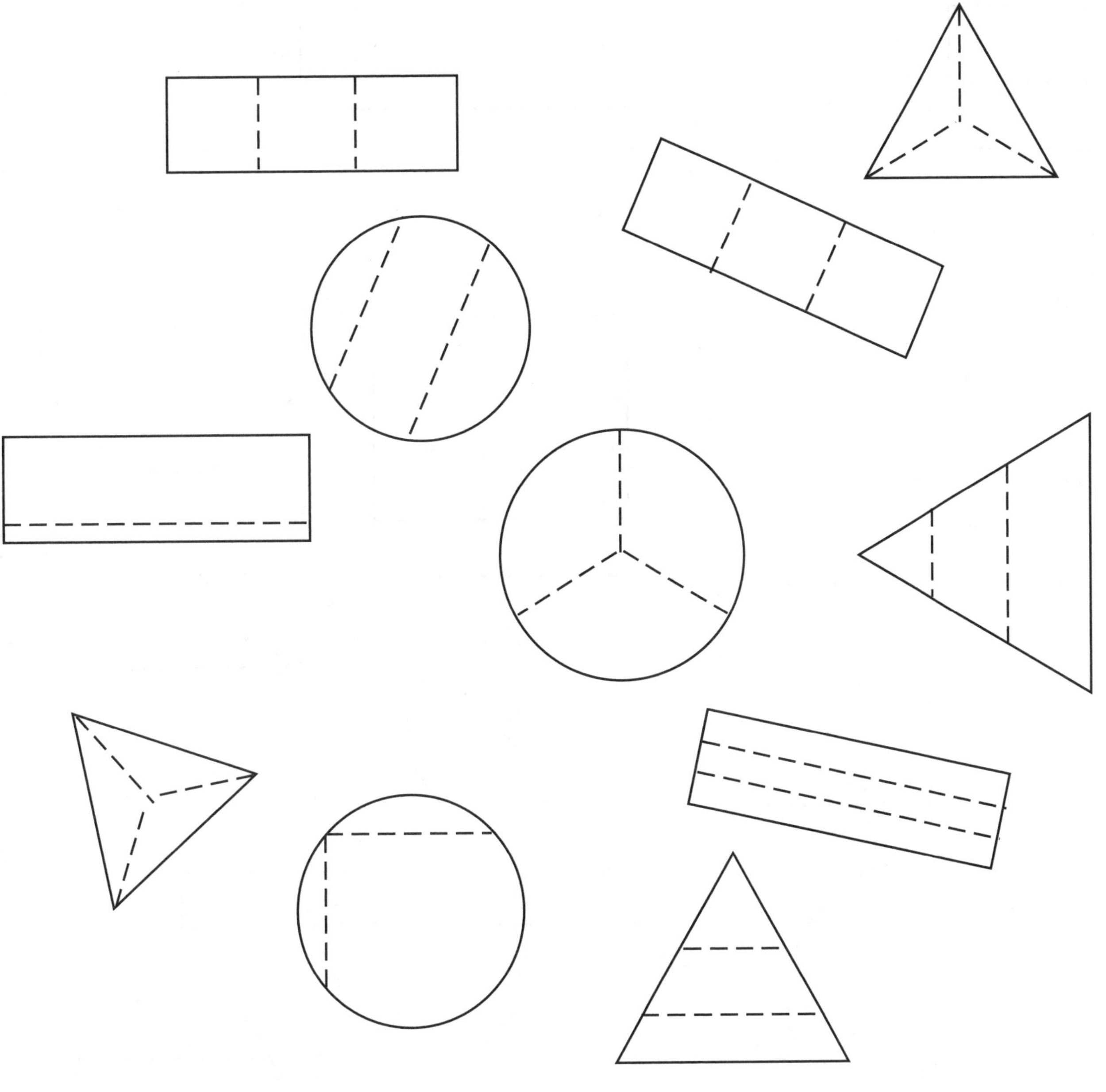

Fractions: Fourths

Circle the objects that have four equal parts.

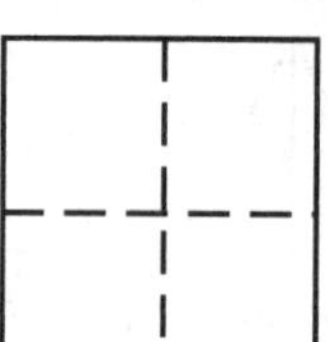
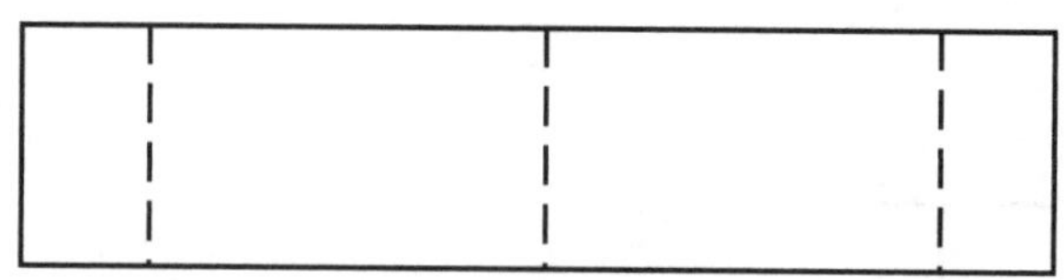
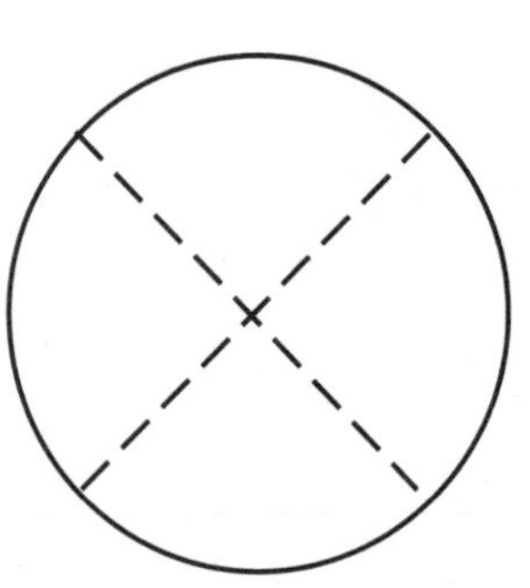
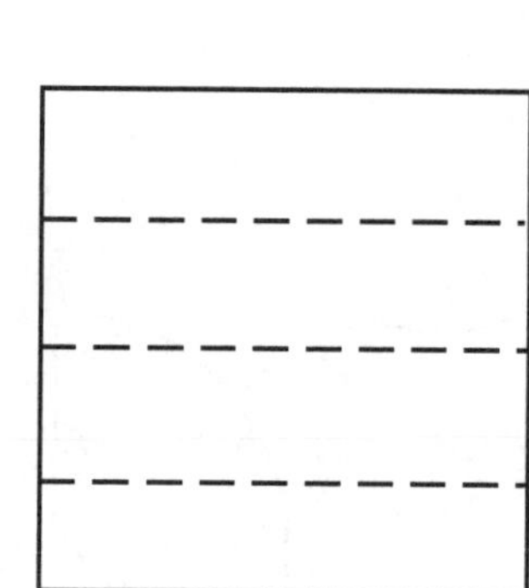
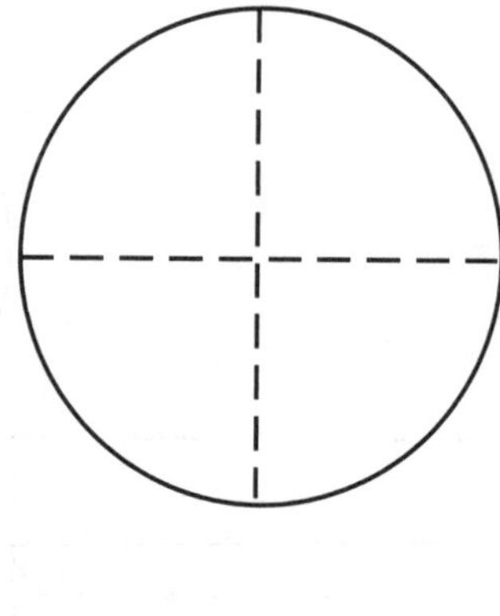
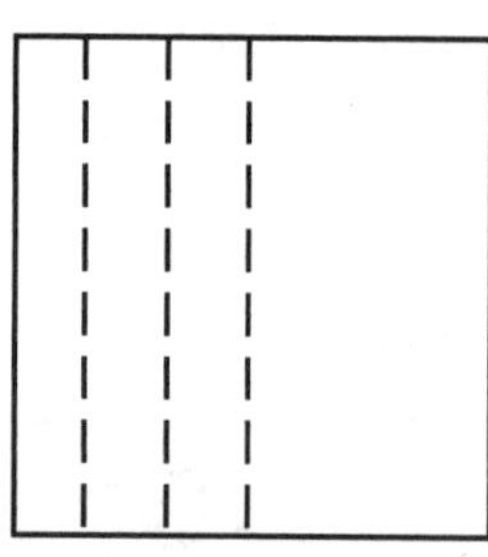
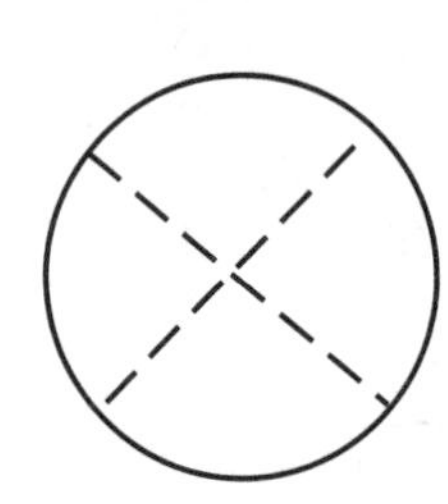
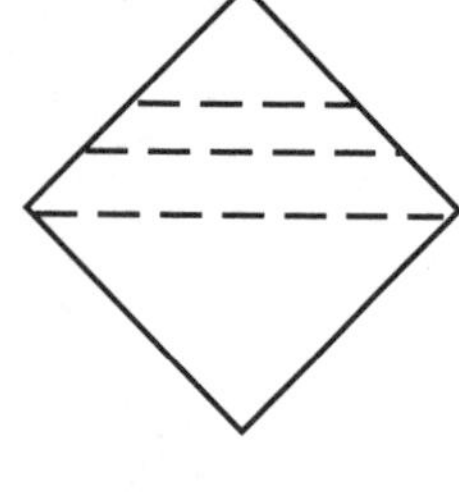
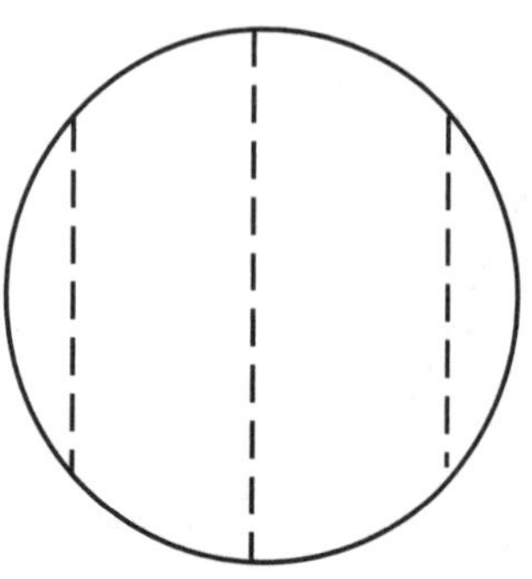
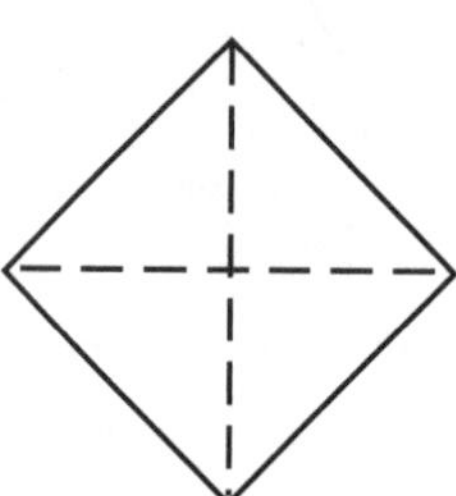
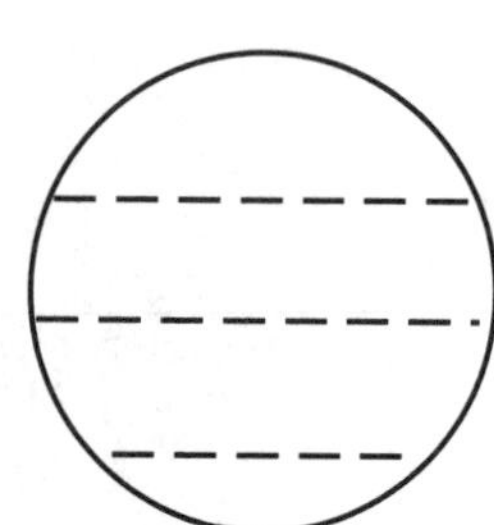

Week 31 Skills

Subject	Skill	Multi-Sensory Learning Activities
Reading and Language Arts	Review statements and questions.	• Complete Practice Pages 330–332. • A riddle can be a question that gives clues to an answer. With your child, read a riddle book. Look for words that begin riddles. Then, have your child write his or her own riddles with answers.
	Understand different characters' points of view.	• Complete Practice Pages 333 and 334. • Help your child form a question that can be answered differently by different people. Ask your child to think of six friends or family members. How might each person answer the question?
Math	Review fractions.	• Complete Practice Pages 335–337. • Draw 10 circles on a piece of paper to represent pizzas. Divide these pizzas to show different fractions—one cut into halves, two cut into thirds, three cut into fourths, and four cut into fifths. Then, cut a piece of paper into 10 slips. On each slip, write one fraction: $\frac{1}{2}$, $\frac{1}{3}$, $\frac{2}{3}$, $\frac{1}{4}$, $\frac{2}{4}$, $\frac{3}{4}$, $\frac{1}{5}$, $\frac{2}{5}$, $\frac{3}{5}$, and $\frac{4}{5}$. Have your child draw a slip of paper from a bowl. If it says $\frac{1}{4}$, he or she gets to "eat" 1 slice of the pizza divided into fourths by coloring it in. Continue pulling more slips of paper from the bowl and coloring in the fractions.

Writing Sentences

Every sentence begins with a capital letter.

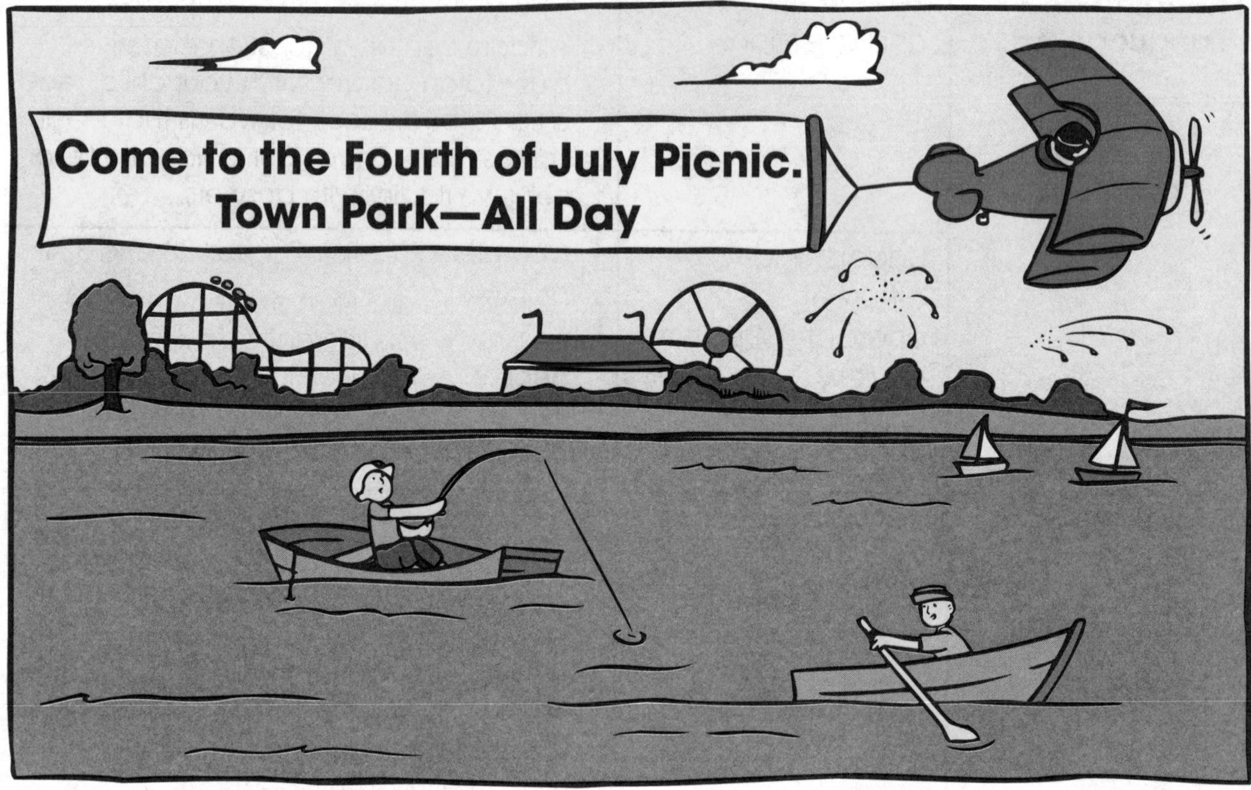

Come to the Fourth of July Picnic.
Town Park—All Day

Write three statements about the picture.

____

____

____

Write three questions about the picture.

____

____

____

Kinds of Sentences

A **statement** ends with a period . (.) A **question** ends with a question mark. (**?**) Write the correct mark in each box.

1. Would you like to help me make an aquarium ☐
2. We can use my brother's big fish tank ☐
3. Will you put this colored sand in the bottom ☐
4. I have three shells to put on the sand ☐
5. Can we use your little toy boat, too ☐
6. Let's go buy some fish for our aquarium ☐
7. Will twelve fish be enough ☐
8. Look, they seem to like their new home ☐
9. How often do we give them fish food ☐
10. Let's tell our friends about our new aquarium ☐

Changing Sentences

The order of words can change a sentence. Read each telling sentence. Change the order of the words to make an asking sentence. **Example:**

The clown is happy.

Is the clown happy?

The boy can swim.

The bell will ring.

The popcorn is hot.

The flowers are lovely.

Making Inferences: Point of View

Chelsea likes to pretend she will meet famous people someday. She would like to ask them many questions.

Write a question you think Chelsea would ask if she met these people.

1. an actor in a popular, new film ______________________________ ?
2. an Olympic gold medal winner ______________________________ ?
3. an alien from outer space ______________________________ ?

Now, write the answers these people might have given to Chelsea's questions.

4. an actor in a popular, new film ______________________________
5. an Olympic Gold medal winner ______________________________
6. an alien from outer space ______________________________

Making Inferences: Point of View

Ellen likes animals. Someday, she might want to be an animal doctor.

Write one question you think Ellen would ask each of these animals if she could speak their language.

1. a giraffe ______________________________?
2. a mouse ______________________________?
3. a shark ______________________________?
4. a hippopotamus ______________________________?
5. a penguin ______________________________?
6. a gorilla ______________________________?
7. an eagle ______________________________?

Now, write the answers you think these animals might have given Ellen.

9. a giraffe ______________________________
10. a mouse ______________________________
11. a shark ______________________________
12. a hippopotamus ______________________________
13. a penguin ______________________________
14. a gorilla ______________________________
15. an eagle ______________________________

Fortunate Fractions

Color the correct number of fortune cookies to show each fraction.

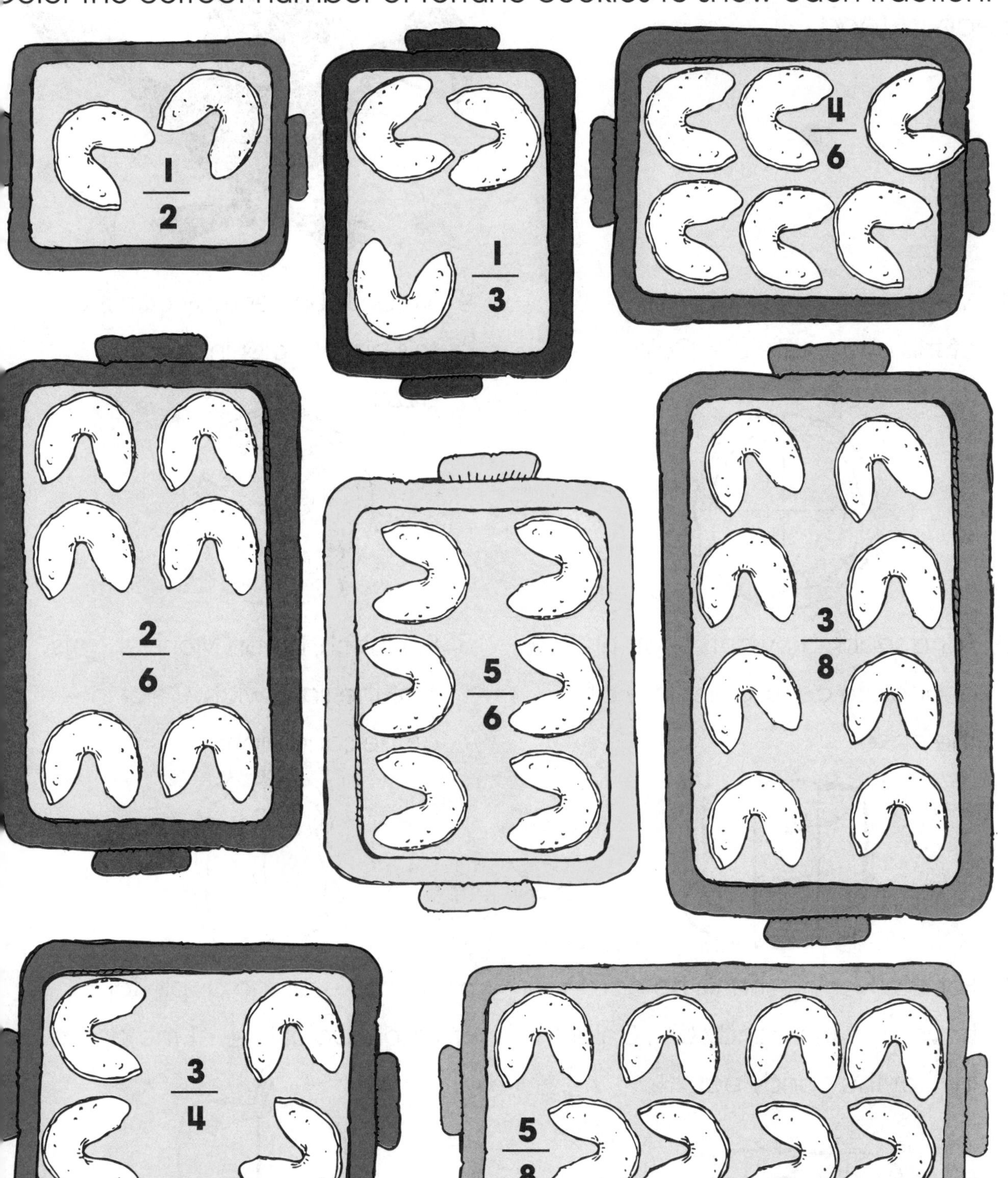

Mean Monster's Diet

Help Mean Monster choose the right piece of food.

1. Mean Monster may have $\frac{1}{4}$ of this chocolate pie. Color in $\frac{1}{4}$ of the pie.

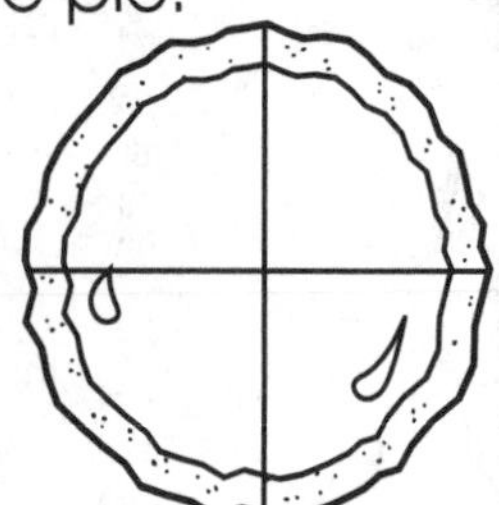

2. For a snack, he wants $\frac{1}{3}$ of this chocolate cake. Color in $\frac{1}{3}$ of the cake.

3. For an evening snack, he can have $\frac{1}{4}$ of the candy bar. Color in $\frac{1}{4}$ of the candy bar.

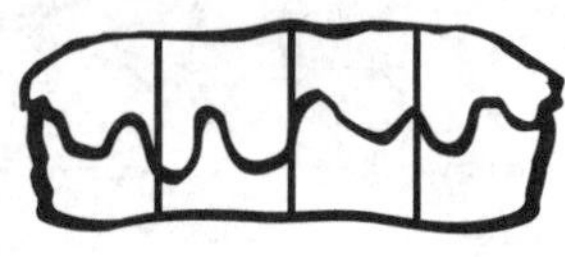

4. Mean Monster may eat $\frac{1}{3}$ of this pizza. Color in $\frac{1}{3}$ of the pizza.

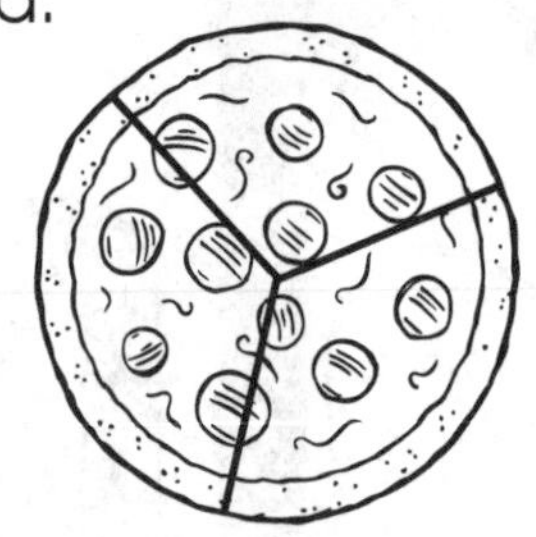

5. For lunch, Mean Monster gets $\frac{1}{2}$ of the sandwich. Color in $\frac{1}{2}$ of the sandwich.

6. He ate $\frac{1}{2}$ of the apple for lunch. Color in $\frac{1}{2}$ of the apple.

Equal and Unequal Parts

Cut out each shape below along the solid lines. Then, fold the shape on the dotted lines. Do you have equal or unequal parts? Sort the shapes by equal and unequal parts.

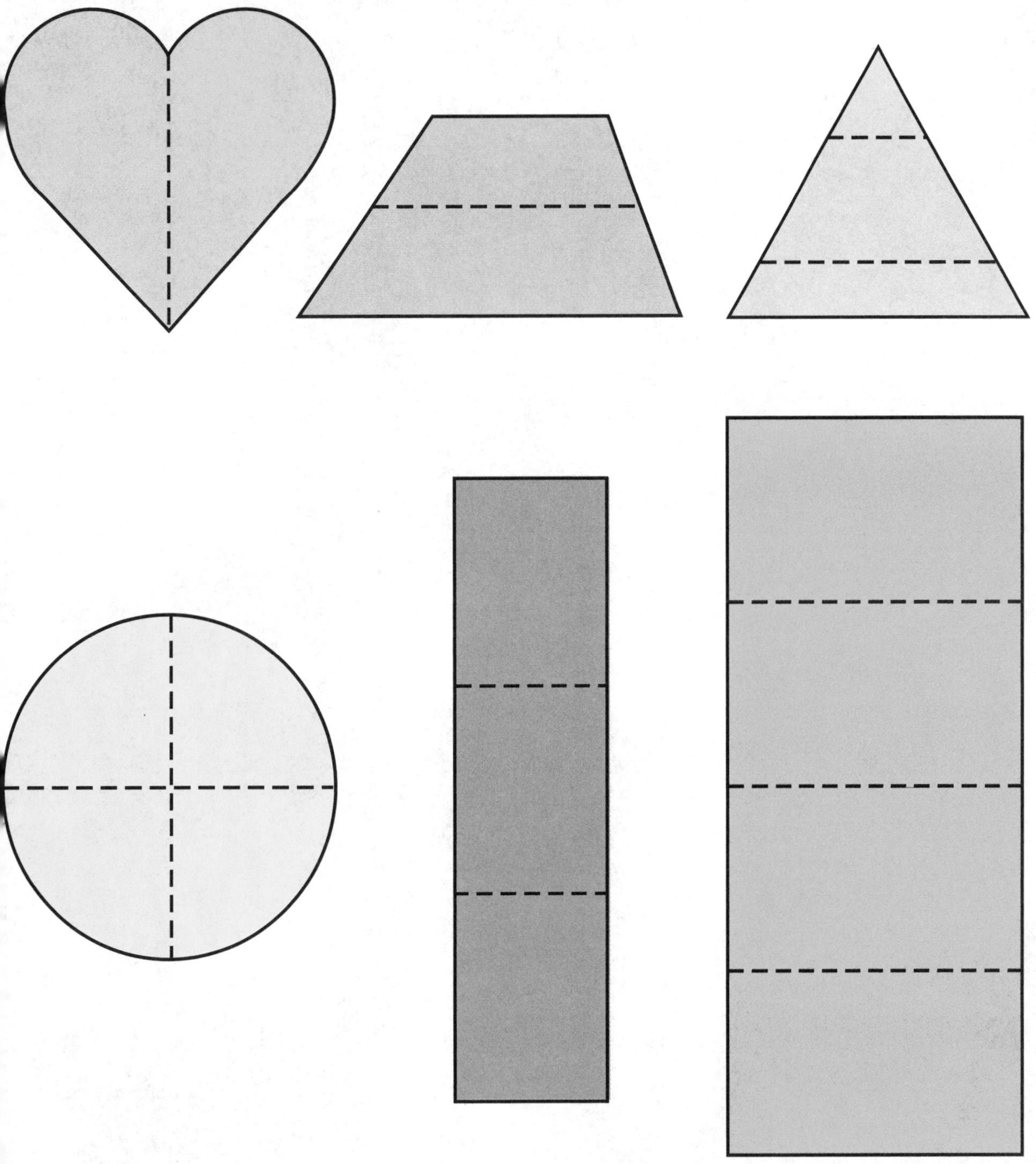

Week 32 Skills

Subject	Skill	Multi-Sensory Learning Activities
Reading and Language Arts	Understand and identify the subject of a sentence.	• Complete Practice Pages 340 and 341. • Write 10 individual sentences on sentence strips. Have your child determine each sentence's subject. Cut the subject of each sentence away from the rest of the sentence strip. Have your child mix and match the strips. They will probably form some silly-sounding sentences!
	Understand compound subjects as sentences that have two or more subjects.	• Complete Practice Page 343. • Write several pairs of sentences that have the same predicate. Have your child write each pair of sentences as one sentence with a compound subject. For example, "The boys went to the park" and "The girls went to the park" could be combined to form "The boys and girls went to the park."
Math	Measure in inches.	• Complete Practice Pages 344–347. • Have your child compare inches on a ruler, yardstick, and tape measure. Point out that an inch is always the same. Have your child show with his or her index finger and thumb the approximate length of an inch. Have an "Inch Scavenger Hunt" by having your child find some objects that measure approximately one inch.

1 2 3 4 5 6 7 8

Subjects of Sentences

The subject of a sentence tells who or what does something.

Example: Some people eat foods that may seem strange to you.

Underline the subject of each sentence.

1. Some people like crocodile steak.
2. The meat tastes like fish.
3. Australians eat kangaroo meat.
4. Kangaroo meat tastes like beef.
5. People in the Southwest eat rattlesnake meat.
6. Snails make a delicious treat for some people.
7. Some Africans think roasted termites are tasty.
8. Bird's-nest soup is a famous Chinese dish.
9. People in Florida serve alligator meat.
10. Almost everyone treats themselves with ice cream.

Sentence Sequence

Sentences can tell a story. Color, cut out and glue the pictures in order to tell a story. Write a sentence on each line that tells what is happening in the pictures.

1

____

____

2

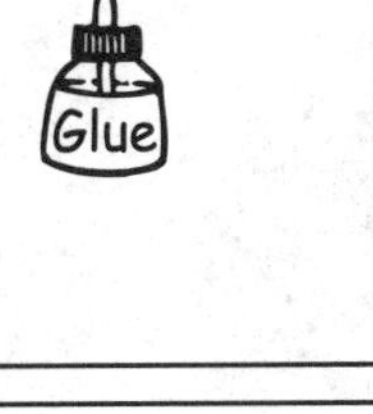

____

____

3

____

____

4

____

____

Compound Subjects

A **compound subject** has two or more subjects joined by the word **and**.

Example: Owls are predators. **Wolves** are predators.
Owls and wolves are predators. (compound subject)

If the sentence has a compound subject, write **CS**. If it does not, write **No**.

_______ 1. A predator is an animal that eats other animals.

_______ 2. Prey is eaten by predators.

_______ 3. Robins and bluejays are predators.

_______ 4. Some predators eat only meat.

_______ 5. Crocodiles and hawks eat meat only.

_______ 6. Raccoons and foxes eat both meat and plants.

Combine the subjects of the two sentences to make a compound subject. Write the new sentence on the line.

1. Snakes are predators. Spiders are predators.

____

2. Frogs prey on insects. Chameleons prey on insects.

____

Jumping Jelly Beans

Use an inch ruler to measure the line segments. Write the total length on each candy jar.

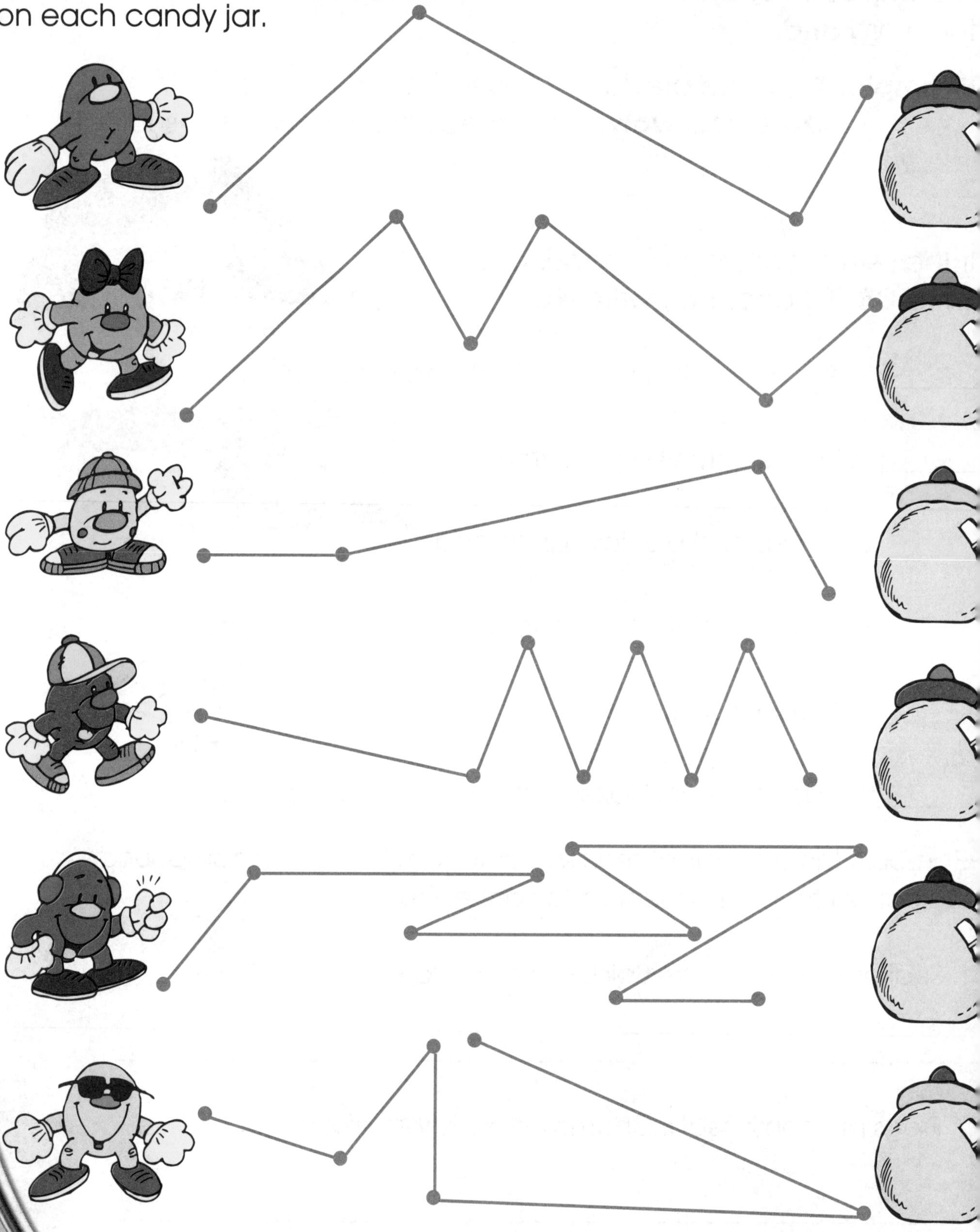

Measurement: Inches

An **inch** is a unit of length in the standard measurement system.

Use a ruler to measure each object to the nearest inch.

1 inch

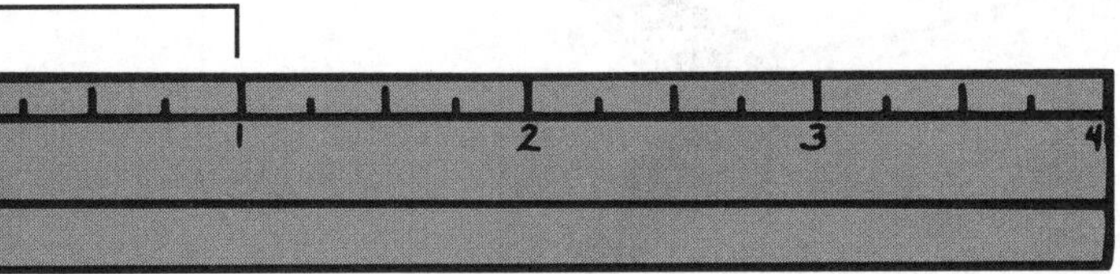

about __1__ inch

about _____ inch

about _____ inches

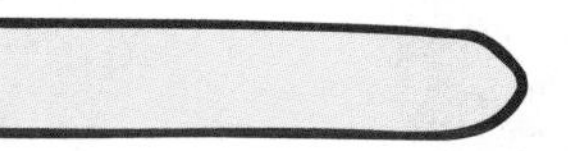

about _____ inches

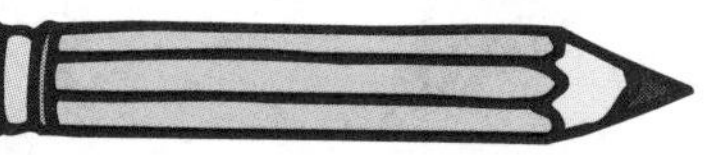

about _____ inches

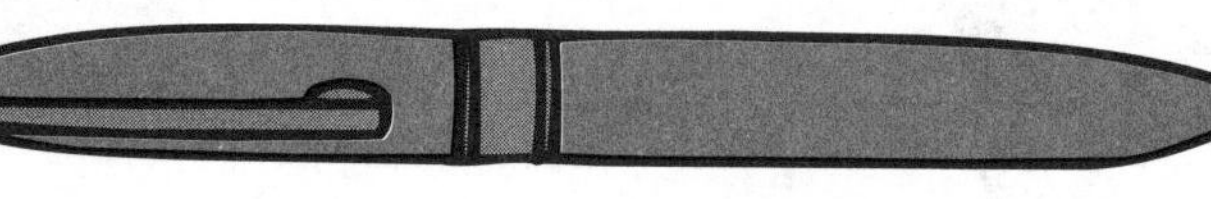

about _____ inches

about _____ inches

Measurement: Inches

Use a ruler to measure the fish to the nearest inch.

about _____inche

about _____inch

about _____inche

about _____inch

about _____inche

about _____inches

Measurement: Inches

Cut out the ruler. Measure each object to the nearest inch.

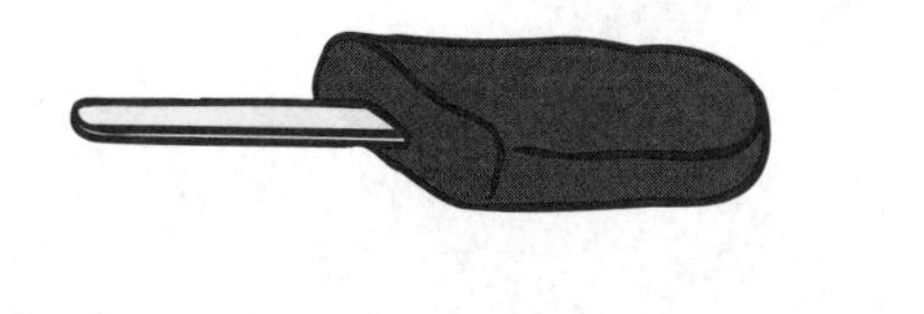

_______ inches

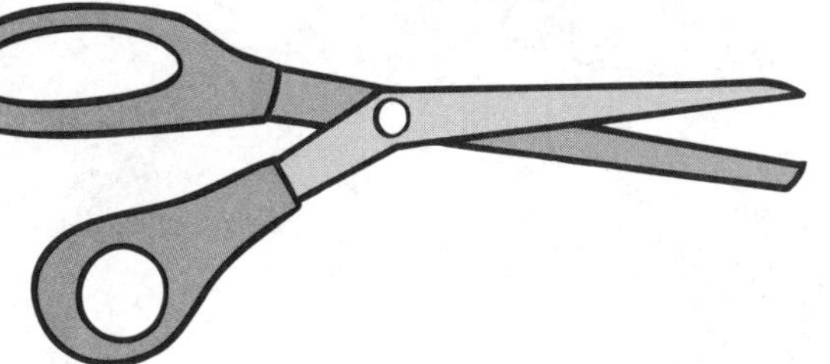

_______ inches

_______ inch

Measure objects around your house.
Write the measurement to the nearest inch.

can of soup _______ inches

pen _______ inches

toothbrush _______ inches

paper clip _______ inches

small toy _______ inches

cut out

1

Week 33 Skills

Subject	Skill	Multi-Sensory Learning Activities
Reading and Language Arts	Understand and identify the predicate of a sentence.	• Complete Practice Pages 350–352. • Cut 10 pictures from an old magazine. Have your child write a sentence about each picture and circle the predicate.
	Understand compound predicates as sentences that have two or more predicates.	• Complete Practice Pages 353 and 354. • Look through your child's favorite book for sentences with compound predicates. Have your child list these sentences and identify the compound predicates.
	Review subjects and predicates.	• Complete Practice Page 355. • Write several subjects on a piece of paper. Ask your child to supply a predicate for each.
Math	Measure in centimeters.	• Complete Practice Pages 356 and 357. • Using a tape measure, measure parts of your child's body in centimeters. Measure around his or her head, the length of an arm or leg, and the distance from head to toe. Have your child record the lengths on a sketch of him- or herself.
	Understand liquid measurements.	• Complete Practice Page 358. • Fill cup, pint, quart, and gallon containers with water. Have your child analyze and compare the different volumes. Which container is the heaviest?

Predicates of Sentences

The **predicate** of a sentence tells what the subject is or does. It is the verb part of the sentence.

Examples: Sally Ride **flew in a space shuttle**.

She **was an astronaut**.

Underline the predicate in each sentence.

1. She was the first American woman astronaut in space.
2. Sally worked hard for many years to become an astronaut.
3. She studied math and science in college.
4. Ms. Ride passed many tests.
5. She learned things quickly.
6. Sally trained to become a jet pilot.
7. This astronaut practiced using a robot arm.
8. Ms. Ride used the robot arm on two space missions.
9. She conducted experiments with it.
10. The robot arm is called a remote manipulator.

Predicates of Sentences

he **predicate** of a sentence tells what the subject is or does.

xample: Cars **pollute the air**.
Cars **are helpful machines**.

Color each piece red that holds a predicate.
Color the other pieces blue.

Predicates

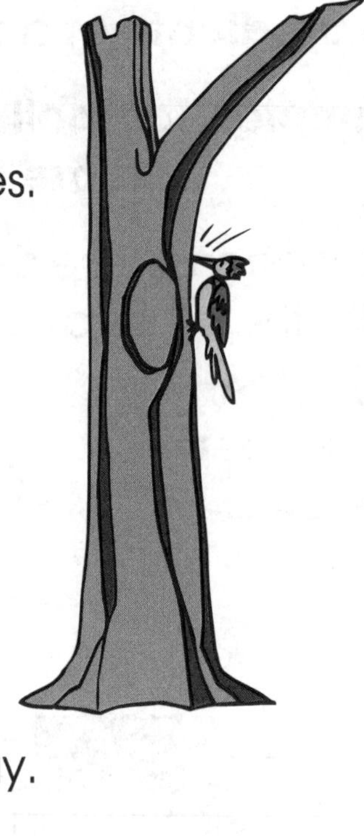

A **predicate** tells what the subject is doing, has done or will do.

Underline the predicate in the following sentences.

Example: Woodpeckers live in trees.

1. They hunt for insects in the trees.

2. Woodpeckers have strong beaks.

3. They can peck through the bark.

4. The pecking sound can be heard from far away.

Circle the groups of words that can be predicates.

have long tongues	pick up insects
hole in bark	sticky substance
help it to climb trees	tree bark

Now, choose the correct predicates from above to finish these sentences.

1. Woodpeckers ______________________.
2. They use their tongues to ______________________.
3. Its strong feet ______________________.

Compound Predicates

Compound predicates have two or more verbs that have the same subject.

Combine the predicates to create one sentence with a compound predicate.

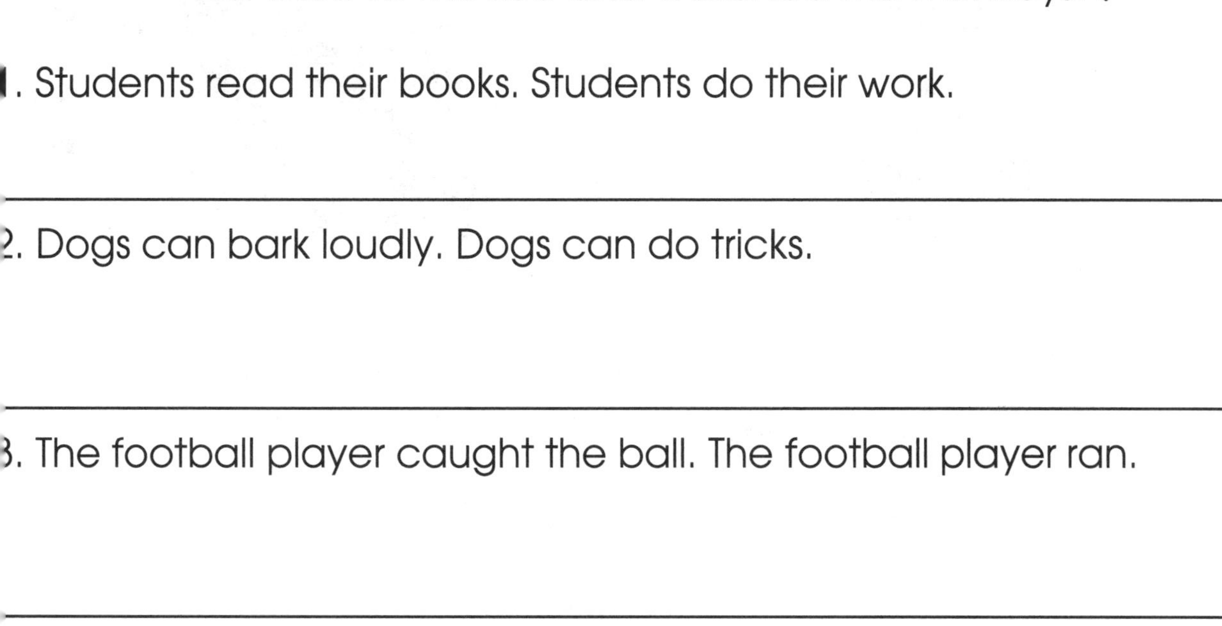

Example: We went to the zoo.
We watched the monkeys.
We went to the zoo and watched the monkeys.

1. Students read their books. Students do their work.

____

2. Dogs can bark loudly. Dogs can do tricks.

____

3. The football player caught the ball. The football player ran.

____

4. My dad sawed wood. My dad stacked wood.

____

5. My teddy bear is soft. My teddy bear likes to be hugged.

____

Compound Predicates

A **compound predicate** has two or more predicates joined by the word **and**.

Example: Abe Lincoln was born in Kentucky. Abe Lincoln lived in a log cabin there.
Abe Lincoln **was born in Kentucky and lived in a log cabin there**.

If the sentence has a compound predicate, write **CP**. If it does not, write **No**.

_________ 1. Abe Lincoln cut trees and chopped wood.

_________ 2. Abe and his sister walked to a spring for water.

_________ 3. Abe's family packed up and left Kentucky.

_________ 4. They crossed the Ohio River to Indiana.

_________ 5. Abe's father built a new home.

_________ 6. Abe's mother became sick and died.

_________ 7. Mr. Lincoln married again.

_________ 8. Abe's new mother loved Abe and his sister and cared for them.

Complete Sentences

sentence is a group of words that tells a whole idea. It has a ubject and a predicate.

xamples: Some animals have stripes.
(sentence)
Help to protect.
(not a sentence)

Vrite **S** in front of each sentence. Write **No** if it is not a sentence.

________ 1. There are different kinds of chipmunks.

________ 2. They all have.

________ 3. They all have stripes to help protect them.

________ 4. The stripes make them hard to see in the forest.

________ 5. Zebras have stripes, too.

________ 6. Some caterpillars also.

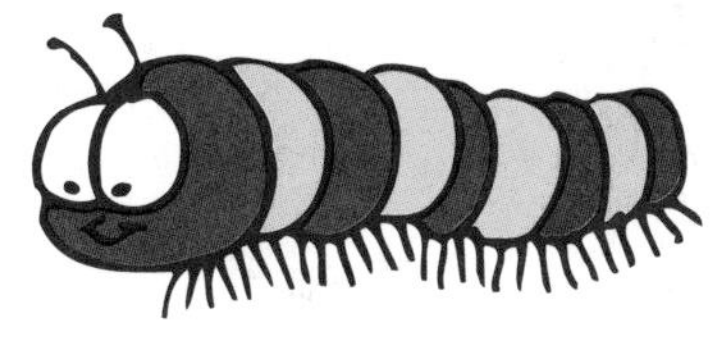

________ 7. Other animals have spots.

________ 8. Some dogs have spots.

________ 9. Beautiful, little fawns.

________ 10. Their spots help to hide them in the woods.

Measurement: Centimeters

A **centimeter** is a unit of length in the metric system. There are 2.54 centimeters in an inch.

Use a centimeter ruler to measure the crayons to the nearest centimeter.

Example: The first crayon is about 7 centimeters long.

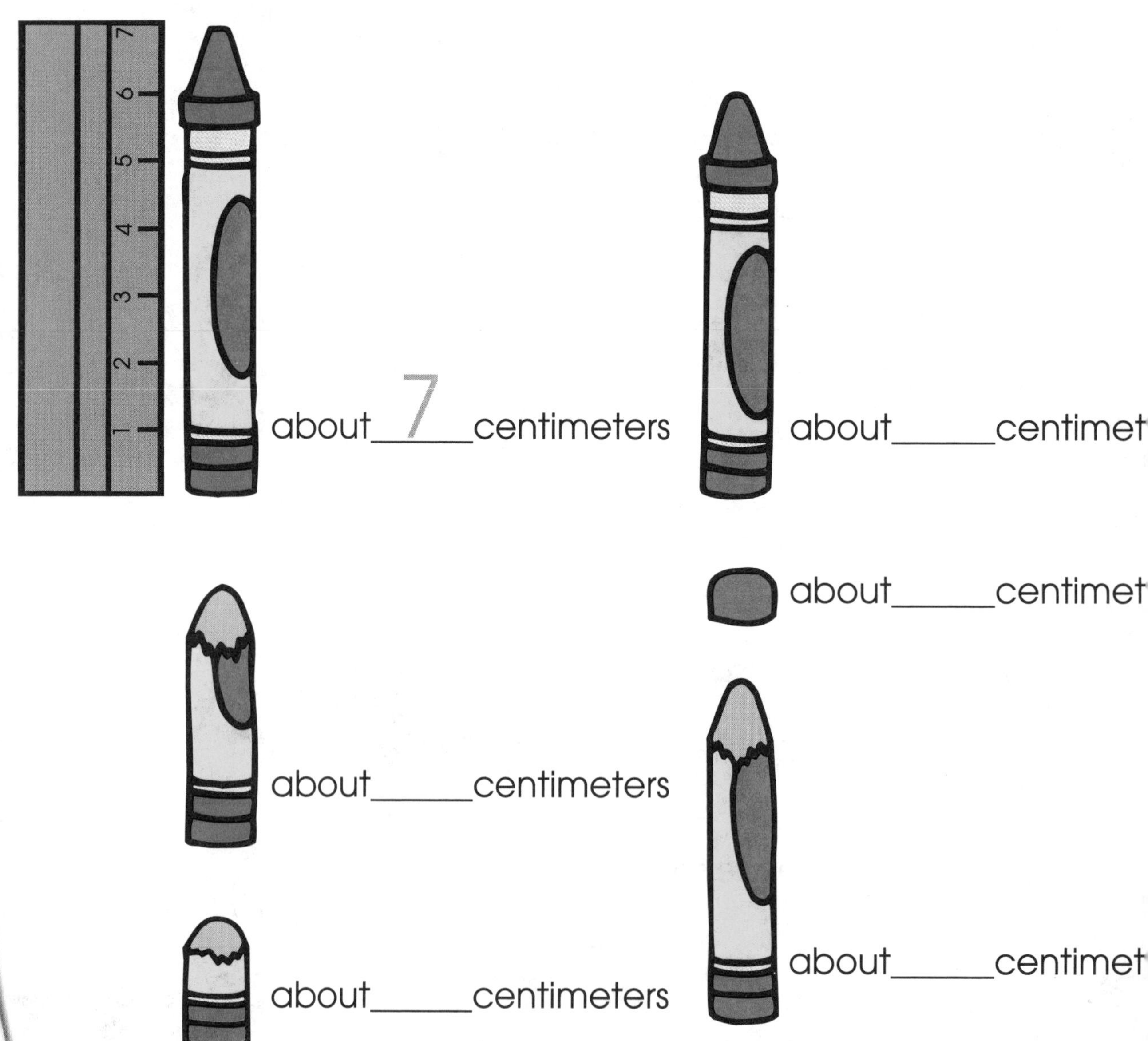

Measurement: Centimeters

ne giraffe is about 8 centimeters high. How many
entimeters (cm) high are the trees? Write your answers in the blanks.

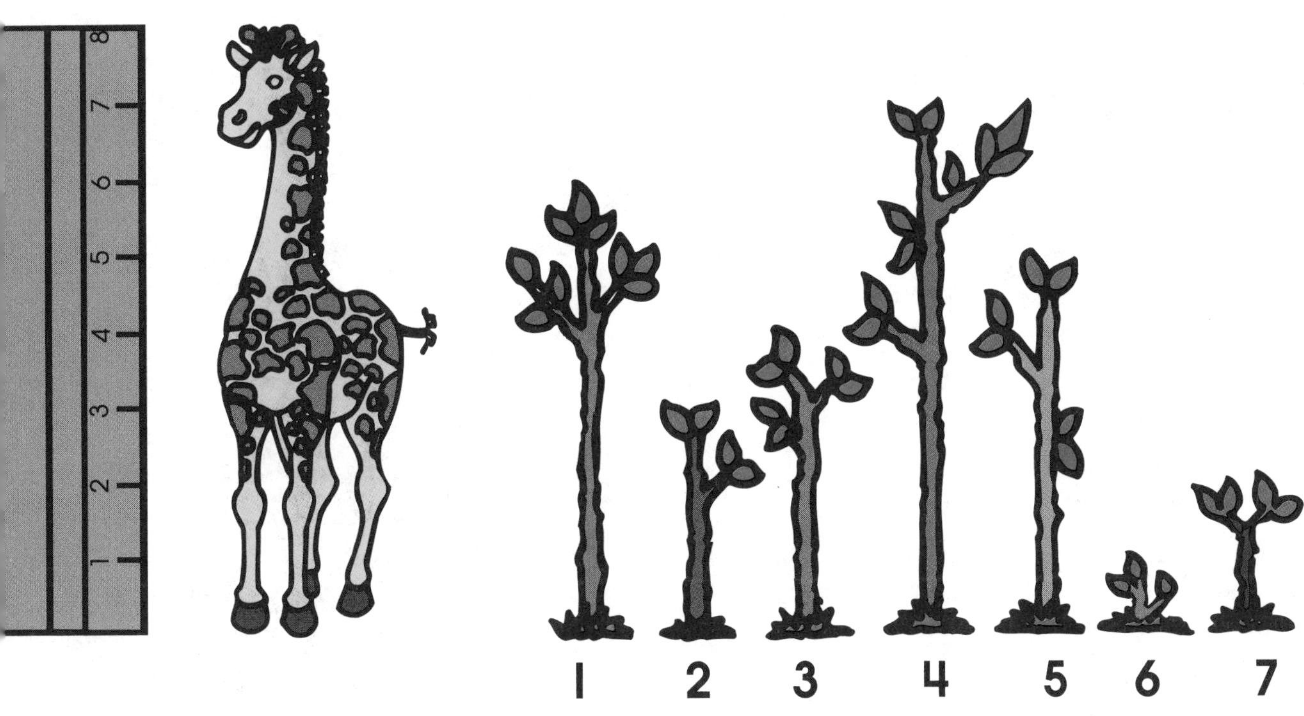

.__________cm 2.__________cm 3.__________cm

.__________cm 5.__________cm 6.__________cm 7.__________cm

Liquid Limits

Draw a line from the containers on the left to the containers on the right that will hold the same amount of liquid. **Hint:** 2 pints = 1 quart

Week 34 Skills

Subject	Skill	Multi-Sensory Learning Activities
Reading and Language Arts	Practice dictionary skills.	• Complete Practice Pages 360–364. • Hang an alphabet line or cards on the wall for reference as your child practices alphabetizing. Pick 10 words that begin with different letters and write them on index cards. Then, have your child arrange them in alphabetical order. • With your child, read *A Girl Named Helen Keller* by Margo Lundell. Practice "The One-Hand Manual Alphabet" shown at the end of the book. Find five words in the book to look up in a dictionary. Read each definition as well as the words defined before and after the word.
Math	Review addition, subtraction, place value, time, money, shapes, and fractions.	• Complete Practice Pages 365–368. • Review three-digit place value. Have your child roll three dice and record the smallest and largest numbers that can be made from the three numerals. • Provide paper shapes for your child to explore and sort. Ask your child to explain how he or she sorted the shapes.

Learning Dictionary Skills

A **dictionary** is a book that gives the meaning of words. It also tells how words sound. Words in a dictionary are in ABC order. That makes them easier to find. A picture dictionary lists a word, a picture of the word and its meaning.

Look at this page from a picture dictionary. Then, answer the questior

baby

A very young child.

band

A group of people who play music.

bank

A place where money is kept.

bark

The sound a dog makes.

berry

A small, juicy fruit.

board

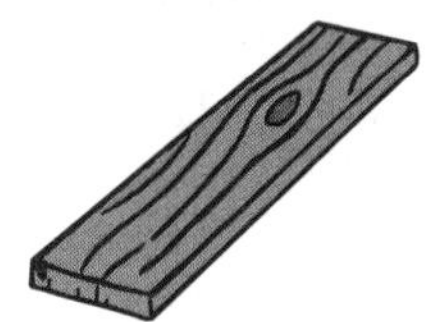

A flat piece of wood.

1. What is a small, juicy fruit? ______________________

2. What is a group of people who play music? ______________

3. What is the name for a very young child? ______________

4. What is a flat piece of wood called? ________________

Learning Dictionary Skills

ook at this page from a picture dictionary. Then, answer
ne questions.

safe

A metal box.

sea

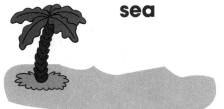

A body of water.

seed

The beginning of a plant.

sheep

An animal that has wool.

store

A place where items are sold.

skate

A shoe with wheels or a blade on it.

snowstorm

A time when much snow falls.

squirrel

A small animal with a bushy tail.

stone

A small rock.

1. What kind of animal has wool? ______________________
2. What do you call a shoe with wheels on it? ______________________
3. When a lot of snow falls, what is it called? ______________________
4. What is a small animal with a bushy tail? ______________________
5. What is a place where items are sold? ______________________
6. When a plant starts, what is it called? ______________________

Learning Dictionary Skills

Look at this page from a picture dictionary. Then, answer the questions.

table

Furniture with legs and a flat top.

tail

A slender part that is on the back of an animal.

teacher

A person who teaches lessons.

telephone

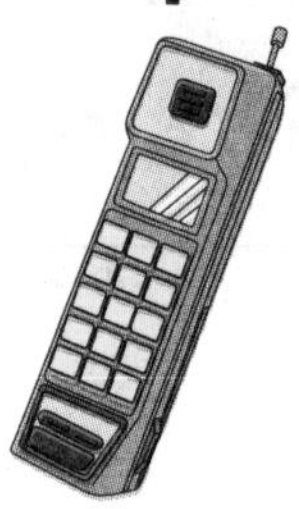

A machine that sends and receives sounds.

ticket

A paper slip or card.

tiger

An animal with stripes.

1. Who is a person who teaches lessons? ____________________

2. What is the name of an animal with stripes? ____________________

3. What is a piece of furniture with legs and a flat top? ____________

4. What is the definition of a ticket?

____

5. What is a machine that sends and receives sounds?

____

Learning Dictionary Skills

The **guide words** at the top of a page in a dictionary tell you what the first and last words on the page will be. Only words that come in ABC order between those two words will be on that page. Guide words help you find the page you need to look up a word.

Write each word from the box in ABC order between each pair of guide words.

faint	far	fence	feed	farmer
fan	feet	farm	family	face

face **fence**

__________	__________
__________	__________
__________	__________
__________	__________
__________	__________

Learning Dictionary Skills

When words have more than one meaning, the meanings are numbered in a dictionary.

Read the meanings of **tag**. Write the number of the correct definition after each sentence.

tag

1. A small strip or tab attached to something else.
2. To label.
3. To follow closely and constantly.
4. A game of chase.

1. We will play a game of tag after we study. ________________
2. I will tag this coat with its price. ________________
3. My little brother will tag along with us. ________________
4. My mother already took off the price tag. ________________
5. The tag on the puppy said, "For Sale." ________________
6. Do not tag that tree. ________________

Review

What time is it?

_____ o'clock

Draw the hands on each clock

2:30

7:30

11:00

How much money?

=______ ¢

=______ ¢

Add or subtract.

9 + 3 = ________ 6 + 8 = ________ 15 - 9 = ________

12 - 8 = ________ 12 + 2 = ________ 7 + 6 = ________

Review

Follow the instructions.

1. How much money?

_____ ¢

		Tens	Ones			Hundreds	Tens	Ones
2.	57 =	_____	_____	128	=	_____	_____	_____

3. What is this shape? Circle the answer.

Square

Triangle

Circle

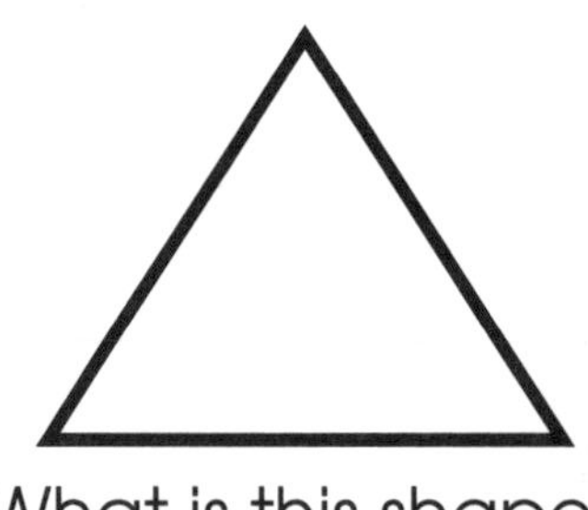

What is this shape? ___________

4.

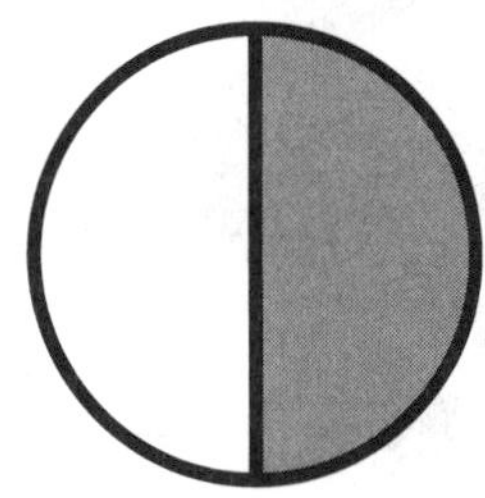

Shaded part = _____

Equal parts = _____

Write ___

Shaded part = _____

Equal parts = _____

Write ___

5. 12 + 3 = _____ 9 + 6 = _____ 15 - 7 = _____

Review

Circle the correct fraction of each shape's white part.

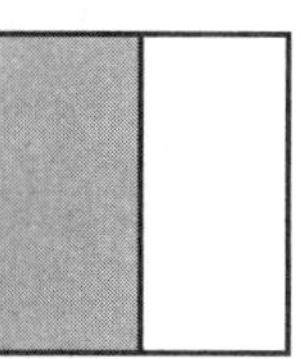

$\frac{1}{2}$ $\frac{1}{3}$ $\frac{1}{4}$

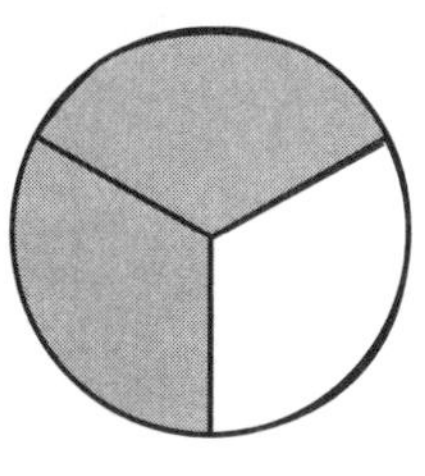

$\frac{1}{4}$ $\frac{1}{3}$ $\frac{1}{2}$

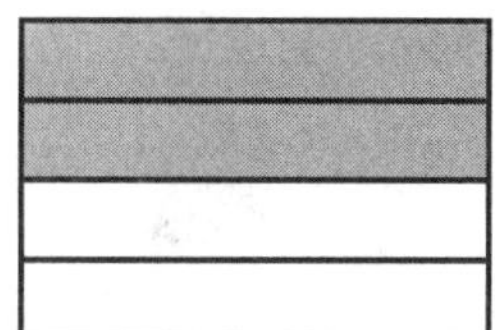

$\frac{2}{3}$ $\frac{2}{4}$ $\frac{1}{3}$

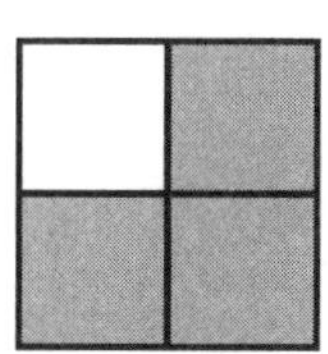

$\frac{1}{4}$ $\frac{1}{2}$ $\frac{3}{4}$

Count the flowers. Color the pots to make a graph that shows the number of flowers.

1 2 3 4 5 6 7 8

Review

Match the shapes.

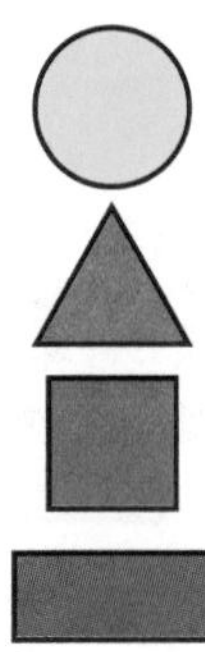

rectangle

square

circle

triangle

Look at the ruler. Measure the objects to the nearest inch.

_______ inch

_______ inch

_______ inch

Tell what time is on each clock.

__________ __________ __________ __________

Week 35 Skills

Subject	Skill	Multi-Sensory Learning Activities
Reading and Language Arts	Sequence and follow directions from reading passages.	• Complete Practice Pages 370–374. • Have your child write a paragraph describing the steps in a familiar process such as brushing teeth, preparing breakfast, or playing a game. Then, complete the task exactly as written to see if your child adequately described each step.
Math	Create and use graphs to determine information.	• Complete Practice Pages 375–378. • Provide pattern blocks or pattern block stickers. Tell your child to create a repeating design or picture with the shapes. On one-inch graph paper, help your child graph how many of each shape were used in the picture.
Bonus: Science		• On a sturdy surface, place a penny on a paper towel. Have your child predict how many drops of water will fit on the penny. Using an eyedropper, add and count drops of water until the water spills onto the paper towel. Allow your child to repeat the experiment with different variations, such as turning the penny over or using a nickel. Ask your child to observe the water on the penny and propose why he or she thinks the water acted as it did.

Following Directions: How to Treat a Ladybu

Read about how to treat ladybugs. Then, follow the instructions.

Ladybugs are shy. If you see a ladybug, sit very still. Hold out your arm. Maybe the ladybug will fly to you. If it does, talk softly. Do not touch it. It will fly away when it is ready.

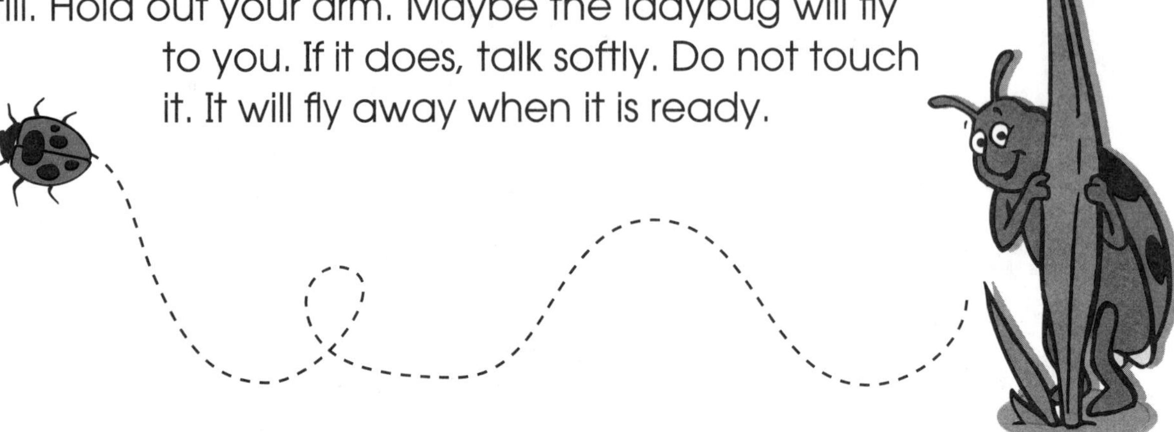

1. Complete the directions on how to treat a ladybug.

   a. Sit very still.

   b. ______________________________

   c. Talk softly.

   d. ______________________________

2. Ladybugs are red. They have black spots. Color the ladybug.

Sequencing: Make a Pencil Holder

Read how to make a pencil holder. Then, follow the instructions.

You can use "junk" to make a pencil holder! First, you need a clean can with one end removed. Make sure there are no sharp edges. Then, you need glue, scissors and paper. Find colorful paper such as wrapping paper, wallpaper or construction paper. Cut the paper to fit the can. Glue the paper around the can. Decorate your can with glitter, buttons and stickers. Then, put your pencils inside!

1. Write **first**, **second**, **third**, **fourth**, **fifth**, **sixth** and **seventh** to put the steps in order.

_______________ Make sure there are no sharp edges.

_______________ Get glue, scissors and paper.

_______________ Cut the paper to fit the can.

_______________ Put your pencils in the can!

_______________ Glue colorful paper to the can.

_______________ Remove one end of a clean can.

_______________ Decorate the can with glitter and stickers.

Sequencing: Follow a Recipe

Here is a recipe for chocolate peanut butter cookies. When you use recipe, you must follow the directions carefully. The sentences below are not in the correct order.

Write the number **1** to show what you would do first. Then, number each step to show the correct sequence.

_____________ Melt the chocolate almond bark in a microsafe bowl.

_____________ Eat!

_____________ While the chocolate is melting, spread peanut butter o a cracker and place another cracker on top.

_____________ Let the melted candy drip off the cracker into the bow before you place it on wax paper.

_____________ Let it cool!

_____________ Carefully use a fork or spoon to dip the crackers into th melted chocolate.

Try the recipe with an adult.

Do you like to cook? _____________

Sequencing: Making Clay

ead about making clay. Then, follow the instructions.

is fun to work with clay. Here is hat you need to make it:

cup salt

cups flour

cup water

Mix the salt and flour. Then, add the water. DO NOT eat the clay. tastes bad. Use your hands to mix and mix. Now, roll it out. What an you make with your clay?

Circle the main idea:

Do not eat clay.

Mix salt, flour and water to make clay.

Write the steps for making clay.

a.________________________________

b. ________________________________

c. Mix the clay.

d. ________________________________

Write why you should not eat clay. ____________________

____

Sequencing: Follow a Recipe

Alana and Marcus are hungry for a snack. They want to make nacho chips and cheese. The steps they need to follow are all mixed up.

Read the steps. Number them in 1, 2, 3 order. Then, color the picture.

____ Bake the chips in the oven for 2 minutes.

____ Get a cookie sheet to bake on.

____ Get out the nacho chips and cheese.

____ Eat the nachos and chips.

____ Put the chips on the cookie sheet.

____ Put grated cheese on the chips.

Honey Bear's Bakery

Fill in the graph to show how many of each treat are in the bakery.

Number of Bakery Treats

12						
11						
10						
9						
8						
7						
6						
5						
4						
3						
2						
1						

Turtle Spots

Color the boxes to show how many spots are on each turtle's shell.

1	2	3	4	5	6	7	8

1	2	3	4	5	6	7	8

1	2	3	4	5	6	7	8

1	2	3	4	5	6	7	8

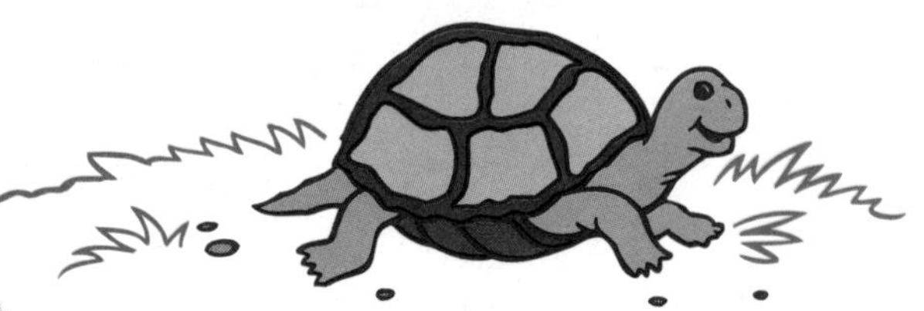

1	2	3	4	5	6	7	8

Food Fun

The table below tells what each animal brought to the picnic. Fill in the missing numbers.

Animal	Vegetables	Fruits	Total
Skunk		6	14
Raccoon	9		17
Squirrel		8	15
Rabbit	6		13
Owl	7		16
Deer		9	18

Write the name of the animal that answers each question.

1. Who brought the same number of vegetables as fruits? ____________

2. Who brought two more fruits than vegetables? ____________

3. Who brought two more vegetables than fruits? ____________

4. Which two animals brought one more fruit than vegetables?

   ____________ and ____________

5. Which two animals brought the most vegetables?

   ____________ and ____________

6. Which two animals brought the most fruit?

   ____________ and ____________

7. Which animal brought the least vegetables? ____________

8. Which animal brought the least fruit? ____________

Television Survey

Ask five people how many hours of television they watch each day. Record the information on the bar graph. Refer to your graph to answer the questions below.

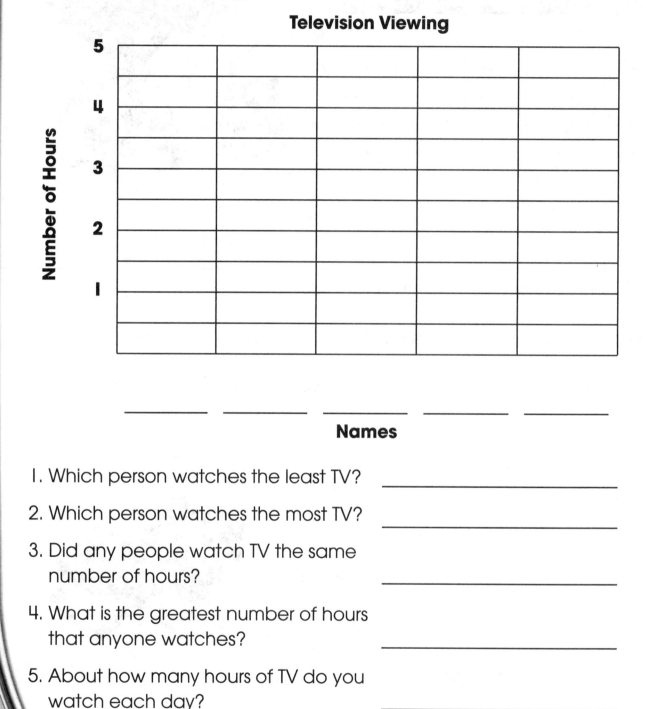

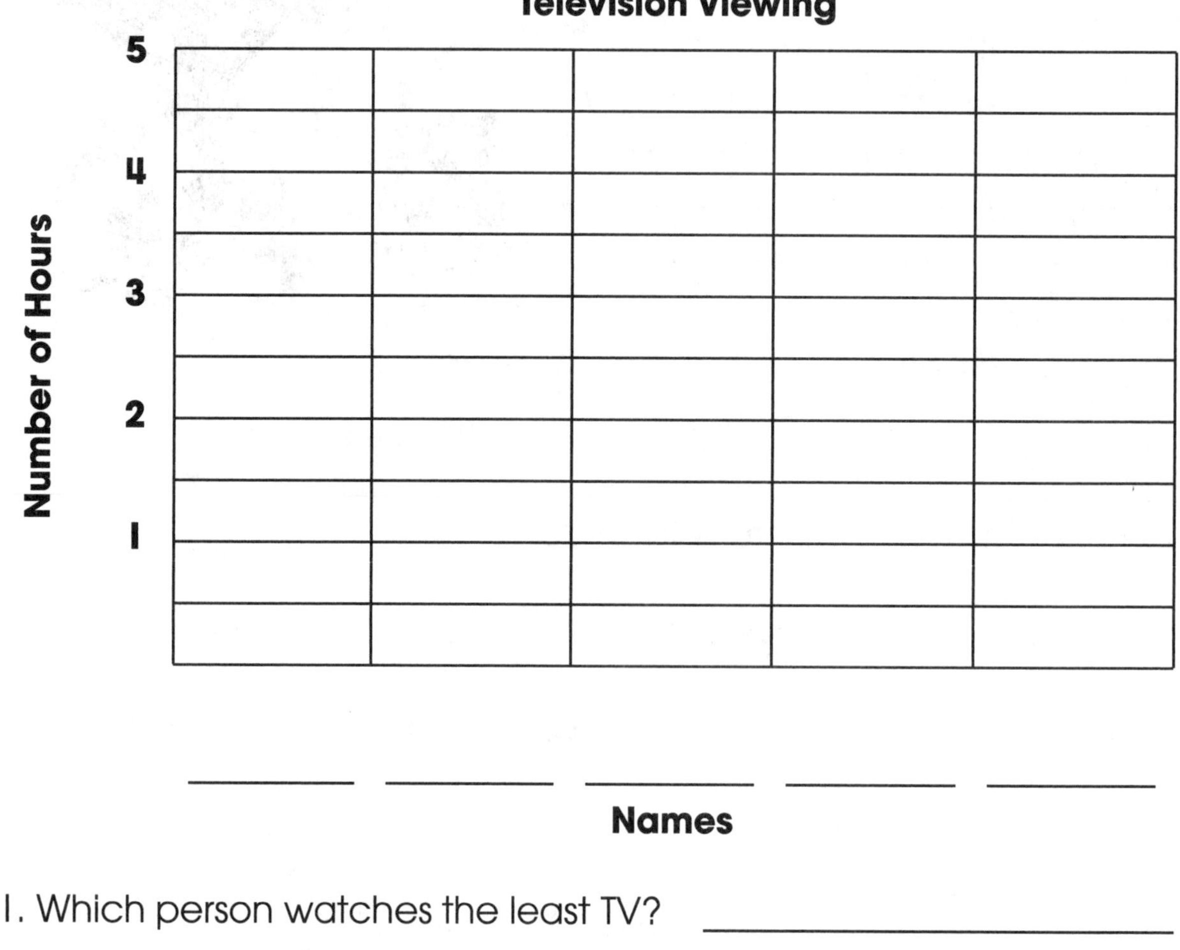

1. Which person watches the least TV? ____________________
2. Which person watches the most TV? ____________________
3. Did any people watch TV the same number of hours? ____________________
4. What is the greatest number of hours that anyone watches? ____________________
5. About how many hours of TV do you watch each day? ____________________

Week 36 Skills

Subject	Skill	Multi-Sensory Learning Activities
Reading and Language Arts	Answer questions about texts to demonstrate reading comprehension.	• Complete Practice Pages 380–384. • Read *Arthur Makes the Team* by Marc Brown with your child. Ask questions to assess comprehension and challenge your child to research more information on a topic related to the book.
Math	Review graphs.	• Complete Practice Pages 385–388. • Have your child make a picture graph to show how many pens, markers, and pencils are found in a desk drawer or junk drawer. Discuss and compare the information shown on the graph. For example, your child may say, "There are ____ more pencils than pens. There are _____ markers and pens together."
Bonus: Social Studies		• Ask your child to define **communication**. Have your child play with a friend for 15 minutes without speaking to demonstrate that communication doesn't necessarily mean words spoken aloud. Then, discuss the fact that communication involves two people: a sender and a receiver. Is there communication if the receiver ignores or doesn't understand the message?

Fiction: Hercules

The **setting** is where a story takes place. The characters are the people in a story or play.

Read about Hercules. Then, answer the questions.

Hercules was born in the warm Atlantic Ocean. He was a very small and weak baby. He wanted to be the strongest hurricane in the world. But he had one problem. He couldn't blow 75-mile-per-hour winds. Hercules blew and blew in the ocean, until one day, his sister, Hola, told him it would be more fun to be a breeze than a hurricane. Hercules agreed. It was a breeze to be a breeze!

1. What is the setting of the story? ______________________

2. Who are the characters? ______________________

3. What is the problem? ______________________

4. How does Hercules solve his problem? ______________________

____

Comprehension: The Puppet Play

Read the play out loud with a friend. Then, answer the questions.

Pip: Hey, Pep. What kind of turkey eats very fast?

Pep: Uh, I don't know.

Pip: A gobbler!

Pep: I have a good joke for you, Pip. What kind of burger does a polar bear eat?

Pip: Uh, a cold burger?

Pep: No, an iceberg-er!

Pip: Hey, that was a great joke!

1. Who are the characters in the play? ______________________________

____

2. Who are the jokes about? ______________________________

____

3. What are the characters in the play doing? ______________________________

____

Comprehension: Sean's Basketball Gam

Read about Sean's basketball game. Then, answer the questions.

Sean really likes to play basketball. One sunny day, he decided to ask his friends to play basketball at the park, but there were six people—Sean, Aki, Lance, Kate, Zac and Oralia. A basketball team only allows five to play at a time. So, Sean decided to be the coach. Sean and his friends had fun.

1. How many kids wanted to play basketball? ____________________

2. Write their names in ABC order:

____________________ ____________________ ____________________

____________________ ____________________ ____________________

3. How many players can play on a basketball team at a time? ____________________

4. Where did they play basketball? ____________________

5. Who decided to be the coach? ____________________

Comprehension: Amazing Ants

Read about ants. Then, answer the questions.

Ants are insects. Ants live in many parts of the world and make their homes in soil, sand, wood and leaves. Most ants live for about 6 to 10 weeks. But the queen ant, who lays the eggs, can live for up to 15 years!

The largest ant is the bulldog ant. This ant can grow to be 5 inches long, and it eats meat! The bulldog ant can be found in Australia.

1. Where do ants make their homes? ______________________________

____

2. How long can a queen ant live? ______________________________

____

3. What is the largest ant? ______________________________

4. What does it eat? ______________________________

Comprehension: Dirty Dogs

Read about dogs. Then, answer the questions.

Like people, dogs get dirty. Some dogs get a bath once a month. Baby soap is a good soap for cleaning dogs. Fill a tub with warm water. Get someone to hold the dog still in the tub. Then, wash the dog fast.

1. How often do some dogs get a bath? ______________________

____

2. What is a good soap to use on dogs? ______________________

3. Do you think most dogs like to take baths?______________________

Graphs

A **graph** is a drawing that shows information about numbers.

Count the apples in each row. Color the boxes to show how many apples have bites taken out of them.

Example:

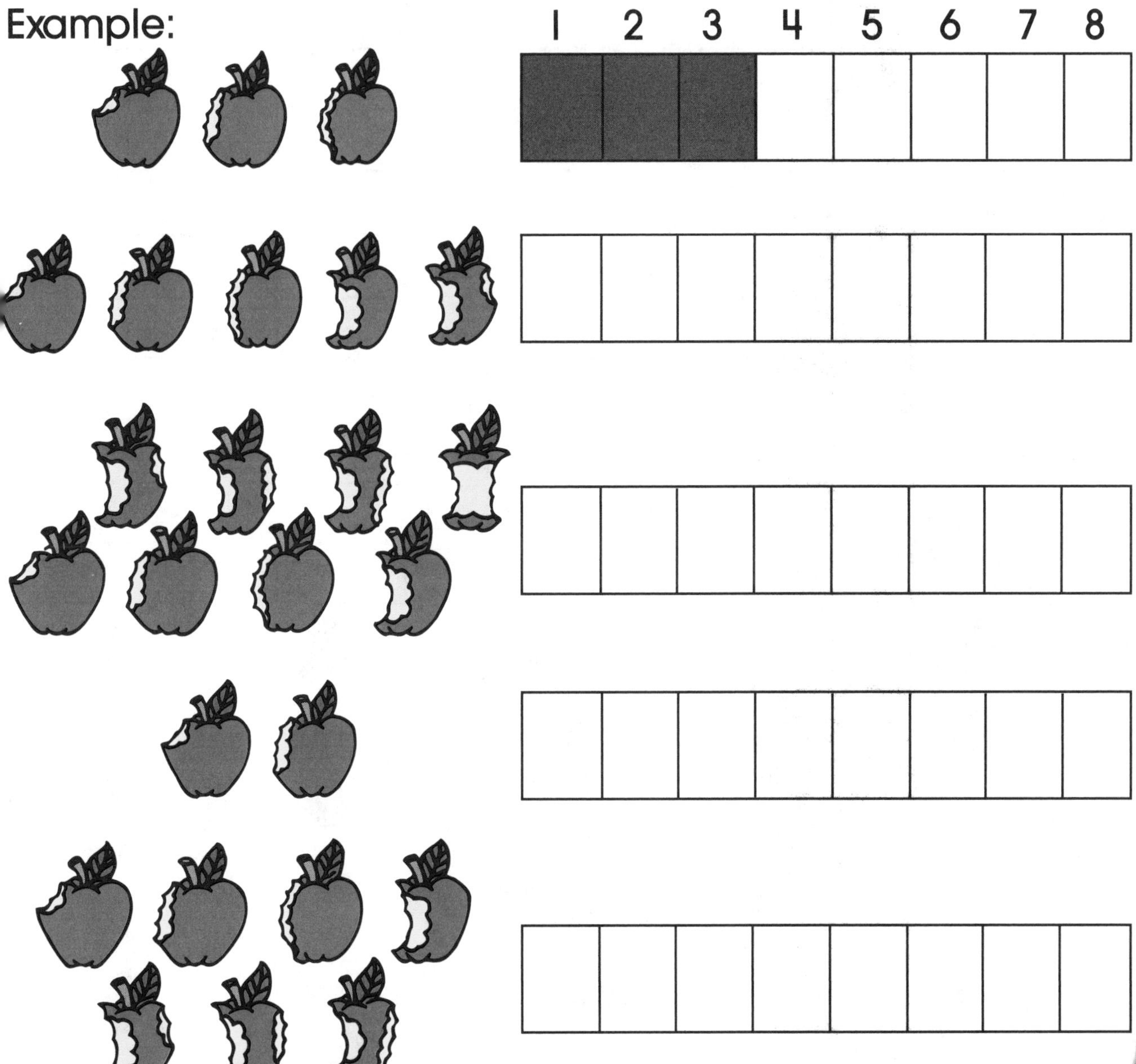

Graphs

Count the bananas in each row. Color the boxes to show how many have been eaten by the monkeys.

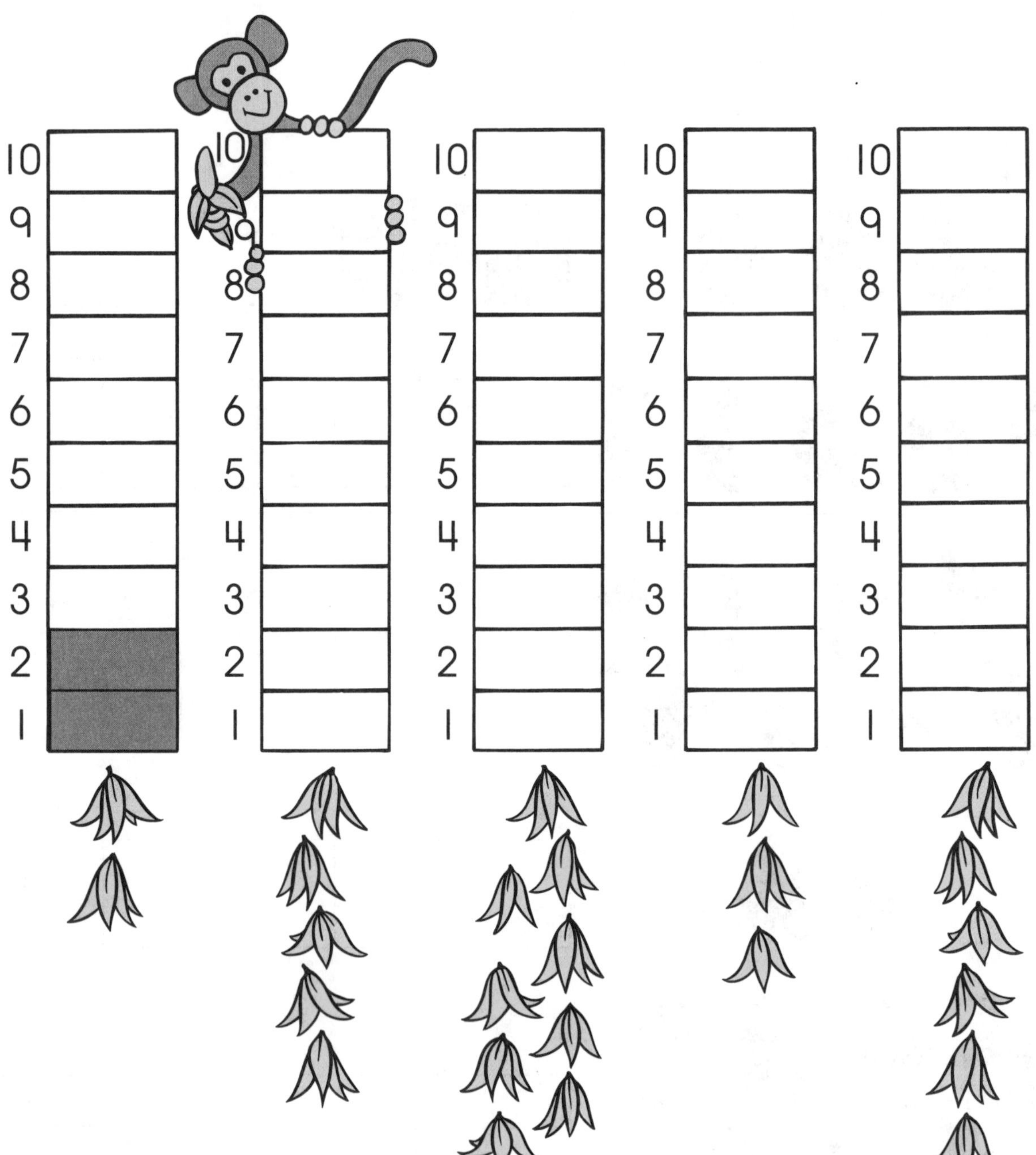

Graphs

Count the fish. Color the bowls to make a graph that shows the number of fish.

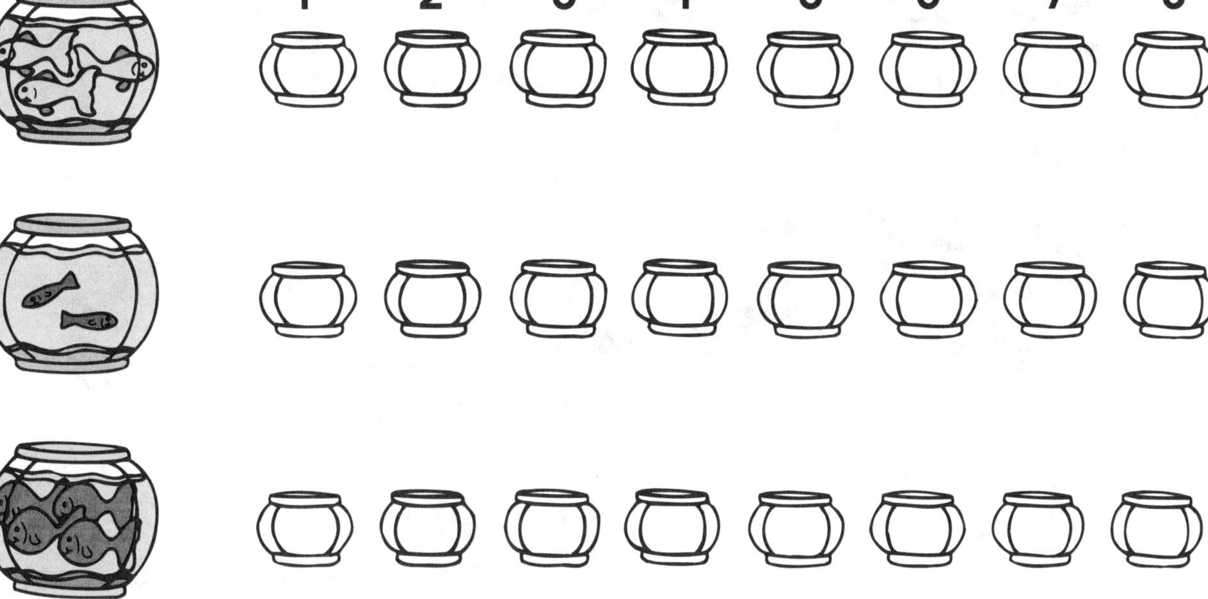

Use your fishbowl graphs to find the answers to the following questions. Draw a line to the correct bowl.

The most fish

The fewest fish

Amy's Things

Fill in the table. Then, answer the questions.

Toy	How Many?

1. How many books and balls are there altogether? ____________
2. How many more teddy bears are there than cars? ____________
3. Are there more dolls or animals? ____________
4. Amy has 4 more ____________ than ____________ .
5. Are there enough cars for each doll? ____________

Fourth Quarter Check-Up

Reading and Language Arts

- ❑ I can add an apostrophe to show ownership in possessive nouns.
- ❑ I can identify statements, questions, commands, and exclamations.
- ❑ I can combine two sentences into one.
- ❑ I can choose words to complete sentences.
- ❑ I understand different characters' points of view.
- ❑ I understand and can identify the subject and predicate of a sentence.
- ❑ I understand compound subjects and compound predicates.
- ❑ I know dictionary skills.
- ❑ I can sequence and follow directions from reading passages.
- ❑ I can answer questions about texts to demonstrate reading comprehension.

Math

- ❑ I can work with wholes, halves, thirds, and fourths.
- ❑ I can solve word problems involving fractions.
- ❑ I can measure in inches and centimeters.
- ❑ I understand liquid measurements.
- ❑ I can create and use graphs to determine information.

Final Project

Collect data and write at least one question you want to answer from the data. Questions may include: Are there more raisins, nuts, or pieces of cereal in this bag of trail mix? How many more blue blocks than red blocks are in this set of blocks? If I collect all the shoes in this closet, how many will there be of each kind? After the information is gathered, graph the data on a bar graph or line graph. Talk with a friend or adult about the information shown on the graph. Then, write at least three statements describing your results.

Student Reference

Aa Bb Cc Dd Ee Ff Gg Hh Ii
Jj Kk Ll Mm Nn Oo Pp Qq Rr
Ss Tt Uu Vv Ww Xx Yy Zz

0 1 2 3 4 5 6 7 8 9 10

Common Consonant Blends

bl	br	tr	sn
cl	cr	sk	sp
fl	dr	sl	st
sl	pr	sm	sw

Common Consonant Digraphs

ch	sh	th	wh

Second Grade Sight Words

always	first	right	very
because	gave	tell	which
before	goes	their	why
does	made	these	would
don't	or	those	your

Recommended Read-Alouds for Second Grade

Tales Our Abuelitas Told: A Hispanic Folktale Collection by F. Isabel Campoy and Alma Flor Ada

My Dad's a Birdman by David Almond

Drooling and Dangerous: The Riot Brothers Return! by Mary Amato

Michael Recycle by Ellie Bethel

The Seven Treasure Hunts by Betsy Byars

It's Test Day, Tiger Turcotte by Pansie Hart Flood

My Father's Dragon by Ruth Stiles Gannett

The Flyer Flew! The Invention of the Airplane by Lee Sullivan Hill

The Puppy Sister by S.E. Hinton

Nim's Island by Wendy Orr

What Presidents Are Made Of by Hanoch Piven

The Busy Body Book: A Kid's Guide to Fitness by Lizzy Rockwell

Paint the Wind by Pam Muñoz Ryan

Water Hole by Zahavit Shalev

Chig and the Second Spread by Gwenyth Swain

Could You? Would You? By Trudy White

Ordinal Numbers

First

Second

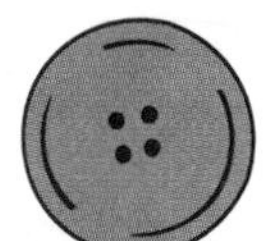
Third

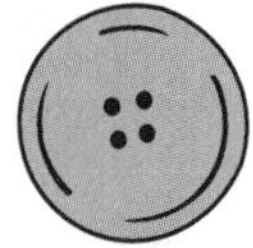
Fourth

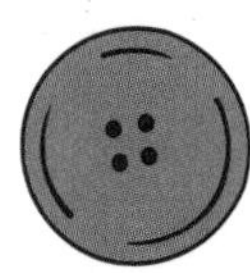
Fifth

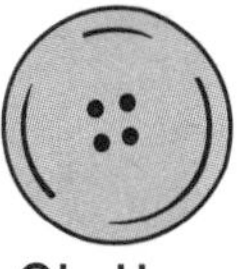
Sixth

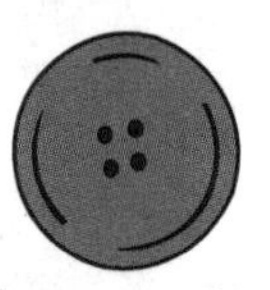
Seventh

Eighth

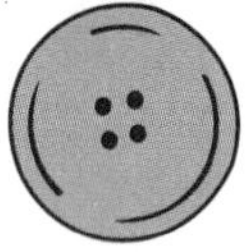
Ninth

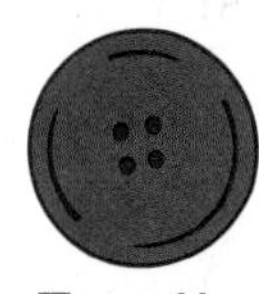
Tenth

Two-Dimensional Shapes

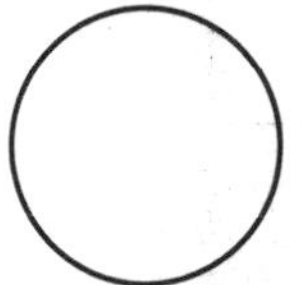
Circle

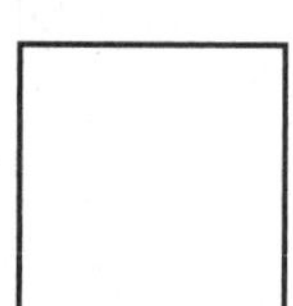
Square

Triangle

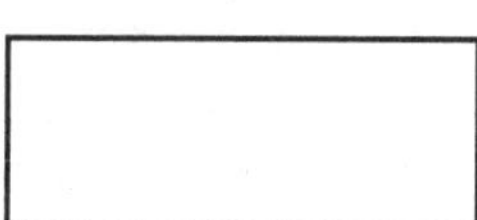
Rectangle

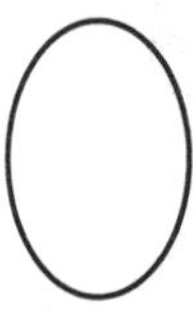
Oval

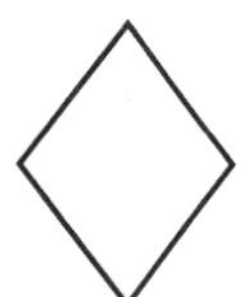
Rhombus

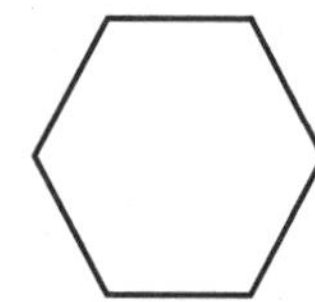
Hexagon

Octagon

Three-Dimensional Shapes

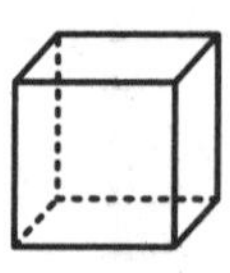
Cube

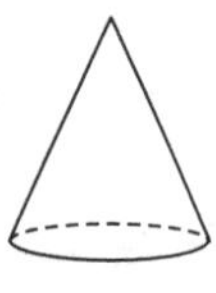
Cone

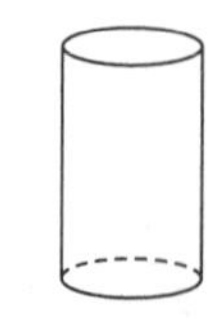
Cylinder

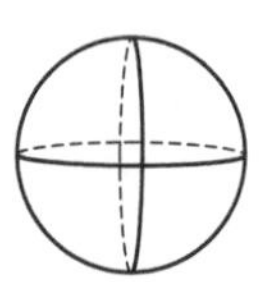
Sphere

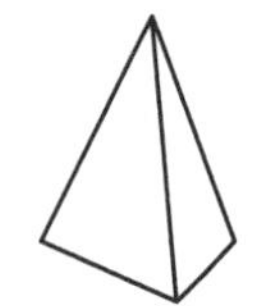
Pyramid

Hundred Chart

1	2	3	4	5	6	7	8	9	10
11	12	13	14	15	16	17	18	19	20
21	22	23	24	25	26	27	28	29	30
31	32	33	34	35	36	37	38	39	40
41	42	43	44	45	46	47	48	49	50
51	52	53	54	55	56	57	58	59	60
61	62	63	64	65	66	67	68	69	70
71	72	73	74	75	76	77	78	79	80
81	82	83	84	85	86	87	88	89	90
91	92	93	94	95	96	97	98	99	100

Student Reference, cont.

Money

Penny

Nickel

Dime

Quarter

Dollar

Time

Fractions

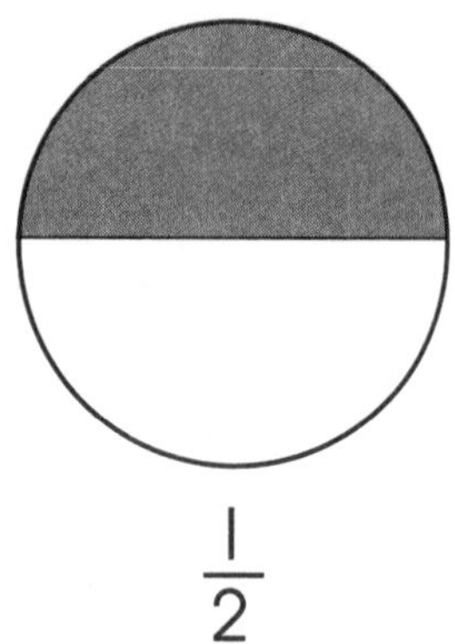
$\frac{1}{2}$

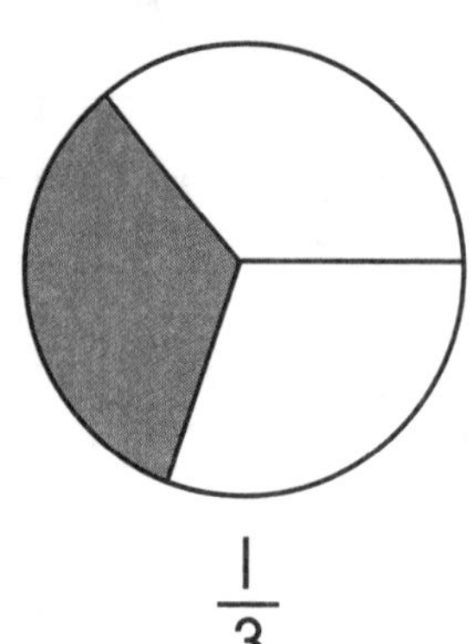
$\frac{1}{3}$

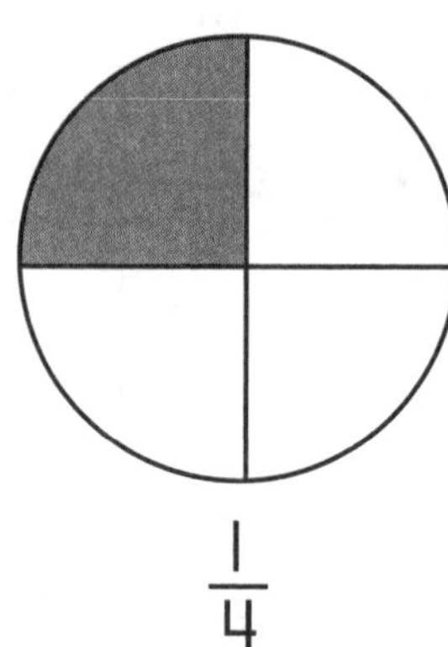
$\frac{1}{4}$

Measurement

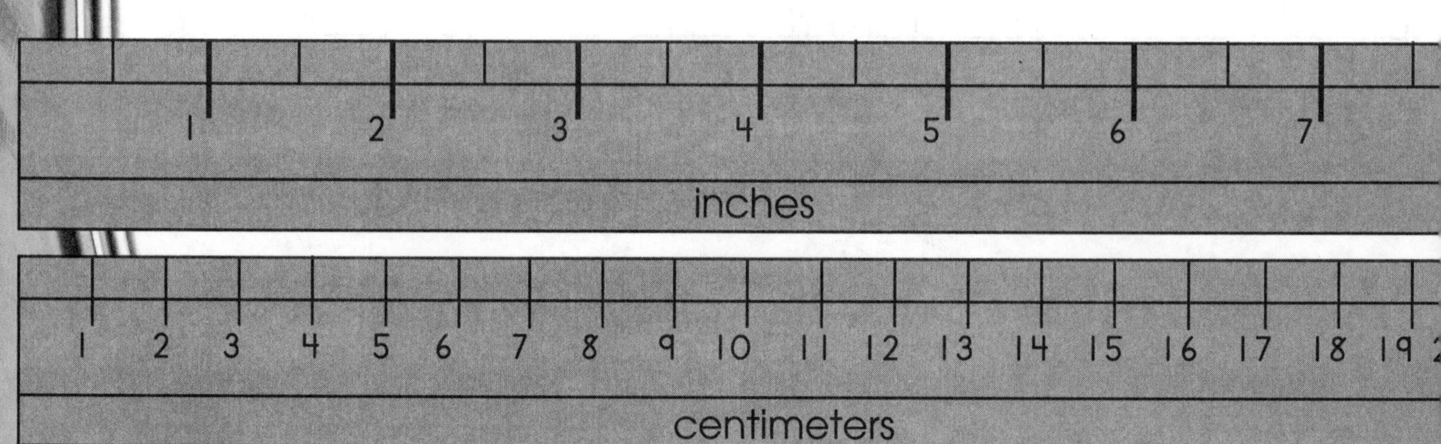

Answer Key

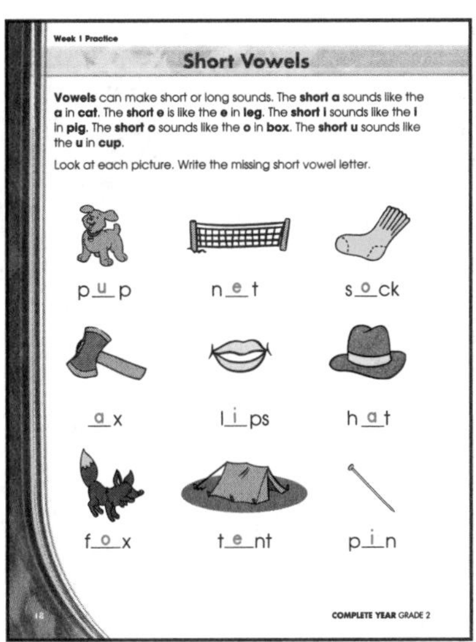

Week 1 Practice

Short Vowels

Vowels can make short or long sounds. The **short a** sounds like the **a** in **cat**. The **short e** is like the **e** in **leg**. The **short i** sounds like the **i** in **pig**. The **short o** sounds like the **o** in **box**. The **short u** sounds like the **u** in **cup**.

Look at each picture. Write the missing short vowel letter.

pup net sock

ax lips hat

fox tent pin

COMPLETE YEAR GRADE 2

18

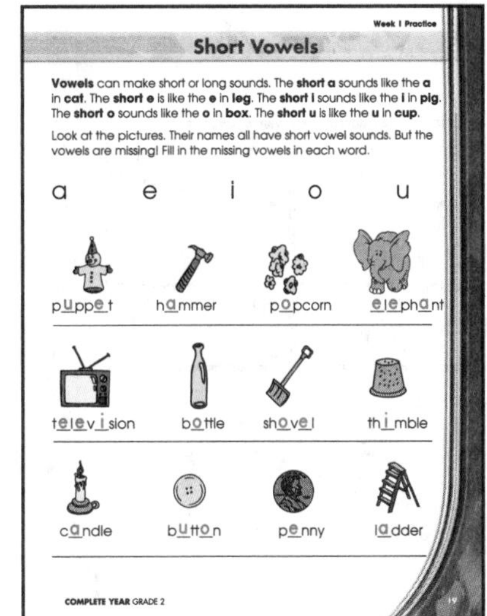

Week 1 Practice

Short Vowels

Vowels can make short or long sounds. The **short a** sounds like the **a** in **cat**. The **short e** is like the **e** in **leg**. The **short i** sounds like the **i** in **pig**. The **short o** sounds like the **o** in **box**. The **short u** is like the **u** in **cup**.

Look at the pictures. Their names all have short vowel sounds. But the vowels are missing! Fill in the missing vowels in each word.

a e i o u

puppet hammer popcorn elephant

television bottle shovel thimble

candle button penny ladder

COMPLETE YEAR GRADE 2

19

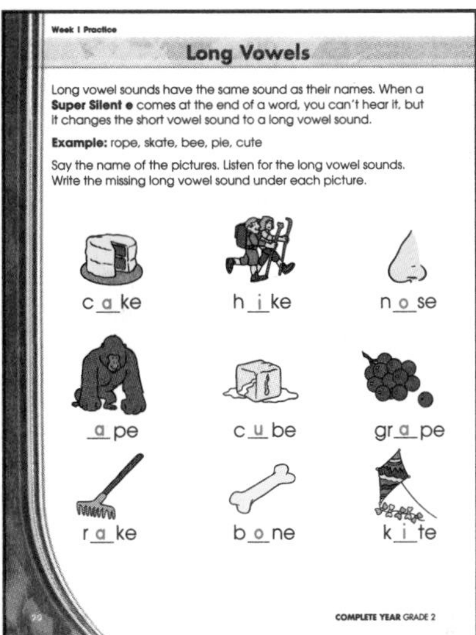

Week 1 Practice

Long Vowels

Long vowel sounds have the same sound as their names. When a **Super Silent e** comes at the end of a word, you can't hear it, but it changes the short vowel sound to a long vowel sound.

Example: rope, skate, bee, pie, cute

Say the name of the pictures. Listen for the long vowel sounds. Write the missing long vowel sound under each picture.

cake hike nose

ape cube grape

rake bone kite

COMPLETE YEAR GRADE 2

20

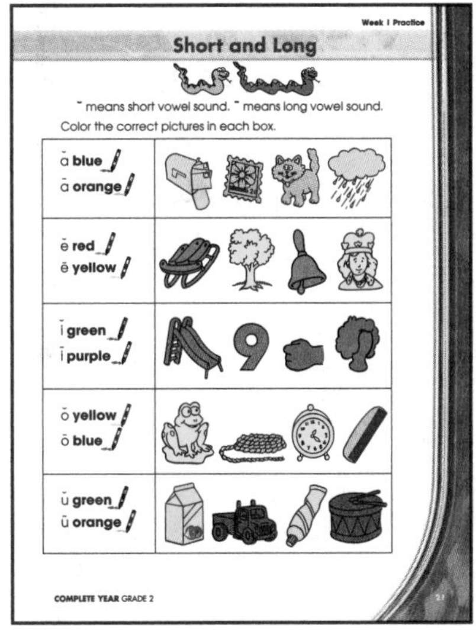

Week 1 Practice

Short and Long

˘ means short vowel sound. ¯ means long vowel sound.

Color the correct pictures in each box.

ă blue, ā orange

ĕ red, ē yellow

ĭ green, ī purple

ŏ yellow, ō blue

ŭ green, ū orange

COMPLETE YEAR GRADE 2

21

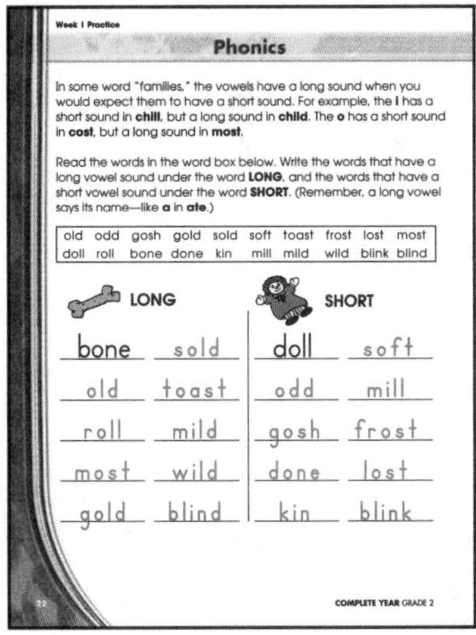

Week 1 Practice

Phonics

In some word "families," the vowels have a long sound when you would expect them to have a short sound. For example, the **i** has a short sound in **chill**, but a long sound in **child**. The **o** has a short sound in **cost**, but a long sound in **most**.

Read the words in the word box below. Write the words that have a long vowel sound under the word **LONG**, and the words that have a short vowel sound under the word **SHORT**. (Remember, a long vowel says its name—like **a** in **ate**.)

old odd gosh gold sold soft toast frost lost most
doll roll bone done kin mill mild wild blink blind

LONG		SHORT	
bone	sold	doll	soft
old	toast	odd	mill
roll	mild	gosh	frost
most	wild	done	lost
gold	blind	kin	blink

COMPLETE YEAR GRADE 2

22

Week 1 Practice

Numbers and Number Words

The word **teen** means "and ten" and **ty** means "tens."

Example: Sixteen means **six and ten**. **Sixty** means **six tens**.

Cut out the word endings and glue them to end the correct numbers.

90	nine ty	13	thir teen
17	seven teen	14	four teen
30	thir ty	40	for ty
19	nine teen	20	twen ty
70	seven ty	15	fif teen
		16	six teen
		60	six ty
		18	eigh teen
		50	fif ty
		80	eigh ty

ty ty ty
ty ty ty
ty ty teen
teen teen teen
teen teen teen

COMPLETE YEAR GRADE 2

23

Answer Key

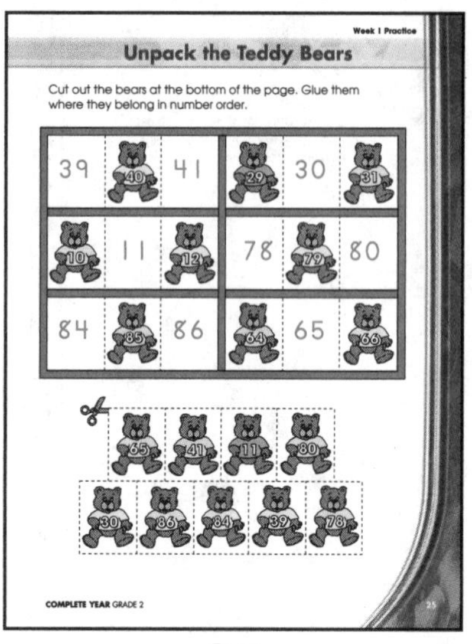
Week 1 Practice

Unpack the Teddy Bears

Cut out the bears at the bottom of the page. Glue them where they belong in number order.

39 40 41 | 29 30 31

10 11 12 | 78 79 80

84 85 86 | 64 65 66

COMPLETE YEAR GRADE 2

25

Week 2 Practice

Sail Away

way pain rain
wait pay say lay
sail day nail

Write the **ai** words that make the **long a** sound.
pain wait nail
rain sail

Write the **ay** words that make the **long a** sound.
way say day
pay lay

Write the missing words in the boxes.

1. It is a good ___ to fly a kite. day
2. Did Mom ___ we may go to the show? say
3. Please ___ here for the bus. wait
4. Sam does not know which ___ to go now. way
5. Ray and Mable will ___ for the tickets. pay
6. Be careful when you hammer the ___ in the wall. nail
7. The ___ splashed in the puddles. rain
8. You may ___ your toy boat in the pond. sail
9. She felt ___ when the bee stung her. pain
10. Please ___ the blankets on the bed. lay

COMPLETE YEAR GRADE 2

28

Week 2 Practice

Catch an Act!

gas mad bag
sat rag had bat
pat bad wag

Write the words that rhyme with each picture.
bag rag wag | bat pat sat | bad mad had

Write the word that did not rhyme. gas

Write the missing words in the boxes.

1. There was no sound when the ___ flew through the cave. bat
2. Be sure to ___ the pie crust into the pan carefully. pat
3. Brad was ___ at his dog when it chewed his mitt. mad
4. The storm was so ___ that it knocked down the trees. bad
5. The puppy likes to jump up and ___ its tail when it meets you. wag
6. Pam ___ to walk home in the rain. had
7. The car is almost out of ___. gas
8. They ___ in the front row. sat
9. The clerk put the box of shoes in the ___. bag
10. Use that old ___ to wipe the dirt off your boots. rag

COMPLETE YEAR GRADE 2

29

Week 2 Practice

Seeing the Sea Life

neat read eat
sea mean seat beam
team meat lean

Write the two letters that make the **long e** sound. ea

Write the words that rhyme with each word below. Circle the letters in each word that make the same sound.

1. wheat — neat, eat, seat, meat
2. tea — sea
3. seam — beam, team
4. bead — read
5. bean — mean, lean

Write the correct word from the word box.

1. Another word for ocean — sea
2. Opposite of **messy** — neat
3. Flashlights throw a ___ of light. — beam
4. You sit on this. — seat
5. You use books to do this. — read
6. Something you can eat — meat
7. You use your mouth to do this. — eat
8. A group of players — team
9. Opposite of **kind** — mean
10. Ladders do this against the side of a house. — lean

COMPLETE YEAR GRADE 2

30

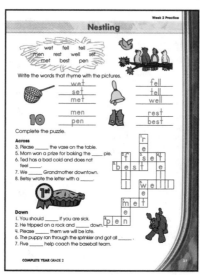

Week 2 Practice

Nestling

wet fell tell
men rest well set
met best pen

Write the words that rhyme with the pictures.
wet set met | fell tell well
men pen | rest best

Complete the puzzle.

Across
3. Please ___ the vase on the table.
5. Mom won a prize for baking the ___ pie.
6. Ted has a bad cold and does not feel ___.
7. We ___ Grandmother downtown.
8. Betsy wrote the letter with a ___.

Down
1. You should ___ if you are sick.
2. He tripped on a rock and ___ down.
4. Please ___ them we will be late.
6. The puppy ran through the sprinkler and got all ___.
7. Five ___ help coach the baseball team.

rest, fell, set, best, tell, well, wet, met, men, pen

COMPLETE YEAR GRADE 2

31

Week 2 Practice

It's a Dilly!

fix still sit
win fin fit hit
will hill bill

Write the words that rhyme with the pictures. Circle the letters that rhyme.
still will hill bill
sit fit hit
win fin

Write the word that did not rhyme. fix

Write the missing words in the boxes.

1. The cat stood ___ as the dog walked by him. still
2. Do the new shoes ___ you? fit
3. My sister helped me ___ the broken toy. fix
4. When ___ we go on our trip? will
5. Willy wants his friend to ___ the contest. win
6. We walked to the top of the ___. hill
7. Minna swung the bat and ___ the ball into the field. hit
8. Some cans are made of ___. tin
9. Mom paid the phone ___. bill
10. We want to ___ next to each other. sit

COMPLETE YEAR GRADE 2

32

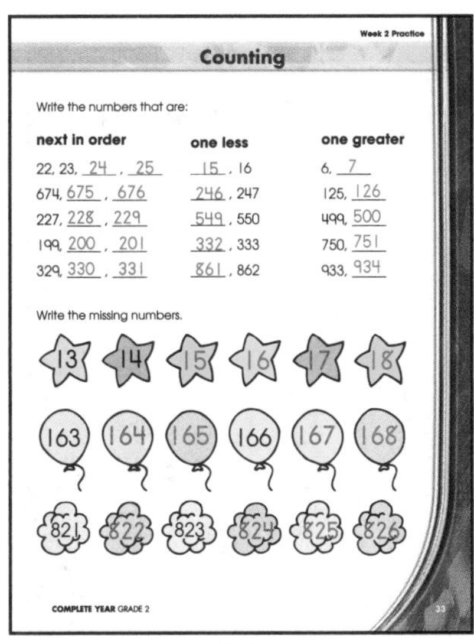
Week 2 Practice

Counting

Write the numbers that are:

next in order	**one less**	**one greater**
22, 23, 24, 25	15, 16	6, 7
674, 675, 676	246, 247	125, 126
227, 228, 229	549, 550	499, 500
199, 200, 201	332, 333	750, 751
329, 330, 331	861, 862	933, 934

Write the missing numbers.

13 14 15 16 17 18

163 164 165 166 167 168

821 822 823 824 825 826

COMPLETE YEAR GRADE 2 33

33

Week 2 Practice

Sequencing Numbers

Sequencing is putting numbers in the correct order.

1, 2, 3, 4, 5, 6, 7, 8, 9, 10

Write the missing numbers.

Example: 4, 5, 6

3, 4, 5 — 7, 8, 9 — 8, 9, 10

6, 7, 8 — 2, 3, 4 — 4, 5, 6

5, 6, 7 — 5, 6, 7 — 2, 3, 4

3, 4, 5 — 6, 7, 8 — 5, 6, 7

2, 3, 4 — 1, 2, 3 — 7, 8, 9

2, 3, 4 — 1, 2, 3 — 4, 5, 6

6, 7, 8 — 3, 4, 5 — 1, 2, 3

7, 8, 9 — 2, 3, 4 — 8, 9, 10

34 COMPLETE YEAR GRADE 2

34

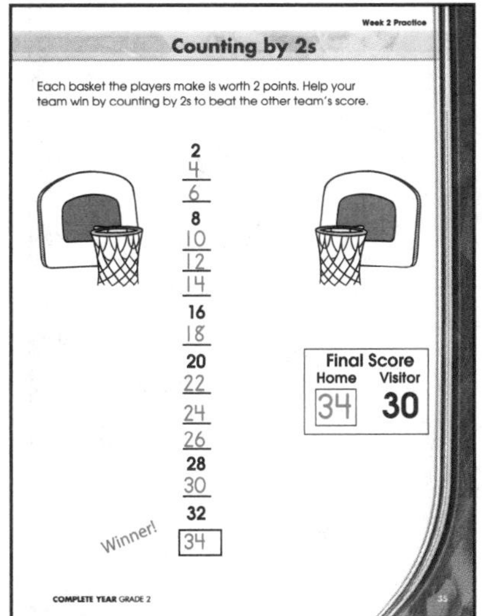
Week 2 Practice

Counting by 2s

Each basket the players make is worth 2 points. Help your team win by counting by 2s to beat the other team's score.

2, 4, 6, 8, 10, 12, 14, 16, 18, 20, 22, 24, 26, 28, 30, 32, 34

Winner!

Final Score

Home	Visitor
34	30

COMPLETE YEAR GRADE 2 35

35

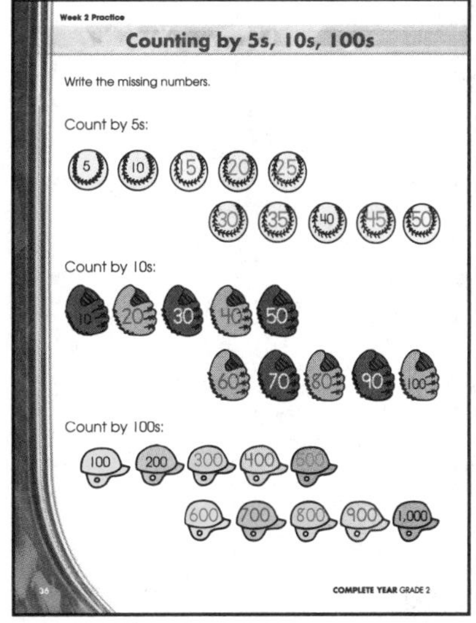
Week 2 Practice

Counting by 5s, 10s, 100s

Write the missing numbers.

Count by 5s:

5 10 15 20 25 30 35 40 45 50

Count by 10s:

10 20 30 40 50 60 70 80 90 100

Count by 100s:

100 200 300 400 500 600 700 800 900 1,000

36 COMPLETE YEAR GRADE 2

36

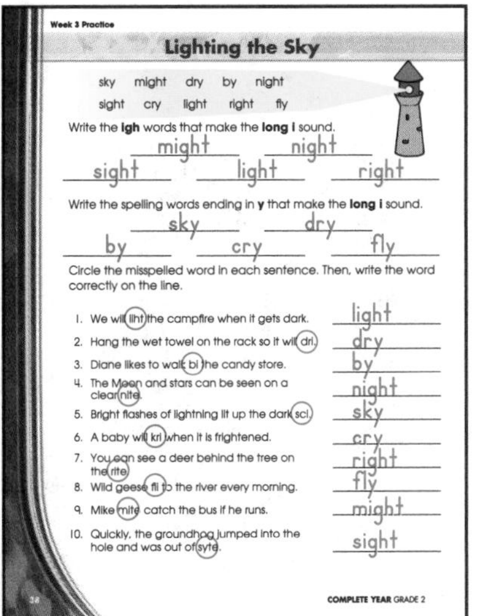
Week 3 Practice

Lighting the Sky

sky might dry by night
sight cry light right fly

Write the **igh** words that make the **long i** sound.

might night sight light right

Write the spelling words ending in **y** that make the **long i** sound.

sky dry by cry fly

Circle the misspelled word in each sentence. Then, write the word correctly on the line.

1. We will lint the campfire when it gets dark. — light
2. Hang the wet towel on the rack so it will dri. — dry
3. Diane likes to walk bi the candy store. — by
4. The Moon and stars can be seen on a clear nite. — night
5. Bright flashes of lightning lit up the dark sci. — sky
6. A baby will kri when it is frightened. — cry
7. You can see a deer behind the tree on the rite. — right
8. Wild geese fli to the river every morning. — fly
9. Mike mite catch the bus if he runs. — might
10. Quickly, the groundhog jumped into the hole and was out of syte. — sight

38 COMPLETE YEAR GRADE 2

38

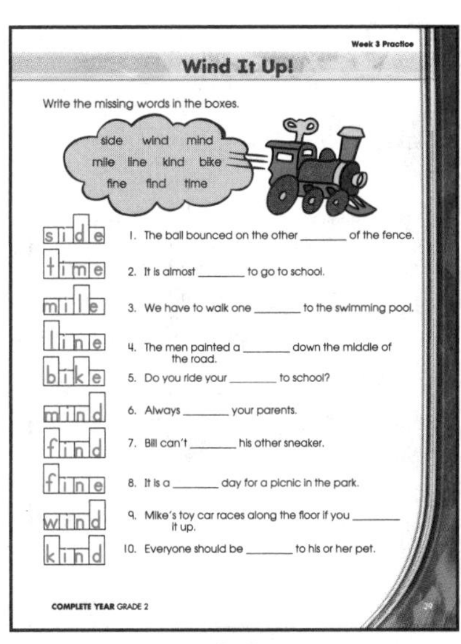
Week 3 Practice

Wind It Up!

Write the missing words in the boxes.

side wind mind
mile line kind bike
fine find time

1. side — The ball bounced on the other ______ of the fence.
2. time — It is almost ______ to go to school.
3. mile — We have to walk one ______ to the swimming pool.
4. line — The men painted a ______ down the middle of the road.
5. bike — Do you ride your ______ to school?
6. mind — Always ______ your parents.
7. find — Bill can't ______ his other sneaker.
8. fine — It is a ______ day for a picnic in the park.
9. wind — Mike's toy car races along the floor if you ______ it up.
10. kind — Everyone should be ______ to his or her pet.

COMPLETE YEAR GRADE 2 39

39

Answer Key

Week 3 Practice

Sow and Grow

sow own hope know show
woke hole grow joke pole

Write the words ending with **e** that make the **long o** sound.

hope woke hole
joke pole

Write the **ow** words that make the **long o** sound.

sow own know
show grow

Read each sentence. Write the missing word on the line.

1. We all laughed at the funny joke.
2. Did you show your mother your pictures?
3. The loud siren woke up the baby.
4. He wants to use his own bike for the race tomorrow.
5. Water and sunshine will make the plants grow.
6. A tiny gray mouse ran into the hole in the ground.
7. They will sow the corn seeds in the spring.
8. Grace helped raise the flag to the top of the pole.
9. Does she know that her report is due today?
10. Cole and Roberta hope that they did well on the test.

COMPLETE YEAR GRADE 2

40

Week 3 Practice

Loading Cargo

coat road fold gold boat
told cold load hold goat

Write the words with **o** followed by **ld** that make the **long o** sound.

fold gold told
cold hold

Write the **oa** words that make the **long o** sound.

coat road boat
load goat

Complete the puzzle.

Across

1. An animal
3. Opposite of **hot**
6. A ship
7. To fill
8. A street

Down

1. You use it to make jewelry.
2. Did tell
3. Something to wear
4. You use your hands to do this.
5. To bend something over

COMPLETE YEAR GRADE 2

41

Week 3 Practice

Submerging Subs

sub but sun
run bus fun nut
cut tub cup

Write the words that rhyme. Circle the letters in each word that make the same sound.

1. bun — sun, run, fun
2. rub — sub, tub
3. hut — but, nut, cut
4. pup — cup
5. us — bus

Write the correct word on each line.

1. To move very fast. run
2. Some kids ride to school in one of these. bus
3. It is in the sky and gives off heat and light. sun
4. A party can be this. fun
5. You do this with a knife. cut
6. You drink out of this. cup
7. A boat that goes under the water. sub
8. You can eat this for a snack. nut
9. One kitten is sleeping, the other is playing. but
10. You take a bath in this. tub

COMPLETE YEAR GRADE 2

42

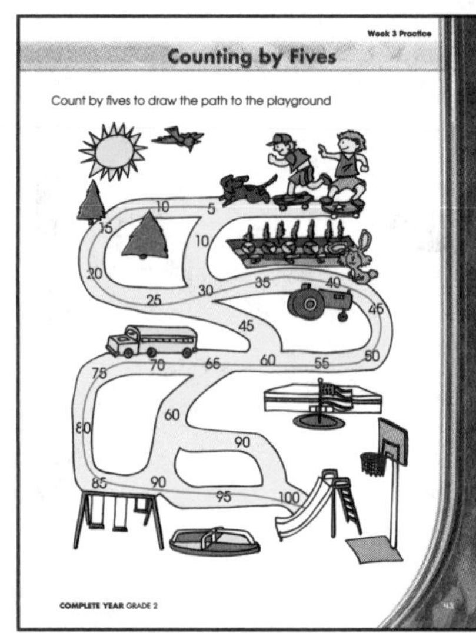
Week 3 Practice

Counting by Fives

Count by fives to draw the path to the playground

COMPLETE YEAR GRADE 2

43

Week 3 Practice

Counting by Fives

Use tally marks to count to fives. Write the number next to the tallies.

Example: A tally mark stands for one = I. Five tally marks look like this = 𝍸

5, 10, 15, 20, 25, 30, 35, 40, 45, 50

COMPLETE YEAR GRADE 2

44

Week 3 Practice

Counting by Tens

Count by tens to draw the path the boy takes to the store.

COMPLETE YEAR GRADE 2

45

Answer Key

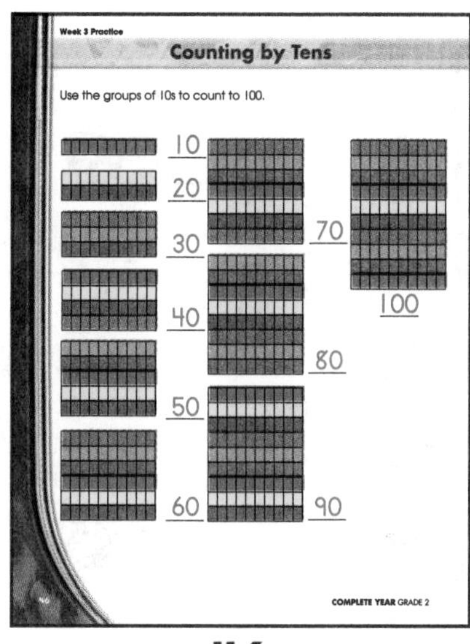

Week 3 Practice

Counting by Tens

Use the groups of 10s to count to 100.

10, 20, 30, 40, 50, 60, 70, 80, 90, 100

COMPLETE YEAR GRADE 2

46

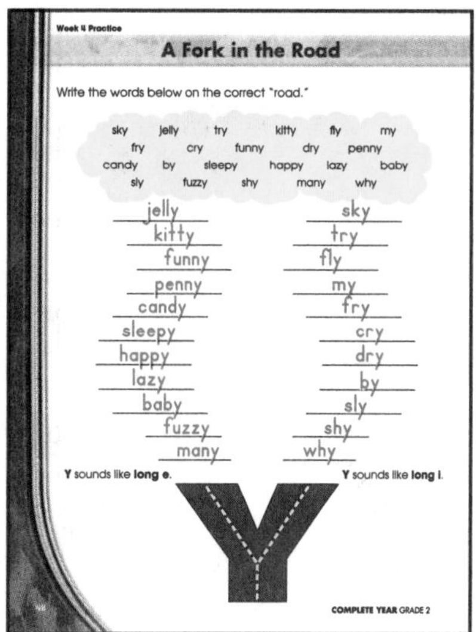

Week 4 Practice

A Fork in the Road

Write the words below on the correct "road."

sky jelly try kitty fly my
fry cry funny dry penny
candy by sleepy happy lazy baby
sly fuzzy shy many why

Y sounds like **long e**.	Y sounds like **long i**.
jelly	sky
kitty	try
funny	fly
penny	my
candy	fry
sleepy	cry
happy	dry
lazy	by
baby	sly
fuzzy	shy
many	why

COMPLETE YEAR GRADE 2

48

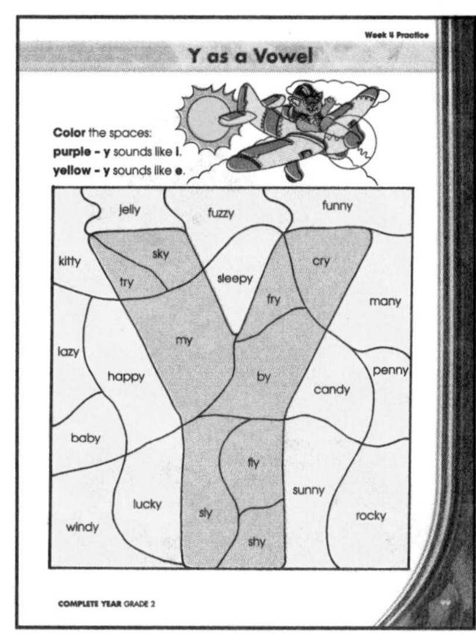

Week 4 Practice

Y as a Vowel

Color the spaces:
purple - y sounds like **i**.
yellow - y sounds like **e**.

COMPLETE YEAR GRADE 2

49

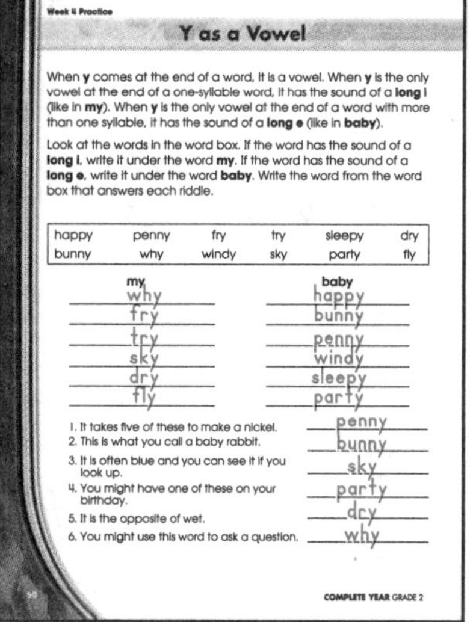

Week 4 Practice

Y as a Vowel

When **y** comes at the end of a word, it is a vowel. When **y** is the only vowel at the end of a one-syllable word, it has the sound of a **long i** (like in **my**). When **y** is the only vowel at the end of a word with more than one syllable, it has the sound of a **long e** (like in **baby**).

Look at the words in the word box. If the word has the sound of a **long i**, write it under the word **my**. If the word has the sound of a **long e**, write it under the word **baby**. Write the word from the word box that answers each riddle.

happy	penny	fry	try	sleepy	dry
bunny	why	windy	sky	party	fly

my	baby
why	happy
fry	bunny
try	penny
sky	windy
dry	sleepy
fly	party

1. It takes five of these to make a nickel. penny
2. This is what you call a baby rabbit. bunny
3. It is often blue and you can see it if you look up. sky
4. You might have one of these on your birthday. party
5. It is the opposite of wet. dry
6. You might use this word to ask a question. why

COMPLETE YEAR GRADE 2

50

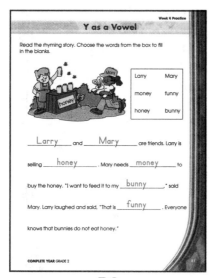

Week 4 Practice

Y as a Vowel

Read the rhyming story. Choose the words from the box to fill in the blanks.

Larry	Mary
money	funny
honey	bunny

Larry and Mary are friends. Larry is selling honey. Mary needs money to buy the honey. "I want to feed it to my bunny," said Mary. Larry laughed and said, "That is funny. Everyone knows that bunnies do not eat honey."

COMPLETE YEAR GRADE 2

51

Week 4 Practice

Y as a Vowel

Read the rhyming story. Choose the words from the box to fill in the blanks.

try	my	Why	cry	shy	fly

Sam is very shy. Ann asks, "Would you like to fly my kite?" Sam starts to cry.

Ann asks, "Why are you crying?"

Sam says, "I am afraid to try."

"Oh, my! You are a very good kite flyer," cries Ann.

COMPLETE YEAR GRADE 2

52

Answer Key

Week 4 Practice

Addition

Complete the facts to 10.

3+1=4, 9+1=10, 6+3=9, 4+2=6, 8+2=10

7+3=10, 6+2=8, 5+5=10, 2+4=6, 1+6=7

4+5=9, 1+4=5, 2+8=10, 4+1=5, 2+2=4, 3+4=7, 6+1=7, 5+1=6, 8+1=9, 1+7=8

5+4=9, 7+1=8, 6+4=10, 5+2=7, 3+7=10, 1+2=3, 2+6=8, 4+3=7, 1+9=10, 2+1=3

5+3=8, 7+2=9, 3+4=7, 1+3=4, 3+7=10, 4+4=8, 3+5=8, 2+7=9, 5+2=7, 2+3=5

3+5=8, 4+3=7, 3+6=9, 4+5=9, 3+2=5

4+6=10, 1+8=9, 2+7=9, 4+6=10, 1+1=2

COMPLETE YEAR GRADE 2 53

53

Week 4 Practice

The Numbers Game

Roll dice to find two addends. Write them on the first two lines. Then, add to find the sum.

1. ____ + ____ = ____
2. ____ + ____ = ____
3. ____ + ____ = ____
4. ____ + ____ = ____
5. ____ + ____ = ____
6. ____ + ____ = ____
7. ____ + ____ = ____
8. ____ + ____ = ____
9. ____ + ____ = ____
10. ____ + ____ = ____

Answers will vary.

54 COMPLETE YEAR GRADE 2

54

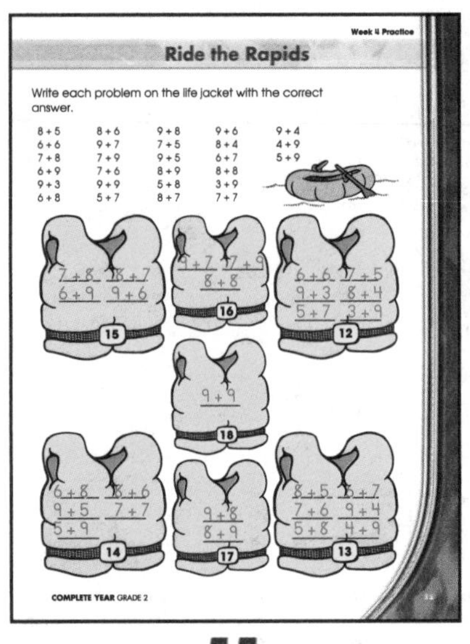

Week 4 Practice

Ride the Rapids

Write each problem on the life jacket with the correct answer.

8+5, 6+6, 7+8, 6+9, 9+3, 6+8

8+6, 9+7, 7+9, 7+6, 9+9, 5+7

9+8, 7+5, 9+5, 8+9, 5+8, 8+7

9+6, 8+4, 6+7, 8+8, 3+9, 7+7

9+4, 4+9, 5+9

15: 7+8, 8+7, 6+9, 9+6

16: 9+7, 7+9, 8+8

12: 6+6, 7+5, 9+3, 8+4, 5+7, 3+9

18: 9+9

14: 6+8, 8+6, 9+5, 7+7, 5+9

17: 9+8, 8+9

13: 8+5, 6+7, 7+6, 9+4, 5+8, 4+9

COMPLETE YEAR GRADE 2 55

55

Week 4 Practice

Addition

Complete the facts to 18.

2+9=11, 6+6=12, 4+9=13, 5+4=9, 8+7=15

5+9=14, 7+7=14, 3+5=8, 9+9=18, 7+9=16

9+8=17, 6+5=11, 8+5=13, 9+6=15, 9+4=13, 4+4=8, 8+6=14, 9+7=16, 4+8=12, 4+7=11

4+6=10, 5+3=8, 4+5=9, 9+9=18, 7+3=10, 6+6=12, 7+8=15, 3+8=11, 6+3=9, 2+6=8

8+3=11, 4+4=8, 6+7=13, 3+2=5, 7+5=12, 3+4=7, 8+8=16, 5+2=7, 3+9=12, 6+8=14

56 COMPLETE YEAR GRADE 2

56

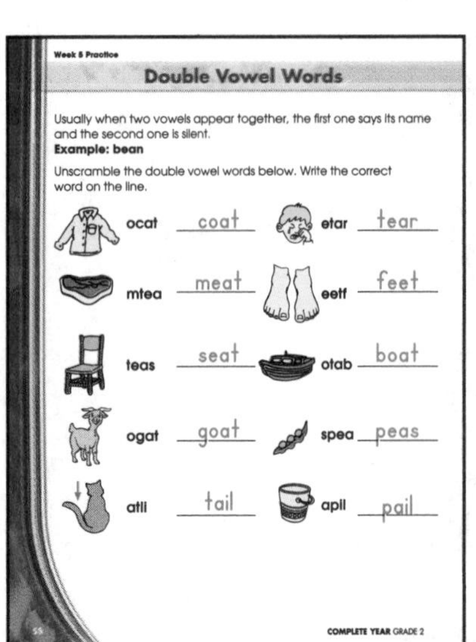

Week 5 Practice

Double Vowel Words

Usually when two vowels appear together, the first one says its name and the second one is silent.
Example: bean

Unscramble the double vowel words below. Write the correct word on the line.

ocat coat | etar tear
mtea meat | eetf feet
teas seat | otab boat
ogat goat | spea peas
atli tail | apli pail

55 COMPLETE YEAR GRADE 2

58

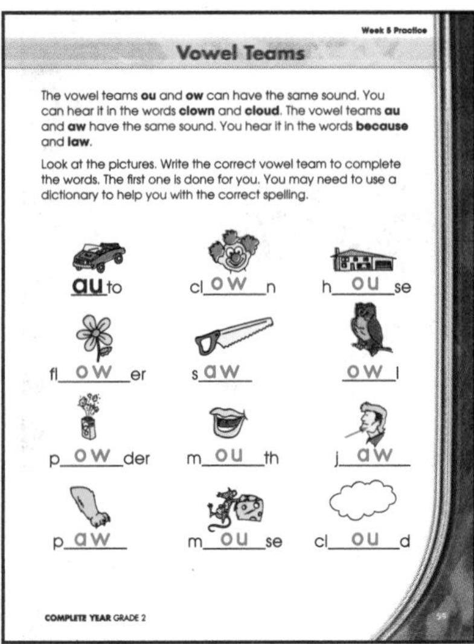

Week 5 Practice

Vowel Teams

The vowel teams **ou** and **ow** can have the same sound. You can hear it in the words **clown** and **cloud**. The vowel teams **au** and **aw** have the same sound. You hear it in the words **because** and **law**.

Look at the pictures. Write the correct vowel team to complete the words. The first one is done for you. You may need to use a dictionary to help you with the correct spelling.

au to | cl ow n | h ou se
fl ow er | s aw | ow l
p ow der | m ou th | j aw
p aw | m ou se | cl ou d

COMPLETE YEAR GRADE 2 56

59

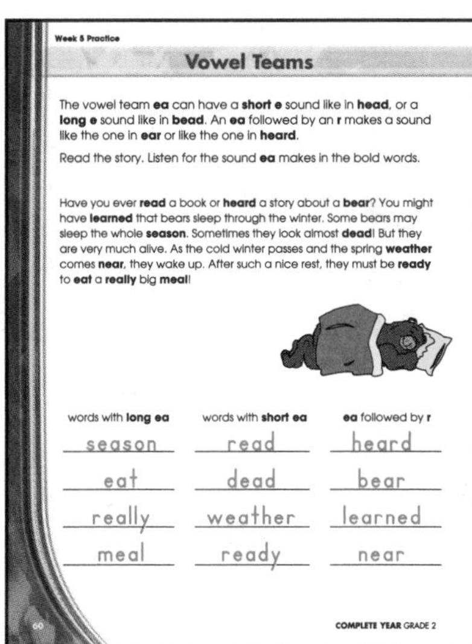
Week 5 Practice

Vowel Teams

The vowel team **ea** can have a **short e** sound like in **head**, or a **long e** sound like in **bead**. An **ea** followed by an **r** makes a sound like the one in **ear** or like the one in **heard**.

Read the story. Listen for the sound **ea** makes in the bold words.

Have you ever **read** a book or **heard** a story about a **bear**? You might have **learned** that bears sleep through the winter. Some bears may sleep the whole **season**. Sometimes they look almost **dead**! But they are very much alive. As the cold winter passes and the spring **weather** comes **near**, they wake up. After such a nice rest, they must be **ready** to **eat** a **really** big **meal**!

words with **long ea**	words with **short ea**	**ea** followed by **r**
season	read	heard
eat	dead	bear
really	weather	learned
meal	ready	near

COMPLETE YEAR GRADE 2

60

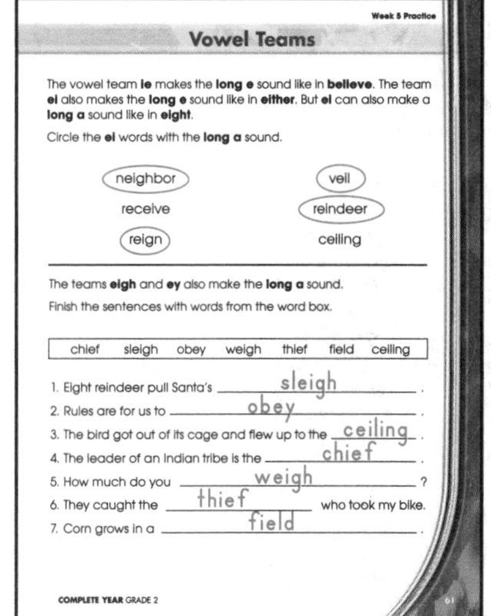
Week 5 Practice

Vowel Teams

The vowel team **ie** makes the **long e** sound like in **believe**. The team **ei** also makes the **long e** sound like in **either**. But **ei** can also make a **long a** sound like in **eight**.

Circle the **ei** words with the **long a** sound.

(neighbor) (veil) receive (reindeer) (reign) ceiling

The teams **eigh** and **ey** also make the **long a** sound.

Finish the sentences with words from the word box.

chief	sleigh	obey	weigh	thief	field	ceiling

1. Eight reindeer pull Santa's sleigh.
2. Rules are for us to obey.
3. The bird got out of its cage and flew up to the ceiling.
4. The leader of an Indian tribe is the chief.
5. How much do you weigh?
6. They caught the thief who took my bike.
7. Corn grows in a field.

COMPLETE YEAR GRADE 2

61

Week 5 Practice

Vowel Teams: oi, oy, ou, ow

Look at the first picture in each row. Circle the pictures that have the same sound.

COMPLETE YEAR GRADE 2

62

Week 5 Practice

Addition

Complete the facts to 18.

3 + 3 = 6, 7 + 4 = 11, 9 + 6 = 15, 5 + 6 = 11, 7 + 4 = 11

9 + 3 = 12, 4 + 6 = 10, 4 + 8 = 12, 5 + 5 = 10, 2 + 4 = 6

5 + 8 = 13, 1 + 7 = 8, 9 + 3 = 12, 6 + 8 = 14, 8 + 9 = 17, 5 + 6 = 11, 3 + 8 = 11, 8 + 7 = 15, 4 + 3 = 7, 6 + 7 = 13

5 + 9 = 14, 7 + 3 = 10, 9 + 4 = 13, 3 + 6 = 9, 2 + 8 = 10, 7 + 6 = 13, 4 + 5 = 9, 3 + 9 = 12, 9 + 7 = 16, 3 + 4 = 7

8 + 6 = 14, 3 + 5 = 8, 5 + 7 = 12, 9 + 9 = 18, 8 + 6 = 14, 8 + 5 = 13, 6 + 7 = 13, 9 + 8 = 17, 7 + 9 = 16, 8 + 4 = 12

COMPLETE YEAR GRADE 2

63

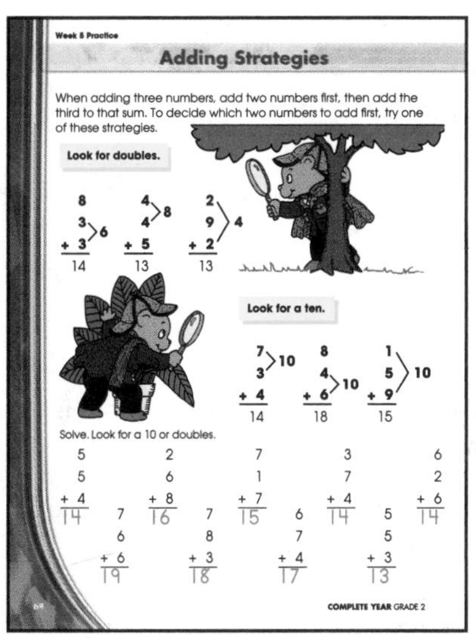
Week 5 Practice

Adding Strategies

When adding three numbers, add two numbers first, then add the third to that sum. To decide which two numbers to add first, try one of these strategies.

Look for doubles.

8 + 3 + 3 (3 + 3 = 6) = 14; 4 + 4 + 5 (4 + 4 = 8) = 13; 2 + 9 + 2 (2 + 2 = 4) = 13

Look for a ten.

7 + 3 + 4 (7 + 3 = 10) = 14; 8 + 4 + 6 (4 + 6 = 10) = 18; 1 + 5 + 9 (10) = 15

Solve. Look for a 10 or doubles.

5 + 5 + 4 = 14; 2 + 6 + 8 = 16; 7 + 1 + 7 = 15; 3 + 7 + 4 = 14; 6 + 2 + 6 = 14

7 + 6 + 6 = 19; 7 + 8 + 3 = 18; 6 + 7 + 4 = 17; 5 + 5 + 3 = 13

COMPLETE YEAR GRADE 2

64

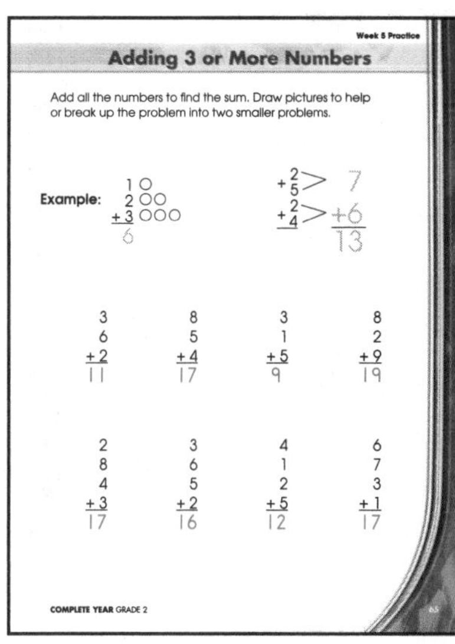
Week 5 Practice

Adding 3 or More Numbers

Add all the numbers to find the sum. Draw pictures to help or break up the problem into two smaller problems.

Example: 1 + 2 + 3 = 6; 2 + 5 = 7, 2 + 4 = 6, 7 + 6 = 13

3 + 6 + 2 = 11; 8 + 5 + 4 = 17; 3 + 1 + 5 = 9; 8 + 2 + 9 = 19

2 + 8 + 4 + 3 = 17; 3 + 6 + 5 + 2 = 16; 4 + 1 + 2 + 5 = 12; 6 + 7 + 3 + 1 = 17

COMPLETE YEAR GRADE 2

65

Answer Key

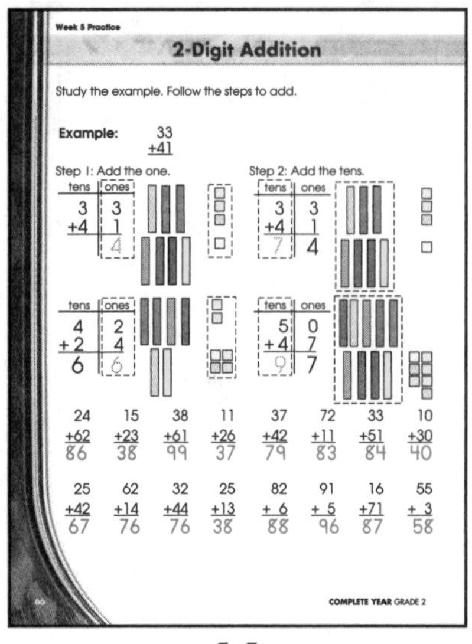
Week 5 Practice

2-Digit Addition

Study the example. Follow the steps to add.

Example: 33 +41

Step 1: Add the one. Step 2: Add the tens.

24 +62 = 86	15 +23 = 38	38 +61 = 99	11 +26 = 37	37 +42 = 79	72 +11 = 83	33 +51 = 84	10 +30 = 40
25 +42 = 67	62 +14 = 76	32 +44 = 76	25 +13 = 38	82 + 6 = 88	91 + 5 = 96	16 +71 = 87	55 + 3 = 58

COMPLETE YEAR GRADE 2

66

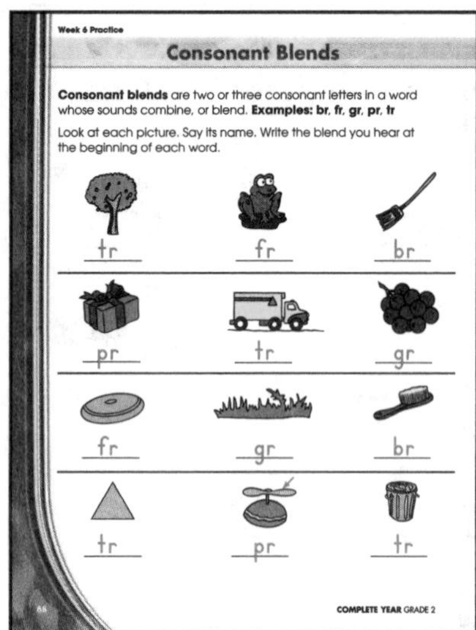
Week 6 Practice

Consonant Blends

Consonant blends are two or three consonant letters in a word whose sounds combine, or blend. **Examples: br, fr, gr, pr, tr**

Look at each picture. Say its name. Write the blend you hear at the beginning of each word.

tr fr br
pr tr gr
fr gr br
tr pr tr

COMPLETE YEAR GRADE 2

68

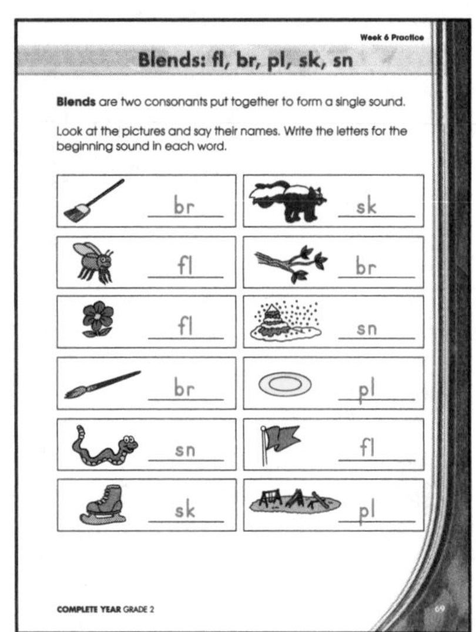
Week 6 Practice

Blends: fl, br, pl, sk, sn

Blends are two consonants put together to form a single sound.

Look at the pictures and say their names. Write the letters for the beginning sound in each word.

br sk
fl br
fl sn
br pl
sn fl
sk pl

COMPLETE YEAR GRADE 2

69

Week 6 Practice

Blends: bl, sl, cr, cl

Look at the pictures and say their names. Write the letters for the beginning sound in each word.

cl own bl anket cr ayon
cl ock sl ide cl oud
sl ed cr ab cr ocodile

COMPLETE YEAR GRADE 2

70

Week 6 Practice

Consonant Blends

Write a word from the word box to answer each riddle.

clock	glass	blow	climb	slipper
sleep	gloves	clap	blocks	flashlight

1. You need me when the lights go out. **What am I?** flashlight
2. People use me to tell the time. **What am I?** clock
3. You put me on your hands in the winter to keep them warm. **What am I?** gloves
4. Cinderella lost one like me at midnight. **What am I?** slipper
5. This is what you do with your hands when you are pleased. **What is it?** clap
6. You can do this with a whistle or with bubble gum. **What is it?** blow
7. These are what you might use to build a castle when you are playing. **What are they?** blocks
8. You do this to get to the top of a hill. **What is it?** climb
9. This is what you use to drink water or milk. **What is it?** glass
10. You do this at night with your eyes closed. **What is it?** sleep

COMPLETE YEAR GRADE 2

71

Week 6 Practice

Consonant Teams

Read the words in the box. Write a word from the word box to finish each sentence. Circle the consonant team in each word.
Hint: There are three letters in each team!

splash	screen	spray	street	scream
screw	shrub	split	strong	string

1. Another word for a bush is a shrub.
2. I tied a string to my tooth to help pull it out.
3. I have many friends who live on my street.
4. We always scream when we ride the roller coaster.
5. A screen helps keep bugs out of the house.
6. It is fun to splash in the water.
7. My father uses an ax to split the firewood.
8. We will need a screw to fix the chair.
9. You must be very strong to lift this heavy box.
10. The firemen spray the fire with water.

COMPLETE YEAR GRADE 2

72

Answer Key

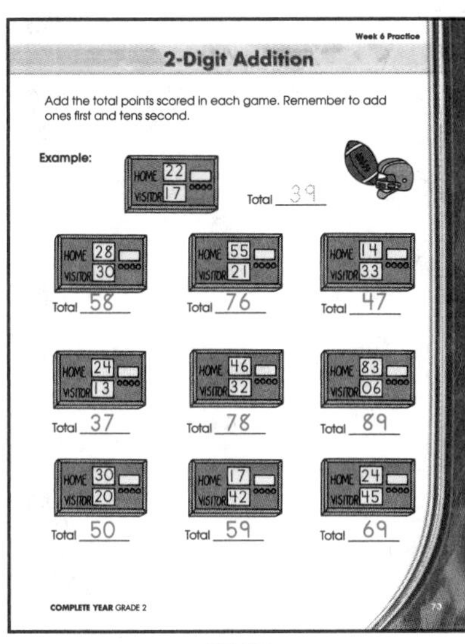

Week 6 Practice

2-Digit Addition

Add the total points scored in each game. Remember to add ones first and tens second.

Example: HOME 22 VISITOR 17 Total 39

HOME 28 VISITOR 30 Total 58
HOME 55 VISITOR 21 Total 76
HOME 14 VISITOR 33 Total 47
HOME 24 VISITOR 13 Total 37
HOME 46 VISITOR 32 Total 78
HOME 83 VISITOR 06 Total 89
HOME 30 VISITOR 20 Total 50
HOME 17 VISITOR 42 Total 59
HOME 24 VISITOR 45 Total 69

COMPLETE YEAR GRADE 2 73

73

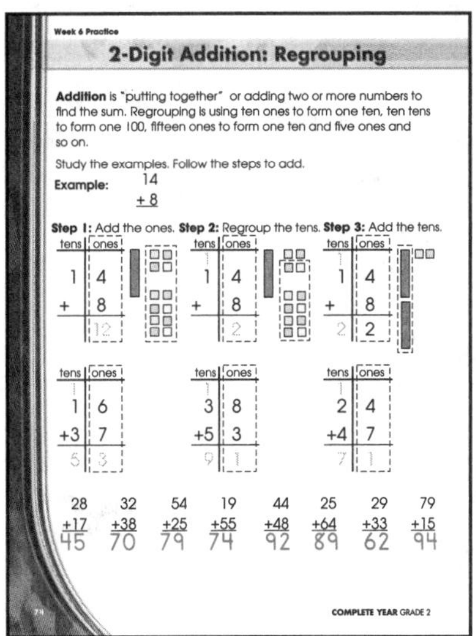

Week 6 Practice

2-Digit Addition: Regrouping

Addition is "putting together" or adding two or more numbers to find the sum. Regrouping is using ten ones to form one ten, ten tens to form one 100, fifteen ones to form one ten and five ones and so on.

Study the examples. Follow the steps to add.

Example: 14 + 8

Step 1: Add the ones. **Step 2:** Regroup the tens. **Step 3:** Add the tens.

14 + 8 = 22

16 + 37 = 53
38 + 53 = 91
24 + 47 = 71

28 + 17 = 45
32 + 38 = 70
54 + 25 = 79
19 + 55 = 74
44 + 48 = 92
25 + 64 = 89
29 + 33 = 62
79 + 15 = 94

74 COMPLETE YEAR GRADE 2

74

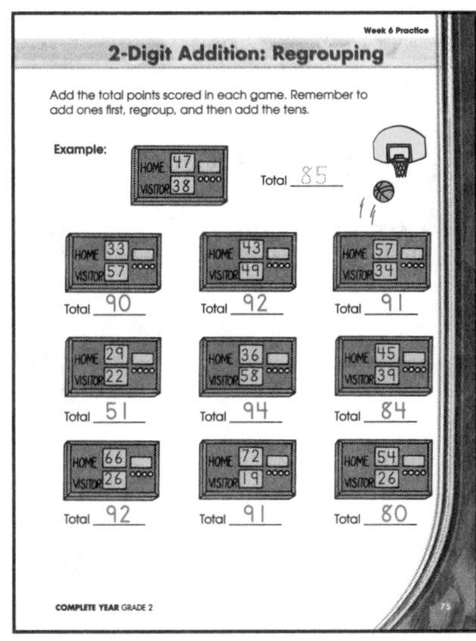

Week 6 Practice

2-Digit Addition: Regrouping

Add the total points scored in each game. Remember to add ones first, regroup, and then add the tens.

Example: HOME 47 VISITOR 38 Total 85

HOME 33 VISITOR 57 Total 90
HOME 43 VISITOR 49 Total 92
HOME 57 VISITOR 34 Total 91
HOME 29 VISITOR 22 Total 51
HOME 36 VISITOR 58 Total 94
HOME 45 VISITOR 39 Total 84
HOME 66 VISITOR 26 Total 92
HOME 72 VISITOR 19 Total 91
HOME 54 VISITOR 26 Total 80

COMPLETE YEAR GRADE 2 75

75

Week 6 Practice

Keep On Truckin'

Write each sum. Connect the sums of 83 to make a road for the truck.

17 + 66 = 83; 48 + 26 = 74; 42 + 19 = 61

28 + 38 = 66; 64 + 19 = 83; 26 + 57 = 83; 58 + 25 = 83; 17 + 75 = 92; 65 + 29 = 94

37 + 39 = 76; 48 + 35 = 83; 58 + 37 = 95; 65 + 16 = 81; 38 + 25 = 63; 39 + 59 = 98

59 + 27 = 86; 55 + 28 = 83; 39 + 44 = 83

76 COMPLETE YEAR GRADE 2

76

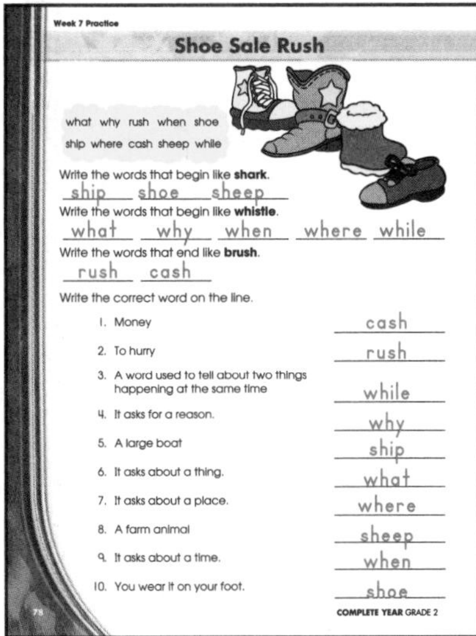

Week 7 Practice

Shoe Sale Rush

what why rush when shoe ship where cash sheep while

Write the words that begin like **shark**. ship shoe sheep

Write the words that begin like **whistle**. what why when where while

Write the words that end like **brush**. rush cash

Write the correct word on the line.

1. Money — cash
2. To hurry — rush
3. A word used to tell about two things happening at the same time — while
4. It asks for a reason. — why
5. A large boat — ship
6. It asks about a thing. — what
7. It asks about a place. — where
8. A farm animal — sheep
9. It asks about a time. — when
10. You wear it on your foot. — shoe

78 COMPLETE YEAR GRADE 2

78

Week 7 Practice

Inching Along

think tooth each child both inch thing change teach thank

Write the words that begin like **cheese**. child change

Write the words that begin like **thumb**. think thing thank

Write the words that end like **branch**. each inch teach

Write the words that end like **teeth**. tooth both

Circle the misspelled word. Then, write the word correctly on the line.

1. Which team do you thick will win the game? — think
2. The dentist filled the cavity in her toth. — tooth
3. We will boht ride on the train. — both
4. A baby kangaroo is about 1 itch long when it is born. — inch
5. There is an apple for eack person. — each
6. Theo had to chanj his clothes after he fell in the mud. — change
7. What is that furry fing under the table? — thing
8. A star soccer player will teech us how to kick the ball. — teach
9. She wrote a letter to tank her grandmother for the gift. — thank
10. Mom helped the lost cilde find his mother. — child

COMPLETE YEAR GRADE 2 79

79

Answer Key

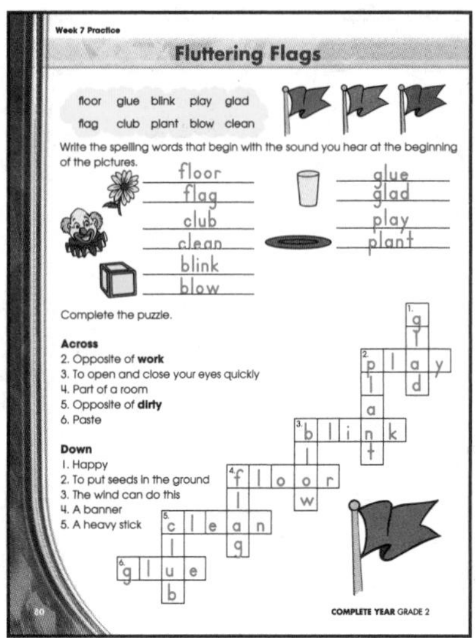

80

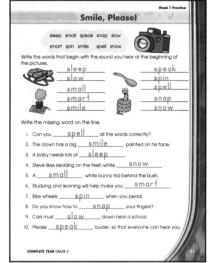

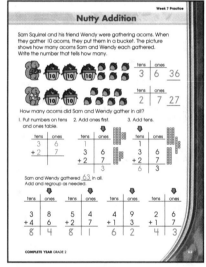

Week 7 Practice

Smile, Please!

sleep small speak snap slow
smart spin smile spell snow

Write the words that begin with the sound you hear at the beginning of the pictures.

sleep, slow, small, smart, smile

speak, spin, spell, snap, snow

Write the missing word on the line.

1. Can you spell all the words correctly?
2. The clown has a big smile painted on his face.
3. A baby needs lots of sleep.
4. Steve likes sledding on the fresh white snow.
5. A small white bunny hid behind the bush.
6. Studying and learning will help make you smart.
7. Bike wheels spin when you pedal.
8. Do you know how to snap your fingers?
9. Cars must slow down near a school.
10. Please speak louder, so that everyone can hear you.

COMPLETE YEAR GRADE 2

81

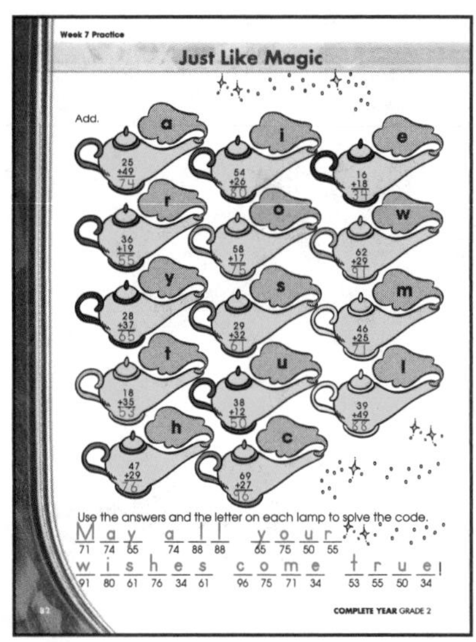

82

Week 7 Practice

Nutty Addition

Sam Squirrel and his friend Wendy were gathering acorns. When they gather 10 acorns, they put them in a bucket. The picture shows how many acorns Sam and Wendy each gathered. Write the number that tells how many.

tens	ones	
3	6	36
2	7	27

How many acorns did Sam and Wendy gather in all?

1. Put numbers on tens and ones table.
2. Add ones first.
3. Add tens.

	tens	ones
	1	
	3	6
+	2	7
	6	3

Sam and Wendy gathered 63 in all.

Add and regroup as needed.

	tens	ones
	3	8
+	4	6
	8	4

	tens	ones
	5	4
+	2	7
	8	1

	tens	ones
	4	9
+	1	3
	6	2

	tens	ones
	2	6
+	1	7
	4	3

COMPLETE YEAR GRADE 2

83

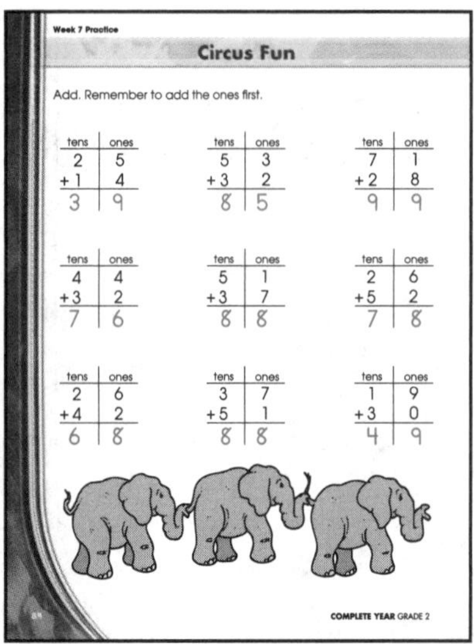

84

Week 7 Practice

Addition

Add.

Example:

Add the ones. 26 + 21 = 7

Add the tens. 26 + 21 = 47

18 + 11 = 29 | 24 + 35 = 59 | 38 + 21 = 59 | 49 + 50 = 99 | 52 + 33 = 85

75 + 12 = 87 | 83 + 16 = 99 | 67 + 32 = 99 | 44 + 25 = 69 | 28 + 41 = 69

68 + 20 = 88 | 54 + 25 = 79 | 71 + 17 = 88

The Lions scored 42 points. The Clippers scored 21 points. How many points were scored in all? 63

COMPLETE YEAR GRADE 2

85

Answer Key

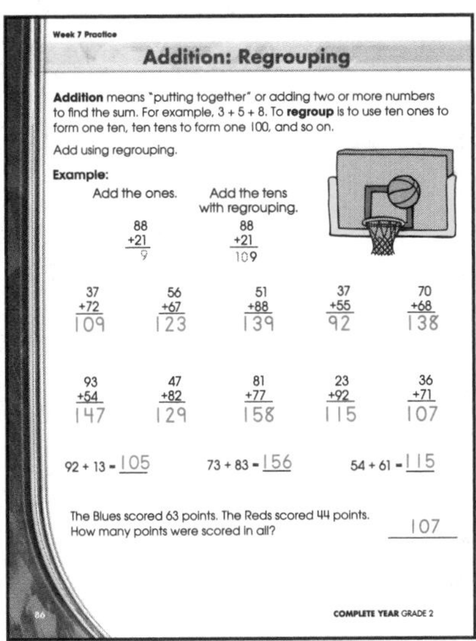

Week 7 Practice

Addition: Regrouping

Addition means "putting together" or adding two or more numbers to find the sum. For example, 3 + 5 + 8. To **regroup** is to use ten ones to form one ten, ten tens to form one 100, and so on.

Add using regrouping.

Example:

Add the ones. 88 + 21 = 9

Add the tens with regrouping. 88 + 21 = 109

37 + 72 = 109 | 56 + 67 = 123 | 51 + 88 = 139 | 37 + 55 = 92 | 70 + 68 = 138

93 + 54 = 147 | 47 + 82 = 129 | 81 + 77 = 158 | 23 + 92 = 115 | 36 + 71 = 107

92 + 13 = 105 | 73 + 83 = 156 | 54 + 61 = 115

The Blues scored 63 points. The Reds scored 44 points. How many points were scored in all? 107

COMPLETE YEAR GRADE 2

86

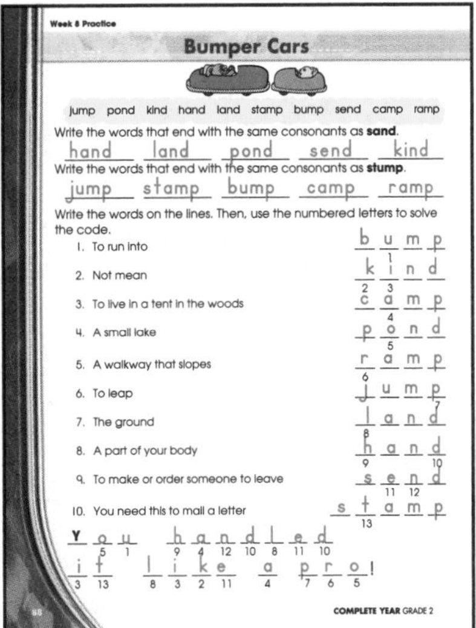

Week 8 Practice

Bumper Cars

jump pond kind hand land stamp bump send camp ramp

Write the words that end with the same consonants as **sand**.

hand land pond send kind

Write the words that end with the same consonants as **stump**.

jump stamp bump camp ramp

Write the words on the lines. Then, use the numbered letters to solve the code.

1. To run into — bump
2. Not mean — kind
3. To live in a tent in the woods — camp
4. A small lake — pond
5. A walkway that slopes — ramp
6. To leap — jump
7. The ground — land
8. A part of your body — hand
9. To make or order someone to leave — send
10. You need this to mail a letter — stamp

You handled it! I like a pro!

COMPLETE YEAR GRADE 2

88

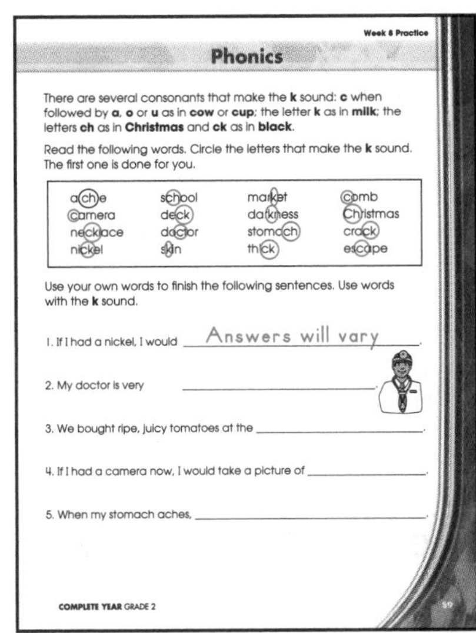

Week 8 Practice

Phonics

There are several consonants that make the **k** sound: **c** when followed by **a**, **o** or **u** as in **cow** or **cup**; the letter **k** as in **milk**; the letters **ch** as in **Christmas** and **ck** as in **black**.

Read the following words. Circle the letters that make the **k** sound. The first one is done for you.

ache, camera, necklace, nickel, school, deck, doctor, skin, market, darkness, stomach, thick, comb, Christmas, crack, escape

Use your own words to finish the following sentences. Use words with the **k** sound.

1. If I had a nickel, I would Answers will vary
2. My doctor is very
3. We bought ripe, juicy tomatoes at the
4. If I had a camera now, I would take a picture of
5. When my stomach aches,

COMPLETE YEAR GRADE 2

89

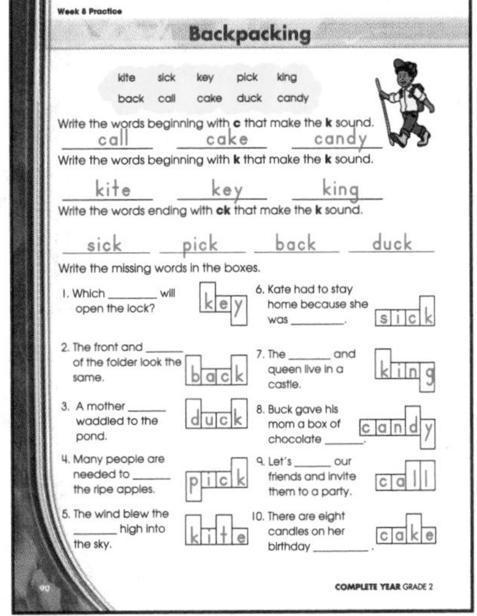

Week 8 Practice

Backpacking

kite sick key pick king back call cake duck candy

Write the words beginning with **c** that make the **k** sound.

call cake candy

Write the words beginning with **k** that make the **k** sound.

kite key king

Write the words ending with **ck** that make the **k** sound.

sick pick back duck

Write the missing words in the boxes.

1. Which ______ will open the lock? key
2. The front and ______ of the folder look the same. back
3. A mother ______ waddled to the pond. duck
4. Many people are needed to ______ the ripe apples. pick
5. The wind blew the ______ high into the sky. kite
6. Kate had to stay home because she was ______. sick
7. The ______ and queen live in a castle. king
8. Buck gave his mom a box of chocolate ______. candy
9. Let's ______ our friends and invite them to a party. call
10. There are eight candles on her birthday ______. cake

COMPLETE YEAR GRADE 2

90

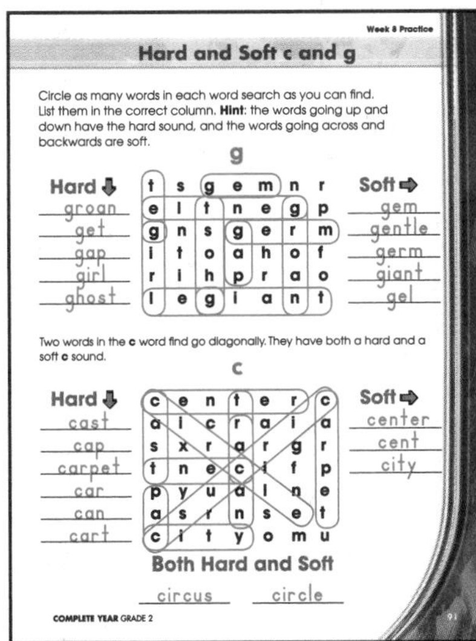

Week 8 Practice

Hard and Soft c and g

Circle as many words in each word search as you can find. List them in the correct column. **Hint:** the words going up and down have the hard sound, and the words going across and backwards are soft.

g

Hard: groan, get, gap, girl, ghost

Soft: gem, gentle, germ, giant, gel

Two words in the **c** word find go diagonally. They have both a hard and a soft **c** sound.

c

Hard: cast, cap, carpet, car, can, cart

Soft: center, cent, city

Both Hard and Soft

circus circle

COMPLETE YEAR GRADE 2

91

Week 8 Practice

3-Digit Addition: Regrouping

Study the examples. Follow the steps to add.

Example:

Step 1: Add the ones — Do you regroup? Yes

Step 2: Add the tens — Do you regroup? No

Step 3: Add the hundreds

348 + 44 = 392

214 + 238 = 452

368 + 213 = 581

119 + 5 = 124

418 + 323 = 741 | 471 + 319 = 790 | 334 + 528 = 862 | 659 + 127 = 786 | 736 + 145 = 881 | 426 + 165 = 591 | 567 + 228 = 795 | 327 + 354 = 681

COMPLETE YEAR GRADE 2

92

Answer Key

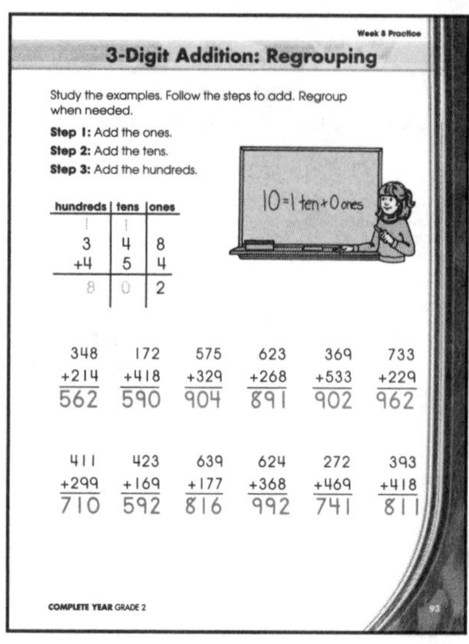

Week 8 Practice

3-Digit Addition: Regrouping

Study the examples. Follow the steps to add. Regroup when needed.

Step 1: Add the ones.
Step 2: Add the tens.
Step 3: Add the hundreds.

hundreds	tens	ones
1	1	
3	4	8
+4	5	4
8	0	2

348	172	575	623	369	733
+214	+418	+329	+268	+533	+229
562	590	904	891	902	962

411	423	639	624	272	393
+299	+169	+177	+368	+469	+418
710	592	816	992	741	811

COMPLETE YEAR GRADE 2 93

93

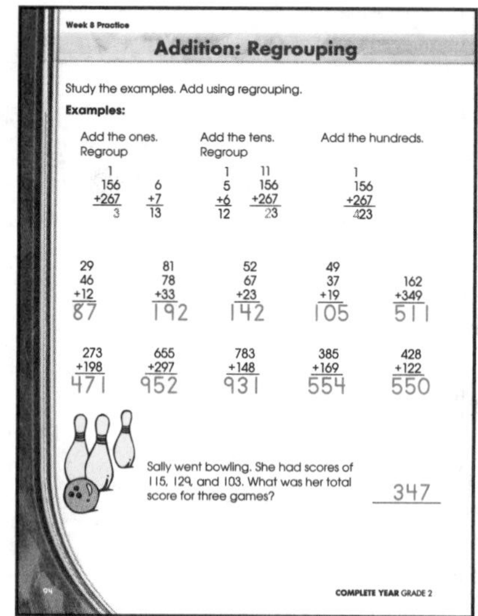

Week 8 Practice

Addition: Regrouping

Study the examples. Add using regrouping.

Examples:

Add the ones. Regroup	Add the tens. Regroup	Add the hundreds.
1 156 + 267 = 3 (6 + 7 = 13)	1 11 156 + 267 = 23 (5 + 6 + 1 = 12)	1 156 + 267 = 423

29 + 46 + 12	81 + 78 + 33	52 + 67 + 23	49 + 37 + 19	162 + 349
87	192	142	105	511

273 + 198	655 + 297	783 + 148	385 + 169	428 + 122
471	952	931	554	550

Sally went bowling. She had scores of 115, 129, and 103. What was her total score for three games? 347

94 COMPLETE YEAR GRADE 2

94

Week 8 Practice

Addition: Mental Math

Try to do theses addition problems in your head without using paper and pencil.

7 +4	6 +3	8 +1	10 +2	2 +9	6 +6
11	9	9	12	11	12

10 +20	40 +20	80 +100	60 +30	50 +70	100 +40
30	60	180	90	120	140

350 +150	300 +500	400 +800	450 +10	680 +100	900 +70
500	800	1,200	460	780	970

1,000 +200	4,000 400 +30	300 200 +80	8,000 500 +60	9,800 +150	7,000 300 +30
1,200	4,430	580	8,560	9,950	7,330

COMPLETE YEAR GRADE 2 95

95

Week 8 Practice

Subtraction

Complete the facts to 10.

10 −5	7 −2	6 −3	4 −3	9 −1
5	5	3	1	8

3 −2	8 −6	10 −7	7 −1	8 −5
1	2	3	6	3

10 −1	7 −4	2 −1	6 −4	8 −4	9 −5	8 −1	9 −2	7 −6	5 −3
9	3	1	2	4	4	7	7	1	2

10 −3	8 −7	9 −6	5 −4	10 −6	7 −3	4 −2	6 −2	9 −7	4 −1
7	1	3	1	4	4	2	4	2	3

10 −8	5 −1	9 −5	9 −3	8 −5	7 −3	6 −4	5 −2	8 −2	7 −4
2	4	4	6	3	4	2	3	6	3

96 COMPLETE YEAR GRADE 2

96

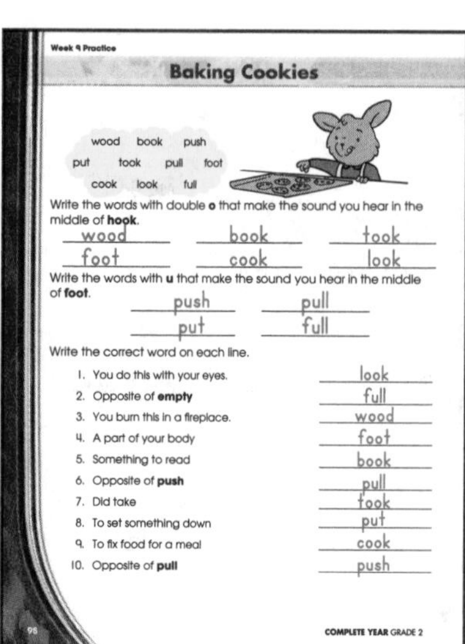

Week 9 Practice

Baking Cookies

wood book push put took pull foot cook look full

Write the words with double **o** that make the sound you hear in the middle of **hook**.

wood book took
foot cook look

Write the words with **u** that make the sound you hear in the middle of **foot**.

push pull
put full

Write the correct word on each line.

1. You do this with your eyes. look
2. Opposite of **empty** full
3. You burn this in a fireplace. wood
4. A part of your body foot
5. Something to read book
6. Opposite of **push** pull
7. Did take took
8. To set something down put
9. To fix food for a meal cook
10. Opposite of **pull** push

98 COMPLETE YEAR GRADE 2

98

Week 9 Practice

Clowning Around

clown our down count how town house about now out

Write the **ou** words that make the vowel sound you hear in **mouse**.

our count house
about out

Write the **ow** words that make the vowel sound you hear in **cow**.

clown down how
town now

Write the missing words in the boxes.

1. Sally lives in the ____ on the corner. house
2. Do you know ____ to make a robot? how
3. Please take the towels ____ of the dryer. out
4. We must leave for the airport ____! now
5. It is ____ time for the race to start. about
6. They rode the elevator ____ to the bottom floor. down
7. This is ____ new four-wheel drive truck. our
8. The big funny ____ rode a tiny bike. clown
9. Can you ____ to 100? count
10. The farmer took his fresh fruit to ____. town

COMPLETE YEAR GRADE 2 99

99

Answer Key

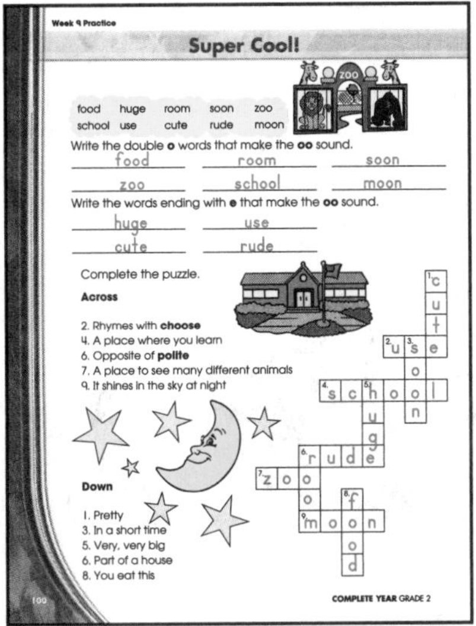

Week 9 Practice

Super Cool!

food huge room soon zoo
school use cute rude moon

Write the double **o** words that make the **oo** sound.

food room soon
zoo school moon

Write the words ending with **e** that make the **oo** sound.

huge use
cute rude

Complete the puzzle.

Across

2. Rhymes with **choose**
4. A place where you learn
6. Opposite of **polite**
7. A place to see many different animals
9. It shines in the sky at night

Down

1. Pretty
3. In a short time
5. Very, very big
6. Part of a house
8. You eat this

COMPLETE YEAR GRADE 2

100

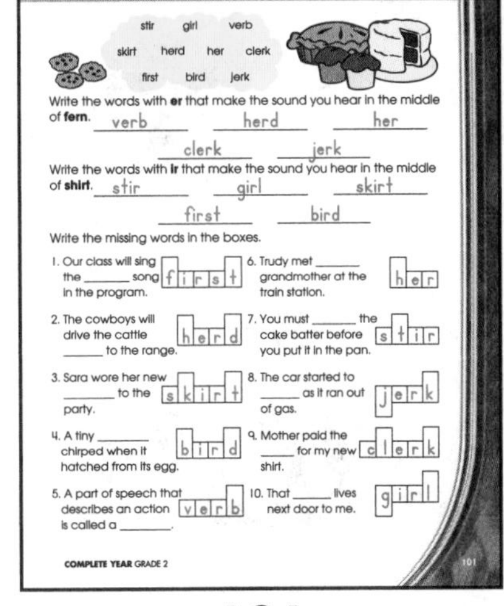

Week 9 Practice

Stir Up a Dessert

stir girl verb
skirt herd her clerk
first bird jerk

Write the words with **er** that make the sound you hear in the middle of **fern**. verb herd her clerk jerk

Write the words with **ir** that make the sound you hear in the middle of **shirt**. stir girl skirt first bird

Write the missing words in the boxes.

1. Our class will sing the ______ song in the program. first
2. The cowboys will drive the cattle ______ to the range. herd
3. Sara wore her new ______ to the party. skirt
4. A tiny ______ chirped when it hatched from its egg. bird
5. A part of speech that describes an action is called a ______. verb
6. Trudy met ______ grandmother at the train station. her
7. You must ______ the cake batter before you put it in the pan. stir
8. The car started to ______ as it ran out of gas. jerk
9. Mother paid the ______ for my new shirt. clerk
10. That ______ lives next door to me. girl

COMPLETE YEAR GRADE 2

101

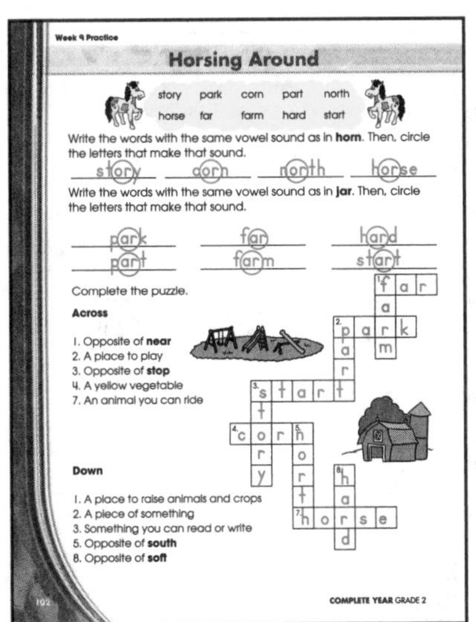

Week 9 Practice

Horsing Around

story park corn part north
horse far farm hard start

Write the words with the same vowel sound as in **horn**. Then, circle the letters that make that sound.

story corn north horse

Write the words with the same vowel sound as in **jar**. Then, circle the letters that make that sound.

park far hard
part farm start

Complete the puzzle.

Across

1. Opposite of **near**
2. A place to play
3. Opposite of **stop**
4. A yellow vegetable
7. An animal you can ride

Down

1. A place to raise animals and crops
2. A piece of something
3. Something you can read or write
5. Opposite of **south**
8. Opposite of **soft**

COMPLETE YEAR GRADE 2

102

Week 9 Practice

Subtraction

Complete the facts to 18.

11 − 9 = 2, 12 − 6 = 6, 13 − 9 = 4, 9 − 4 = 5, 15 − 7 = 8

14 − 9 = 5, 14 − 7 = 7, 8 − 5 = 3, 11 − 2 = 9, 14 − 9 = 5

17 − 1 = 16, 11 − 5 = 6, 13 − 5 = 8, 15 − 6 = 9, 13 − 4 = 9, 8 − 4 = 4, 14 − 6 = 8, 16 − 7 = 9, 12 − 8 = 4, 11 − 7 = 4

10 − 6 = 4, 8 − 3 = 5, 9 − 5 = 4, 18 − 9 = 9, 10 − 3 = 7, 14 − 8 = 6, 15 − 8 = 7, 11 − 8 = 3, 9 − 3 = 6, 8 − 6 = 2

11 − 3 = 8, 14 − 4 = 10, 13 − 7 = 6, 5 − 2 = 3, 12 − 5 = 7, 7 − 4 = 3, 16 − 8 = 8, 7 − 2 = 5, 12 − 9 = 3, 11 − 6 = 5

COMPLETE YEAR GRADE 2

103

Week 9 Practice

Connect the Facts

Subtract. Write the answer.

17 − 9 = 8, 14 − 7 = 7, 16 − 9 = 7, 12 − 6 = 6, 14 − 8 = 6, 15 − 8 = 7, 16 − 8 = 8, 11 − 3 = 8, 14 − 9 = 5, 18 − 9 = 9, 15 − 9 = 6, 13 − 7 = 6, 16 − 8 = 8, 15 − 8 = 7, 13 − 8 = 5, 12 − 4 = 8, 14 − 6 = 8, 13 − 3 = 10, 16 − 7 = 9, 11 − 7 = 4

COMPLETE YEAR GRADE 2

104

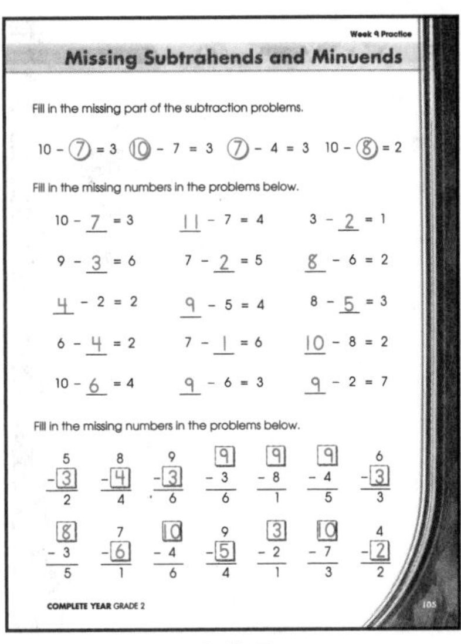

Week 9 Practice

Missing Subtrahends and Minuends

Fill in the missing part of the subtraction problems.

10 − 7 = 3   10 − 7 = 3   7 − 4 = 3   10 − 8 = 2

Fill in the missing numbers in the problems below.

10 − 7 = 3   11 − 7 = 4   3 − 2 = 1
9 − 3 = 6   7 − 2 = 5   8 − 6 = 2
4 − 2 = 2   9 − 5 = 4   8 − 5 = 3
6 − 4 = 2   7 − 1 = 6   10 − 8 = 2
10 − 6 = 4   9 − 6 = 3   9 − 2 = 7

Fill in the missing numbers in the problems below.

5 − 3 = 2, 8 − 4 = 4, 9 − 3 = 6, 9 − 3 = 6, 9 − 8 = 1, 9 − 4 = 5, 6 − 3 = 3

8 − 3 = 5, 7 − 6 = 1, 10 − 4 = 6, 9 − 5 = 4, 3 − 2 = 1, 10 − 7 = 3, 4 − 2 = 2

COMPLETE YEAR GRADE 2

105

Answer Key

Week 9 Practice

Subtraction

Complete the facts to 18.

6 − 3 = 3	11 − 4 = 7	15 − 6 = 9	11 − 6 = 5	11 − 4 = 7					
12 − 3 = 9	10 − 6 = 4	12 − 4 = 8	10 − 5 = 5	6 − 4 = 2					
13 − 5 = 8	8 − 7 = 1	12 − 3 = 9	14 − 8 = 6	17 − 9 = 8	11 − 6 = 5	11 − 8 = 3	15 − 7 = 8	7 − 3 = 4	13 − 7 = 6
14 − 9 = 5	10 − 3 = 7	13 − 4 = 9	9 − 6 = 3	10 − 8 = 2	13 − 6 = 7	9 − 6 = 3	12 − 9 = 3	16 − 7 = 9	7 − 4 = 3
14 − 6 = 8	8 − 5 = 3	12 − 7 = 5	18 − 9 = 9	14 − 6 = 8	13 − 8 = 5	13 − 6 = 7	17 − 8 = 9	16 − 9 = 7	12 − 4 = 8

106 COMPLETE YEAR GRADE 2

106

Week 10 Practice

Singular Nouns

A **singular noun** names one person, place or thing.

Example: My **mother** unlocked the old **trunk** in the **attic**.

If the noun is singular, draw a line from it to the trunk. If the noun is not singular, draw an **X** on the word.

teddy bear	hammer	picture	sweater
bonnet	letters	seashells	fiddle
kite	ring	feather	books
postcard	crayon	doll	dishes
blocks	hats	bicycle	blanket

112 COMPLETE YEAR GRADE 2

112

Week 10 Practice

Common Nouns

A **common noun** names a person, place or thing.

Example: The **boy** had several **chores** to do.

Fill in the circle below each common noun.

1. First, the boy had to feed his puppy.
2. He got fresh water for his pet.
3. Next, the boy poured some dry food into a bowl.
4. He set the dish on the floor in the kitchen.
5. Then, he called his dog to come to dinner.
6. The boy and his dad worked in the garden.
7. The father turned the dirt with a shovel.
8. The boy carefully dropped seeds into little holes.
9. Soon, tiny plants would sprout from the soil.
10. Sunshine and showers would help the radishes grow.

COMPLETE YEAR GRADE 2 113

113

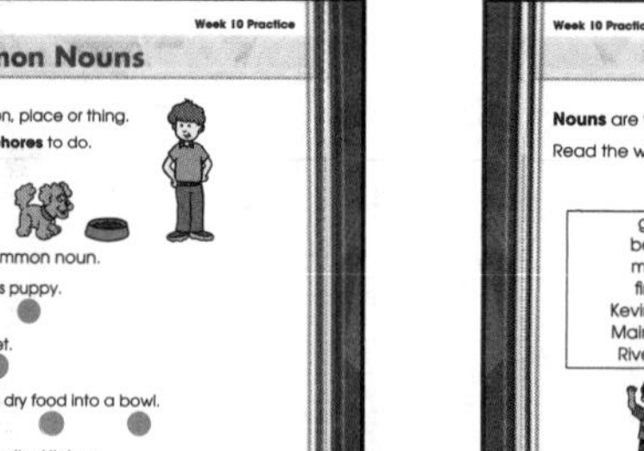

Week 10 Practice

Nouns

Nouns are words that tell the names of people, places or things.

Read the words below. Then, write them in the correct column.

goat	Mrs. Jackson	girl
beach	tree	song
mouth	park	Jean Rivers
finger	flower	New York
Kevin Jones	Elm City	Frank Gates
Main Street	theater	skates
River Park	father	boy

Person	Place	Thing
Kevin Jones	beach	goat
Mrs. Jackson	Main Street	mouth
father	River Park	finger
girl	park	tree
Jean Rivers	Elm City	flower
Frank Gates	theater	song
boy	New York	skates

114 COMPLETE YEAR GRADE 2

114

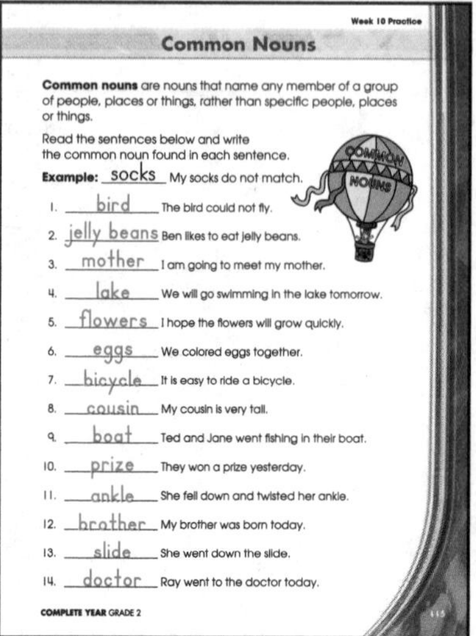

Week 10 Practice

Common Nouns

Common nouns are nouns that name any member of a group of people, places or things, rather than specific people, places or things.

Read the sentences below and write the common noun found in each sentence.

Example: socks My socks do not match.

1. bird The bird could not fly.
2. jelly beans Ben likes to eat jelly beans.
3. mother I am going to meet my mother.
4. lake We will go swimming in the lake tomorrow.
5. flowers I hope the flowers will grow quickly.
6. eggs We colored eggs together.
7. bicycle It is easy to ride a bicycle.
8. cousin My cousin is very tall.
9. boat Ted and Jane went fishing in their boat.
10. prize They won a prize yesterday.
11. ankle She fell down and twisted her ankle.
12. brother My brother was born today.
13. slide She went down the slide.
14. doctor Ray went to the doctor today.

COMPLETE YEAR GRADE 2 115

115

Week 10 Practice

Subtraction

Subtraction is "taking away" or subtracting one number from another to find the difference.

Subtract.

Example: 4 − 3 = 1

5 − 3 = 2	6 − 1 = 5	4 − 3 = 1	3 − 1 = 2	2 − 0 = 2	1 − 1 = 0
9 − 2 = 7	7 − 4 = 3	10 − 5 = 5	14 − 6 = 8	15 − 9 = 6	12 − 3 = 9
18 − 8 = 10	13 − 5 = 8	14 − 7 = 7	11 − 4 = 7	17 − 9 = 8	16 − 8 = 8

116 COMPLETE YEAR GRADE 2

116

Answer Key

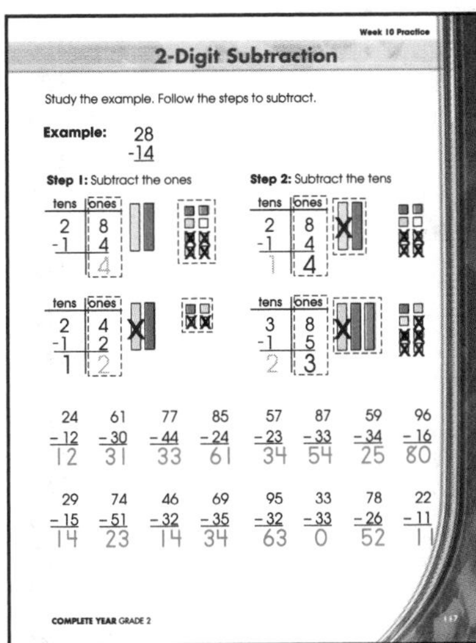

Week 10 Practice

2-Digit Subtraction

Study the example. Follow the steps to subtract.

Example: 28 − 14

Step 1: Subtract the ones **Step 2:** Subtract the tens

24 − 12	61 − 30	77 − 44	85 − 24	57 − 23	87 − 33	59 − 34	96 − 16
12	31	33	61	34	54	25	80

29 − 15	74 − 51	46 − 32	69 − 35	95 − 32	33 − 33	78 − 26	22 − 11
14	23	14	34	63	0	52	11

COMPLETE YEAR GRADE 2

117

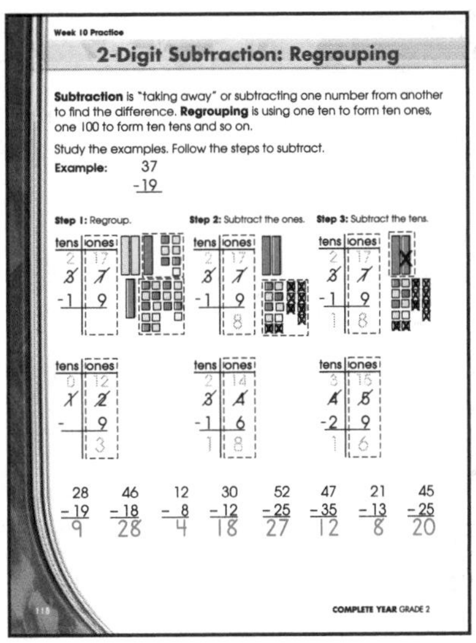

Week 10 Practice

2-Digit Subtraction: Regrouping

Subtraction is "taking away" or subtracting one number from another to find the difference. **Regrouping** is using one ten to form ten ones, one 100 to form ten tens and so on.

Study the examples. Follow the steps to subtract.

Example: 37 − 19

Step 1: Regroup. **Step 2:** Subtract the ones. **Step 3:** Subtract the tens.

28 − 19	46 − 18	12 − 8	30 − 12	52 − 25	47 − 35	21 − 13	45 − 25
9	28	4	18	27	12	8	20

COMPLETE YEAR GRADE 2

118

Week 10 Practice

2-Digit Subtraction: Regrouping

Study the steps for subtracting. Solve the problems using the steps.

STEPS FOR SUBTRACTING

1. DO YOU REGROUP? YES, WHEN BOTTOM NUMBER IS BIGGER THAN THE TOP.
2. SUBTRACT THE ONES.
3. SUBTRACT THE TENS.

47 − 28	64 − 34	53 − 39
19	30	14

56 − 27	83 − 47	43 − 39	75 − 53	91 − 18
29	36	4	22	73

73 − 66	35 − 14	67 − 58	26 − 7	68 − 45
7	21	9	19	23

COMPLETE YEAR GRADE 2

119

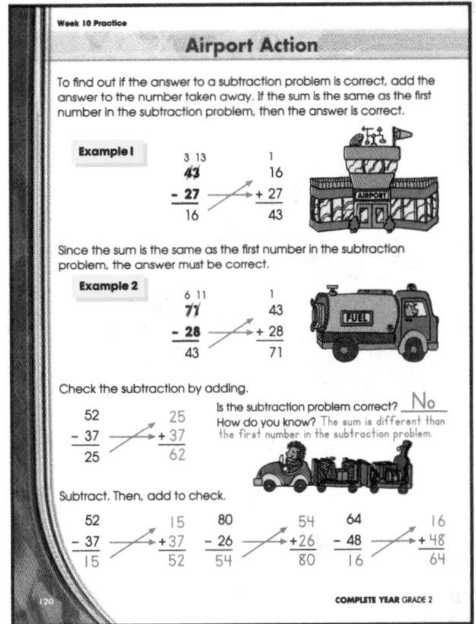

Week 10 Practice

Airport Action

To find out if the answer to a subtraction problem is correct, add the answer to the number taken away. If the sum is the same as the first number in the subtraction problem, then the answer is correct.

Example 1 43 − 27 = 16; 16 + 27 = 43

Since the sum is the same as the first number in the subtraction problem, the answer must be correct.

Example 2 71 − 28 = 43; 43 + 28 = 71

Check the subtraction by adding.

52 − 37 = 25; 25 + 37 = 62

Is the subtraction problem correct? No

How do you know? The sum is different than the first number in the subtraction problem.

Subtract. Then, add to check.

52 − 37 = 15; 15 + 37 = 52 | 80 − 26 = 54; 54 + 26 = 80 | 64 − 48 = 16; 16 + 48 = 64

COMPLETE YEAR GRADE 2

120

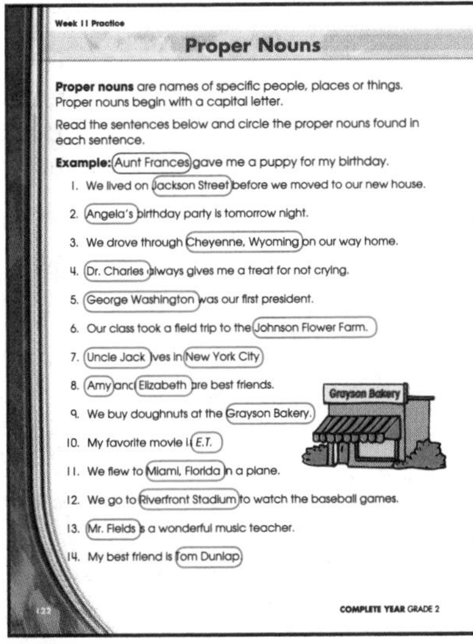

Week 11 Practice

Proper Nouns

Proper nouns are names of specific people, places or things. Proper nouns begin with a capital letter.

Read the sentences below and circle the proper nouns found in each sentence.

Example: (Aunt Frances) gave me a puppy for my birthday.

1. We lived on (Jackson Street) before we moved to our new house.
2. (Angela's) birthday party is tomorrow night.
3. We drove through (Cheyenne, Wyoming) on our way home.
4. (Dr. Charles) always gives me a treat for not crying.
5. (George Washington) was our first president.
6. Our class took a field trip to the (Johnson Flower Farm.)
7. (Uncle Jack) lives in (New York City)
8. (Amy) and (Elizabeth) are best friends.
9. We buy doughnuts at the (Grayson Bakery.)
10. My favorite movie is (E.T.)
11. We flew to (Miami, Florida) in a plane.
12. We go to (Riverfront Stadium) to watch the baseball games.
13. (Mr. Fields) is a wonderful music teacher.
14. My best friend is (Tom Dunlap)

COMPLETE YEAR GRADE 2

122

Week 11 Practice

Proper Nouns

Rewrite each sentence, capitalizing the proper nouns.

1. mike's birthday is in september.

Mike's birthday is in September.

2. aunt katie lives in detroit, michigan.

Aunt Katie lives in Detroit, Michigan.

3. In july, we went to canada.

In July, we went to Canada.

4. kathy jones moved to utah in january.

Kathy Jones moved to Utah in January.

5. My favorite holiday is valentine's day in february.

My favorite holiday is Valentine's Day in February.

6. On friday, mr. polzin gave the smith family a tour.

On Friday, Mr. Polzin gave the Smith family a tour.

7. saturday, uncle cliff and I will go to the mall of america in minnesota.

Saturday, Uncle Cliff and I will go to the Mall of America in Minnesota.

COMPLETE YEAR GRADE 2

123

Answer Key

Week 11 Practice

Proper Nouns

Write about you! Write a proper noun for each category below. Capitalize the first letter of each proper noun.

1. Your first name: ____________
2. Your last name: ____________
3. Your street: ____________
4. ____________
5. ____________
6. Your school: ____________
7. Your best friend's name: ____________
8. Your teacher: ____________
9. Your favorite book character: ____________
10. Your favorite vacation place: ____________

Answers will vary.

COMPLETE YEAR GRADE 2

124

Week 11 Practice

Proper Nouns

A **proper noun** names a specific or certain person, place or thing. A proper noun always begins with a capital letter.

Example: Becky flew to **St. Louis** in a **Boeing 747**.

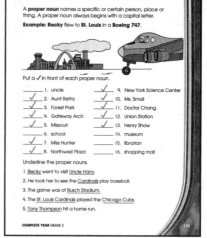

Put a ✓ in front of each proper noun.

____	1. uncle	✓	9. New York Science Center
✓	2. Aunt Retta	✓	10. Ms. Small
✓	3. Forest Park	✓	11. Doctor Chang
✓	4. Gateway Arch	✓	12. Union Station
✓	5. Missouri	✓	13. Henry Shaw
____	6. school	____	14. museum
✓	7. Miss Hunter	____	15. librarian
✓	8. Northwest Plaza	____	16. shopping mall

Underline the proper nouns.

1. Becky went to visit Uncle Harry.
2. He took her to see the Cardinals play baseball.
3. The game was at Busch Stadium.
4. The St. Louis Cardinals played the Chicago Cubs.
5. Tony Thompson hit a home run.

COMPLETE YEAR GRADE 2

125

Week 11 Practice

Subtraction on the Beach

Subtract. Regroup as needed. Color the spaces with differences of:

10–19 **red** 20–29 **blue** 30–39 **green**
40–49 **yellow** 50–59 **brown** 60–69 **orange**

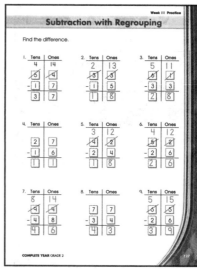

33 − 14 = 19
96 − 47 = 49
67 − 49 = 18
42 − 16 = 26
75 − 53 = 22
80 − 53 = 27
88 − 29 = 59
69 − 24 = 45
85 − 36 = 49
93 − 47 = 46
91 − 25 = 66
70 − 39 = 31
86 − 18 = 68
74 − 26 = 48
73 − 27 = 46

COMPLETE YEAR GRADE 2

126

Week 11 Practice

Subtraction with Regrouping

Find the difference.

1. 54 − 17 = 37 (regrouped: 4 tens 14 ones)
2. 35 − 15 = 18 (regrouped: 2 tens 13 ones)
3. 61 − 33 = 28 (regrouped: 5 tens 11 ones)
4. 27 − 16 = 11
5. 42 − 24 = 18 (regrouped: 3 tens 12 ones)
6. 52 − 26 = 26 (regrouped: 4 tens 12 ones)
7. 94 − 48 = 46 (regrouped: 8 tens 14 ones)
8. 77 − 34 = 43
9. 65 − 26 = 39 (regrouped: 5 tens 15 ones)

COMPLETE YEAR GRADE 2

127

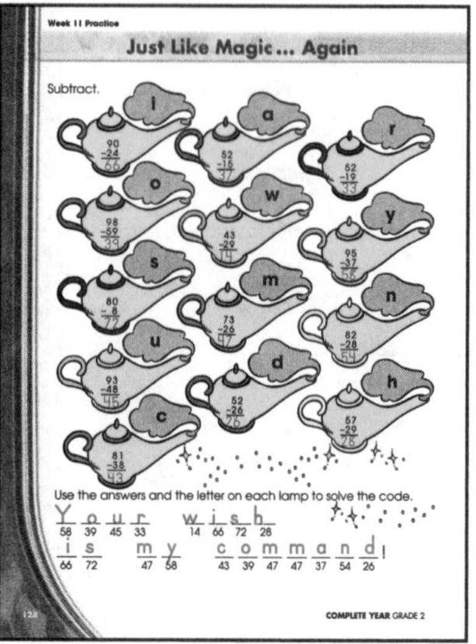
Week 11 Practice

Just Like Magic... Again

Subtract.

l: 90 − 24 = 66
a: 52 − 15 = 37
r: 52 − 19 = 33
o: 98 − 59 = 39
w: 43 − 29 = 14
y: 95 − 37 = 58
s:
m:
n:
c: 80 − 8 = 72
u: 93 − 48 = 45
i: 73 −
d: 52 − 26 = 26
h: 62 − 28 = 34
c: 81 − 38 = 43
h: 67 − 39 = 28

Use the answers and the letter on each lamp to solve the code.

Your wish is my command!

COMPLETE YEAR GRADE 2

128

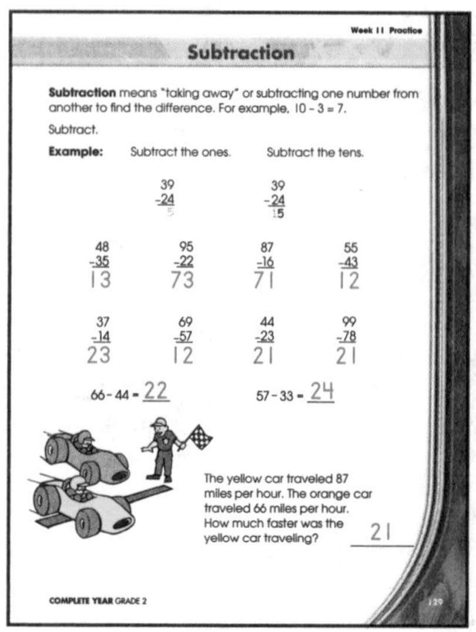
Week 11 Practice

Subtraction

Subtraction means "taking away" or subtracting one number from another to find the difference. For example, 10 − 3 = 7.

Subtract.

Example: Subtract the ones. Subtract the tens.

39 − 24 = 5 (ones); 39 − 24 = 15

48 − 35 = 13 95 − 22 = 73 87 − 16 = 71 55 − 43 = 12

37 − 14 = 23 69 − 57 = 12 44 − 23 = 21 99 − 78 = 21

66 − 44 = 22 57 − 33 = 24

The yellow car traveled 87 miles per hour. The orange car traveled 66 miles per hour. How much faster was the yellow car traveling? 21

COMPLETE YEAR GRADE 2

129

Answer Key

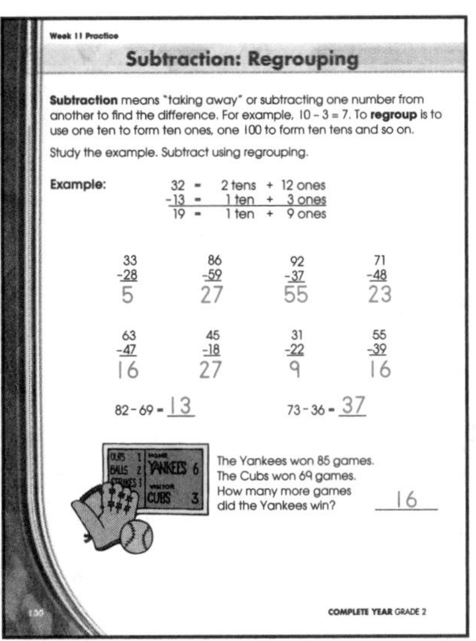

Week 11 Practice

Subtraction: Regrouping

Subtraction means "taking away" or subtracting one number from another to find the difference. For example, 10 - 3 = 7. To **regroup** is to use one ten to form ten ones, one 100 to form ten tens and so on.

Study the example. Subtract using regrouping.

Example: 32 = 2 tens + 12 ones; -13 = 1 ten + 3 ones; 19 = 1 ten + 9 ones

33 - 28 = 5; 86 - 59 = 27; 92 - 37 = 55; 71 - 48 = 23

63 - 47 = 16; 45 - 18 = 27; 31 - 22 = 9; 55 - 39 = 16

82 - 69 = 13   73 - 36 = 37

The Yankees won 85 games. The Cubs won 69 games. How many more games did the Yankees win? 16

COMPLETE YEAR GRADE 2

130

Week 12 Practice

Pronouns

Rewrite each sentence. Replace the underlined words with the correct pronoun.

Tommy packed sandwiches and apples.

He packed sandwiches and apples.

Tommy hiked along the trail.

Tommy hiked along it.

Ed and Larry caught up with Tommy.

They caught up with Tommy.

Rita met the boys at the trail's end.

She met the boys at the trail's end.

Tommy sent Bill one of his photos later.

Tommy sent him one of his photos later.

The boys ate their lunches under a tree.

They ate their lunches under a tree.

After lunch, Rita gave the boys a cookie.

After lunch, she gave the boys a cookie.

COMPLETE YEAR GRADE 2

132

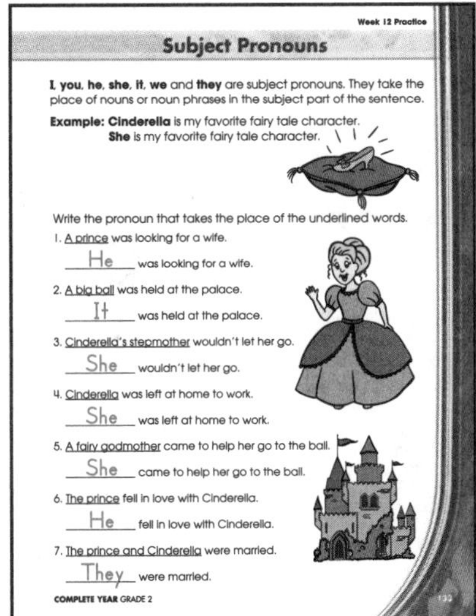

Week 12 Practice

Subject Pronouns

I, you, he, she, it, we and **they** are subject pronouns. They take the place of nouns or noun phrases in the subject part of the sentence.

Example: Cinderella is my favorite fairy tale character.
She is my favorite fairy tale character.

Write the pronoun that takes the place of the underlined words.

1. A prince was looking for a wife.
   He was looking for a wife.
2. A big ball was held at the palace.
   It was held at the palace.
3. Cinderella's stepmother wouldn't let her go.
   She wouldn't let her go.
4. Cinderella was left at home to work.
   She was left at home to work.
5. A fairy godmother came to help her go to the ball.
   She came to help her go to the ball.
6. The prince fell in love with Cinderella.
   He fell in love with Cinderella.
7. The prince and Cinderella were married.
   They were married.

COMPLETE YEAR GRADE 2

133

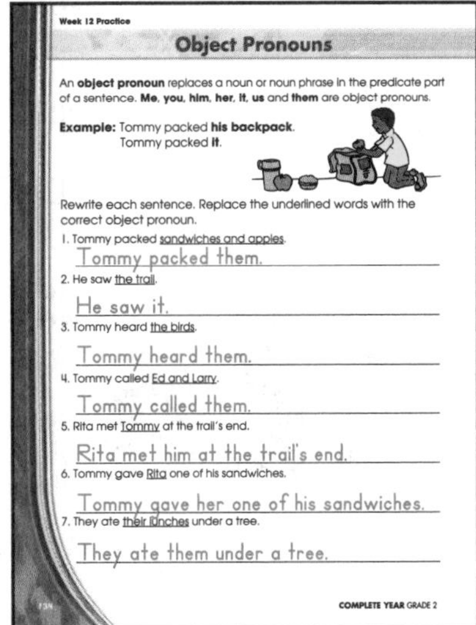

Week 12 Practice

Object Pronouns

An **object pronoun** replaces a noun or noun phrase in the predicate part of a sentence. **Me, you, him, her, it, us** and **them** are object pronouns.

Example: Tommy packed **his backpack**.
Tommy packed **it**.

Rewrite each sentence. Replace the underlined words with the correct object pronoun.

1. Tommy packed sandwiches and apples.
   Tommy packed them.
2. He saw the trail.
   He saw it.
3. Tommy heard the birds.
   Tommy heard them.
4. Tommy called Ed and Larry.
   Tommy called them.
5. Rita met Tommy at the trail's end.
   Rita met him at the trail's end.
6. Tommy gave Rita one of his sandwiches.
   Tommy gave her one of his sandwiches.
7. They ate their lunches under a tree.
   They ate them under a tree.

COMPLETE YEAR GRADE 2

134

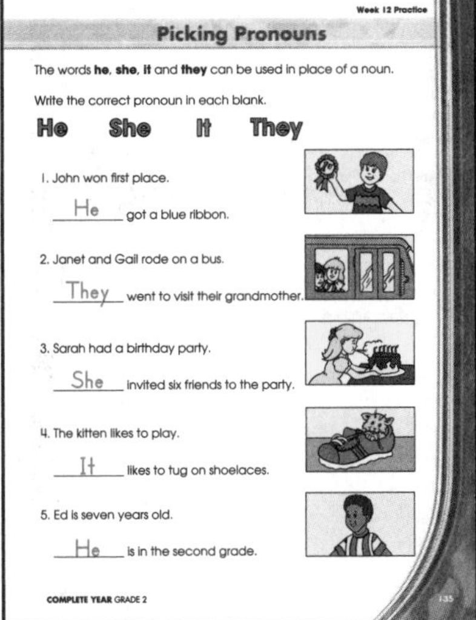

Week 12 Practice

Picking Pronouns

The words **he, she, it** and **they** can be used in place of a noun.

Write the correct pronoun in each blank.

He   She   It   They

1. John won first place.
   He got a blue ribbon.
2. Janet and Gail rode on a bus.
   They went to visit their grandmother.
3. Sarah had a birthday party.
   She invited six friends to the party.
4. The kitten likes to play.
   It likes to tug on shoelaces.
5. Ed is seven years old.
   He is in the second grade.

COMPLETE YEAR GRADE 2

135

Week 12 Practice

Pronouns

Pronouns are words that are used in place of nouns.

Examples: he, she, it, they, him, them, her, him

Read each sentence. Write the pronoun that takes the place of each noun.

Example:
The **monkey** dropped the banana. It

1. **Dad** washed the car last night. He
2. **Mary and David** took a walk in the park. They
3. **Peggy** spent the night at her grandmother's house. She
4. The baseball **players** lost their game. they
5. **Mike Van Meter** is a great soccer player. He
6. The **parrot** can say five different words. It
7. **Megan** wrote a story in class today. She
8. They gave a party for **Teresa**. her
9. Everyone in the class was happy for **Ted**. him
10. The children petted the **giraffe**. it
11. Linda put the **kittens** near the warm stove. them
12. **Gina** made a chocolate cake for my birthday. She
13. **Pete and Matt** played baseball on the same team. They
14. Give the books to **Herbie**. him

COMPLETE YEAR GRADE 2

136

Answer Key

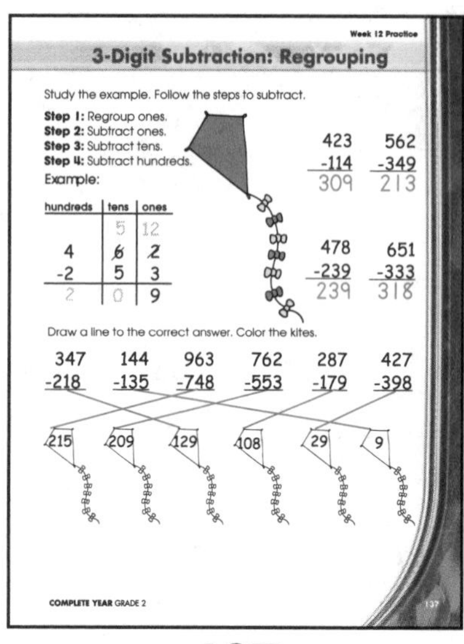

Week 12 Practice

3-Digit Subtraction: Regrouping

Study the example. Follow the steps to subtract.

Step 1: Regroup ones.
Step 2: Subtract ones.
Step 3: Subtract tens.
Step 4: Subtract hundreds.

Example:

	hundreds	tens	ones
		5	12
	4	6	2
-	2	5	3
	2	0	9

423 − 114 = 309
562 − 349 = 213
478 − 239 = 239
651 − 333 = 318

Draw a line to the correct answer. Color the kites.

347 − 218, 144 − 135, 963 − 748, 762 − 553, 287 − 179, 427 − 398

215, 209, 129, 108, 29, 9

COMPLETE YEAR GRADE 2 137

137

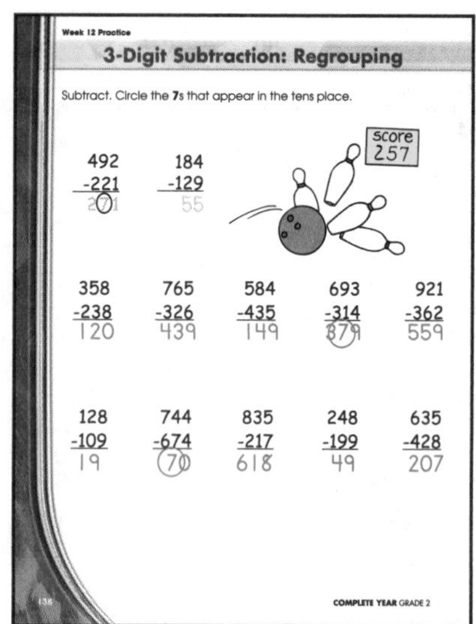

Week 12 Practice

3-Digit Subtraction: Regrouping

Subtract. Circle the **7**s that appear in the tens place.

492 − 221 = 271
184 − 129 = 55

358 − 238 = 120
765 − 326 = 439
584 − 435 = 149
693 − 314 = 379
921 − 362 = 559

128 − 109 = 19
744 − 674 = 70
835 − 217 = 618
248 − 199 = 49
635 − 428 = 207

138 COMPLETE YEAR GRADE 2

138

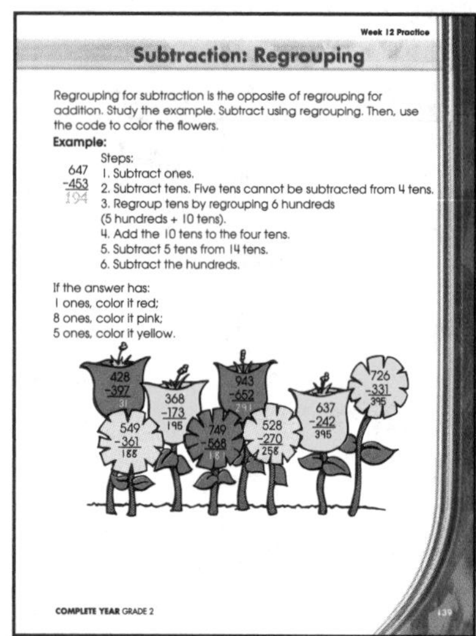

Week 12 Practice

Subtraction: Regrouping

Regrouping for subtraction is the opposite of regrouping for addition. Study the example. Subtract using regrouping. Then, use the code to color the flowers.

Example:

647 − 453 = 194

Steps:
1. Subtract ones.
2. Subtract tens. Five tens cannot be subtracted from 4 tens.
3. Regroup tens by regrouping 6 hundreds (5 hundreds + 10 tens).
4. Add the 10 tens to the four tens.
5. Subtract 5 tens from 14 tens.
6. Subtract the hundreds.

If the answer has:
1 ones, color it red;
8 ones, color it pink;
5 ones, color it yellow.

COMPLETE YEAR GRADE 2 139

139

Week 12 Practice

Subtraction: Regrouping

Study the example. Follow the steps. Subtract using regrouping.

Example:

634 − 455 = 179

Steps:
1. Subtract ones. You cannot subtract five ones from 4 ones.
2. Regroup ones by regrouping 3 tens to 2 tens + 10 ones.
3. Subtract 5 ones from 14 ones.
4. Regroup tens by regrouping hundreds (5 hundreds + 10 tens).
5. Subtract 5 tens from 12 tens.
6. Subtract hundreds.

635 − 169 = 466
553 − 174 = 379
832 − 563 = 269
944 − 578 = 366

423 − 268 = 155
941 − 872 = 69
733 − 498 = 235
266 − 197 = 69

387 − 198 = 189
594 − 385 = 209
960 − 759 = 201
887 − 598 = 289

Sue goes to school 185 days a year. Yoko goes to school 313 days a year. How many more days of school does Yoko attend each year? 128

140 COMPLETE YEAR GRADE 2

140

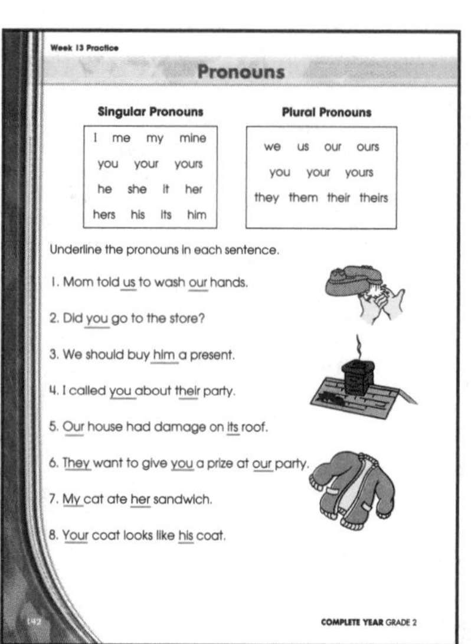

Week 13 Practice

Pronouns

Singular Pronouns			
I	me	my	mine
you	your	yours	
he	she	it	her
hers	his	its	him

Plural Pronouns			
we	us	our	ours
you	your	yours	
they	them	their	theirs

Underline the pronouns in each sentence.

1. Mom told us to wash our hands.
2. Did you go to the store?
3. We should buy him a present.
4. I called you about their party.
5. Our house had damage on its roof.
6. They want to give you a prize at our party.
7. My cat ate her sandwich.
8. Your coat looks like his coat.

142 COMPLETE YEAR GRADE 2

142

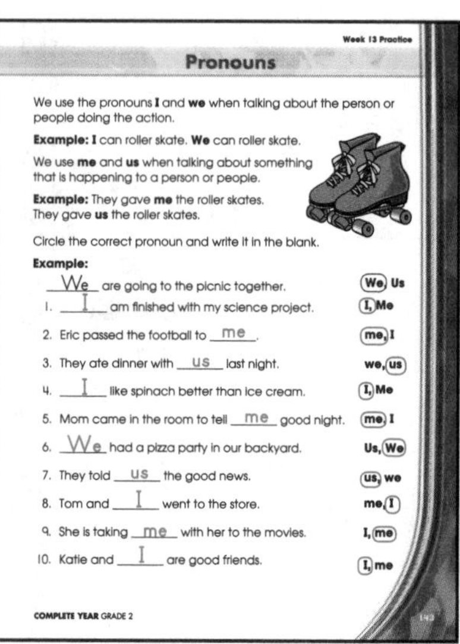

Week 13 Practice

Pronouns

We use the pronouns **I** and **we** when talking about the person or people doing the action.

Example: I can roller skate. **We** can roller skate.

We use **me** and **us** when talking about something that is happening to a person or people.

Example: They gave **me** the roller skates. They gave **us** the roller skates.

Circle the correct pronoun and write it in the blank.

Example:
We are going to the picnic together. **We, Us**

1. I am finished with my science project. **I, Me**
2. Eric passed the football to me. **me, I**
3. They ate dinner with us last night. **we, us**
4. I like spinach better than ice cream. **I, Me**
5. Mom came in the room to tell me good night. **me, I**
6. We had a pizza party in our backyard. **Us, We**
7. They told us the good news. **us, we**
8. Tom and I went to the store. **me, I**
9. She is taking me with her to the movies. **I, me**
10. Katie and I are good friends. **I, me**

COMPLETE YEAR GRADE 2 143

143

Answer Key

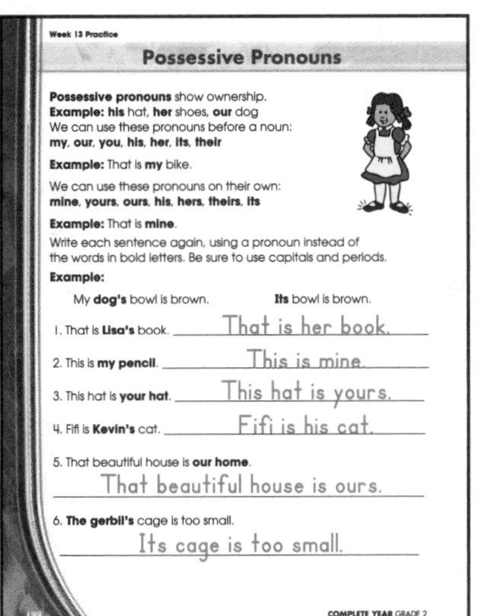

Week 13 Practice

Possessive Pronouns

Possessive pronouns show ownership.
Example: his hat, **her** shoes, **our** dog
We can use these pronouns before a noun:
my, our, you, his, her, its, their

Example: That is **my** bike.

We can use these pronouns on their own:
mine, yours, ours, his, hers, theirs, its

Example: That is **mine**.

Write each sentence again, using a pronoun instead of the words in bold letters. Be sure to use capitals and periods.

Example:

My **dog's** bowl is brown. **Its** bowl is brown.

1. That is **Lisa's** book. That is her book.
2. This is **my pencil**. This is mine.
3. This hat is **your hat**. This hat is yours.
4. Fifi is **Kevin's** cat. Fifi is his cat.
5. That beautiful house is **our home**. That beautiful house is ours.
6. **The gerbil's** cage is too small. Its cage is too small.

COMPLETE YEAR GRADE 2

144

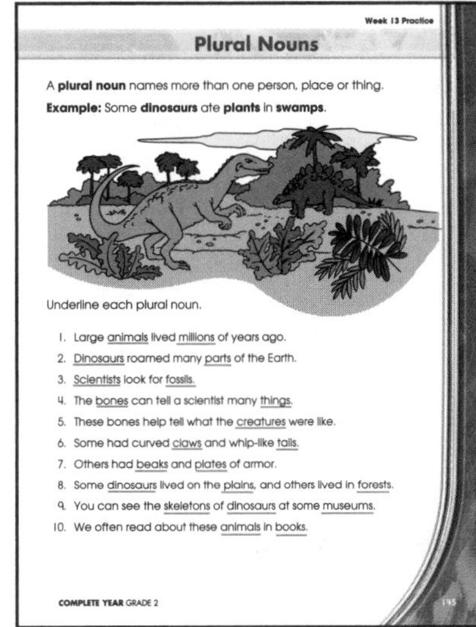

Week 13 Practice

Plural Nouns

A **plural noun** names more than one person, place or thing.
Example: Some **dinosaurs** ate **plants** in **swamps**.

Underline each plural noun.

1. Large animals lived millions of years ago.
2. Dinosaurs roamed many parts of the Earth.
3. Scientists look for fossils.
4. The bones can tell a scientist many things.
5. These bones help tell what the creatures were like.
6. Some had curved claws and whip-like tails.
7. Others had beaks and plates of armor.
8. Some dinosaurs lived on the plains, and others lived in forests.
9. You can see the skeletons of dinosaurs at some museums.
10. We often read about these animals in books.

COMPLETE YEAR GRADE 2

145

Week 13 Practice

Plural Nouns

A **plural** is more than one person, place or thing. We usually add an **s** to show that a noun names more than one. If a noun ends in **x, ch, sh** or **s**, we add an **es** to the word.

Example: pizza pizzas

Write the plural of the words below.

Example: dog + s = dogs
cat cats
boot boots
house houses

Example: peach + es = peaches
lunch lunches
bunch bunches
punch punches

Example: ax + es = axes
fox foxes
tax taxes
box boxes

Example: glass + es = glasses
mess messes
guess guesses
class classes

Example: dish + es = dishes
bush bushes
ash ashes
brush brushes

walrus
walruses

COMPLETE YEAR GRADE 2

146

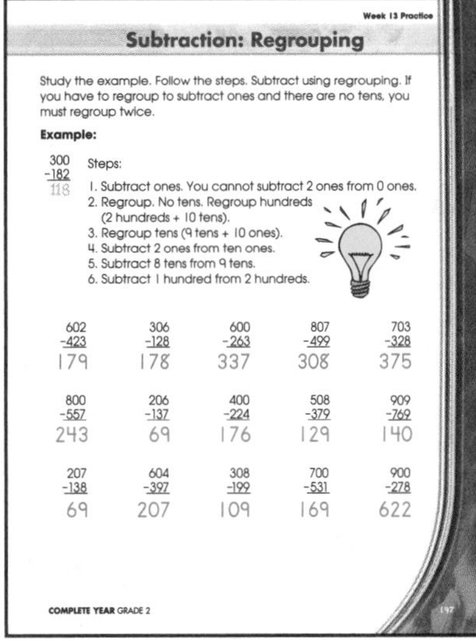

Week 13 Practice

Subtraction: Regrouping

Study the example. Follow the steps. Subtract using regrouping. If you have to regroup to subtract ones and there are no tens, you must regroup twice.

Example:

300 − 182 = 118

Steps:
1. Subtract ones. You cannot subtract 2 ones from 0 ones.
2. Regroup. No tens. Regroup hundreds (2 hundreds + 10 tens).
3. Regroup tens (9 tens + 10 ones).
4. Subtract 2 ones from ten ones.
5. Subtract 8 tens from 9 tens.
6. Subtract 1 hundred from 2 hundreds.

602 −423 = 179	306 −128 = 178	600 −263 = 337	807 −499 = 308	703 −328 = 375
800 −557 = 243	206 −137 = 69	400 −224 = 176	508 −379 = 129	909 −769 = 140
207 −138 = 69	604 −397 = 207	308 −199 = 109	700 −531 = 169	900 −278 = 622

COMPLETE YEAR GRADE 2

147

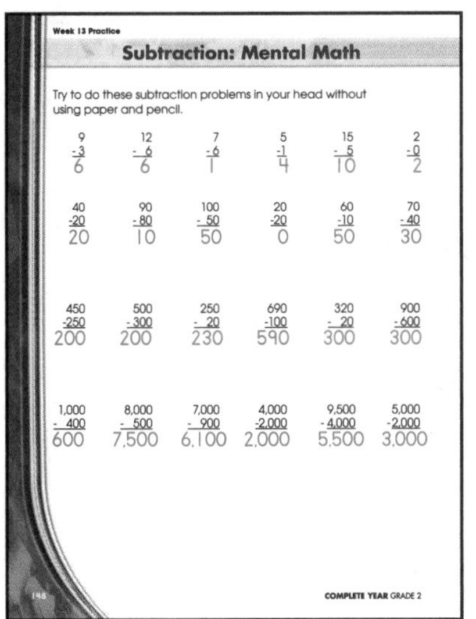

Week 13 Practice

Subtraction: Mental Math

Try to do these subtraction problems in your head without using paper and pencil.

9 −3 = 6	12 −6 = 6	7 −6 = 1	5 −1 = 4	15 −5 = 10	2 −0 = 2
40 −20 = 20	90 −80 = 10	100 −50 = 50	20 −20 = 0	60 −10 = 50	70 −40 = 30
450 −250 = 200	500 −300 = 200	250 −20 = 230	690 −100 = 590	320 −20 = 300	900 −600 = 300
1,000 −400 = 600	8,000 −500 = 7,500	7,000 −900 = 6,100	4,000 −2,000 = 2,000	9,500 −4,000 = 5,500	5,000 −2,000 = 3,000

COMPLETE YEAR GRADE 2

148

Week 13 Practice

Addition and Subtraction

Complete the facts to 10.

10 −6 = 4	7 +3 = 10	4 −2 = 2	6 −2 = 4	9 −7 = 2
4 +1 = 5	10 −8 = 2	5 −1 = 4	6 +4 = 10	3 −2 = 1
5 +4 = 9	7 −1 = 6	6 −3 = 3	5 +2 = 7	3 +7 = 10

9 −2 = 7	2 +6 = 8	4 +3 = 7	1 +9 = 10	2 −1 = 1	8 −6 = 2	2 +1 = 3	10 −3 = 7	4 +2 = 6	7 +2 = 9
9 −4 = 5	3 +5 = 8	2 +8 = 10	6 −3 = 3	5 +5 = 10	5 −3 = 2	8 +2 = 10	5 −4 = 1	3 +7 = 10	8 −1 = 7

COMPLETE YEAR GRADE 2

149

Answer Key

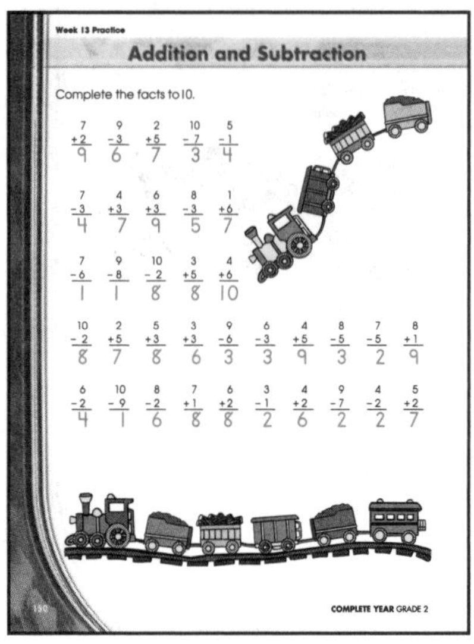

Week 13 Practice

Addition and Subtraction

Complete the facts to 10.

7 + 2 = 9 | 9 − 3 = 6 | 2 + 5 = 7 | 10 − 7 = 3 | 5 − 1 = 4

7 − 3 = 4 | 4 + 3 = 7 | 6 + 3 = 9 | 8 − 3 = 5 | 1 + 6 = 7

7 − 6 = 1 | 9 − 8 = 1 | 10 − 2 = 8 | 3 + 5 = 8 | 4 + 6 = 10

10 − 2 = 8 | 2 + 5 = 7 | 5 + 3 = 8 | 3 + 3 = 6 | 9 − 6 = 3 | 6 − 3 = 3 | 4 + 5 = 9 | 8 − 5 = 3 | 7 − 5 = 2 | 8 + 1 = 9

6 − 2 = 4 | 10 − 9 = 1 | 8 − 2 = 6 | 7 + 1 = 8 | 6 + 2 = 8 | 3 − 1 = 2 | 4 + 2 = 6 | 9 − 7 = 2 | 4 − 2 = 2 | 5 + 2 = 7

150 COMPLETE YEAR GRADE 2

150

Week 14 Practice

Plural Nouns

Write the plural of each noun to complete the sentences below. Remember to change the **y** to **ie** before you add **s**!

1. I am going to two birthday parties (party) this week.
2. Sandy picked some cherries (cherry) for Mom's pie.
3. At the store, we saw lots of bunnies (bunny).
4. My change at the candy store was three pennies (penny).
5. All the ladies (lady) baked cookies for the bake sale.
6. Thanksgiving is a special time for families (family) to gather together.
7. Boston and New York are very large cities (city).

152 COMPLETE YEAR GRADE 2

152

Week 14 Practice

Plural Nouns

To write the plural forms of words ending in **y**, we change the **y** to **ie** and add **s**.

Example: pony ponies

Write the plural of each noun on the lines below.

berry berries
cherry cherries
bunny bunnies
penny pennies
family families
candy candies
party parties

Now, write a story using some of the words that end in **y**. Remember to use capital letters and periods.

Answers will vary.

COMPLETE YEAR GRADE 2 153

153

Week 14 Practice

Plural Nouns

Some words have special plural forms.

Example: leaf leaves

tooth	teeth
child	children
foot	feet
mouse	mice
woman	women
man	men

Some of the words in the box are special plurals. Complete each sentence with a plural from the box. Then, write the letters from the boxes in the blanks below to solve the puzzle.

1. I lost my two front t e e t h.
2. My sister has two pet m i c e.
3. Her favorite book is Little W o m e n.
4. The circus clown had big f e e t.
5. The teacher played a game with the c h i l d r e n.

Take good care of this pearly plural!

t e e t h
1 2 3 4 5

154 COMPLETE YEAR GRADE 2

154

Week 14 Practice

Plural Nouns

Plural nouns name more than one person, place or thing.

Read the words in the box. Write the words in the correct column.

children	girl	mice	kittens	cake
feet	glass	book	horse	teeth

one	more than one
girl	children
glass	feet
book	mice
horse	kittens
cake	teeth

COMPLETE YEAR GRADE 2 155

155

Week 14 Practice

Plural Pronouns

The **singular form** of a word shows one person, place or thing. Write the singular form of each noun on the lines below.

cherries cherry
lunches lunch
countries country
leaves leaf
churches church
arms arm
boxes box
men man
wheels wheel
pictures picture
cities city
places place
ostriches ostrich
glasses glass

156 COMPLETE YEAR GRADE 2

156

Answer Key

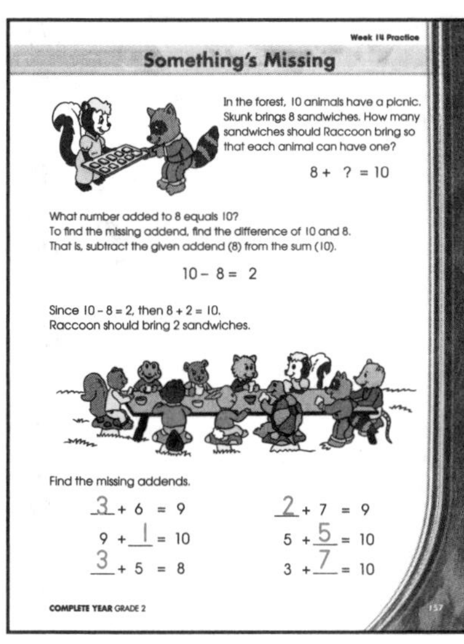

Week 14 Practice

Something's Missing

In the forest, 10 animals have a picnic. Skunk brings 8 sandwiches. How many sandwiches should Raccoon bring so that each animal can have one?

8 + ? = 10

What number added to 8 equals 10?
To find the missing addend, find the difference of 10 and 8.
That is, subtract the given addend (8) from the sum (10).

10 − 8 = 2

Since 10 − 8 = 2, then 8 + 2 = 10.
Raccoon should bring 2 sandwiches.

Find the missing addends.

3 + 6 = 9 | 2 + 7 = 9
9 + 1 = 10 | 5 + 5 = 10
3 + 5 = 8 | 3 + 7 = 10

COMPLETE YEAR GRADE 2 157

157

Week 14 Practice

A Hidden Message

Add or subtract. Use the code to find out your new motto!

Code:

9	18	6	15	13	12	16	11	8	7	14	17
H	Y	D	E	V	T	S	O	A	M	N	I

9 +8	16 −7	16 −8	8 +5	6 +9	14 −7	9 +9
17	9	8	13	15	7	18
I	H	A	V	E	M	Y

17 −8	15 −7	9 +5	13 −7	8 +8
9	8	14	6	16
H	A	N	D	S

4 +7	6 +8	12 −5	17 −9	6 +6	15 −6
11	14	7	8	12	9
O	N	M	A	T	H

158 COMPLETE YEAR GRADE 2

158

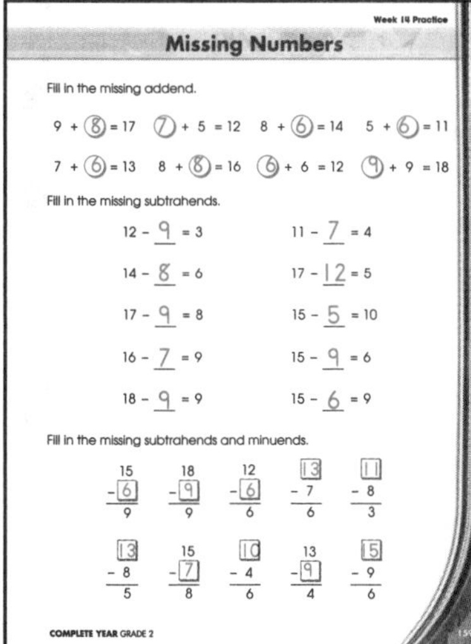

Week 14 Practice

Missing Numbers

Fill in the missing addend.

9 + (8) = 17 (7) + 5 = 12 8 + (6) = 14 5 + (6) = 11

7 + (6) = 13 8 + (8) = 16 (6) + 6 = 12 (9) + 9 = 18

Fill in the missing subtrahends.

12 − 9 = 3 | 11 − 7 = 4
14 − 8 = 6 | 17 − 12 = 5
17 − 9 = 8 | 15 − 5 = 10
16 − 7 = 9 | 15 − 9 = 6
18 − 9 = 9 | 15 − 6 = 9

Fill in the missing subtrahends and minuends.

15 − [6] = 9 18 − [9] = 9 12 − [6] = 6 [13] − 7 = 6 [11] − 8 = 3

[13] − 8 = 5 15 − [7] = 8 [10] − 4 = 6 13 − [9] = 4 [15] − 9 = 6

COMPLETE YEAR GRADE 2 159

159

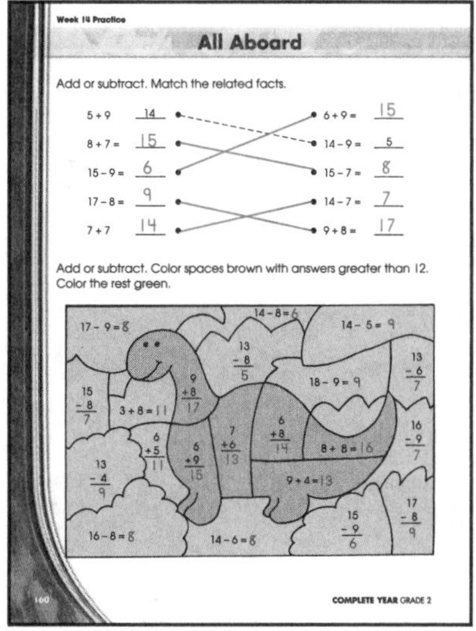

Week 14 Practice

All Aboard

Add or subtract. Match the related facts.

5 + 9 14 • • 6 + 9 = 15
8 + 7 = 15 • • 14 − 9 = 5
15 − 9 = 6 • • 15 − 7 = 8
17 − 8 = 9 • • 14 − 7 = 7
7 + 7 14 • • 9 + 8 = 17

Add or subtract. Color spaces brown with answers greater than 12. Color the rest green.

160 COMPLETE YEAR GRADE 2

160

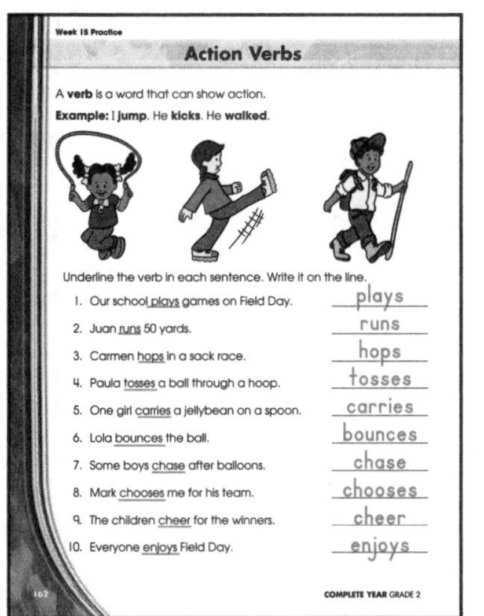

Week 15 Practice

Action Verbs

A **verb** is a word that can show action.
Example: I jump. He **kicks.** He **walked.**

Underline the verb in each sentence. Write it on the line.

1. Our school plays games on Field Day. plays
2. Juan runs 50 yards. runs
3. Carmen hops in a sack race. hops
4. Paula tosses a ball through a hoop. tosses
5. One girl carries a jellybean on a spoon. carries
6. Lola bounces the ball. bounces
7. Some boys chase after balloons. chase
8. Mark chooses me for his team. chooses
9. The children cheer for the winners. cheer
10. Everyone enjoys Field Day. enjoys

162 COMPLETE YEAR GRADE 2

162

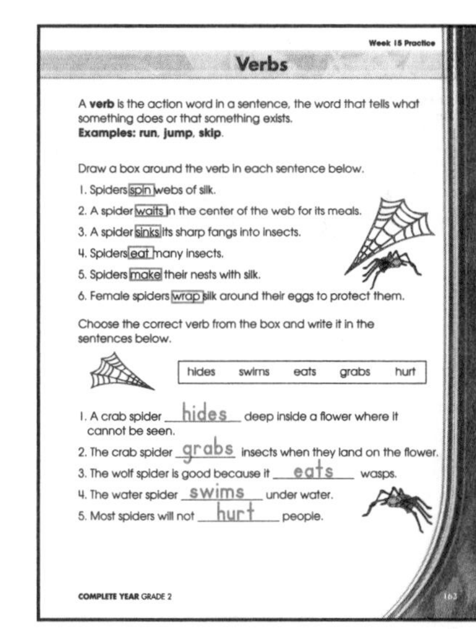

Week 15 Practice

Verbs

A **verb** is the action word in a sentence, the word that tells what something does or that something exists.
Examples: run, jump, skip

Draw a box around the verb in each sentence below.

1. Spiders [spin] webs of silk.
2. A spider [waits] in the center of the web for its meals.
3. A spider [sinks] its sharp fangs into insects.
4. Spiders [eat] many insects.
5. Spiders [make] their nests with silk.
6. Female spiders [wrap] silk around their eggs to protect them.

Choose the correct verb from the box and write it in the sentences below.

hides	swims	eats	grabs	hurt

1. A crab spider hides deep inside a flower where it cannot be seen.
2. The crab spider grabs insects when they land on the flower.
3. The wolf spider is good because it eats wasps.
4. The water spider swims under water.
5. Most spiders will not hurt people.

COMPLETE YEAR GRADE 2 163

163

Answer Key

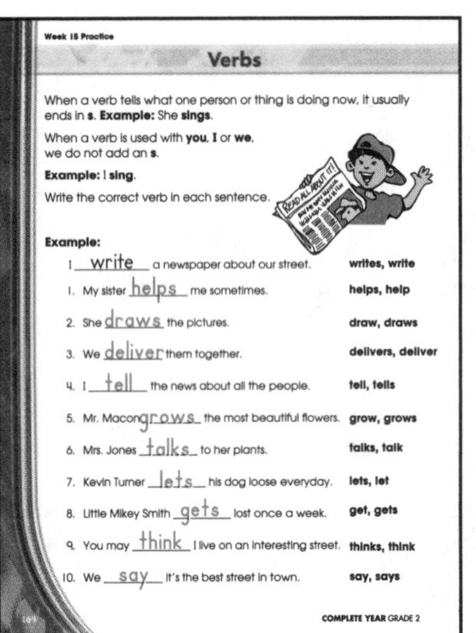

Week 15 Practice

Verbs

When a verb tells what one person or thing is doing now, it usually ends in **s**. **Example:** She **sings**.

When a verb is used with **you**, **I** or **we**, we do not add an **s**.

Example: I **sing**.

Write the correct verb in each sentence.

Example:

I write a newspaper about our street. — **writes, write**

1. My sister helps me sometimes. — **helps, help**
2. She draws the pictures. — **draw, draws**
3. We deliver them together. — **delivers, deliver**
4. I tell the news about all the people. — **tell, tells**
5. Mr. Macon grows the most beautiful flowers. — **grow, grows**
6. Mrs. Jones talks to her plants. — **talks, talk**
7. Kevin Turner lets his dog loose everyday. — **lets, let**
8. Little Mikey Smith gets lost once a week. — **get, gets**
9. You may think I live on an interesting street. — **thinks, think**
10. We say it's the best street in town. — **say, says**

COMPLETE YEAR GRADE 2

164

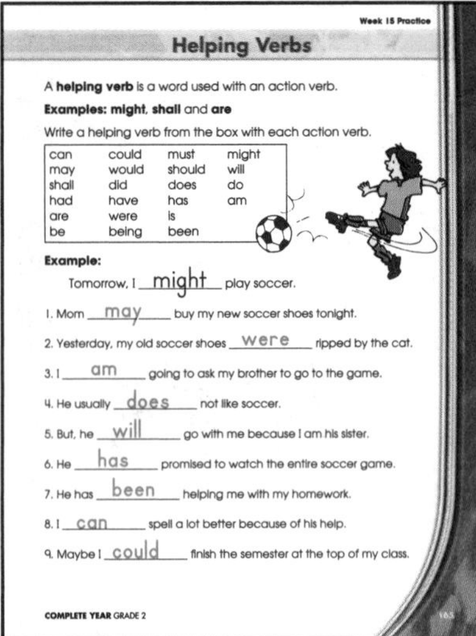

Week 15 Practice

Helping Verbs

A **helping verb** is a word used with an action verb.

Examples: might, **shall** and **are**

Write a helping verb from the box with each action verb.

can	could	must	might
may	would	should	will
shall	did	does	do
had	have	has	am
are	were	is	
be	being	been	

Example:

Tomorrow, I might play soccer.

1. Mom may buy my new soccer shoes tonight.
2. Yesterday, my old soccer shoes were ripped by the cat.
3. I am going to ask my brother to go to the game.
4. He usually does not like soccer.
5. But, he will go with me because I am his sister.
6. He has promised to watch the entire soccer game.
7. He has been helping me with my homework.
8. I can spell a lot better because of his help.
9. Maybe I could finish the semester at the top of my class.

COMPLETE YEAR GRADE 2

165

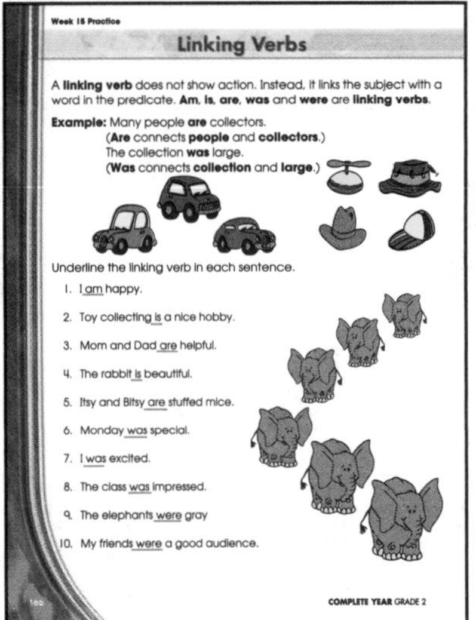

Week 15 Practice

Linking Verbs

A **linking verb** does not show action. Instead, it links the subject with a word in the predicate. **Am**, **is**, **are**, **was** and **were** are **linking verbs**.

Example: Many people **are** collectors.
(**Are** connects **people** and **collectors**.)
The collection **was** large.
(**Was** connects **collection** and **large**.)

Underline the linking verb in each sentence.

1. I am happy.
2. Toy collecting is a nice hobby.
3. Mom and Dad are helpful.
4. The rabbit is beautiful.
5. Itsy and Bitsy are stuffed mice.
6. Monday was special.
7. I was excited.
8. The class was impressed.
9. The elephants were gray
10. My friends were a good audience.

COMPLETE YEAR GRADE 2

166

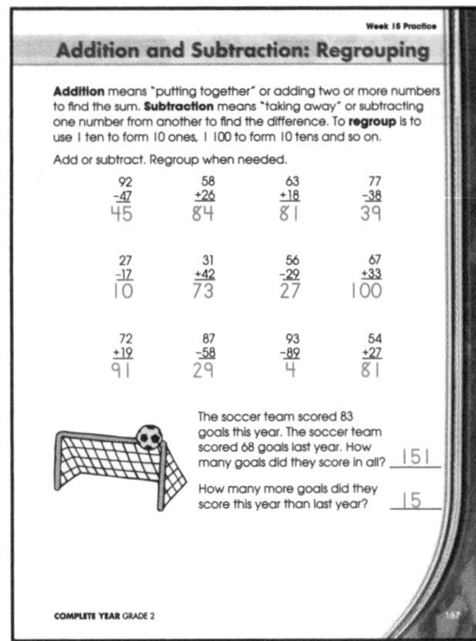

Week 15 Practice

Addition and Subtraction: Regrouping

Addition means "putting together" or adding two or more numbers to find the sum. **Subtraction** means "taking away" or subtracting one number from another to find the difference. To **regroup** is to use 1 ten to form 10 ones, 1 100 to form 10 tens and so on.

Add or subtract. Regroup when needed.

92 − 47 = 45	58 + 26 = 84	63 + 18 = 81	77 − 38 = 39
27 − 17 = 10	31 + 42 = 73	56 − 29 = 27	67 + 33 = 100
72 + 19 = 91	87 − 58 = 29	93 − 89 = 4	54 + 27 = 81

The soccer team scored 83 goals this year. The soccer team scored 68 goals last year. How many goals did they score in all? 151

How many more goals did they score this year than last year? 15

COMPLETE YEAR GRADE 2

167

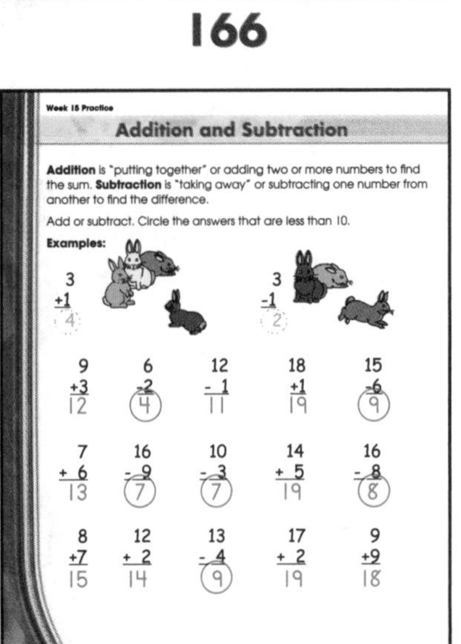

Week 15 Practice

Addition and Subtraction

Addition is "putting together" or adding two or more numbers to find the sum. **Subtraction** is "taking away" or subtracting one number from another to find the difference.

Add or subtract. Circle the answers that are less than 10.

Examples: 3 + 1 = (4) 3 − 1 = (2)

9 + 3 = 12	6 − 2 = (4)	12 − 1 = 11	18 + 1 = 19	15 − 6 = (9)
7 + 6 = 13	16 − 9 = (7)	10 − 3 = (7)	14 + 5 = 19	16 − 8 = (8)
8 + 7 = 15	12 + 2 = 14	13 − 4 = (9)	17 + 2 = 19	9 + 9 = 18

COMPLETE YEAR GRADE 2

168

Week 15 Practice

Review

Add or subtract. Use regrouping when needed. Always do ones first and tens last.

tens ones	tens ones	tens ones	tens ones
93 − 25 = 68	30 + 27 = 57	65 + 17 = 82	71 − 36 = 35
76 − 28 = 48	82 + 19 = 101	56 − 28 = 28	25 − 16 = 9
43 − 14 = 29	53 − 15 = 38	24 + 57 = 81	48 + 28 = 76
33 + 47 = 80	52 + 29 = 81	46 − 37 = 9	97 − 68 = 29

COMPLETE YEAR GRADE 2

169

Answer Key

Week 16 Practice

2-Digit Addition and Subtraction

Addition is "putting together" or adding two or more numbers to find the sum. **Subtraction** is "taking away" or subtracting one number from another to find the difference. **Regrouping** is using 1 ten to form 10 ones, 1 100 to form 10 tens, and so on.

Add or subtract using regrouping.

Example:

tens	ones
2	15
3	5
-2	7
	8

56	40	35	42	53	97	44	93
− 27	− 16	+ 27	− 14	+38	− 48	+ 27	− 39
29	24	62	28	91	49	71	54

56	44	68	73	33	49	77	27
− 17	+ 28	− 49	− 24	+ 18	+ 32	− 68	+ 19
39	72	19	49	51	81	9	46

170 COMPLETE YEAR GRADE 2

170

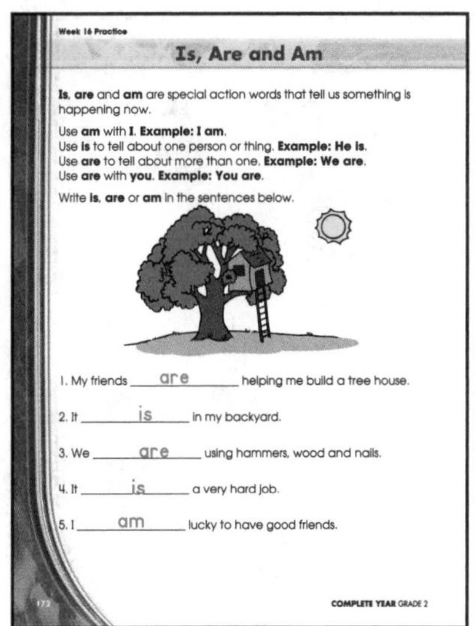
Week 16 Practice

Is, Are and Am

Is, **are** and **am** are special action words that tell us something is happening now.

Use **am** with **I**. **Example: I am.**
Use **is** to tell about one person or thing. **Example: He is.**
Use **are** to tell about more than one. **Example: We are.**
Use **are** with **you**. **Example: You are.**
Write **is**, **are** or **am** in the sentences below.

1. My friends ___are___ helping me build a tree house.
2. It ___is___ in my backyard.
3. We ___are___ using hammers, wood and nails.
4. It ___is___ a very hard job.
5. I ___am___ lucky to have good friends.

172 COMPLETE YEAR GRADE 2

172

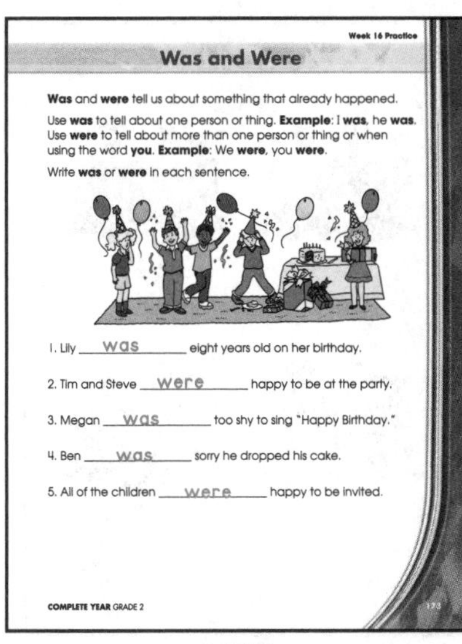
Week 16 Practice

Was and Were

Was and **were** tell us about something that already happened.

Use **was** to tell about one person or thing. **Example**: I **was**, he **was**.
Use **were** to tell about more than one person or thing or when using the word **you**. **Example**: We **were**, you **were**.

Write **was** or **were** in each sentence.

1. Lily ___was___ eight years old on her birthday.
2. Tim and Steve ___were___ happy to be at the party.
3. Megan ___was___ too shy to sing "Happy Birthday."
4. Ben ___was___ sorry he dropped his cake.
5. All of the children ___were___ happy to be invited.

COMPLETE YEAR GRADE 2 173

173

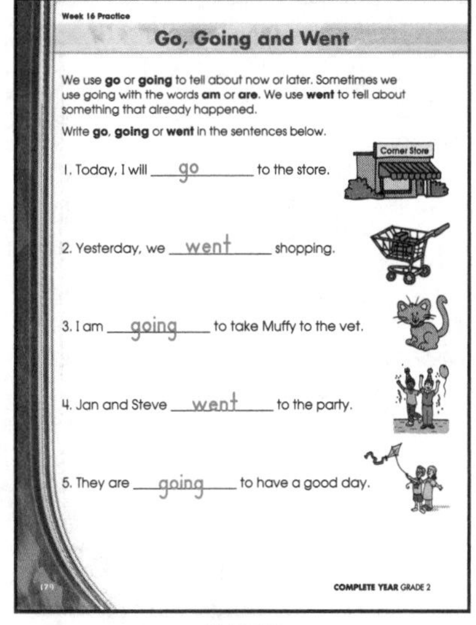
Week 16 Practice

Go, Going and Went

We use **go** or **going** to tell about now or later. Sometimes we use going with the words **am** or **are**. We use **went** to tell about something that already happened.

Write **go**, **going** or **went** in the sentences below.

1. Today, I will ___go___ to the store.
2. Yesterday, we ___went___ shopping.
3. I am ___going___ to take Muffy to the vet.
4. Jan and Steve ___went___ to the party.
5. They are ___going___ to have a good day.

174 COMPLETE YEAR GRADE 2

174

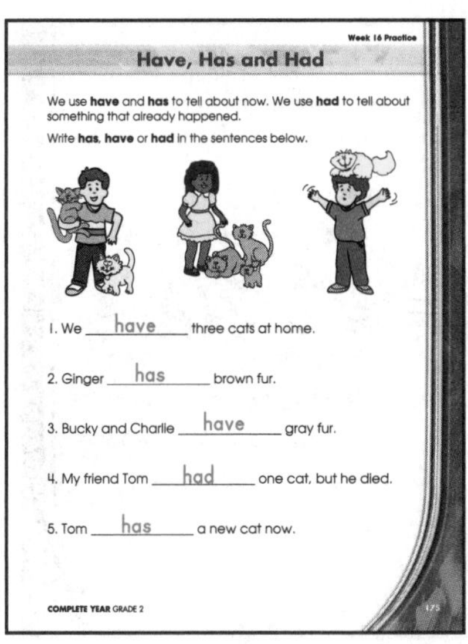
Week 16 Practice

Have, Has and Had

We use **have** and **has** to tell about now. We use **had** to tell about something that already happened.

Write **has**, **have** or **had** in the sentences below.

1. We ___have___ three cats at home.
2. Ginger ___has___ brown fur.
3. Bucky and Charlie ___have___ gray fur.
4. My friend Tom ___had___ one cat, but he died.
5. Tom ___has___ a new cat now.

COMPLETE YEAR GRADE 2 175

175

Week 16 Practice

See, Saw and Sees

We use **see** or **sees** to tell about now. We use **saw** to tell about something that already happened.

Write **see**, **sees** or **saw** in the sentences below.

1. Last night, we ___saw___ the stars.
2. John can ___see___ the stars from his window.
3. He ___sees___ them every night.
4. Last week, he ___saw___ the Big Dipper.
5. Can you ___see___ it in the night sky, too?
6. If you ___saw___ it, you would remember it!
7. John ___sees___ it often now.
8. How often do you ___see___ it?

176 COMPLETE YEAR GRADE 2

176

Answer Key

Week 16 Practice

2-Digit Addition and Subtraction

Add or subtract using regrouping

23 +48 = 71	84 -56 = 28	69 +29 = 98	41 -17 = 24
52 -28 = 24	73 +18 = 91	84 -27 = 57	57 -39 = 18
33 -15 = 18	64 +17 = 81	37 +58 = 95	36 -19 = 17
65 -28 = 37	48 -30 = 18	33 +18 = 51	25 +35 = 60

COMPLETE YEAR GRADE 2 177

177

Week 16 Practice

Review

Counting

Write the number that is:

next	one less	one greater
68, 69, 70	56, 57	12, 13
786, 787, 788	649, 650	843, 844

Place Value: Tens and Ones

Draw a line to the correct number.

4 tens + 7 ones — 47
2 tens + 0 ones — 20
7 tens + 3 ones — 73
5 tens + 1 one — 51

Addition and Subtraction

Add or subtract.

15 + 5 = 20	14 - 4 = 10	7 + 3 = 10	8 - 6 = 2	10 + 7 = 17	14 - 5 = 9

178 COMPLETE YEAR GRADE 2

178

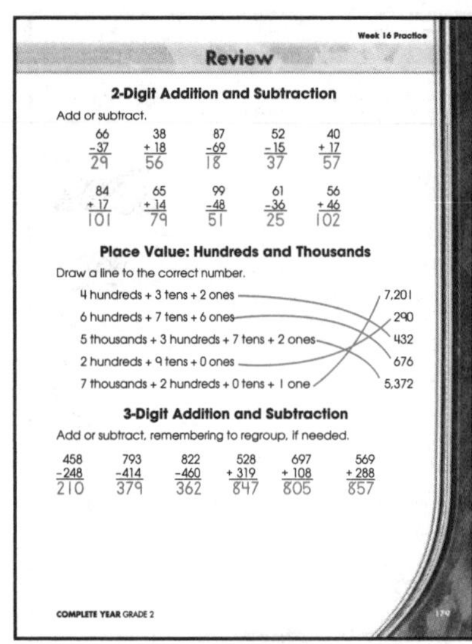
Week 16 Practice

Review

2-Digit Addition and Subtraction

Add or subtract.

66 -37 = 29	38 +18 = 56	87 -69 = 18	52 -15 = 37	40 +17 = 57
84 +17 = 101	65 +14 = 79	99 -48 = 51	61 -36 = 25	56 +46 = 102

Place Value: Hundreds and Thousands

Draw a line to the correct number.

4 hundreds + 3 tens + 2 ones — 432
6 hundreds + 7 tens + 6 ones — 676
5 thousands + 3 hundreds + 7 tens + 2 ones — 5,372
2 hundreds + 9 tens + 0 ones — 290
7 thousands + 2 hundreds + 0 tens + 1 one — 7,201

3-Digit Addition and Subtraction

Add or subtract, remembering to regroup, if needed.

458 -248 = 210	793 -414 = 379	822 -460 = 362	528 +319 = 847	697 +108 = 805	569 +288 = 857

COMPLETE YEAR GRADE 2 179

179

Week 16 Practice

Training With Facts

Use the numbers on each train to write the fact families.

6 + 8 = 14
8 + 6 = 14
14 - 6 = 8
14 - 8 = 6

6 + 9 = 15
9 + 6 = 15
15 - 6 = 9
15 - 9 = 6

8 + 9 = 17
9 + 8 = 17
17 - 9 = 8
17 - 8 = 9

5 + 9 = 14
9 + 5 = 14
14 - 5 = 9
14 - 9 = 5

180 COMPLETE YEAR GRADE 2

180

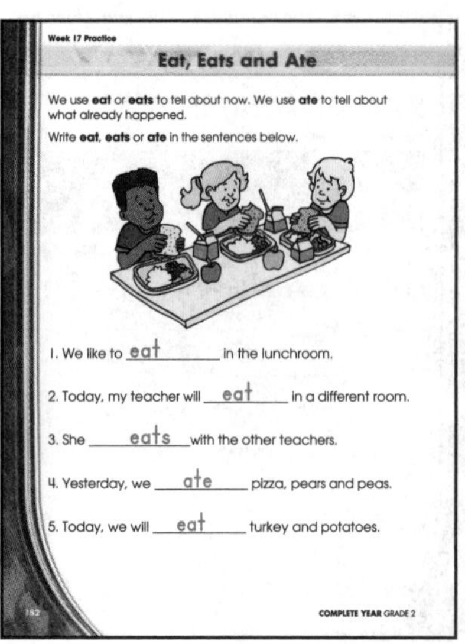
Week 17 Practice

Eat, Eats and Ate

We use **eat** or **eats** to tell about now. We use **ate** to tell about what already happened.

Write **eat, eats** or **ate** in the sentences below.

1. We like to eat in the lunchroom.
2. Today, my teacher will eat in a different room.
3. She eats with the other teachers.
4. Yesterday, we ate pizza, pears and peas.
5. Today, we will eat turkey and potatoes.

182 COMPLETE YEAR GRADE 2

182

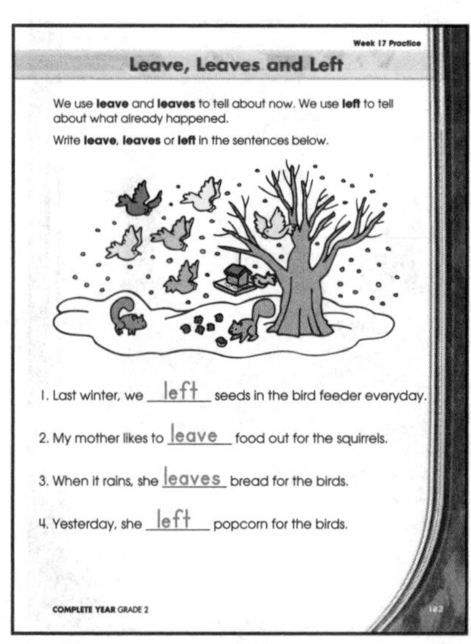
Week 17 Practice

Leave, Leaves and Left

We use **leave** and **leaves** to tell about now. We use **left** to tell about what already happened.

Write **leave, leaves** or **left** in the sentences below.

1. Last winter, we left seeds in the bird feeder everyday.
2. My mother likes to leave food out for the squirrels.
3. When it rains, she leaves bread for the birds.
4. Yesterday, she left popcorn for the birds.

COMPLETE YEAR GRADE 2 183

183

Answer Key

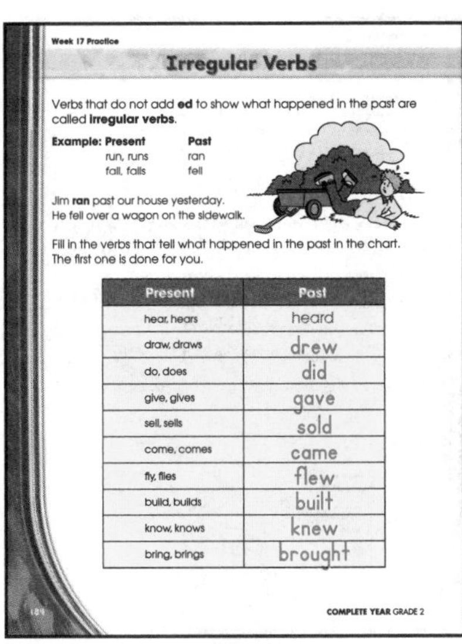

Week 17 Practice

Irregular Verbs

Verbs that do not add **ed** to show what happened in the past are called **irregular verbs**.

Example: Present — **Past**
run, runs — ran
fall, falls — fell

Jim **ran** past our house yesterday.
He fell over a wagon on the sidewalk.

Fill in the verbs that tell what happened in the past in the chart. The first one is done for you.

Present	Past
hear, hears	heard
draw, draws	drew
do, does	did
give, gives	gave
sell, sells	sold
come, comes	came
fly, flies	flew
build, builds	built
know, knows	knew
bring, brings	brought

COMPLETE YEAR GRADE 2

184

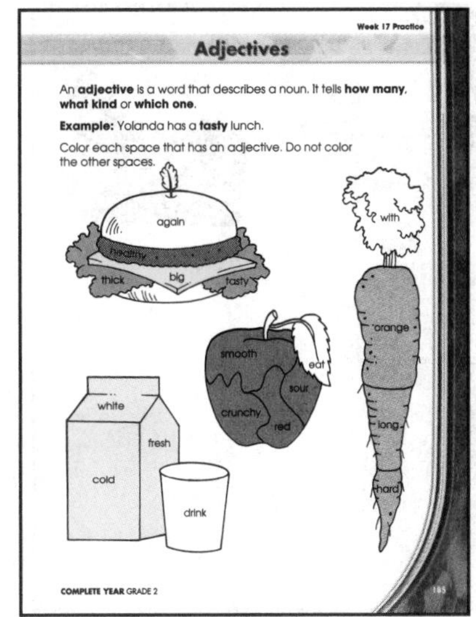

Week 17 Practice

Adjectives

An **adjective** is a word that describes a noun. It tells **how many, what kind** or **which one**.

Example: Yolanda has a **tasty** lunch.

Color each space that has an adjective. Do not color the other spaces.

COMPLETE YEAR GRADE 2

185

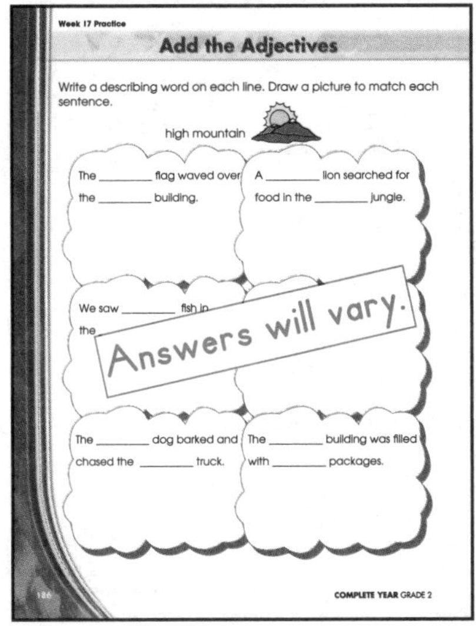

Week 17 Practice

Add the Adjectives

Write a describing word on each line. Draw a picture to match each sentence.

high mountain

The ________ flag waved over the ________ building.

A ________ lion searched for food in the ________ jungle.

We saw ________ fish in the ________

The ________ dog barked and chased the ________ truck.

The ________ building was filled with ________ packages.

Answers will vary.

COMPLETE YEAR GRADE 2

186

Week 17 Practice

Problems! Problems! Problems!

Read and solve these problems.

1. Craig went to the pond. He kept a tally of the animals he saw there. Which kind of animal did he see most often? bug Which kind of animal did he see least often? lizard

Frog ~~IIII~~ 5 Duck III 3 Bug ~~IIII~~ ~~IIII~~ II 12 Bird ~~IIII~~ II 7 Lizard II 2 Fish ~~IIII~~ III 8

2. Ellen went to the library. She checked out five books on zoo animals, three books on fish, eight books on airplanes and two books on dogs. How many animal books did Ellen check out? 10 How many books did she check out altogether? 18 If she returns the books on dogs and airplanes, how many books will she have then? 8

3. Complete this sequence of numbers: 14, 24, 34, 44, 54, 64

COMPLETE YEAR GRADE 2

187

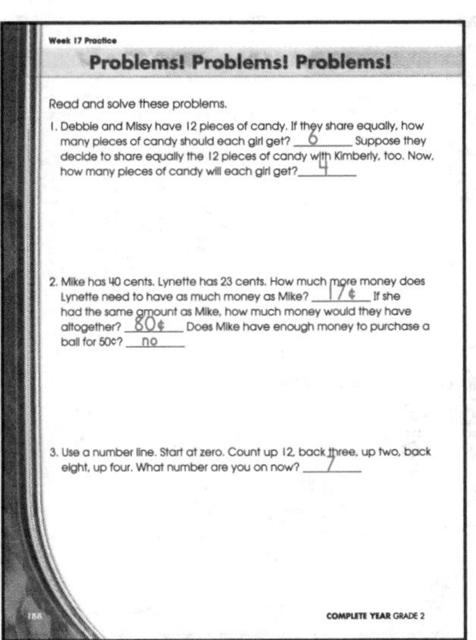

Week 17 Practice

Problems! Problems! Problems!

Read and solve these problems.

1. Debbie and Missy have 12 pieces of candy. If they share equally, how many pieces of candy should each girl get? 6 Suppose they decide to share equally the 12 pieces of candy with Kimberly, too. Now, how many pieces of candy will each girl get? 4

2. Mike has 40 cents. Lynette has 23 cents. How much more money does Lynette need to have as much money as Mike? 17¢ If she had the same amount as Mike, how much money would they have altogether? 80¢ Does Mike have enough money to purchase a ball for 50¢? no

3. Use a number line. Start at zero. Count up 12, back three, up two, back eight, up four. What number are you on now? 7

COMPLETE YEAR GRADE 2

188

Week 17 Practice

Problem-Solving

Tell whether you should add or subtract. "In all" is a clue to add. "Left" is a clue to subtract. Draw pictures to help you.

Example: Jane's dog has 5 bones. He ate 3 bones. How many bones are left?

subtract — 5 − 3 = 2 bones

Lucky the cat had 5 mice. She got 4 more for her birthday. How many mice did she have in all?

add — 5 + 4 = 9 mice

Sam bought 6 fish. She gave 2 fish to a friend. How many fish does she have left?

subtract — 6 − 2 = 4 fish

COMPLETE YEAR GRADE 2

189

Answer Key

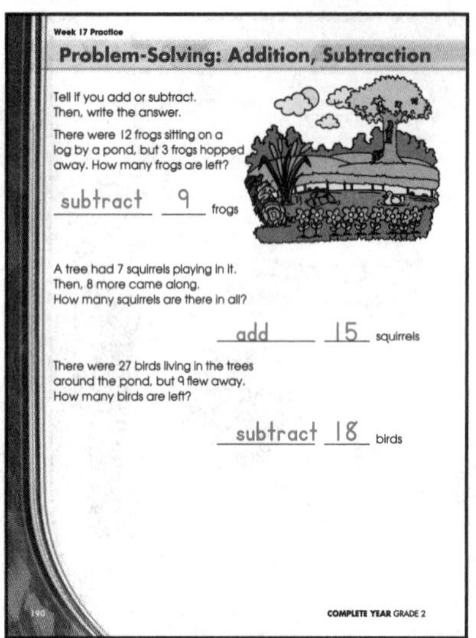

Week 17 Practice

Problem-Solving: Addition, Subtraction

Tell if you add or subtract. Then, write the answer.

There were 12 frogs sitting on a log by a pond, but 3 frogs hopped away. How many frogs are left?

subtract 9 frogs

A tree had 7 squirrels playing in it. Then, 8 more came along. How many squirrels are there in all?

add 15 squirrels

There were 27 birds living in the trees around the pond, but 9 flew away. How many birds are left?

subtract 18 birds

190 COMPLETE YEAR GRADE 2

190

Week 18 Practice

Adjectives

Adjectives are words that tell more about nouns, such as a **happy** child, a **cold** day or a **hard** problem. Adjectives can tell how many (**one** airplane) or which one (**those** shoes).

The nouns are in bold letters. Circle the adjectives that describe the nouns.

Example: Some people have (unusual) **pets**.

1. Some people keep (wild) **animals**, like lions and bears.
2. (These) **pets** need special care.
3. (These) **animals** want to be free when they get older.
4. Even (small) **animals** can be difficult if they are wild.
5. Raccoons and squirrels are not (tame) **pets**.
6. Never touch a (wild) **animal** that may be sick.

Complete the story below by writing in your own adjectives. Use your imagination.

My Cat

My cat is a very ________ animal. She has ...

and ________ fur. Her fa...

She ha...

She ... ________ whiskers.

I thi... ________ cat in the world!

Answers will vary.

192 COMPLETE YEAR GRADE 2

192

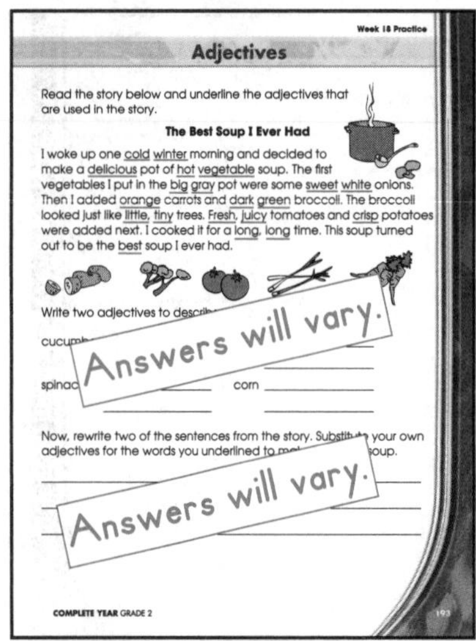

Week 18 Practice

Adjectives

Read the story below and underline the adjectives that are used in the story.

The Best Soup I Ever Had

I woke up one cold winter morning and decided to make a delicious pot of hot vegetable soup. The first vegetables I put in the big gray pot were some sweet white onions. Then I added orange carrots and dark green broccoli. The broccoli looked just like little, tiny trees. Fresh, juicy tomatoes and crisp potatoes were added next. I cooked it for a long, long time. This soup turned out to be the best soup I ever had.

Write two adjectives to descri...

cucum...

spinac... corn

Answers will vary.

Now, rewrite two of the sentences from the story. Substitute your own adjectives for the words you underlined to ma... soup.

Answers will vary.

COMPLETE YEAR GRADE 2 193

193

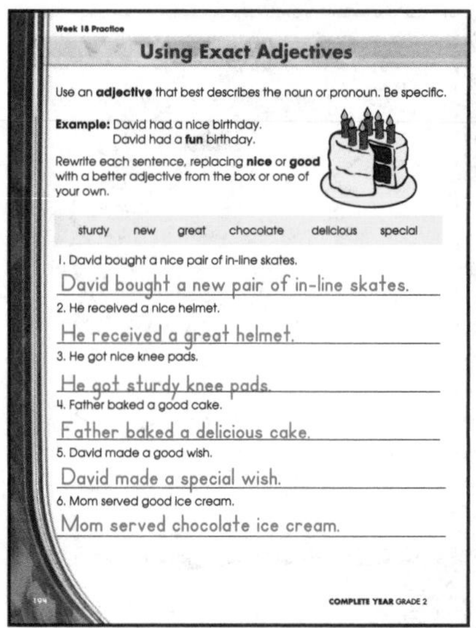

Week 18 Practice

Using Exact Adjectives

Use an **adjective** that best describes the noun or pronoun. Be specific.

Example: David had a nice birthday.
David had a **fun** birthday.

Rewrite each sentence, replacing **nice** or **good** with a better adjective from the box or one of your own.

sturdy new great chocolate delicious special

1. David bought a nice pair of in-line skates.
   David bought a new pair of in-line skates.
2. He received a nice helmet.
   He received a great helmet.
3. He got nice knee pads.
   He got sturdy knee pads.
4. Father baked a good cake.
   Father baked a delicious cake.
5. David made a good wish.
   David made a special wish.
6. Mom served good ice cream.
   Mom served chocolate ice cream.

194 COMPLETE YEAR GRADE 2

194

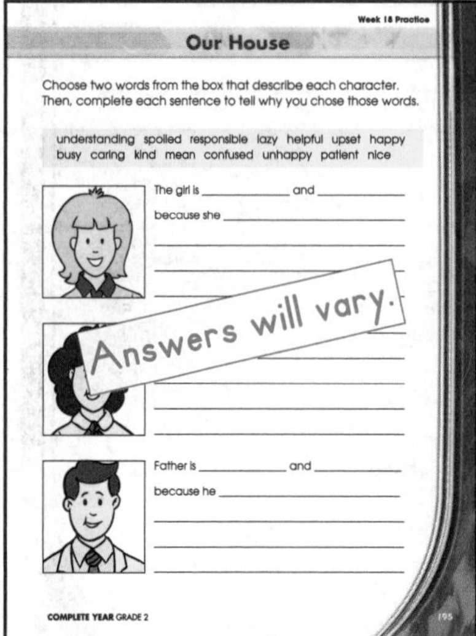

Week 18 Practice

Our House

Choose two words from the box that describe each character. Then, complete each sentence to tell why you chose those words.

understanding spoiled responsible lazy helpful upset happy busy caring kind mean confused unhappy patient nice

The girl is ________ and ________ because she ________

Answers will vary.

Father is ________ and ________ because he ________

COMPLETE YEAR GRADE 2 195

195

Week 18 Practice

Better Sentences

Describing words like adjectives can make a better sentence. Write a word on each line to make the sentences more interesting. Draw a picture of your sentence.

1. The skater won a medal.
   The ________ skater won a ________ medal.
2. The jewels were in the safe.
   The ________ jewe... ...e.
3. The ...
   The ... ...rough the ________ storm.
4. A fi... ...d into the house.
   A ________ fireman rushed into the ________ house.
5. The detective hid behind the tree.
   The ________ detective hid behind the ________ tree.

Answers will vary.

1. 2. 3.

Pictures should match sentences above.

196 COMPLETE YEAR GRADE 2

196

Answer Key

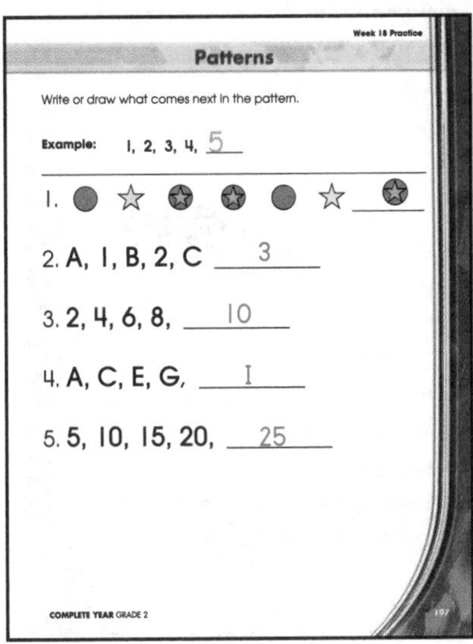
Week 18 Practice

Patterns

Write or draw what comes next in the pattern.

Example: 1, 2, 3, 4, 5

1\.

2\. A, 1, B, 2, C 3

3\. 2, 4, 6, 8, 10

4\. A, C, E, G, I

5\. 5, 10, 15, 20, 25

COMPLETE YEAR GRADE 2 197

197

Week 18 Practice

Finding Patterns: Numbers

Mia likes to count by twos, threes, fours, fives, tens and hundreds. Complete the number patterns.

1 2 3 4 5

1\. 5, 10, 15, 20, 25, 30, 35, 40, 45, 50

2\. 100, 200, 300, 400, 500, 600, 700, 800, 900

3\. 2, 4, 6, 8, 10, 12, 14, 16, 18, 20

4\. 10, 20, 30, 40, 50, 60, 70, 80, 90

5\. 4, 8, 12, 16, 20, 24, 28, 32, 36, 40

6\. 3, 6, 9, 12, 15, 18, 21, 24, 27, 30

Make up two of your own number patterns.

Answers will vary.

198 COMPLETE YEAR GRADE 2

198

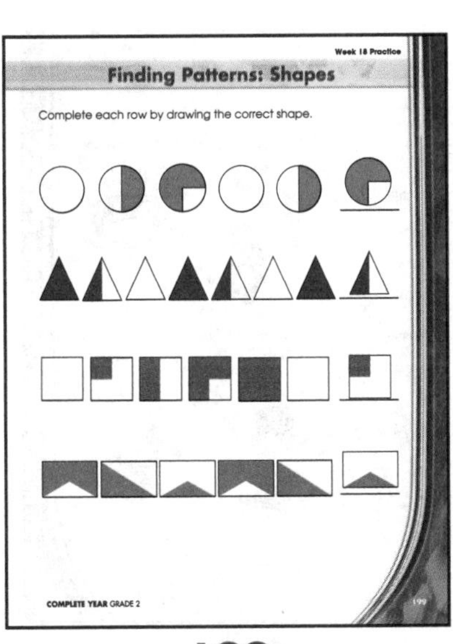
Week 18 Practice

Finding Patterns: Shapes

Complete each row by drawing the correct shape.

COMPLETE YEAR GRADE 2 199

199

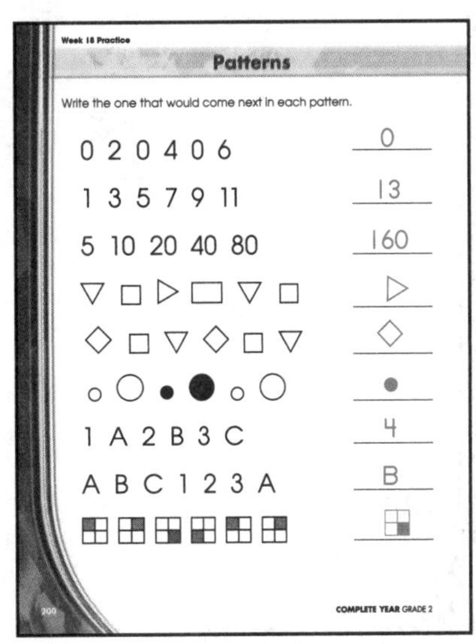
Week 18 Practice

Patterns

Write the one that would come next in each pattern.

0 2 0 4 0 6 — 0

1 3 5 7 9 11 — 13

5 10 20 40 80 — 160

▽ □ ▷ □ ▽ □ — ▷

◇ □ ▽ ◇ □ ▽ — ◇

○ ◯ ● ⬤ ○ ◯ — ●

1 A 2 B 3 C — 4

A B C 1 2 3 A — B

200 COMPLETE YEAR GRADE 2

200

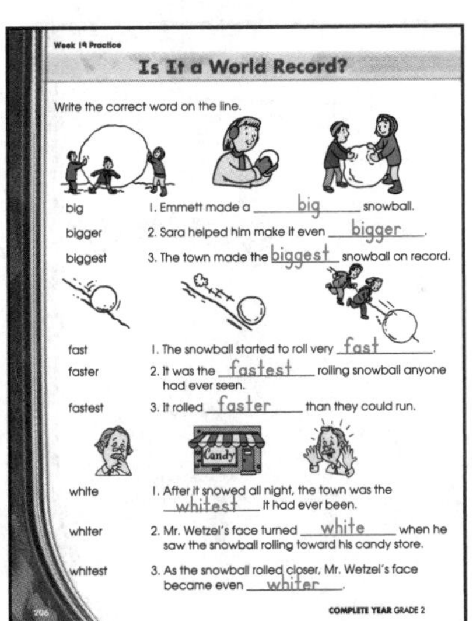
Week 19 Practice

Is It a World Record?

Write the correct word on the line.

big / bigger / biggest

1\. Emmett made a big snowball.

2\. Sara helped him make it even bigger.

3\. The town made the biggest snowball on record.

fast / faster / fastest

1\. The snowball started to roll very fast.

2\. It was the fastest rolling snowball anyone had ever seen.

3\. It rolled faster than they could run.

white / whiter / whitest

1\. After it snowed all night, the town was the whitest it had ever been.

2\. Mr. Wetzel's face turned white when he saw the snowball rolling toward his candy store.

3\. As the snowball rolled closer, Mr. Wetzel's face became even whiter.

206 COMPLETE YEAR GRADE 2

206

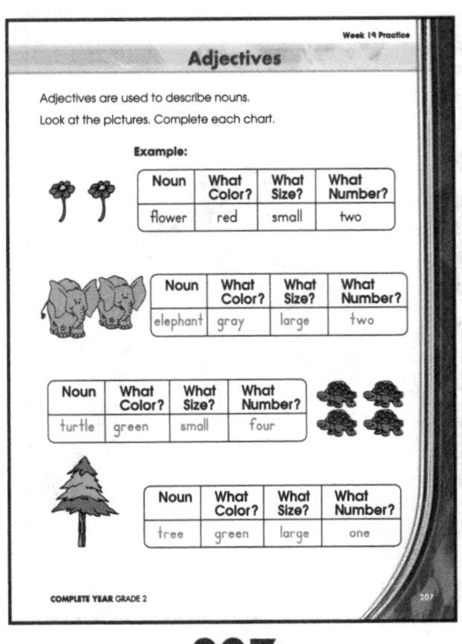
Week 19 Practice

Adjectives

Adjectives are used to describe nouns.

Look at the pictures. Complete each chart.

Example:

Noun	What Color?	What Size?	What Number?
flower	red	small	two

Noun	What Color?	What Size?	What Number?
elephant	gray	large	two

Noun	What Color?	What Size?	What Number?
turtle	green	small	four

Noun	What Color?	What Size?	What Number?
tree	green	large	one

COMPLETE YEAR GRADE 2 207

207

Answer Key

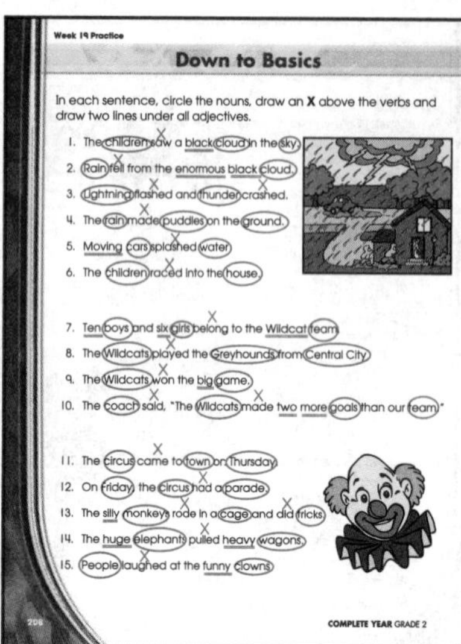

Week 19 Practice

Down to Basics

In each sentence, circle the nouns, draw an **X** above the verbs and draw two lines under all adjectives.

1. The children saw a black cloud in the sky.
2. Rain fell from the enormous black cloud.
3. Lightning flashed and thunder crashed.
4. The rain made puddles on the ground.
5. Moving cars splashed water.
6. The children raced into the house.
7. Ten boys and six girls belong to the Wildcat team.
8. The Wildcats played the Greyhounds from Central City.
9. The Wildcats won the big game.
10. The coach said, "The Wildcats made two more goals than our team."
11. The circus came to town on Thursday.
12. On Friday, the circus had a parade.
13. The silly monkeys rode in a cage and did tricks.
14. The huge elephants pulled heavy wagons.
15. People laughed at the funny clowns.

208 COMPLETE YEAR GRADE 2

208

Week 19 Practice

Adjectives

Underline the nouns in each sentence below. Then, draw an arrow from each adjective to the noun it describes.

Example:

A platypus is a furry animal that lives in Australia.

1. This animal likes to swim.
2. The nose looks like a duck's bill.
3. It has a broad tail like a beaver.
4. Platypuses are great swimmers.
5. They have webbed feet which help them swim.
6. Their flat tails also help them move through the water.
7. The platypus is an unusual mammal because it lays eggs.
8. The eggs look like reptile eggs.
9. Platypuses can lay three eggs at a time.
10. These babies do not leave their mothers for one year.
11. This animal spends most of its time hunting near streams.

COMPLETE YEAR GRADE 2 209

209

Week 19 Practice

Adverbs

An **adverb** describes a verb. It tells how, when or where an action takes place.

Example:

The space shuttle blasted off **yesterday**. (when)
It rose **quickly** into the sky. (how)
We watched **outdoors**. (where)

Write **how**, **when** or **where** to explain what each adverb tells.

1. I run **today**.	when	8. I run **far**.	where
2. I run **outside**.	where	9. I run **happily**.	how
3. I run **tomorrow**.	when	10. I run **weekly**.	when
4. I run **around**.	where	11. I run **swiftly**.	how
5. I run **nearby**.	where	12. I run **first**.	when
6. I run **sometimes**.	when	13. I run **next**.	when
7. I run **there**.	where	14. I run **gracefully**.	how

Circle the adverb in each pair of words. Remember, an adverb describes an action.

1. soon, supper	4. help, easily	7. finally, feather
2. neatly, nine	5. warmly, wonder	8. quietly, quacks
3. proudly, prove	6. quilt, quickly	9. sail, safely

210 COMPLETE YEAR GRADE 2

210

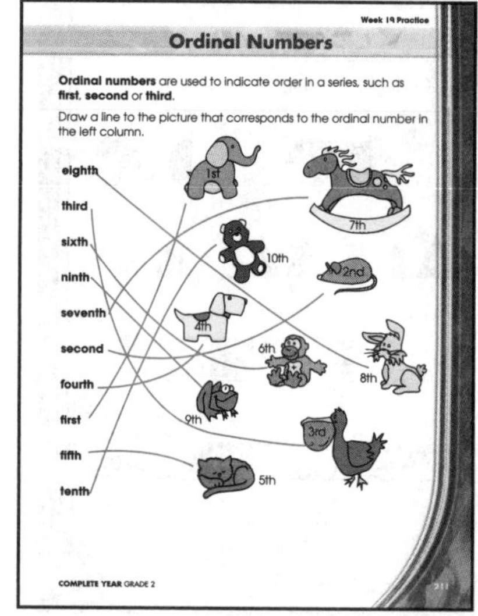

Week 19 Practice

Ordinal Numbers

Ordinal numbers are used to indicate order in a series, such as **first**, **second** or **third**.

Draw a line to the picture that corresponds to the ordinal number in the left column.

eighth
third
sixth
ninth
seventh
second
fourth
first
fifth
tenth

COMPLETE YEAR GRADE 2 211

211

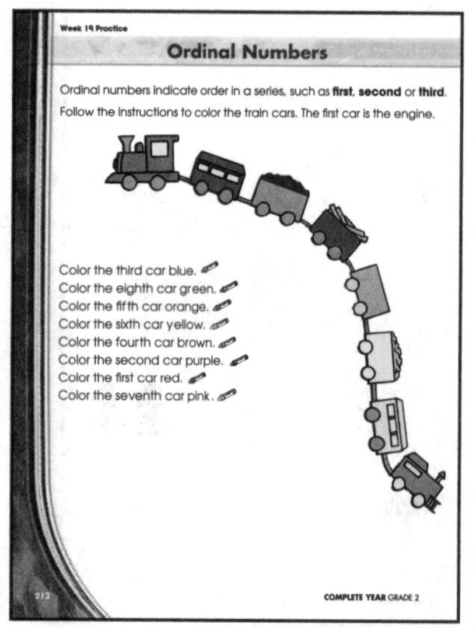

Week 19 Practice

Ordinal Numbers

Ordinal numbers indicate order in a series, such as **first**, **second** or **third**.

Follow the instructions to color the train cars. The first car is the engine.

Color the third car blue.
Color the eighth car green.
Color the fifth car orange.
Color the sixth car yellow.
Color the fourth car brown.
Color the second car purple.
Color the first car red.
Color the seventh car pink.

212 COMPLETE YEAR GRADE 2

212

Week 19 Practice

Ordinal Numbers

Follow the instructions.

Draw glasses on the second one.
Put a hat on the fourth one.
Color blonde hair on the third one.
Draw a tie on the first one.
Draw ears on the fifth one.
Draw black hair on the seventh one.
Put a bow on the head of the sixth one.

COMPLETE YEAR GRADE 2 213

213

Answer Key

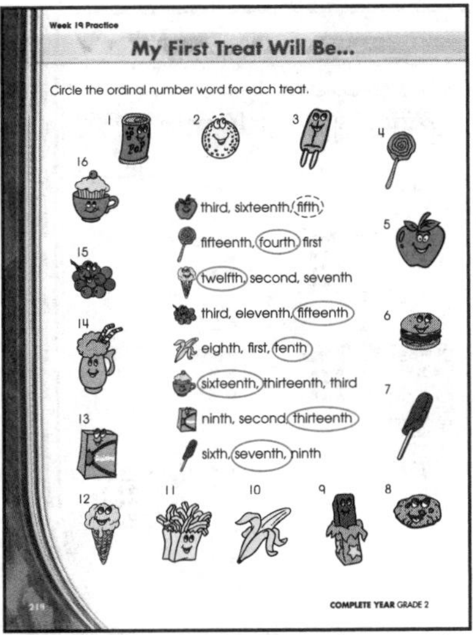

Week 19 Practice

My First Treat Will Be...

Circle the ordinal number word for each treat.

third, sixteenth, fifth

fifteenth, fourth, first

twelfth, second, seventh

third, eleventh, fifteenth

eighth, first, tenth

sixteenth, thirteenth, third

ninth, second, thirteenth

sixth, seventh, ninth

COMPLETE YEAR GRADE 2

214

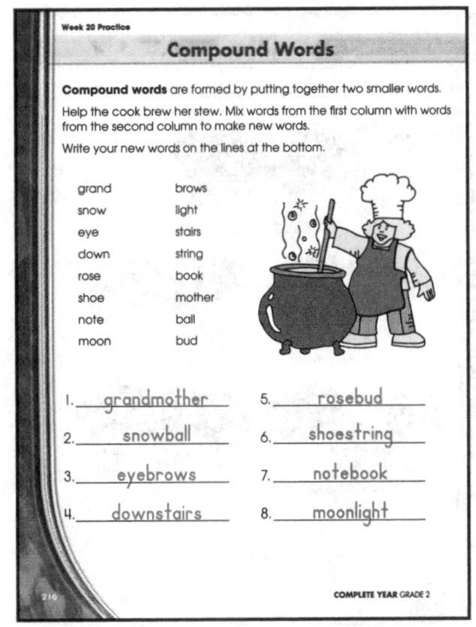

Week 20 Practice

Compound Words

Compound words are formed by putting together two smaller words.

Help the cook brew her stew. Mix words from the first column with words from the second column to make new words.

Write your new words on the lines at the bottom.

grand	brows
snow	light
eye	stairs
down	string
rose	book
shoe	mother
note	ball
moon	bud

1. grandmother
2. snowball
3. eyebrows
4. downstairs
5. rosebud
6. shoestring
7. notebook
8. moonlight

COMPLETE YEAR GRADE 2

216

Week 20 Practice

Compound Words

Compound words are two words that are put together to make one new word.

Read the sentences. Fill in the blank with a compound word from the box.

raincoat	bedroom	lunchbox	hallway	sandbox

1. A box with sand is a sandbox.
2. The way through a hall is a hallway.
3. A box for lunch is a lunchbox.
4. A coat for the rain is a raincoat.
5. A room with a bed is a bedroom.

COMPLETE YEAR GRADE 2 217

217

Week 20 Practice

Compound Words

Draw a line under the compound word in each sentence. On the line, write the two words that make up the compound word.

1. A firetruck came to help put out the fire. fire truck
2. I will be nine years old on my next birthday. birth day
3. We built a treehouse at the back. tree house
4. Dad put a scarecrow in his garden. scare crow
5. It is fun to make footprints in the snow. foot prints
6. I like to read the comics in the newspaper. news paper
7. Cowboys ride horses and use lassos. cow boys

COMPLETE YEAR GRADE 2

218

Week 20 Practice

Compound Words

Cut out the words below. Glue them together in the box to make compound words.

COMPOUND WORDS

sunflower, football, mailbox, watermelon, classroom, airplane, bathroom, bodyguard

Can you think of any more compound words?

sun	air	mail	ball
box	room	water	guard
foot	bath	class	flower
plane	room	melon	body

COMPLETE YEAR GRADE 2 219

219

Week 20 Practice

Tens and Ones

Write the number indicated by tally marks.

13, 17, 20, 42, 36, 20, 8, 25, 34, 36

Using tally marks, draw the numbers named.

35, 15, 45, 11, 30, 18, 41, 22, 7, 29, 26, 10

COMPLETE YEAR GRADE 2 221

221

Answer Key

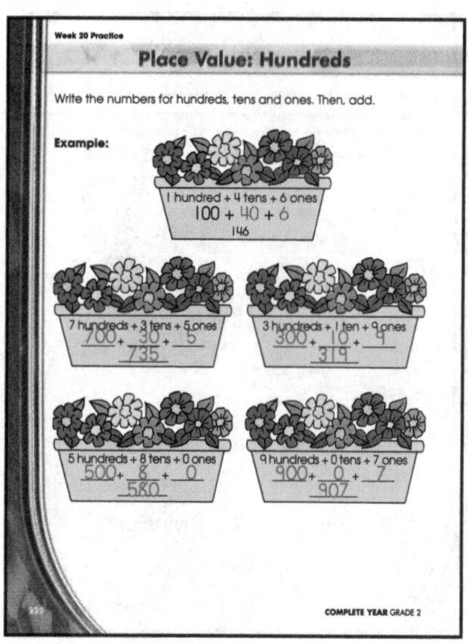

Week 20 Practice

Place Value: Hundreds

Write the numbers for hundreds, tens and ones. Then, add.

Example:

1 hundred + 4 tens + 6 ones
100 + 40 + 6
146

7 hundreds + 3 tens + 5 ones
700 + 30 + 5
735

3 hundreds + 1 ten + 9 ones
300 + 10 + 9
319

5 hundreds + 8 tens + 0 ones
500 + 8 + 0
580

9 hundreds + 0 tens + 7 ones
900 + 0 + 7
907

COMPLETE YEAR GRADE 2

222

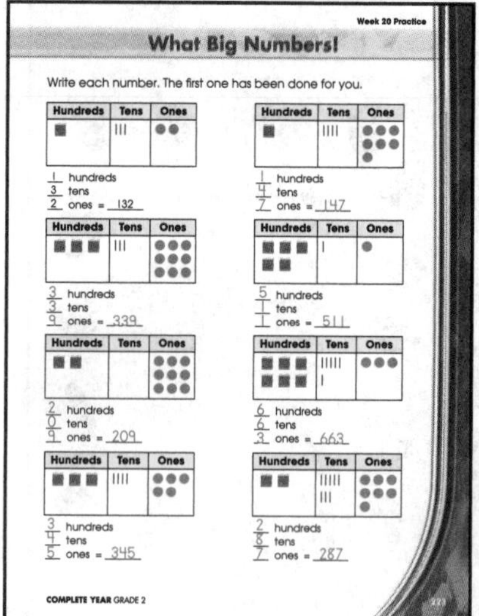

Week 20 Practice

What Big Numbers!

Write each number. The first one has been done for you.

1 hundreds, 3 tens, 2 ones = 132

1 hundreds, 4 tens, 7 ones = 147

3 hundreds, 3 tens, 9 ones = 339

5 hundreds, 1 tens, 1 ones = 511

2 hundreds, 0 tens, 9 ones = 209

6 hundreds, 6 tens, 3 ones = 663

3 hundreds, 4 tens, 5 ones = 345

2 hundreds, 8 tens, 7 ones = 287

COMPLETE YEAR GRADE 2

223

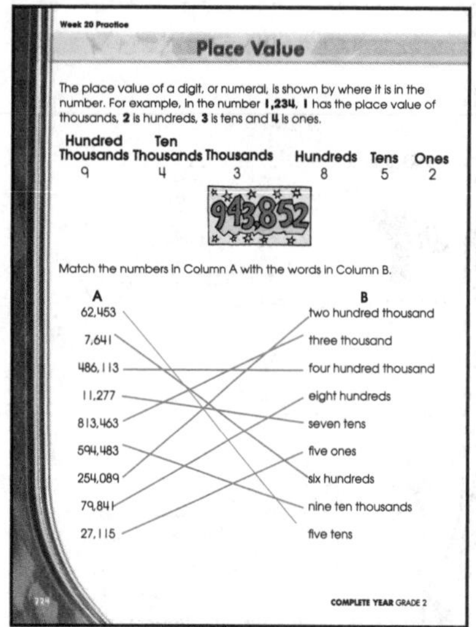

Week 20 Practice

Place Value

The place value of a digit, or numeral, is shown by where it is in the number. For example, in the number **1,234**, **1** has the place value of thousands, **2** is hundreds, **3** is tens and **4** is ones.

Hundred Thousands	Ten Thousands	Thousands	Hundreds	Tens	Ones
9	4	3	8	5	2

943,852

Match the numbers in Column A with the words in Column B.

A	B
62,453	two hundred thousand
7,641	three thousand
486,113	four hundred thousand
11,277	eight hundreds
813,463	seven tens
594,483	five ones
254,089	six hundreds
79,841	nine ten thousands
27,115	five tens

COMPLETE YEAR GRADE 2

224

Week 21 Practice

Word Magic

Maggie Magician announced, "One plus one equals one!" The audience giggled. So Maggie put two words into a hat and waved her magic wand. When she reached into the hat, Maggie pulled out one word and a picture. "See," said Maggie, "I was right!"

Use the box to help write a compound word for each picture below.

ball	door	rain	star	shirt	bell	fish	shoe	book	foot	basket
bow	lace	box	stool	light	sun	cup	mail	tail	cake	worm

shoelace, cupcake, doorbell

basketball, mailbox, footstool

rainbow, shirttail, starfish

bookworm, sunlight

COMPLETE YEAR GRADE 2

226

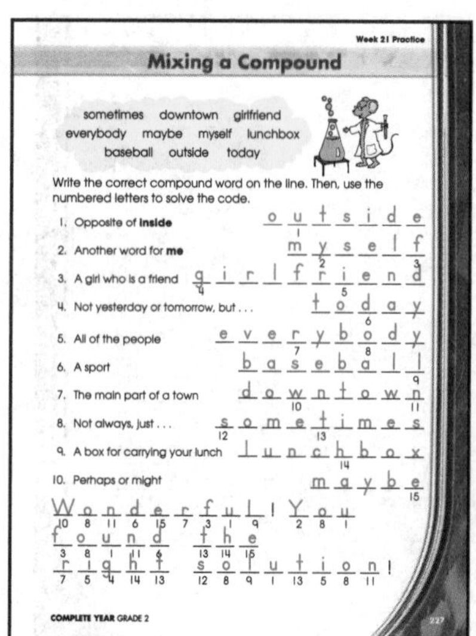

Week 21 Practice

Mixing a Compound

sometimes downtown girlfriend everybody maybe myself lunchbox baseball outside today

Write the correct compound word on the line. Then, use the numbered letters to solve the code.

1. Opposite of **inside** — outside
2. Another word for **me** — myself
3. A girl who is a friend — girlfriend
4. Not yesterday or tomorrow, but . . . — today
5. All of the people — everybody
6. A sport — baseball
7. The main part of a town — downtown
8. Not always, just . . . — sometimes
9. A box for carrying your lunch — lunchbox
10. Perhaps or might — maybe

Wonderful! You found the right solution!

COMPLETE YEAR GRADE 2

227

Week 21 Practice

Compound Your Effort

Find the word in the word box that goes with the words numbered below to make a compound word. Cross it out. Then, write the compound word on the line.

board writing class room book where thing hopper work side toe out bag ball basket

1. coat coatroom
2. snow snowball
3. home homework
4. waste wastebasket
5. tip tiptoe
6. chalk chalkboard
7. note notebook
8. grass grasshopper
9. school schoolbag
10. with without

Look at the words in the word box that you did not use. Use those words to make your own compound words.

1. outside
2. something
3. nowhere
4. classroom
5. handwriting

Answers will vary.

COMPLETE YEAR GRADE 2

228

Answer Key

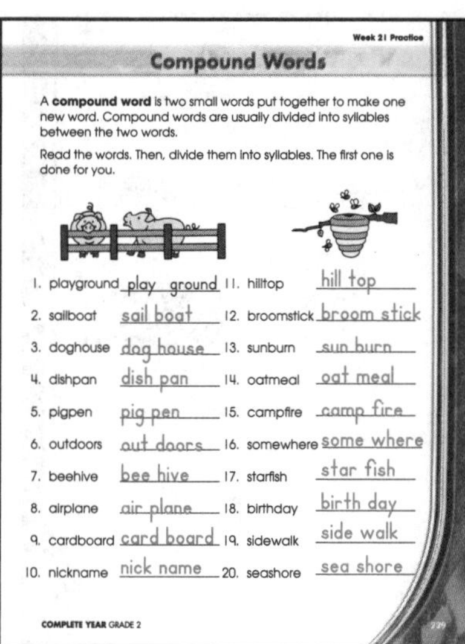

Week 21 Practice

Compound Words

A **compound word** is two small words put together to make one new word. Compound words are usually divided into syllables between the two words.

Read the words. Then, divide them into syllables. The first one is done for you.

1. playground play ground
2. sailboat sail boat
3. doghouse dog house
4. dishpan dish pan
5. pigpen pig pen
6. outdoors out doors
7. beehive bee hive
8. airplane air plane
9. cardboard card board
10. nickname nick name
11. hilltop hill top
12. broomstick broom stick
13. sunburn sun burn
14. oatmeal oat meal
15. campfire camp fire
16. somewhere some where
17. starfish star fish
18. birthday birth day
19. sidewalk side walk
20. seashore sea shore

COMPLETE YEAR GRADE 2 229

229

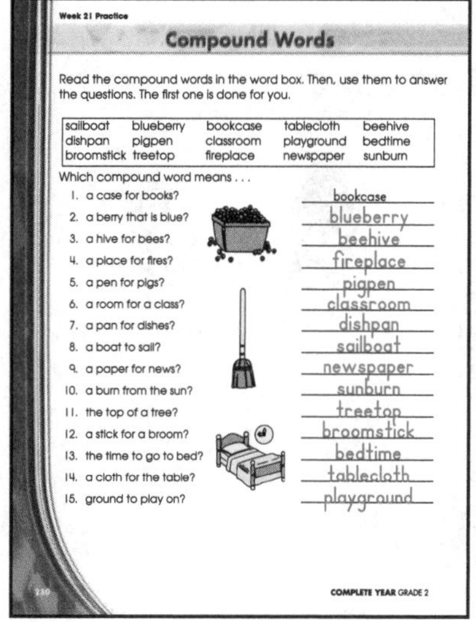

Week 21 Practice

Compound Words

Read the compound words in the word box. Then, use them to answer the questions. The first one is done for you.

sailboat	blueberry	bookcase	tablecloth	beehive
dishpan	pigpen	classroom	playground	bedtime
broomstick	treetop	fireplace	newspaper	sunburn

Which compound word means . . .

1. a case for books? bookcase
2. a berry that is blue? blueberry
3. a hive for bees? beehive
4. a place for fires? fireplace
5. a pen for pigs? pigpen
6. a room for a class? classroom
7. a pan for dishes? dishpan
8. a boat to sail? sailboat
9. a paper for news? newspaper
10. a burn from the sun? sunburn
11. the top of a tree? treetop
12. a stick for a broom? broomstick
13. the time to go to bed? bedtime
14. a cloth for the table? tablecloth
15. ground to play on? playground

230 COMPLETE YEAR GRADE 2

230

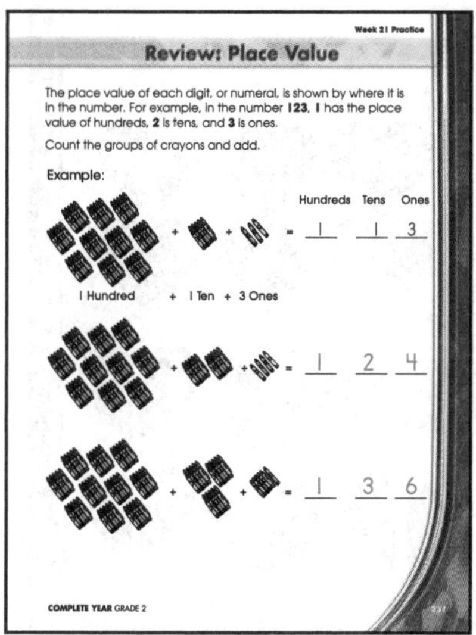

Week 21 Practice

Review: Place Value

The place value of each digit, or numeral, is shown by where it is in the number. For example, in the number **123**, **1** has the place value of hundreds, **2** is tens, and **3** is ones.

Count the groups of crayons and add.

Example:

	Hundreds	Tens	Ones
1 Hundred + 1 Ten + 3 Ones =	1	1	3
=	1	2	4
=	1	3	6

COMPLETE YEAR GRADE 2 231

231

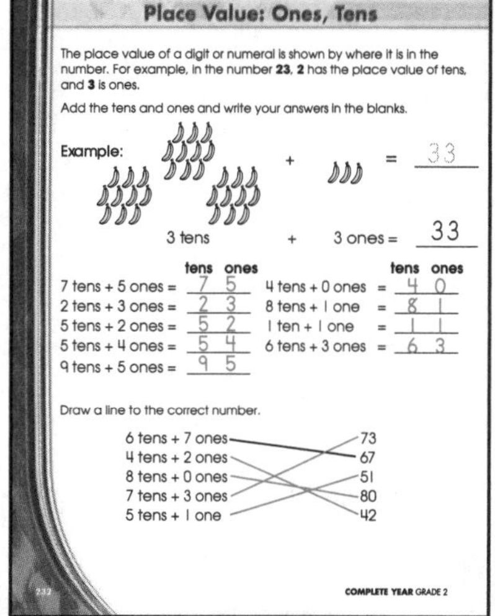

Week 21 Practice

Place Value: Ones, Tens

The place value of a digit or numeral is shown by where it is in the number. For example, in the number **23**, **2** has the place value of tens, and **3** is ones.

Add the tens and ones and write your answers in the blanks.

Example: 3 tens + 3 ones = 33

	tens	ones
7 tens + 5 ones =	7	5
2 tens + 3 ones =	2	3
5 tens + 2 ones =	5	2
5 tens + 4 ones =	5	4
9 tens + 5 ones =	9	5

	tens	ones
4 tens + 0 ones =	4	0
8 tens + 1 one =	8	1
1 ten + 1 one =	1	1
6 tens + 3 ones =	6	3

Draw a line to the correct number.

6 tens + 7 ones — 73
4 tens + 2 ones — 67
8 tens + 0 ones — 51
7 tens + 3 ones — 80
5 tens + 1 one — 42

232 COMPLETE YEAR GRADE 2

232

Week 21 Practice

Place Value: Ones, Tens

Write the numbers for the tens and ones. Then, add.

Example: 2 tens + 7 ones, 20 + 7, 27

6 tens + 2 ones, 60 + 2, 62

3 tens + 4 ones, 30 + 4, 34

8 tens + 3 ones, 80 + 3, 83

5 tens + 0 ones, 50 + 0, 50

COMPLETE YEAR GRADE 2 233

233

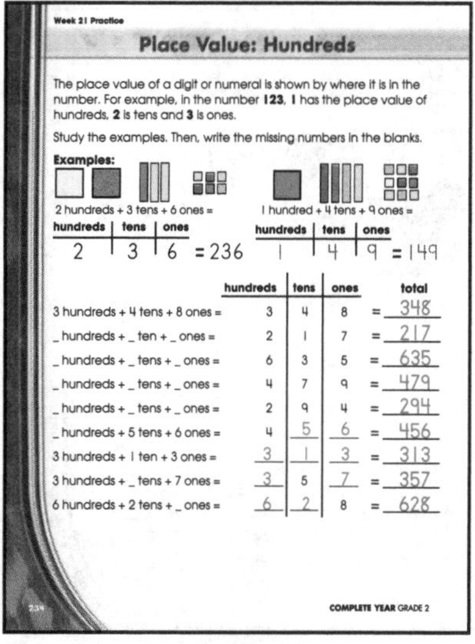

Week 21 Practice

Place Value: Hundreds

The place value of a digit or numeral is shown by where it is in the number. For example, in the number **123**, **1** has the place value of hundreds, **2** is tens and **3** is ones.

Study the examples. Then, write the missing numbers in the blanks.

Examples:

2 hundreds + 3 tens + 6 ones =

hundreds	tens	ones	
2	3	6	= 236

1 hundred + 4 tens + 9 ones =

hundreds	tens	ones	
1	4	9	= 149

	hundreds	tens	ones	total
3 hundreds + 4 tens + 8 ones =	3	4	8	= 348
_ hundreds + _ ten + _ ones =	2	1	7	= 217
_ hundreds + _ tens + _ ones =	6	3	5	= 635
_ hundreds + _ tens + _ ones =	4	7	9	= 479
_ hundreds + _ tens + _ ones =	2	9	4	= 294
_ hundreds + 5 tens + 6 ones =	4	5	6	= 456
3 hundreds + 1 ten + 3 ones =	3	1	3	= 313
3 hundreds + _ tens + 7 ones =	3	5	7	= 357
6 hundreds + 2 tens + _ ones =	6	2	8	= 628

234 COMPLETE YEAR GRADE 2

234

Answer Key

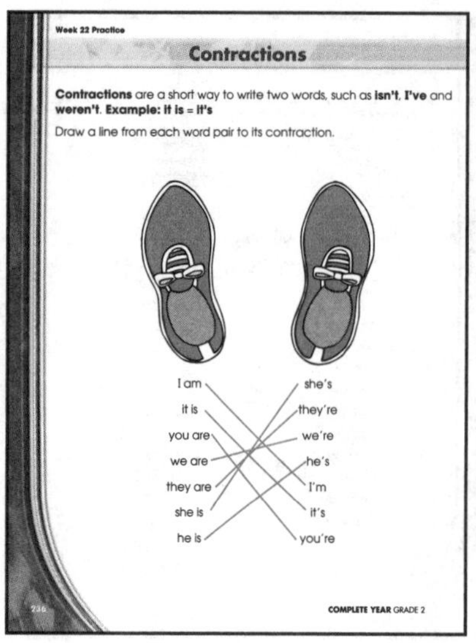
Week 22 Practice

Contractions

Contractions are a short way to write two words, such as **isn't**, **I've** and **weren't**. **Example: It is = it's**

Draw a line from each word pair to its contraction.

COMPLETE YEAR GRADE 2

236

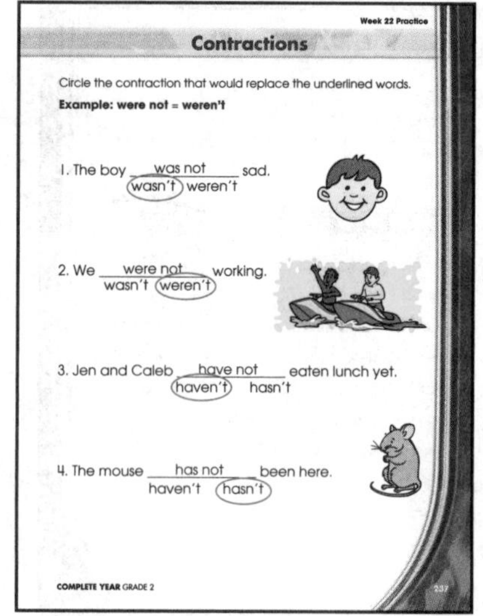
Week 22 Practice

Contractions

Circle the contraction that would replace the underlined words.

Example: were not = weren't

1. The boy was not sad.
   wasn't weren't
2. We were not working.
   wasn't weren't
3. Jen and Caleb have not eaten lunch yet.
   haven't hasn't
4. The mouse has not been here.
   haven't hasn't

COMPLETE YEAR GRADE 2

237

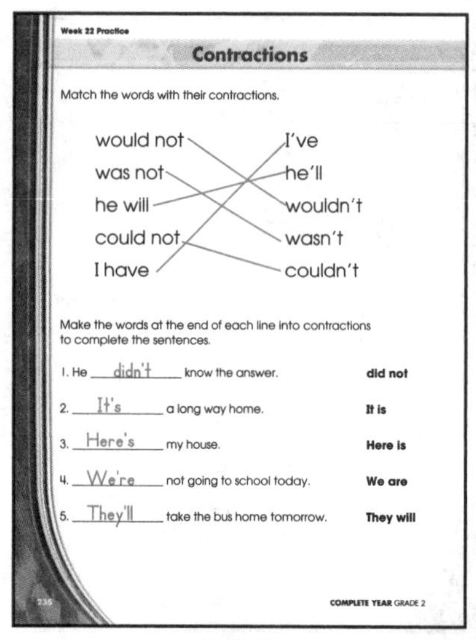
Week 22 Practice

Contractions

Match the words with their contractions.

Make the words at the end of each line into contractions to complete the sentences.

1. He didn't know the answer. **did not**
2. It's a long way home. **It is**
3. Here's my house. **Here is**
4. We're not going to school today. **We are**
5. They'll take the bus home tomorrow. **They will**

COMPLETE YEAR GRADE 2

238

Week 22 Practice

Contractions

Cut out the heart halves and put them together to show what two words make the contraction. Glue them over the contraction.

COMPLETE YEAR GRADE 2

239

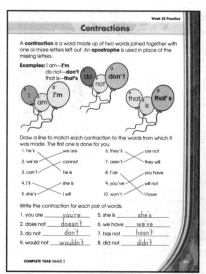

Week 22 Practice

Contractions

A **contraction** is a word made up of two words joined together with one or more letters left out. An **apostrophe** is used in place of the missing letters.

Examples: I am—**I'm**
do not—**don't**
that is—**that's**

I am I'm do not don't that is that's

Draw a line to match each contraction to the words from which it was made. The first one is done for you.

1. he's	we are	6. they'll	are not
2. we're	cannot	7. aren't	they will
3. can't	he is	8. I've	you have
4. I'll	she is	9. you've	will not
5. she's	I will	10. won't	I have

Write the contraction for each pair of words.

1. you are you're	5. she is she's
2. does not doesn't	6. we have we've
3. do not don't	7. has not hasn't
4. would not wouldn't	8. did not didn't

COMPLETE YEAR GRADE 2

241

241

Week 22 Practice

"Mouth" Math

Write < or > in each circle. Make sure the "mouth" is open toward the greater number!

36 < 49	35 < 53
20 > 18	74 > 21
53 < 76	68 < 80
29 > 26	45 > 19
90 > 89	70 > 67

242

COMPLETE YEAR GRADE 2

242

Answer Key

Week 22 Practice

Number Lines

Write the circled numbers in the correct order on the lines.

A. 0 1 2 3 4 (5) 6 7 8 9 10 11 (12) 13 14 15 16 17 18 19 20
12 > 5

B. 10 11 12 13 14 15 16 17 (18) 19 20 21 22 23 24 25 26 27 28 29 (30)
18 < 30

C. 20 (21) 22 (23) 24 25 26 27 28 29 30 31 32 33 34 35 36 37 38 39 40
23 > 21

D. 30 31 32 33 34 35 36 37 38 (39) 40 41 42 (43) 44 45 46 47 48 49 50
39 < 43

E. 40 41 (42) 43 44 45 46 47 (48) 49 50 51 52 53 54 55 56 57 58 59 60
48 > 42

F. 50 51 52 53 54 55 (56) 57 58 59 60 (61) 62 63 64 65 66 67 68 69 70
56 < 61

COMPLETE YEAR GRADE 2 243

243

Week 22 Practice

Less Than, Greater Than

The open mouth points to the larger number. The small point goes to the smaller number. Draw the symbol < or > to the correct number.

Example: 5 (>) 3 — This means that 5 is greater than 3, and 3 is less than 5.

12 (>) 2	16 (>) 6
16 (>) 15	1 (<) 2
7 (>) 1	19 (>) 5
9 (>) 6	11 (<) 13

244 COMPLETE YEAR GRADE 2

244

Week 23 Practice

Prefixes

Change the meaning of the sentences by adding the prefixes to the **bold** words.

The boy was **lucky** because he guessed the answer **correctly**.
The boy was (un) unlucky because he guessed the answer (in) incorrectly.

When Mary **behaved**, she felt **happy**.
When Mary (mis) misbehaved, she felt (un) unhappy.

Mike wore his jacket **buttoned** because the dance was **formal**.
Mike wore his jacket (un) unbuttoned because the dance was (in) informal.

Tim **understood** because he was **familiar** with the book.
Tim (mis) misunderstood because he was (un) unfamiliar with the book.

246 COMPLETE YEAR GRADE 2

246

Week 23 Practice

Prefixes

Read the story. Change the story by removing the prefix **re** from the **bold** words. Write the new words in the new story.

Repete is a **rewriter** who has to **redo** every story. He has to **rethink** up the ideas. He has to **rewrite** the sentences. He has to **redraw** the pictures. He even has to **retype** the pages. Who will **repay** **Repete** for all the work he **redoes**?

Pete is a writer who has to do every story. He has to think up the ideas. He has to write the sentences. He has to draw the pictures. He even has to type the pages. Who will pay Pete for all the work he does?

COMPLETE YEAR GRADE 2 247

247

Week 23 Practice

Prefixes

Read each sentence. Look at the words in **bold**. Circle the prefix and write the root word on the line.

1. The **preview** of the movie was funny. — view
2. We always drink **nonfat** milk. — fat
3. We will have to **reschedule** the trip. — schedule
4. Are you tired of **reruns** on television? — run
5. I have **outgrown** my new shoes already. — grow
6. You must have **misplaced** the papers. — place
7. Police **enforce** the laws of the city. — force
8. I **disliked** that book. — like
9. The boy **distrusted** the big dog. — trust
10. Try to **enjoy** yourself at the party. — joy
11. Please try to keep the cat **inside** the house. — side
12. That song is total **nonsense**! — sense
13. We will **replace** any parts that we lost. — place
14. Can you help me **unzip** this jacket? — zip
15. Let's **rework** today's arithmetic problems. — work

248 COMPLETE YEAR GRADE 2

248

Week 23 Practice

Prefixes

pre mis un re dis

Prefixes are special word parts added to the beginnings of words. Prefixes change the meaning of words.

Prefix	Meaning	Example
un	not	**un**happy
re	again	**re**do
pre	before	**pre**view
mis	wrong	**mis**understanding
dis	opposite	**dis**obey

Circle the word that begins with a prefix. Then, write the prefix and the root word.

1. The dog was (unfriendly). — un + friendly
2. The movie (preview) was interesting. — pre + view
3. The referee called an (unfair) penalty. — un + fair
4. Please do not (misbehave). — mis + behave
5. My parents (disapprove) of that show. — dis + approve
6. I had to (redo) the assignment. — re + do

COMPLETE YEAR GRADE 2 249

249

Answer Key

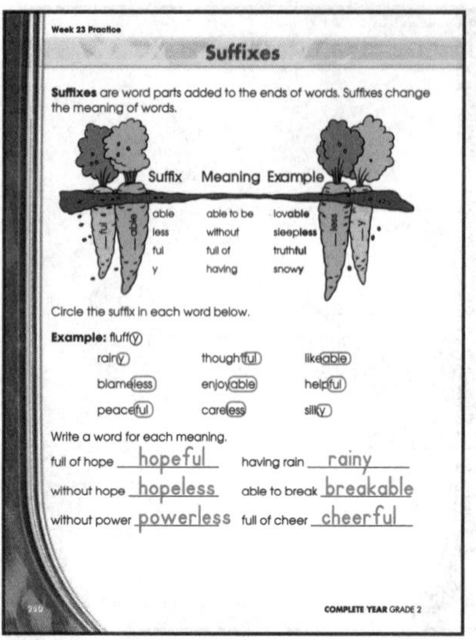

Week 23 Practice

Suffixes

Suffixes are word parts added to the ends of words. Suffixes change the meaning of words.

Suffix	Meaning	Example
able	able to be	lovable
less	without	sleepless
ful	full of	truthful
y	having	snowy

Circle the suffix in each word below.

Example: fluffy

rainy thoughtful likeable
blameless enjoyable helpful
peaceful careless silky

Write a word for each meaning.

full of hope hopeful — having rain rainy
without hope hopeless — able to break breakable
without power powerless — full of cheer cheerful

COMPLETE YEAR GRADE 2

250

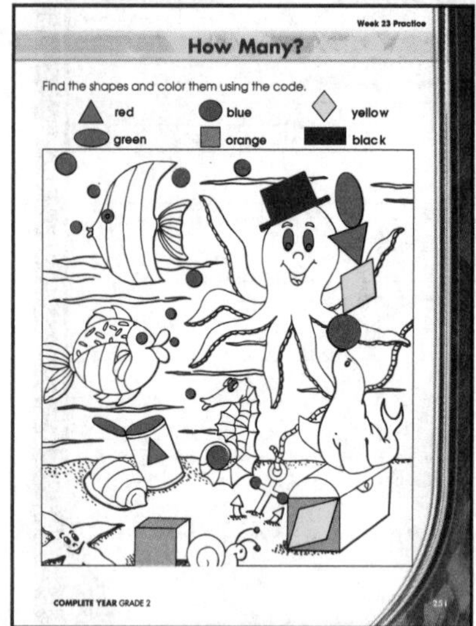

Week 23 Practice

How Many?

Find the shapes and color them using the code.

red blue yellow
green orange black

COMPLETE YEAR GRADE 2

251

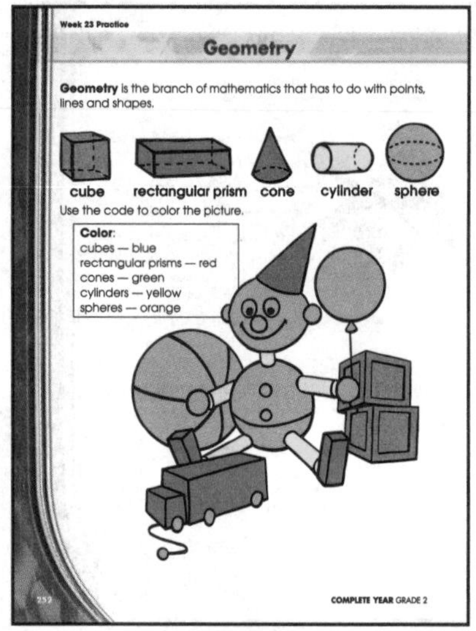

Week 23 Practice

Geometry

Geometry is the branch of mathematics that has to do with points, lines and shapes.

cube rectangular prism cone cylinder sphere

Use the code to color the picture.

Color:
cubes — blue
rectangular prisms — red
cones — green
cylinders — yellow
spheres — orange

COMPLETE YEAR GRADE 2

252

Week 24 Practice

Syllables

Write **1** or **2** on the line to tell how many syllables are in each word. If the word has two syllables, draw a line between the syllables.
Example: supper

dog	1	timber	2
bedroom	2	cat	1
slipper	2	street	1
tree	1	chalk	1
batter	2	blanket	2
chair	1	marker	2
fish	1	brush	1
master	2	rabbit	2

COMPLETE YEAR GRADE 2

256

Week 24 Practice

Syllables

When a double consonant is used in the middle of a word, the word can usually be divided between the consonants.

Look at the words in the word box. Divide each word into two syllables. Leave space between each syllable. One is done for you.

butter	puppy	kitten	yellow
dinner	chatter	ladder	happy
pillow	letter	mitten	summer

but ter — chat ter — mit ten
din ner — let ter — yel low
pil low — kit ten — hap py
pup py — lad der — sum mer

Many words are divided between two consonants that are not alike.

Look at the words in the word box. Divide each word into two syllables. One is done for you.

window	doctor	number	carpet
mister	winter	pencil	candle
barber	sister	picture	under

win dow — win ter — pic ture
mis ter — sis ter — car pet
bar ber — num ber — can dle
doc tor — pen cil — un der

COMPLETE YEAR GRADE 2

257

Week 24 Practice

Syllables

One way to help you read a word you don't know is to divide it into parts called **syllables**. Every syllable has a vowel sound.

Say the words. Write the number of syllables. The first one is done for you.

straw • ber • ry

bird	1	rabbit	2
apple	2	elephant	3
balloon	2	family	3
basketball	3	fence	1
breakfast	2	ladder	2
block	1	open	2
candy	2	puddle	2
popcorn	2	Saturday	3
yellow	2	wind	1
understand	3	butterfly	3

COMPLETE YEAR GRADE 2

258

Answer Key

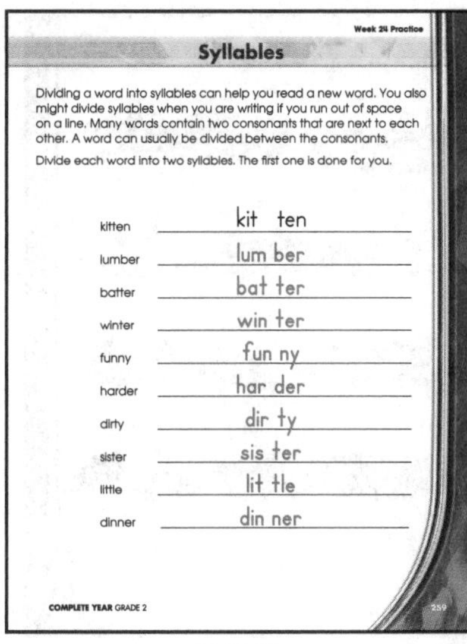

Week 24 Practice

Syllables

Dividing a word into syllables can help you read a new word. You also might divide syllables when you are writing if you run out of space on a line. Many words contain two consonants that are next to each other. A word can usually be divided between the consonants.

Divide each word into two syllables. The first one is done for you.

kitten kit ten
lumber lum ber
batter bat ter
winter win ter
funny fun ny
harder har der
dirty dir ty
sister sis ter
little lit tle
dinner din ner

COMPLETE YEAR GRADE 2 259

259

Week 24 Practice

Syllables

Words are made up of parts called **syllables**. Each syllable has a vowel sound. One way to count syllables is to clap as you say the word.

Example:

cat	1 clap	1 syllable
table	2 claps	2 syllables
butterfly	3 claps	3 syllables

"Clap out" the words below. Write how many syllables each word has.

movie	2	dog	1
piano	3	basket	2
tree	1	swimmer	2
bicycle	3	rainbow	2
sun	1	paper	2
cabinet	3	picture	2
football	2	run	1
television	4	enter	2

260 COMPLETE YEAR GRADE 2

260

Week 24 Practice

It's About Time!

Trace each mouse with red if it has a time word.

Circle the correct answer.

1. There are 60 seconds in a (minute) year.
2. There are 60 minutes in an second (hour).
3. There are 24 hours in a minute (day).
4. There are 365 days in a (year) week.
5. There are 7 days in a (week) hour.
6. There are 12 months in a (year) week.

COMPLETE YEAR GRADE 2 261

261

Week 24 Practice

Turtle Time

Write the time each clock shows.

9:10 8:25

10:05 8:20 1:45 7:55

8:15 3:50 2:35 7:30

262 COMPLETE YEAR GRADE 2

262

Week 24 Practice

Time: Hour, Half-Hour

An **hour** is sixty minutes. The short hand of a clock tells the hour. It is written **0:00**, such as **5:00**. A **half-hour** is thirty minutes. When the long hand of the clock is pointing to the six, the time is on the half-hour. It is written **:30**, such as **5:30**.

Study the examples. Tell what time it is on each clock.

Example: 9:00 4:30

The minute hand is on the 12. The hour hand is on the 9. It is 9 o'clock.

The minute hand is on the 6. The hour hand is *between* the 4 and 5. It is 4:30.

2:00 3:30 1:00 5:30 8:00

10:30 12:00 9:30 2:30 3:00

COMPLETE YEAR GRADE 2 263

263

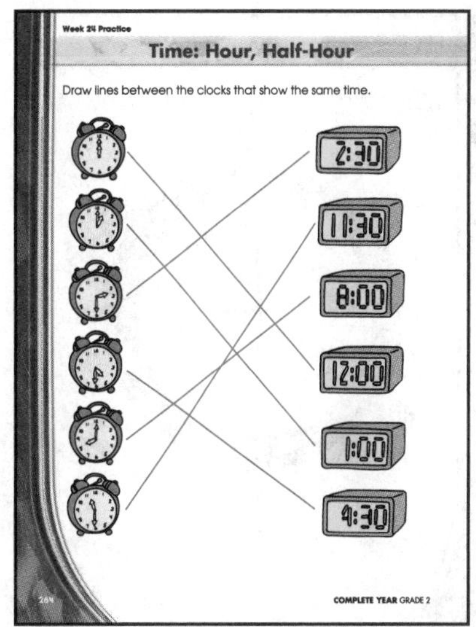

Week 24 Practice

Time: Hour, Half-Hour

Draw lines between the clocks that show the same time.

264 COMPLETE YEAR GRADE 2

264

Answer Key

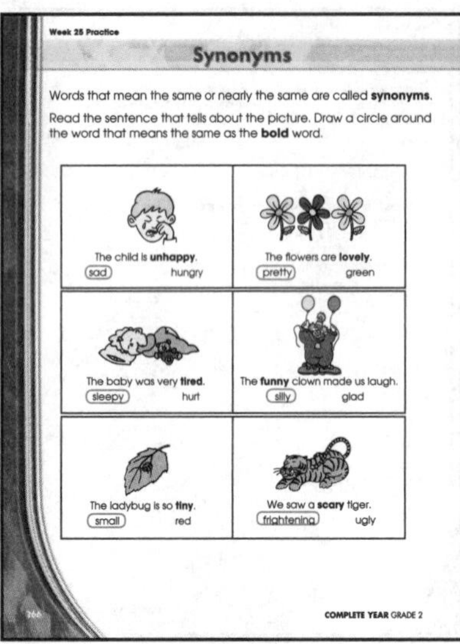

Week 25 Practice

Synonyms

Words that mean the same or nearly the same are called **synonyms**.

Read the sentence that tells about the picture. Draw a circle around the word that means the same as the **bold** word.

The child is **unhappy**. (sad) hungry	The flowers are **lovely**. (pretty) green
The baby was very **tired**. (sleepy) hurt	The **funny** clown made us laugh. (silly) glad
The ladybug is so **tiny**. (small) red	We saw a **scary** tiger. (frightening) ugly

266 COMPLETE YEAR GRADE 2

266

Week 25 Practice

Flower Fun

Write the words from the box that are **synonyms** for the words in the flower pots.

pick start easy sky kind rain afraid fall close hard scream awake put whisper dirt tired

yell scream; begin start; scared afraid; drop fall; nice kind; sleepy tired; soil dirt; near close; place put; difficult hard

COMPLETE YEAR GRADE 2 267

267

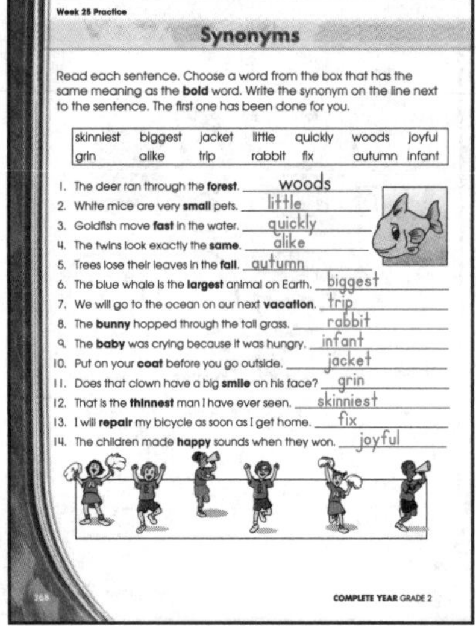

Week 25 Practice

Synonyms

Read each sentence. Choose a word from the box that has the same meaning as the **bold** word. Write the synonym on the line next to the sentence. The first one has been done for you.

skinniest	biggest	jacket	little	quickly	woods	joyful
grin	alike	trip	rabbit	fix	autumn	infant

1. The deer ran through the **forest**. woods
2. White mice are very **small** pets. little
3. Goldfish move **fast** in the water. quickly
4. The twins look exactly the **same**. alike
5. Trees lose their leaves in the **fall**. autumn
6. The blue whale is the **largest** animal on Earth. biggest
7. We will go to the ocean on our next **vacation**. trip
8. The **bunny** hopped through the tall grass. rabbit
9. The **baby** was crying because it was hungry. infant
10. Put on your **coat** before you go outside. jacket
11. Does that clown have a big **smile** on his face? grin
12. That is the **thinnest** man I have ever seen. skinniest
13. I will **repair** my bicycle as soon as I get home. fix
14. The children made **happy** sounds when they won. joyful

268 COMPLETE YEAR GRADE 2

268

Week 25 Practice

Synonyms

Match the pairs of synonyms.

delight	discover
speak	tidy
lovely	start
find	talk
nearly	beautiful
neat	almost
big	joy
sad	unhappy
begin	large

Read each sentence. Write the synonym pairs from each sentence in the boxes.

1. That unusual clock is a rare antique.

unusual | rare

2. I am glad you are so happy!

glad | happy

3. Becky felt unhappy when she heard the sad news.

unhappy | sad

COMPLETE YEAR GRADE 2 269

269

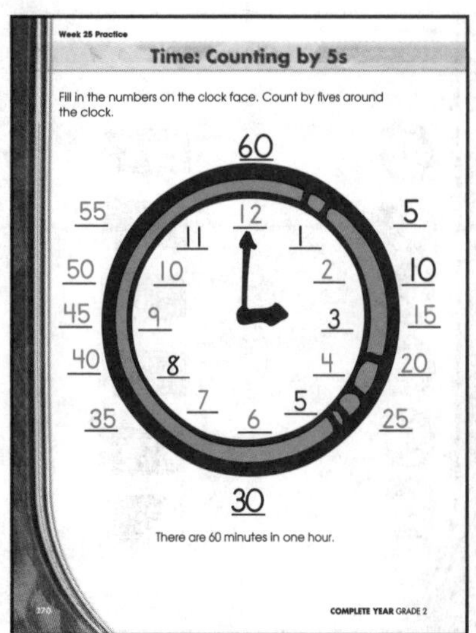

Week 25 Practice

Time: Counting by 5s

Fill in the numbers on the clock face. Count by fives around the clock.

60, 5, 10, 15, 20, 25, 30, 35, 40, 45, 50, 55

12, 1, 2, 3, 4, 5, 6, 7, 8, 9, 10, 11

There are 60 minutes in one hour.

270 COMPLETE YEAR GRADE 2

270

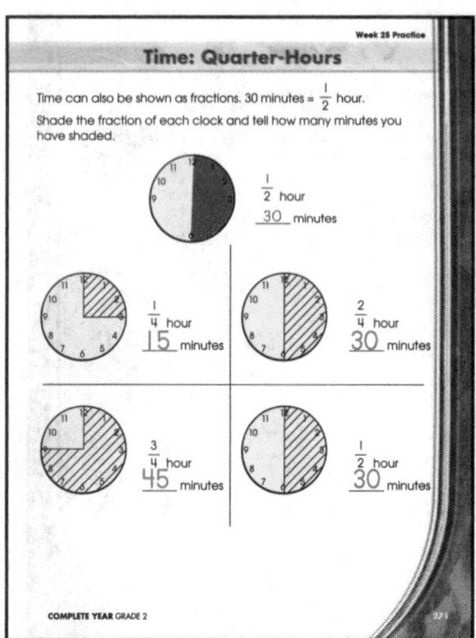

Week 25 Practice

Time: Quarter-Hours

Time can also be shown as fractions. 30 minutes = $\frac{1}{2}$ hour.

Shade the fraction of each clock and tell how many minutes you have shaded.

$\frac{1}{2}$ hour 30 minutes

$\frac{1}{4}$ hour 15 minutes

$\frac{2}{4}$ hour 30 minutes

$\frac{3}{4}$ hour 45 minutes

$\frac{1}{2}$ hour 30 minutes

COMPLETE YEAR GRADE 2 271

271

Answer Key

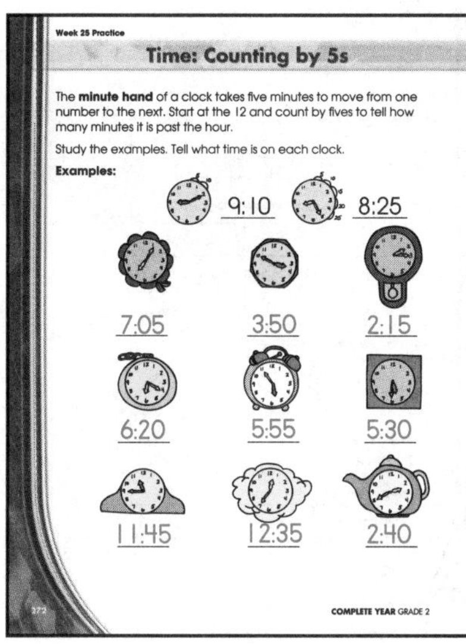

Week 25 Practice

Time: Counting by 5s

The **minute hand** of a clock takes five minutes to move from one number to the next. Start at the 12 and count by fives to tell how many minutes it is past the hour.

Study the examples. Tell what time is on each clock.

Examples:

9:10 8:25

7:05 3:50 2:15

6:20 5:55 5:30

11:45 12:35 2:40

272 COMPLETE YEAR GRADE 2

272

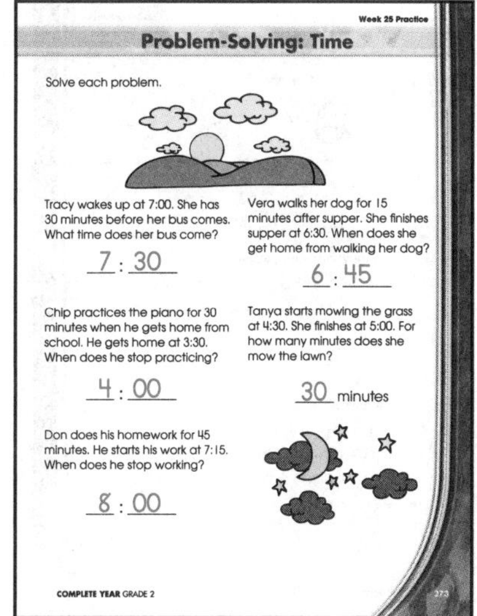

Week 25 Practice

Problem-Solving: Time

Solve each problem.

Tracy wakes up at 7:00. She has 30 minutes before her bus comes. What time does her bus come?

7 : 30

Vera walks her dog for 15 minutes after supper. She finishes supper at 6:30. When does she get home from walking her dog?

6 : 45

Chip practices the piano for 30 minutes when he gets home from school. He gets home at 3:30. When does he stop practicing?

4 : 00

Tanya starts mowing the grass at 4:30. She finishes at 5:00. For how many minutes does she mow the lawn?

30 minutes

Don does his homework for 45 minutes. He starts his work at 7:15. When does he stop working?

8 : 00

COMPLETE YEAR GRADE 2 273

273

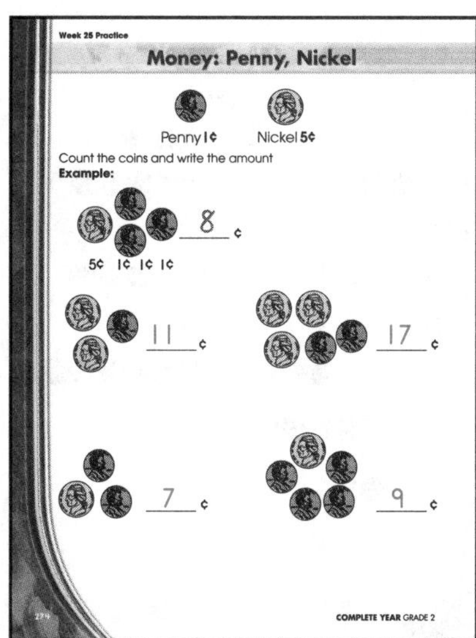

Week 25 Practice

Money: Penny, Nickel

Penny 1¢ Nickel 5¢

Count the coins and write the amount

Example:

8 ¢

5¢ 1¢ 1¢ 1¢

11 ¢

17 ¢

7 ¢

9 ¢

274 COMPLETE YEAR GRADE 2

274

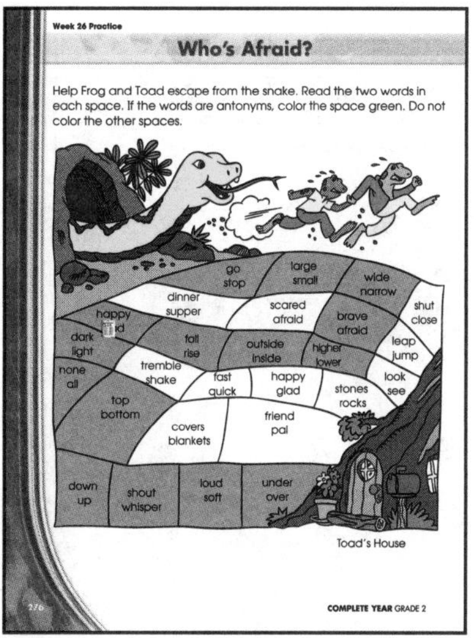

Week 26 Practice

Who's Afraid?

Help Frog and Toad escape from the snake. Read the two words in each space. If the words are antonyms, color the space green. Do not color the other spaces.

276 COMPLETE YEAR GRADE 2

276

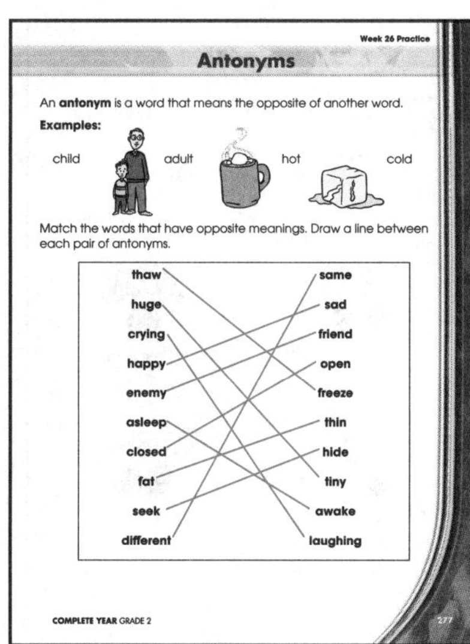

Week 26 Practice

Antonyms

An **antonym** is a word that means the opposite of another word.

Examples:

child adult hot cold

Match the words that have opposite meanings. Draw a line between each pair of antonyms.

thaw	same
huge	sad
crying	friend
happy	open
enemy	freeze
asleep	thin
closed	hide
fat	tiny
seek	awake
different	laughing

COMPLETE YEAR GRADE 2 277

277

Week 26 Practice

Antonyms

Complete each sentence with an antonym pair from page 277. Some pairs will not be used.

Example: Usually we wear different clothes, but today we are dressed the same.

1. A child is allowed in the museum if he or she is with an adult.
2. Mom was happy it rained since her garden was very dry, but I was sad because I had to stay inside.
3. The huge crowd of people tried to fit into the tiny room.
4. The crying baby was soon laughing and playing in the crib.
5. We'll freeze the meat for now, and Dad will thaw it when we need it.
6. The windows were wide open, but the door was closed.

Now, write your own sentence using one of the antonym pairs.

Answers will vary.

278 COMPLETE YEAR GRADE 2

278

Answer Key

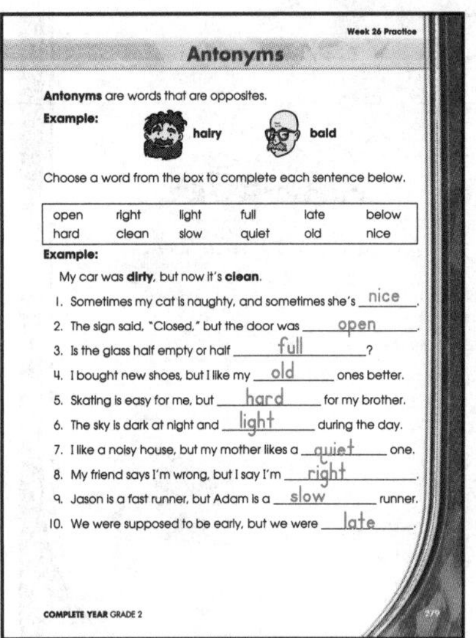

Week 26 Practice

Antonyms

Antonyms are words that are opposites.

Example: hairy bald

Choose a word from the box to complete each sentence below.

open	right	light	full	late	below
hard	clean	slow	quiet	old	nice

Example:

My car was **dirty**, but now it's **clean**.

1. Sometimes my cat is naughty, and sometimes she's nice.
2. The sign said, "Closed," but the door was open.
3. Is the glass half empty or half full?
4. I bought new shoes, but I like my old ones better.
5. Skating is easy for me, but hard for my brother.
6. The sky is dark at night and light during the day.
7. I like a noisy house, but my mother likes a quiet one.
8. My friend says I'm wrong, but I say I'm right.
9. Jason is a fast runner, but Adam is a slow runner.
10. We were supposed to be early, but we were late.

COMPLETE YEAR GRADE 2 279

279

Week 26 Practice

Antonyms

Write the antonym pairs from each sentence in the boxes.

Example: Many things are bought and sold at the market.

bought | sold

1. I thought I lost my dog, but someone found him.

lost | found

2. The teacher will ask questions for the students to answer.

ask | answer

3. Airplanes arrive and depart from the airport.

arrive | depart

4. The water in the pool was cold compared to the warm water in the whirlpool.

cold | warm

5. The tortoise was slow, but the hare was fast.

slow | fast

280 COMPLETE YEAR GRADE 2

280

Week 26 Practice

Money: Penny, Nickel, Dime

Penny 1¢ Nickel 5¢ Dime 10¢

Count the coins and write the amount.

16 ¢

27 ¢

38 ¢

26 ¢

21 ¢

COMPLETE YEAR GRADE 2 281

281

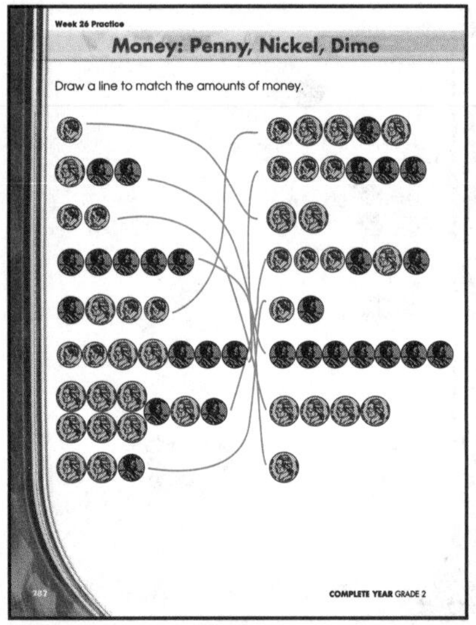

Week 26 Practice

Money: Penny, Nickel, Dime

Draw a line to match the amounts of money.

282 COMPLETE YEAR GRADE 2

282

Week 26 Practice

Money: Quarter

A **quarter** is worth 25¢.

Count the coins and write the amounts.

25 ¢

25 ¢

30 ¢

25 ¢

30 ¢

25 ¢

28 ¢

36 ¢

COMPLETE YEAR GRADE 2 283

283

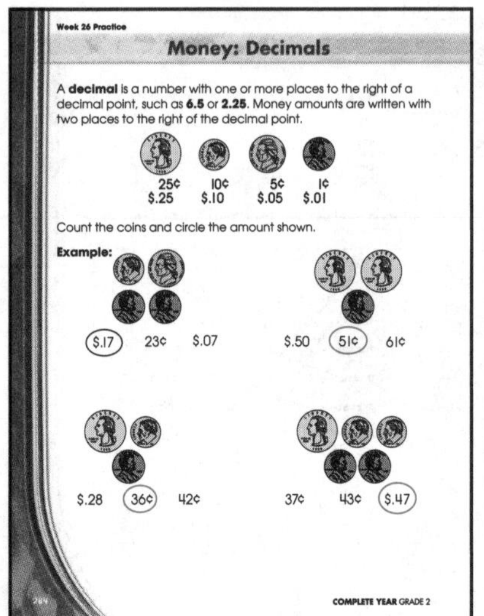

Week 26 Practice

Money: Decimals

A **decimal** is a number with one or more places to the right of a decimal point, such as **6.5** or **2.25**. Money amounts are written with two places to the right of the decimal point.

25¢ $.25 10¢ $.10 5¢ $.05 1¢ $.01

Count the coins and circle the amount shown.

Example:

($.17) 23¢ $.07

$.50 (51¢) 61¢

$.28 (36¢) 42¢

37¢ 43¢ ($.47)

284 COMPLETE YEAR GRADE 2

284

Answer Key

Week 27 Practice

Capitalization

Proper nouns are the names of specific people, places and pets. Proper nouns begin with a capital letter.

Write the proper nouns on the lines below. Use capital letters at the beginning of each word.

logan, utah — Logan, Utah

mike smith — Mike Smith

lynn cramer — Lynn Cramer

buster — Buster

fluffy — Fluffy

chicago, illinois — Chicago, Illinois

286 COMPLETE YEAR GRADE 2

286

Week 27 Practice

Capitalization

Write capital letters where they should appear in the sentences below.

Example: joe can play in january.
Joe can play in January.

1. we celebrate thanksgiving on the fourth thursday in november.
We celebrate Thanksgiving on the fourth Thursday in November.

2. in june, michelle and mark will go camping every friday.
In June, Michelle and Mark will go camping every Friday.

3. on mondays in october, i will take piano lessons.
On Mondays in October, I will take piano lessons.

COMPLETE YEAR GRADE 2 287

287

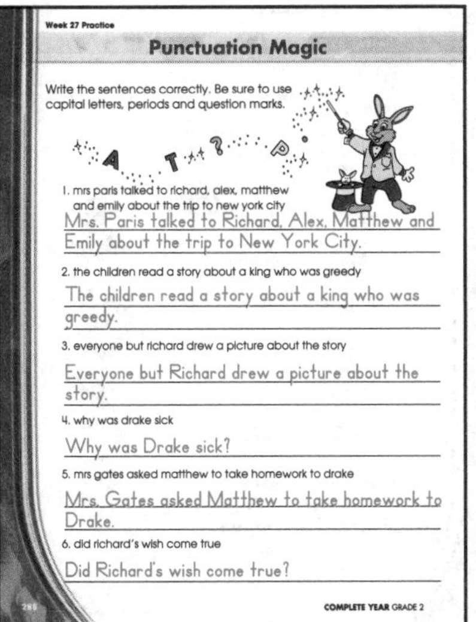

Week 27 Practice

Punctuation Magic

Write the sentences correctly. Be sure to use capital letters, periods and question marks.

1. mrs paris talked to richard, alex, matthew and emily about the trip to new york city
Mrs. Paris talked to Richard, Alex, Matthew and Emily about the trip to New York City.
2. the children read a story about a king who was greedy
The children read a story about a king who was greedy.
3. everyone but richard drew a picture about the story
Everyone but Richard drew a picture about the story.
4. why was drake sick
Why was Drake sick?
5. mrs gates asked matthew to take homework to drake
Mrs. Gates asked Matthew to take homework to Drake.
6. did richard's wish come true
Did Richard's wish come true?

288 COMPLETE YEAR GRADE 2

288

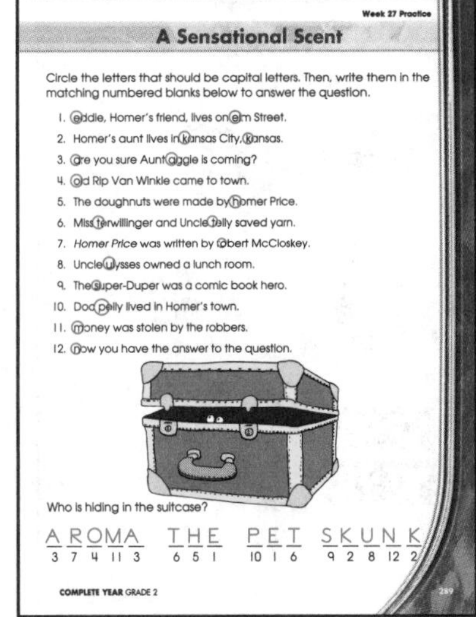

Week 27 Practice

A Sensational Scent

Circle the letters that should be capital letters. Then, write them in the matching numbered blanks below to answer the question.

1. eddie, Homer's friend, lives on elm Street.
2. Homer's aunt lives in kansas City, kansas.
3. are you sure Aunt aggie is coming?
4. old Rip Van Winkle came to town.
5. The doughnuts were made by homer Price.
6. Miss terwillinger and Uncle telly saved yarn.
7. *Homer Price* was written by robert McCloskey.
8. Uncle ulysses owned a lunch room.
9. The super-Duper was a comic book hero.
10. Doc pelly lived in Homer's town.
11. money was stolen by the robbers.
12. now you have the answer to the question.

Who is hiding in the suitcase?

A R O M A (3 7 4 11 3) T H E (6 5 1) P E T (10 1 6) S K U N K (9 2 8 12 2)

COMPLETE YEAR GRADE 2 289

289

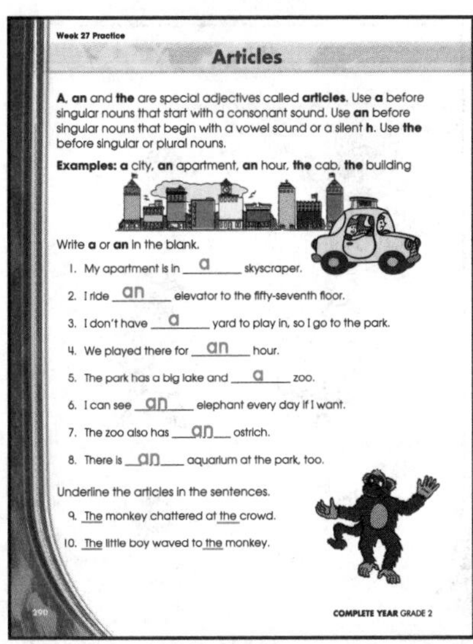

Week 27 Practice

Articles

A, **an** and **the** are special adjectives called **articles**. Use **a** before singular nouns that start with a consonant sound. Use **an** before singular nouns that begin with a vowel sound or a silent **h**. Use **the** before singular or plural nouns.

Examples: **a** city, **an** apartment, **an** hour, **the** cab, **the** building

Write **a** or **an** in the blank.

1. My apartment is in a skyscraper.
2. I ride an elevator to the fifty-seventh floor.
3. I don't have a yard to play in, so I go to the park.
4. We played there for an hour.
5. The park has a big lake and a zoo.
6. I can see an elephant every day if I want.
7. The zoo also has an ostrich.
8. There is an aquarium at the park, too.

Underline the articles in the sentences.

9. The monkey chattered at the crowd.
10. The little boy waved to the monkey.

290 COMPLETE YEAR GRADE 2

290

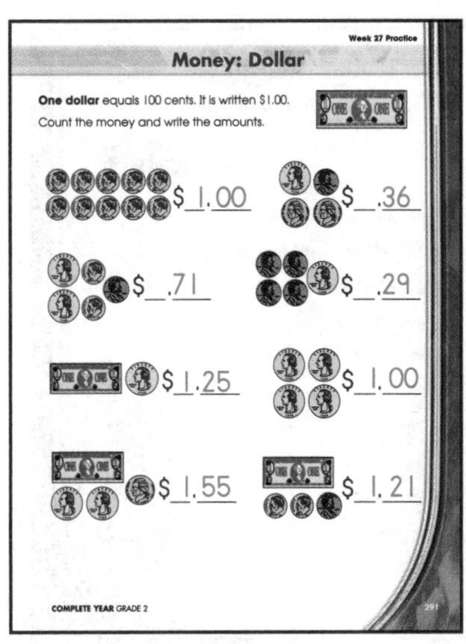

Week 27 Practice

Money: Dollar

One dollar equals 100 cents. It is written $1.00.

Count the money and write the amounts.

$ 1.00 $ .36

$ .71 $ .29

$ 1.25 $ 1.00

$ 1.55 $ 1.21

COMPLETE YEAR GRADE 2 291

291

Answer Key

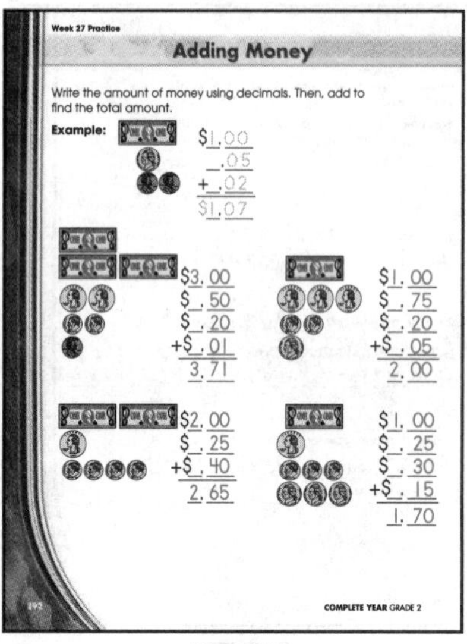
Week 27 Practice

Adding Money

Write the amount of money using decimals. Then, add to find the total amount.

Example: $1.00 / .05 / + .02 / $1.07

$3.00 / $.50 / $.20 / + $.01 / 3.71

$1.00 / $.75 / $.20 / + $.05 / 2.00

$2.00 / $.25 / + $.40 / 2.65

$1.00 / $.25 / $.30 / + $.15 / 1.70

292 COMPLETE YEAR GRADE 2

292

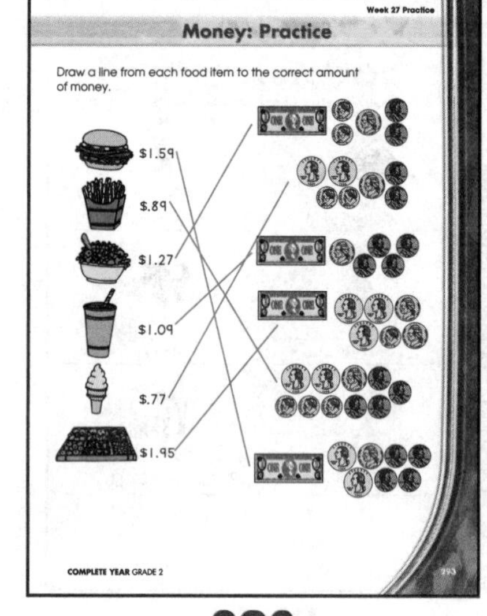
Week 27 Practice

Money: Practice

Draw a line from each food item to the correct amount of money.

$1.59

$.89

$1.27

$1.09

$.77

$1.95

COMPLETE YEAR GRADE 2 293

293

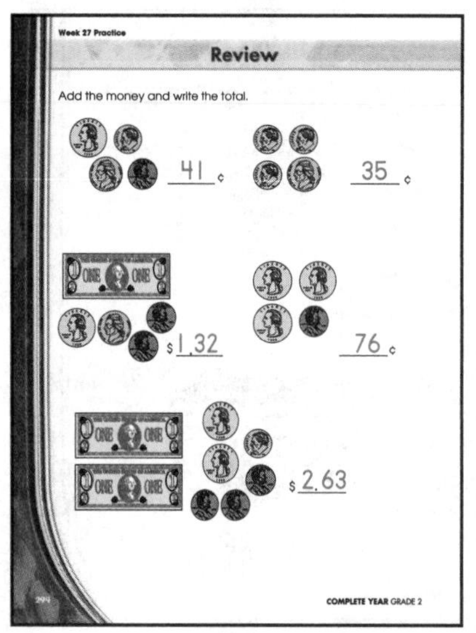
Week 27 Practice

Review

Add the money and write the total.

41 ¢

35 ¢

$1.32

76 ¢

$2.63

294 COMPLETE YEAR GRADE 2

294

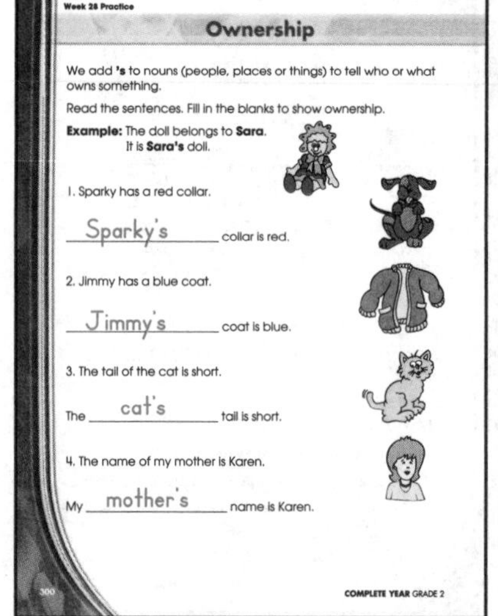
Week 28 Practice

Ownership

We add **'s** to nouns (people, places or things) to tell who or what owns something.

Read the sentences. Fill in the blanks to show ownership.

Example: The doll belongs to **Sara**.
It is **Sara's** doll.

1. Sparky has a red collar.
Sparky's collar is red.

2. Jimmy has a blue coat.
Jimmy's coat is blue.

3. The tail of the cat is short.
The cat's tail is short.

4. The name of my mother is Karen.
My mother's name is Karen.

300 COMPLETE YEAR GRADE 2

300

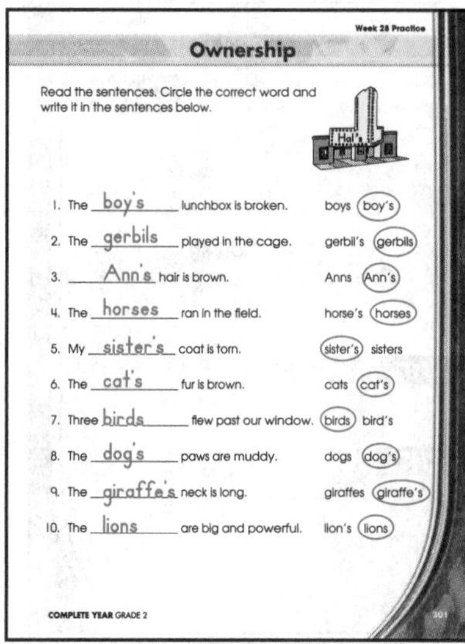
Week 28 Practice

Ownership

Read the sentences. Circle the correct word and write it in the sentences below.

1. The boy's lunchbox is broken. boys (boy's)
2. The gerbils played in the cage. gerbil's (gerbils)
3. Ann's hair is brown. Anns (Ann's)
4. The horses ran in the field. horse's (horses)
5. My sister's coat is torn. (sister's) sisters
6. The cat's fur is brown. cats (cat's)
7. Three birds flew past our window. (birds) bird's
8. The dog's paws are muddy. dogs (dog's)
9. The giraffe's neck is long. giraffes (giraffe's)
10. The lions are big and powerful. lion's (lions)

COMPLETE YEAR GRADE 2 301

301

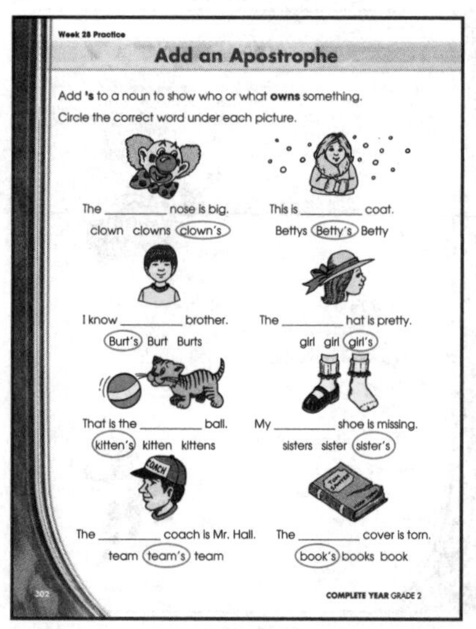
Week 28 Practice

Add an Apostrophe

Add **'s** to a noun to show who or what **owns** something.

Circle the correct word under each picture.

The ________ nose is big. clown clowns (clown's)

This is ________ coat. Bettys (Betty's) Betty

I know ________ brother. (Burt's) Burt Burts

The ________ hat is pretty. girl girl (girl's)

That is the ________ ball. (kitten's) kitten kittens

My ________ shoe is missing. sisters sister (sister's)

The ________ coach is Mr. Hall. team (team's) team

The ________ cover is torn. (book's) books book

302 COMPLETE YEAR GRADE 2

302

Answer Key

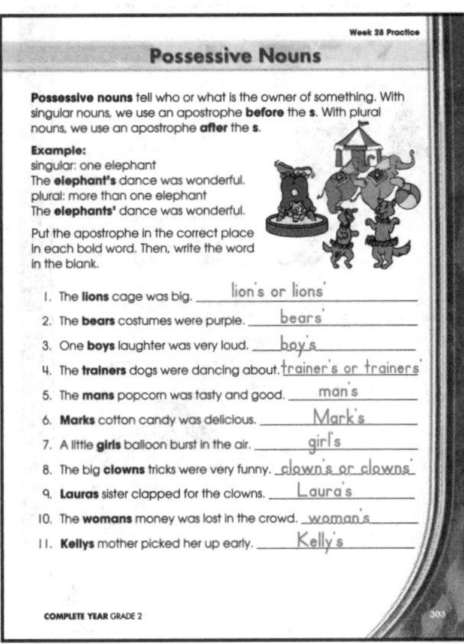

Week 28 Practice

Possessive Nouns

Possessive nouns tell who or what is the owner of something. With singular nouns, we use an apostrophe **before** the **s**. With plural nouns, we use an apostrophe **after** the **s**.

Example:
singular: one elephant
The **elephant's** dance was wonderful.
plural: more than one elephant
The **elephants'** dance was wonderful.

Put the apostrophe in the correct place in each bold word. Then, write the word in the blank.

1. The **lions** cage was big. lion's or lions'
2. The **bears** costumes were purple. bears'
3. One **boys** laughter was very loud. boy's
4. The **trainers** dogs were dancing about. trainer's or trainers'
5. The **mans** popcorn was tasty and good. man's
6. **Marks** cotton candy was delicious. Mark's
7. A little **girls** balloon burst in the air. girl's
8. The big **clowns** tricks were very funny. clown's or clowns'
9. **Lauras** sister clapped for the clowns. Laura's
10. The **womans** money was lost in the crowd. woman's
11. **Kellys** mother picked her up early. Kelly's

COMPLETE YEAR GRADE 2 303

303

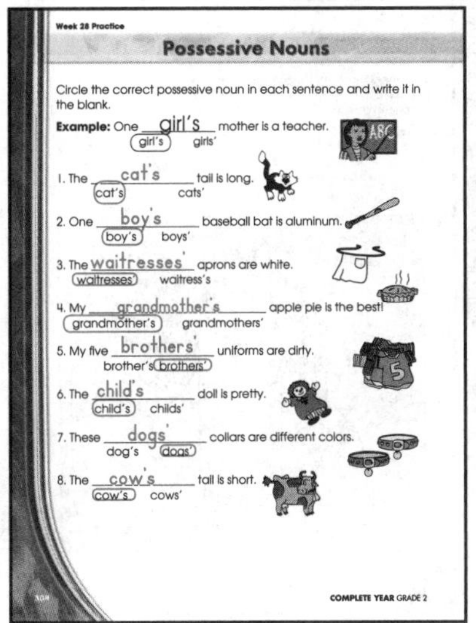

Week 28 Practice

Possessive Nouns

Circle the correct possessive noun in each sentence and write it in the blank.

Example: One girl's mother is a teacher. (girl's) girls'

1. The cat's tail is long. (cat's) cats'
2. One boy's baseball bat is aluminum. (boy's) boys'
3. The waitresses' aprons are white. (waitresses') waitress's
4. My grandmother's apple pie is the best! (grandmother's) grandmothers'
5. My five brothers' uniforms are dirty. brother's (brothers')
6. The child's doll is pretty. (child's) childs'
7. These dogs' collars are different colors. dog's (dogs')
8. The cow's tail is short. (cow's) cows'

304 COMPLETE YEAR GRADE 2

304

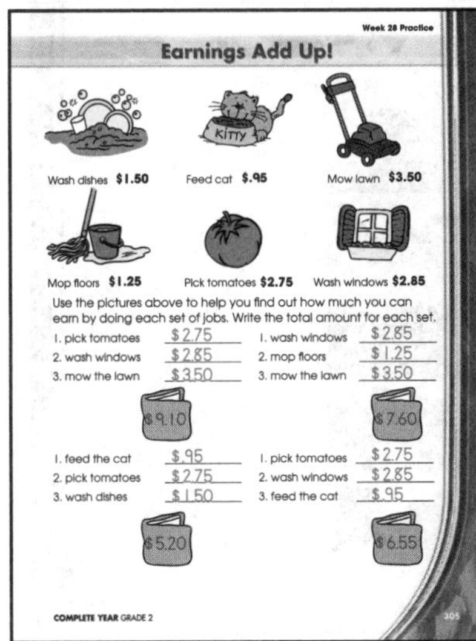

Week 28 Practice

Earnings Add Up!

Wash dishes **$1.50** Feed cat **$.95** Mow lawn **$3.50**
Mop floors **$1.25** Pick tomatoes **$2.75** Wash windows **$2.85**

Use the pictures above to help you find out how much you can earn by doing each set of jobs. Write the total amount for each set.

1. pick tomatoes	$2.75	1. wash windows	$2.85
2. wash windows	$2.85	2. mop floors	$1.25
3. mow the lawn	$3.50	3. mow the lawn	$3.50
	$9.10		$7.60
1. feed the cat	$.95	1. pick tomatoes	$2.75
2. pick tomatoes	$2.75	2. wash windows	$2.85
3. wash dishes	$1.50	3. feed the cat	$.95
	$5.20		$6.55

COMPLETE YEAR GRADE 2 305

305

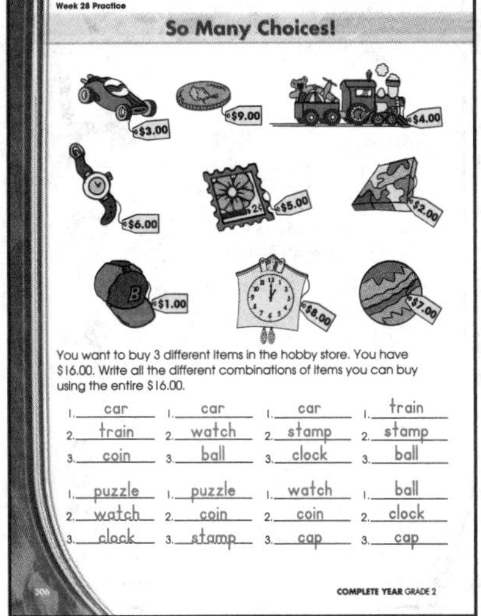

Week 28 Practice

So Many Choices!

You want to buy 3 different items in the hobby store. You have $16.00. Write all the different combinations of items you can buy using the entire $16.00.

1. car	1. car	1. car	1. train
2. train	2. watch	2. stamp	2. stamp
3. coin	3. ball	3. clock	3. ball
1. puzzle	1. puzzle	1. watch	1. ball
2. watch	2. coin	2. coin	2. clock
3. clock	3. stamp	3. cap	3. cap

306 COMPLETE YEAR GRADE 2

306

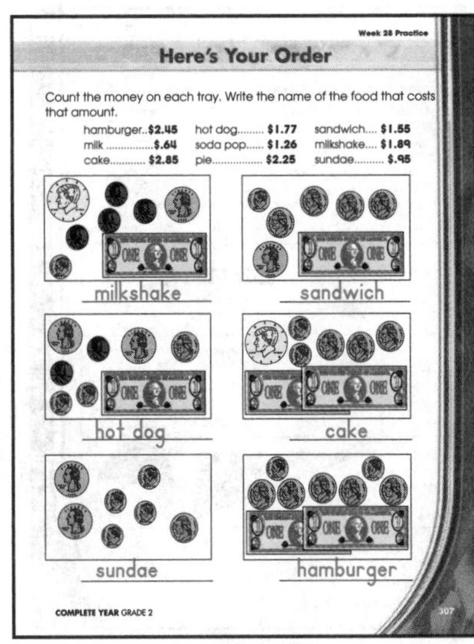

Week 28 Practice

Here's Your Order

Count the money on each tray. Write the name of the food that costs that amount.

hamburger.. **$2.45**	hot dog........ **$1.77**	sandwich.... **$1.55**
milk .... **$.64**	soda pop...... **$1.26**	milkshake.... **$1.89**
cake............ **$2.85**	pie................ **$2.25**	sundae......... **$.95**

milkshake — sandwich
hot dog — cake
sundae — hamburger

COMPLETE YEAR GRADE 2 307

307

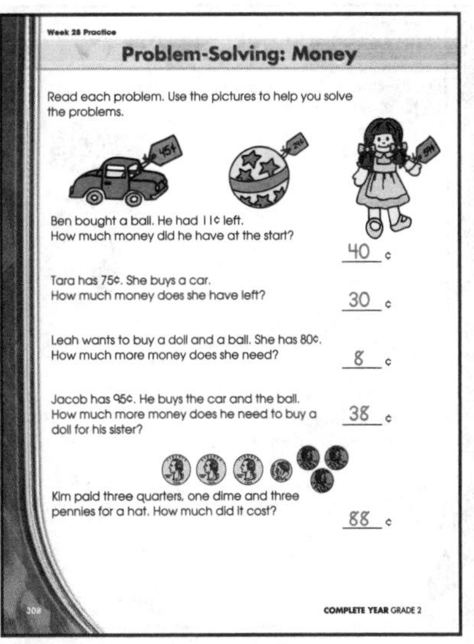

Week 28 Practice

Problem-Solving: Money

Read each problem. Use the pictures to help you solve the problems.

Ben bought a ball. He had 11¢ left. How much money did he have at the start? 40 ¢

Tara has 75¢. She buys a car. How much money does she have left? 30 ¢

Leah wants to buy a doll and a ball. She has 80¢. How much more money does she need? 8 ¢

Jacob has 95¢. He buys the car and the ball. How much more money does he need to buy a doll for his sister? 38 ¢

Kim paid three quarters, one dime and three pennies for a hat. How much did it cost? 88 ¢

308 COMPLETE YEAR GRADE 2

308

Answer Key

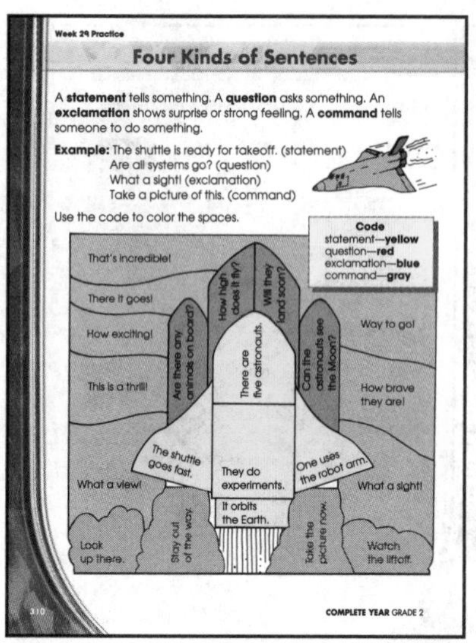

Week 29 Practice

Four Kinds of Sentences

A **statement** tells something. A **question** asks something. An **exclamation** shows surprise or strong feeling. A **command** tells someone to do something.

Example: The shuttle is ready for takeoff. (statement)
Are all systems go? (question)
What a sight! (exclamation)
Take a picture of this. (command)

Use the code to color the spaces.

Code
statement—**yellow**
question—**red**
exclamation—**blue**
command—**gray**

That's incredible!
There it goes!
How exciting!
This is a thrill!
What a view!
Look up there.
How high does it fly?
Will they land soon?
Are there any animals on board?
There are five astronauts.
Can the astronauts see the Moon?
Way to go!
How brave they are!
The shuttle goes fast.
They do experiments.
One uses the robot arm.
What a sight!
It orbits the Earth.
Stay out of the way.
Take the picture now.
Watch the liftoff.

COMPLETE YEAR GRADE 2

310

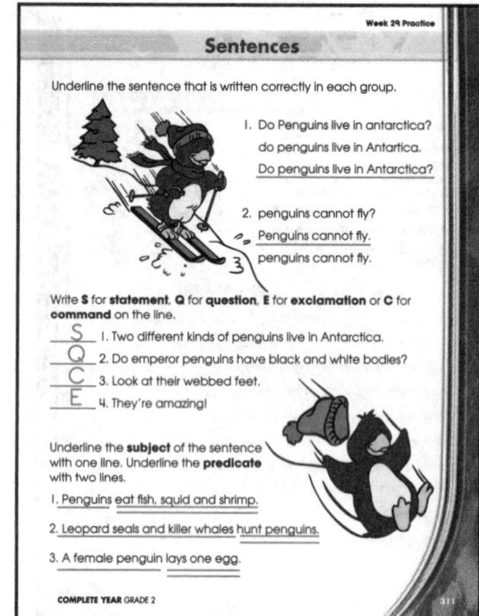

Week 29 Practice

Sentences

Underline the sentence that is written correctly in each group.

1. Do Penguins live in antarctica?
   do penguins live in Antartica.
   Do penguins live in Antarctica?
2. penguins cannot fly?
   Penguins cannot fly.
   penguins cannot fly.

Write **S** for **statement**, **Q** for **question**, **E** for **exclamation** or **C** for **command** on the line.

S 1. Two different kinds of penguins live in Antarctica.
Q 2. Do emperor penguins have black and white bodies?
C 3. Look at their webbed feet.
E 4. They're amazing!

Underline the **subject** of the sentence with one line. Underline the **predicate** with two lines.

1. Penguins eat fish, squid and shrimp.
2. Leopard seals and killer whales hunt penguins.
3. A female penguin lays one egg.

COMPLETE YEAR GRADE 2

311

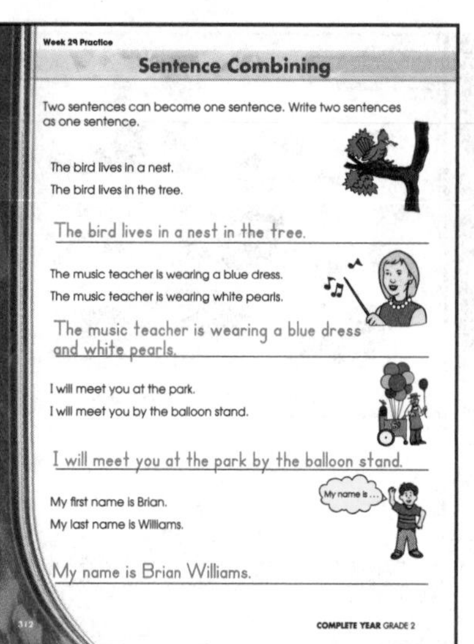

Week 29 Practice

Sentence Combining

Two sentences can become one sentence. Write two sentences as one sentence.

The bird lives in a nest.
The bird lives in the tree.

The bird lives in a nest in the tree.

The music teacher is wearing a blue dress.
The music teacher is wearing white pearls.

The music teacher is wearing a blue dress and white pearls.

I will meet you at the park.
I will meet you by the balloon stand.

I will meet you at the park by the balloon stand.

My first name is Brian.
My last name is Williams.

My name is Brian Williams.

My name is . . .

COMPLETE YEAR GRADE 2

312

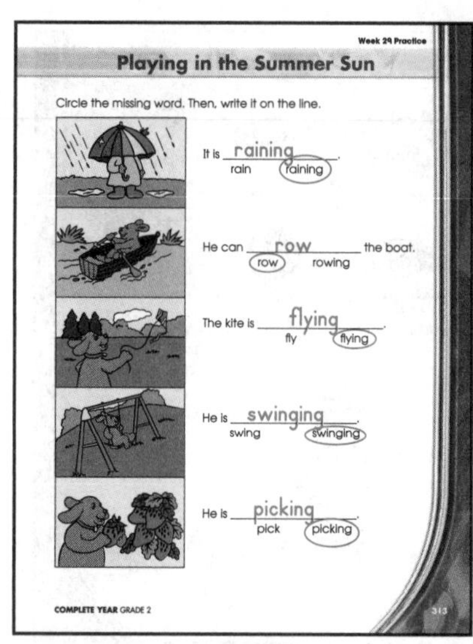

Week 29 Practice

Playing in the Summer Sun

Circle the missing word. Then, write it on the line.

It is raining. (rain / raining)

He can row the boat. (row / rowing)

The kite is flying. (fly / flying)

He is swinging. (swing / swinging)

He is picking. (pick / picking)

COMPLETE YEAR GRADE 2

313

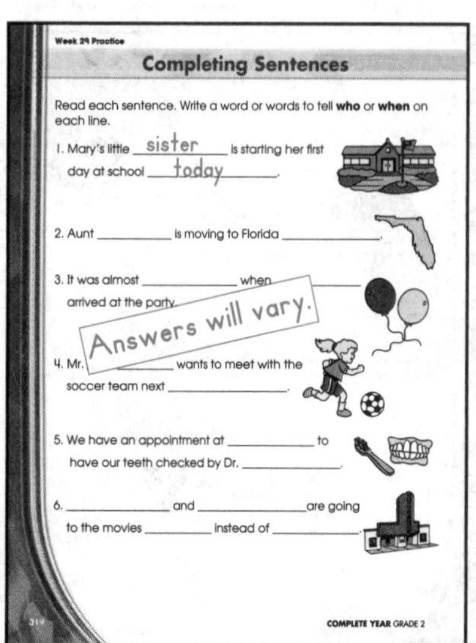

Week 29 Practice

Completing Sentences

Read each sentence. Write a word or words to tell **who** or **when** on each line.

1. Mary's little sister is starting her first day at school today.
2. Aunt __________ is moving to Florida __________.
3. It was almost __________ when __________ arrived at the party.
4. Mr. __________ wants to meet with the soccer team next __________.
5. We have an appointment at __________ to have our teeth checked by Dr. __________.
6. __________ and __________ are going to the movies __________ instead of __________.

Answers will vary.

COMPLETE YEAR GRADE 2

314

Week 29 Practice

Fractions: Half, Third, Fourth

A **fraction** is a number that names part of a whole, such as $\frac{1}{2}$ or $\frac{1}{3}$.

Study the examples. Color the correct fraction of each shape.

Examples:

shaded part 1 equal parts 2 $\frac{1}{2}$ (one-half) shaded	shaded part 1 equal parts 3 $\frac{1}{3}$ (one-third) shaded	shaded part 1 equal parts 4 $\frac{1}{4}$ (one-fourth) shaded

Color: $\frac{1}{3}$ red

Color: $\frac{1}{4}$ blue

Color: $\frac{1}{2}$ orange

COMPLETE YEAR GRADE 2

315

Answer Key

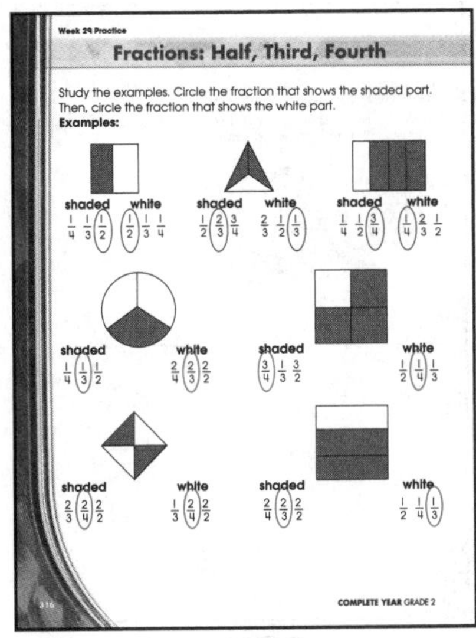

Week 29 Practice

Fractions: Half, Third, Fourth

Study the examples. Circle the fraction that shows the shaded part. Then, circle the fraction that shows the white part.

Examples:

shaded white

COMPLETE YEAR GRADE 2

316

Week 29 Practice

Fractions: Half, Third, Fourth

Draw a line from the fraction to the correct shape.

$\frac{1}{4}$ shaded

$\frac{2}{4}$ shaded

$\frac{1}{2}$ shaded

$\frac{1}{3}$ shaded

$\frac{2}{3}$ shaded

COMPLETE YEAR GRADE 2

317

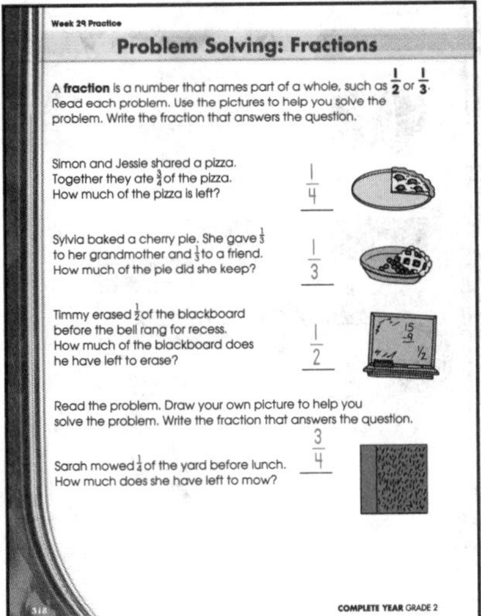

Week 29 Practice

Problem Solving: Fractions

A **fraction** is a number that names part of a whole, such as $\frac{1}{2}$ or $\frac{1}{3}$. Read each problem. Use the pictures to help you solve the problem. Write the fraction that answers the question.

Simon and Jessie shared a pizza. Together they ate $\frac{3}{4}$ of the pizza. How much of the pizza is left? $\frac{1}{4}$

Sylvia baked a cherry pie. She gave $\frac{1}{3}$ to her grandmother and $\frac{1}{3}$ to a friend. How much of the pie did she keep? $\frac{1}{3}$

Timmy erased $\frac{1}{2}$ of the blackboard before the bell rang for recess. How much of the blackboard does he have left to erase? $\frac{1}{2}$

Read the problem. Draw your own picture to help you solve the problem. Write the fraction that answers the question.

Sarah mowed $\frac{1}{4}$ of the yard before lunch. How much does she have left to mow? $\frac{3}{4}$

COMPLETE YEAR GRADE 2

318

Week 30 Practice

Summer Camp

A **statement** is a telling sentence. It begins with a capital letter and ends with a period. Write each statement correctly on the lines.

1. everyone goes to breakfast at 6:30 each morning
   Everyone goes to breakfast at 6:30 each morning.
2. only three people can ride in one canoe
   Only three people can ride in one canoe.
3. each person must help clean the cabins
   Each person must help clean the cabins.
4. older campers should help younger campers
   Older campers should help younger campers.
5. all lights are out by 9:00 each night
   All lights are out by 9:00 each night.
6. everyone should write home at least once a week
   Everyone should write home at least once a week.

COMPLETE YEAR GRADE 2

320

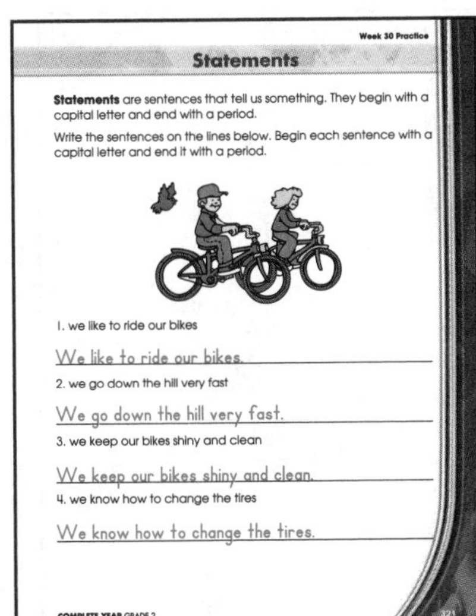

Week 30 Practice

Statements

Statements are sentences that tell us something. They begin with a capital letter and end with a period.

Write the sentences on the lines below. Begin each sentence with a capital letter and end it with a period.

1. we like to ride our bikes
   We like to ride our bikes.
2. we go down the hill very fast
   We go down the hill very fast.
3. we keep our bikes shiny and clean
   We keep our bikes shiny and clean.
4. we know how to change the tires
   We know how to change the tires.

COMPLETE YEAR GRADE 2

321

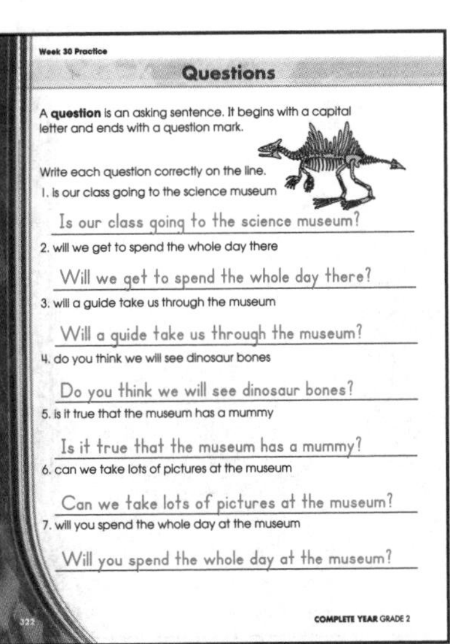

Week 30 Practice

Questions

A **question** is an asking sentence. It begins with a capital letter and ends with a question mark.

Write each question correctly on the line.

1. is our class going to the science museum
   Is our class going to the science museum?
2. will we get to spend the whole day there
   Will we get to spend the whole day there?
3. will a guide take us through the museum
   Will a guide take us through the museum?
4. do you think we will see dinosaur bones
   Do you think we will see dinosaur bones?
5. is it true that the museum has a mummy
   Is it true that the museum has a mummy?
6. can we take lots of pictures at the museum
   Can we take lots of pictures at the museum?
7. will you spend the whole day at the museum
   Will you spend the whole day at the museum?

COMPLETE YEAR GRADE 2

322

Answer Key

Week 30 Practice

More Questions

Write five questions about the picture.

Example: What color is she painting the front door?

COMPLETE YEAR GRADE 2 323

323

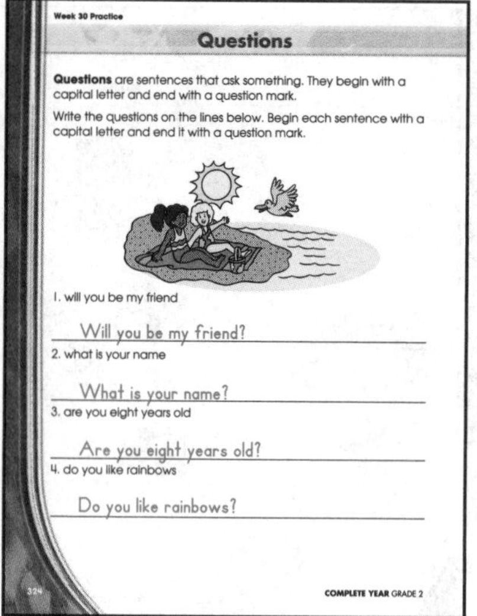

Week 30 Practice

Questions

Questions are sentences that ask something. They begin with a capital letter and end with a question mark.

Write the questions on the lines below. Begin each sentence with a capital letter and end it with a question mark.

1. will you be my friend

   Will you be my friend?

2. what is your name

   What is your name?

3. are you eight years old

   Are you eight years old?

4. do you like rainbows

   Do you like rainbows?

324 COMPLETE YEAR GRADE 2

324

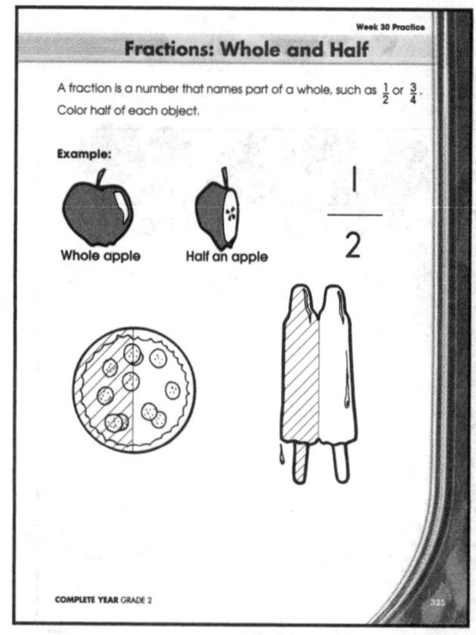

Week 30 Practice

Fractions: Whole and Half

A fraction is a number that names part of a whole, such as $\frac{1}{2}$ or $\frac{3}{4}$. Color half of each object.

Example:

Whole apple Half an apple $\frac{1}{2}$

COMPLETE YEAR GRADE 2 325

325

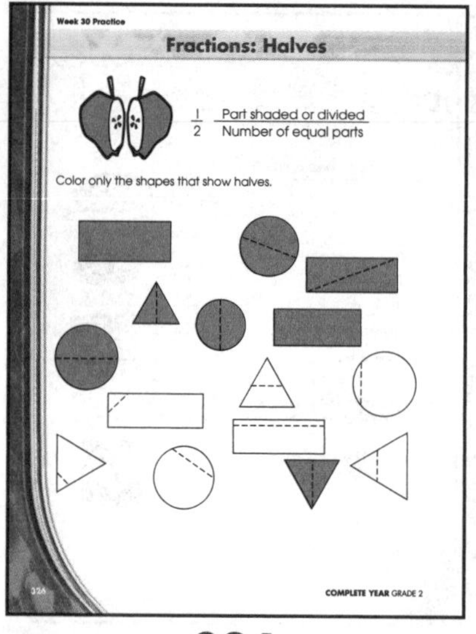

Week 30 Practice

Fractions: Halves

$\frac{1}{2}$ Part shaded or divided / Number of equal parts

Color only the shapes that show halves.

326 COMPLETE YEAR GRADE 2

326

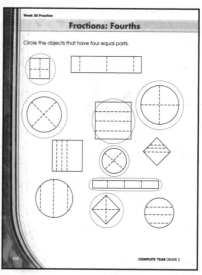

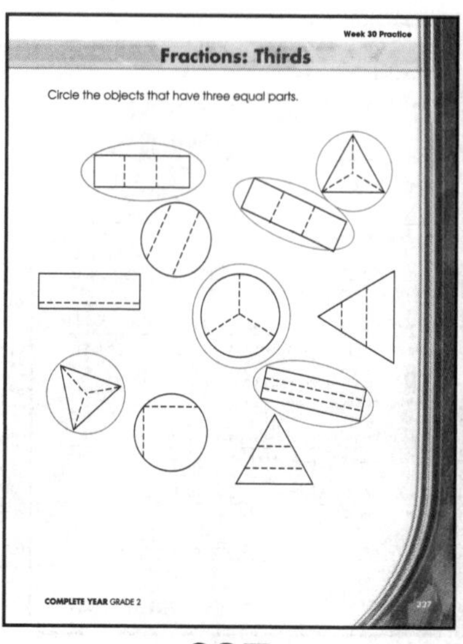

Week 30 Practice

Fractions: Thirds

Circle the objects that have three equal parts.

COMPLETE YEAR GRADE 2 327

327

Week 30 Practice

Fractions: Fourths

Circle the objects that have four equal parts.

328 COMPLETE YEAR GRADE 2

328

Answer Key

Week 31 Practice

Writing Sentences

Every sentence begins with a capital letter.

Come to the Fourth of July Picnic,
Town Park—All Day

Write three statements about the picture.

Example: The red airplane is pulling a sign.

Write three questions about the picture.

Example: Will the girl catch a fish?

330 COMPLETE YEAR GRADE 2

330

Week 31 Practice

Kinds of Sentences

A **statement** ends with a period . (.) A **question** ends with a question mark. (?) Write the correct mark in each box.

1. Would you like to help me make an aquarium ?
2. We can use my brother's big fish tank .
3. Will you put this colored sand in the bottom ?
4. I have three shells to put on the sand .
5. Can we use your little toy boat, too ?
6. Let's go buy some fish for our aquarium .
7. Will twelve fish be enough ?
8. Look, they seem to like their new home .
9. How often do we give them fish food ?
10. Let's tell our friends about our new aquarium .

COMPLETE YEAR GRADE 2 331

331

Week 31 Practice

Changing Sentences

The order of words can change a sentence. Read each telling sentence. Change the order of the words to make an asking sentence. **Example:**

The clown is happy.

Is the clown happy?

The boy can swim.

Can the boy swim?

The bell will ring.

Will the bell ring?

The popcorn is hot.

Is the popcorn hot?

The flowers are lovely.

Are the flowers lovely?

332 COMPLETE YEAR GRADE 2

332

Week 31 Practice

Making Inferences: Point of View

Chelsea likes to pretend she will meet famous people someday. She would like to ask them many questions.

Write a question you think Chelsea would ask if she met these people.

1. an actor in a popular, new film ?
2. an Oly... ?
3. an alien from outer space ?

Questions will vary.

Now, write the answers these people might have given to Chelsea's questions.

4. an actor in a popular, new film
5. an Olympic ...
6. an alien from outer space

Answers will vary.

COMPLETE YEAR GRADE 2 333

333

Week 31 Practice

Making Inferences: Point of View

Ellen likes animals. Someday, she might want to be an animal doctor.

Write one question you think Ellen would ask each of these animals if she could speak their language.

1. a giraffe ?
2. a mouse ?
3. a shark ?
4. a hippopotam... ?
5. a penguin ?
6. a gorilla ?
7. an eagle ?

Questions will vary.

Now, write the answers you think these animals might have given Ellen.

9. a giraffe
10. a mouse
11. a shark
12. a hippopotamus
13. a penguin
14. a gorilla
15. an eagle

Answers will vary.

334 COMPLETE YEAR GRADE 2

334

Week 31 Practice

Fortunate Fractions

Color the correct number of fortune cookies to show each fraction.

$\frac{1}{2}$ $\frac{1}{3}$ $\frac{4}{6}$ $\frac{2}{6}$ $\frac{5}{6}$ $\frac{3}{8}$ $\frac{3}{4}$ $\frac{5}{8}$

COMPLETE YEAR GRADE 2 335

335

Answer Key

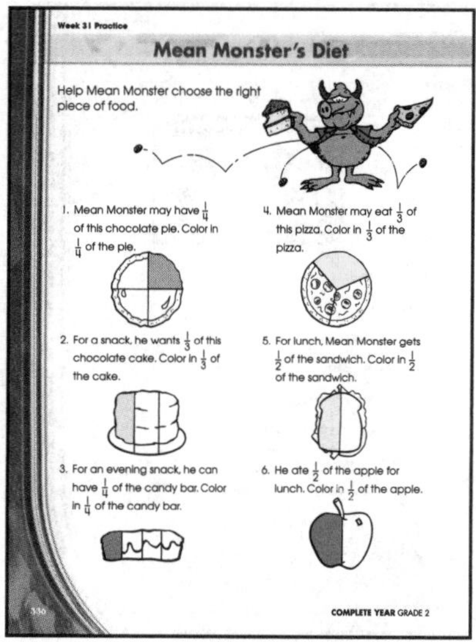

Week 31 Practice

Mean Monster's Diet

Help Mean Monster choose the right piece of food.

1. Mean Monster may have $\frac{1}{4}$ of this chocolate pie. Color in $\frac{1}{4}$ of the pie.
2. For a snack, he wants $\frac{1}{3}$ of this chocolate cake. Color in $\frac{1}{3}$ of the cake.
3. For an evening snack, he can have $\frac{1}{4}$ of the candy bar. Color in $\frac{1}{4}$ of the candy bar.
4. Mean Monster may eat $\frac{1}{3}$ of this pizza. Color in $\frac{1}{3}$ of the pizza.
5. For lunch, Mean Monster gets $\frac{1}{2}$ of the sandwich. Color in $\frac{1}{2}$ of the sandwich.
6. He ate $\frac{1}{2}$ of the apple for lunch. Color in $\frac{1}{2}$ of the apple.

336 COMPLETE YEAR GRADE 2

336

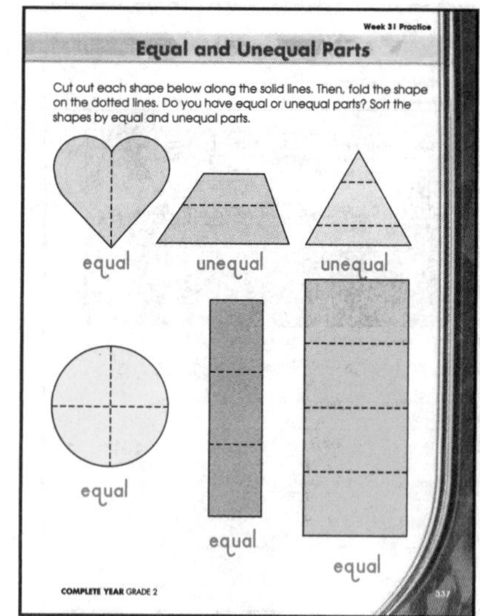

Week 31 Practice

Equal and Unequal Parts

Cut out each shape below along the solid lines. Then, fold the shape on the dotted lines. Do you have equal or unequal parts? Sort the shapes by equal and unequal parts.

COMPLETE YEAR GRADE 2 337

337

Week 32 Practice

Subjects of Sentences

The subject of a sentence tells who or what does something.

Example: Some people eat foods that may seem strange to you.

Underline the subject of each sentence.

1. Some people like crocodile steak.
2. The meat tastes like fish.
3. Australians eat kangaroo meat.
4. Kangaroo meat tastes like beef.
5. People in the Southwest eat rattlesnake meat.
6. Snails make a delicious treat for some people.
7. Some Africans think roasted termites are tasty.
8. Bird's-nest soup is a famous Chinese dish.
9. People in Florida serve alligator meat.
10. Almost everyone treats themselves with ice cream.

340 COMPLETE YEAR GRADE 2

340

Week 32 Practice

Sentence Sequence

Sentences can tell a story. Color, cut out and glue the pictures in order to tell a story. Write a sentence on each line that tells what is happening in the pictures.

Answers will vary.

COMPLETE YEAR GRADE 2 341

341

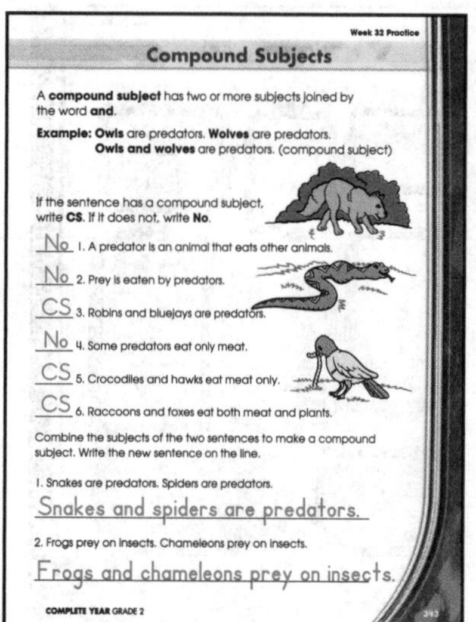

Week 32 Practice

Compound Subjects

A **compound subject** has two or more subjects joined by the word **and**.

Example: Owls are predators. **Wolves** are predators.
Owls and wolves are predators. (compound subject)

If the sentence has a compound subject, write **CS**. If it does not, write **No**.

No 1. A predator is an animal that eats other animals.
No 2. Prey is eaten by predators.
CS 3. Robins and bluejays are predators.
No 4. Some predators eat only meat.
CS 5. Crocodiles and hawks eat meat only.
CS 6. Raccoons and foxes eat both meat and plants.

Combine the subjects of the two sentences to make a compound subject. Write the new sentence on the line.

1. Snakes are predators. Spiders are predators.
Snakes and spiders are predators.

2. Frogs prey on insects. Chameleons prey on insects.
Frogs and chameleons prey on insects.

COMPLETE YEAR GRADE 2 343

343

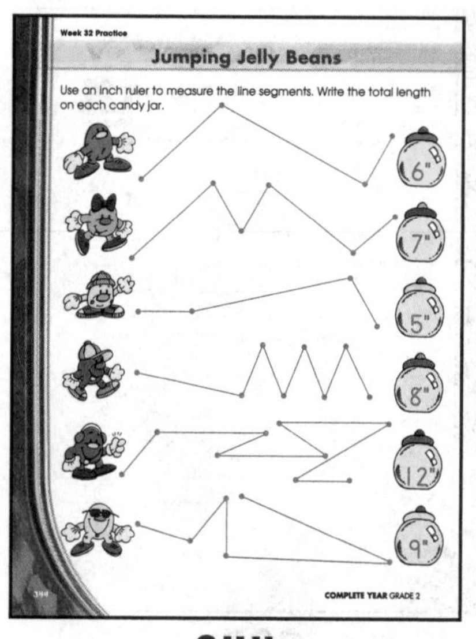

Week 32 Practice

Jumping Jelly Beans

Use an inch ruler to measure the line segments. Write the total length on each candy jar.

344 COMPLETE YEAR GRADE 2

344

Answer Key

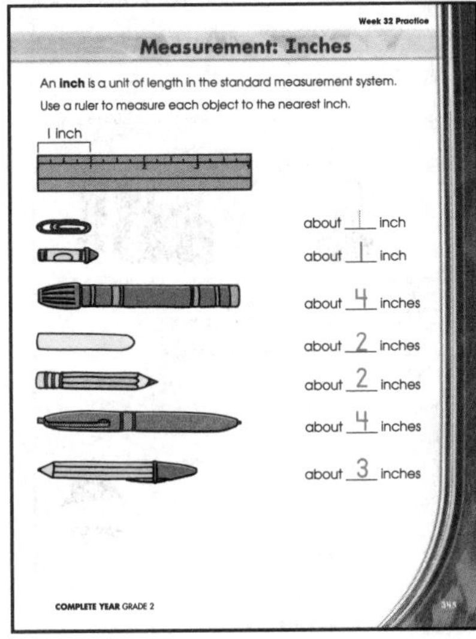

Week 32 Practice

Measurement: Inches

An **inch** is a unit of length in the standard measurement system.
Use a ruler to measure each object to the nearest inch.

1 inch

about 1 inch
about 1 inch
about 4 inches
about 2 inches
about 2 inches
about 4 inches
about 3 inches

COMPLETE YEAR GRADE 2 345

345

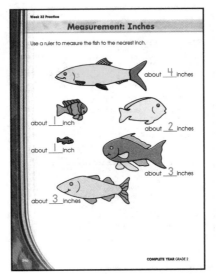

Week 32 Practice

Measurement: Inches

Use a ruler to measure the fish to the nearest inch.

about 4 inches
about 1 inch
about 2 inches
about 1 inch
about 3 inches
about 3 inches

346 COMPLETE YEAR GRADE 2

346

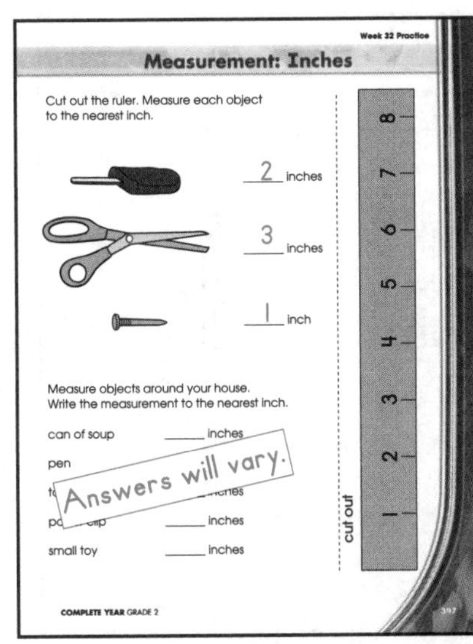

Week 32 Practice

Measurement: Inches

Cut out the ruler. Measure each object to the nearest inch.

2 inches
3 inches
1 inch

Measure objects around your house.
Write the measurement to the nearest inch.

can of soup ____ inches
pen ____ inches
t... ____ inches
pa... clip ____ inches
small toy ____ inches

Answers will vary.

cut out

1 2 3 4 5 6 7 8

COMPLETE YEAR GRADE 2 347

347

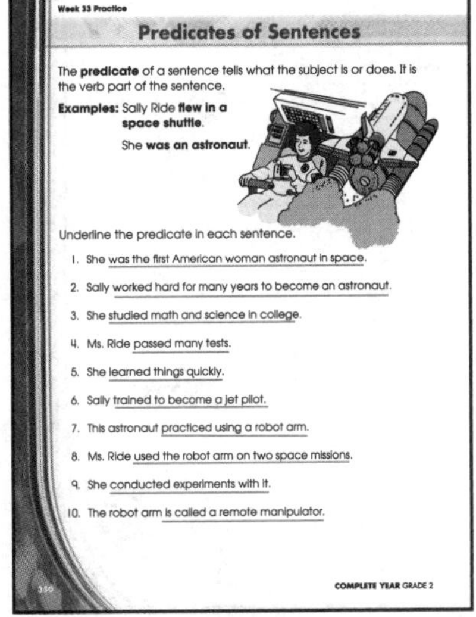

Week 33 Practice

Predicates of Sentences

The **predicate** of a sentence tells what the subject is or does. It is the verb part of the sentence.

Examples: Sally Ride **flew in a space shuttle.**
She **was an astronaut.**

Underline the predicate in each sentence.

1. She was the first American woman astronaut in space.
2. Sally worked hard for many years to become an astronaut.
3. She studied math and science in college.
4. Ms. Ride passed many tests.
5. She learned things quickly.
6. Sally trained to become a jet pilot.
7. This astronaut practiced using a robot arm.
8. Ms. Ride used the robot arm on two space missions.
9. She conducted experiments with it.
10. The robot arm is called a remote manipulator.

350 COMPLETE YEAR GRADE 2

350

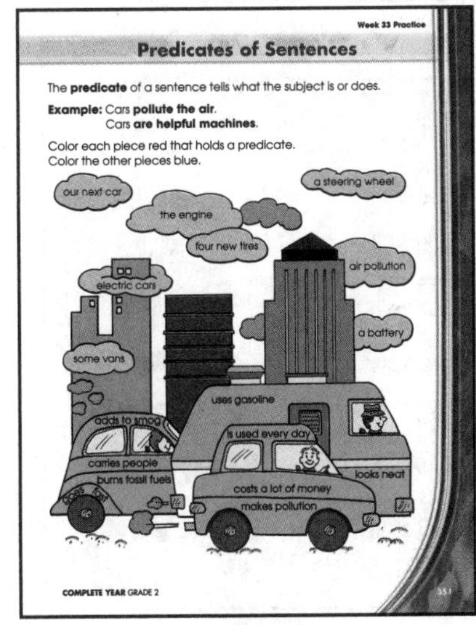

Week 33 Practice

Predicates of Sentences

The **predicate** of a sentence tells what the subject is or does.

Example: Cars **pollute the air.**
Cars **are helpful machines.**

Color each piece red that holds a predicate.
Color the other pieces blue.

COMPLETE YEAR GRADE 2 351

351

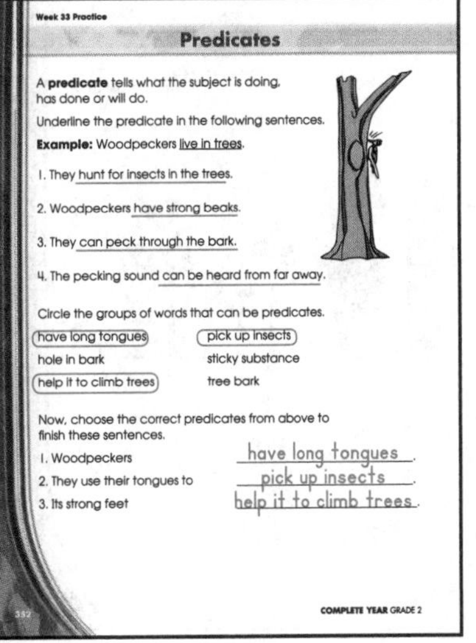

Week 33 Practice

Predicates

A **predicate** tells what the subject is doing, has done or will do.

Underline the predicate in the following sentences.

Example: Woodpeckers live in trees.

1. They hunt for insects in the trees.
2. Woodpeckers have strong beaks.
3. They can peck through the bark.
4. The pecking sound can be heard from far away.

Circle the groups of words that can be predicates.

have long tongues | pick up insects
hole in bark | sticky substance
help it to climb trees | tree bark

Now, choose the correct predicates from above to finish these sentences.

1. Woodpeckers have long tongues.
2. They use their tongues to pick up insects.
3. Its strong feet help it to climb trees.

352 COMPLETE YEAR GRADE 2

352

Answer Key

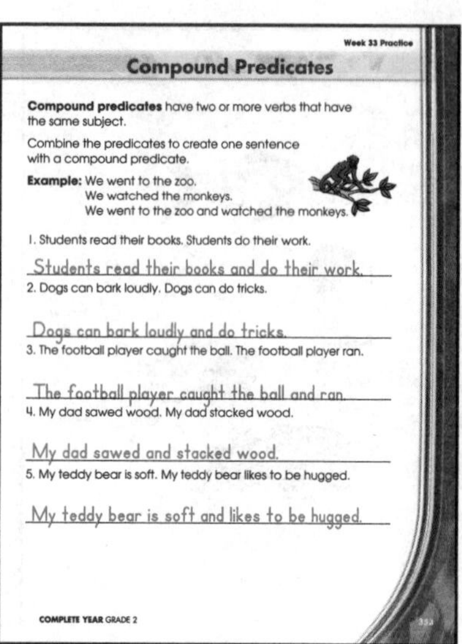

Week 33 Practice

Compound Predicates

Compound predicates have two or more verbs that have the same subject.

Combine the predicates to create one sentence with a compound predicate.

Example: We went to the zoo.
We watched the monkeys.
We went to the zoo and watched the monkeys.

1. Students read their books. Students do their work.
Students read their books and do their work.
2. Dogs can bark loudly. Dogs can do tricks.
Dogs can bark loudly and do tricks.
3. The football player caught the ball. The football player ran.
The football player caught the ball and ran.
4. My dad sawed wood. My dad stacked wood.
My dad sawed and stacked wood.
5. My teddy bear is soft. My teddy bear likes to be hugged.
My teddy bear is soft and likes to be hugged.

COMPLETE YEAR GRADE 2

353

Week 33 Practice

Compound Predicates

A **compound predicate** has two or more predicates joined by the word **and**.

Example: Abe Lincoln was born in Kentucky. Abe Lincoln lived in a log cabin there.
Abe Lincoln **was born in Kentucky and lived in a log cabin there.**

Kentucky

If the sentence has a compound predicate, write **CP**. If it does not, write **No**.

CP 1. Abe Lincoln cut trees and chopped wood.
No 2. Abe and his sister walked to a spring for water.
CP 3. Abe's family packed up and left Kentucky.
No 4. They crossed the Ohio River to Indiana.
No 5. Abe's father built a new home.
CP 6. Abe's mother became sick and died.
No 7. Mr. Lincoln married again.
CP 8. Abe's new mother loved Abe and his sister and cared for them.

COMPLETE YEAR GRADE 2

354

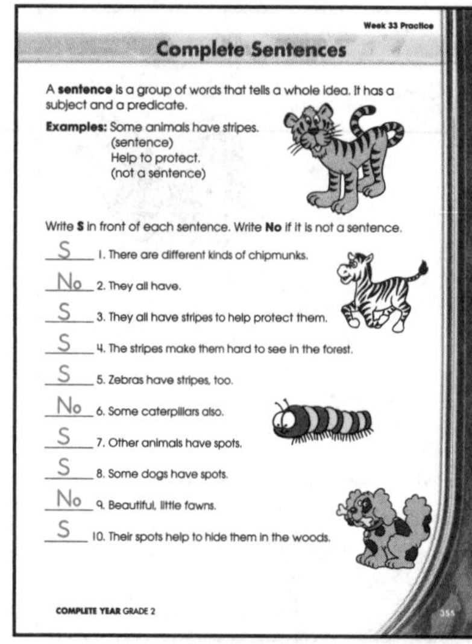

Week 33 Practice

Complete Sentences

A **sentence** is a group of words that tells a whole idea. It has a subject and a predicate.

Examples: Some animals have stripes.
(sentence)
Help to protect.
(not a sentence)

Write **S** in front of each sentence. Write **No** if it is not a sentence.

S 1. There are different kinds of chipmunks.
No 2. They all have.
S 3. They all have stripes to help protect them.
S 4. The stripes make them hard to see in the forest.
S 5. Zebras have stripes, too.
No 6. Some caterpillars also.
S 7. Other animals have spots.
S 8. Some dogs have spots.
No 9. Beautiful, little fawns.
S 10. Their spots help to hide them in the woods.

COMPLETE YEAR GRADE 2

355

Week 33 Practice

Measurement: Centimeters

A **centimeter** is a unit of length in the metric system. There are 2.54 centimeters in an inch.

Use a centimeter ruler to measure the crayons to the nearest centimeter.

Example: The first crayon is about 7 centimeters long.

about 7 centimeters
about 6 centimeters
about 1 centimeter
about 4 centimeters
about 2 centimeters
about 5 centimeters

COMPLETE YEAR GRADE 2

356

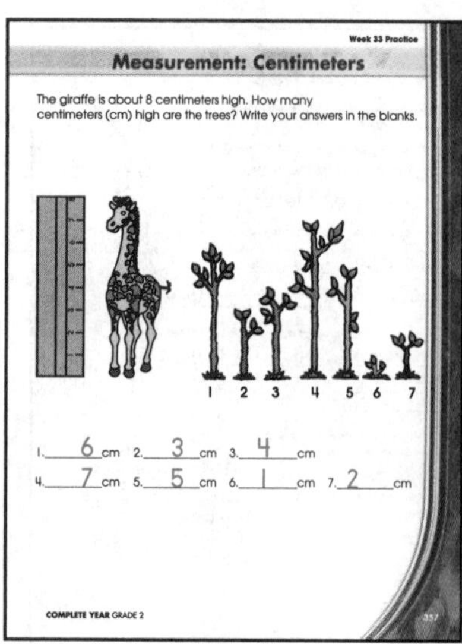

Week 33 Practice

Measurement: Centimeters

The giraffe is about 8 centimeters high. How many centimeters (cm) high are the trees? Write your answers in the blanks.

1 2 3 4 5 6 7

1. 6 cm 2. 3 cm 3. 4 cm
4. 7 cm 5. 5 cm 6. 1 cm 7. 2 cm

COMPLETE YEAR GRADE 2

357

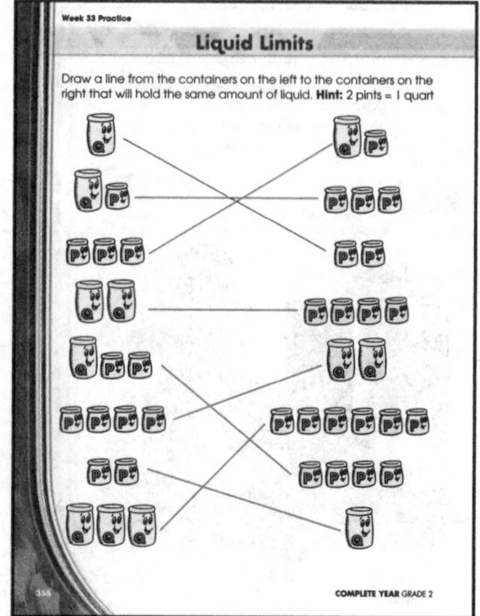

Week 33 Practice

Liquid Limits

Draw a line from the containers on the left to the containers on the right that will hold the same amount of liquid. **Hint:** 2 pints = 1 quart

COMPLETE YEAR GRADE 2

358

Answer Key

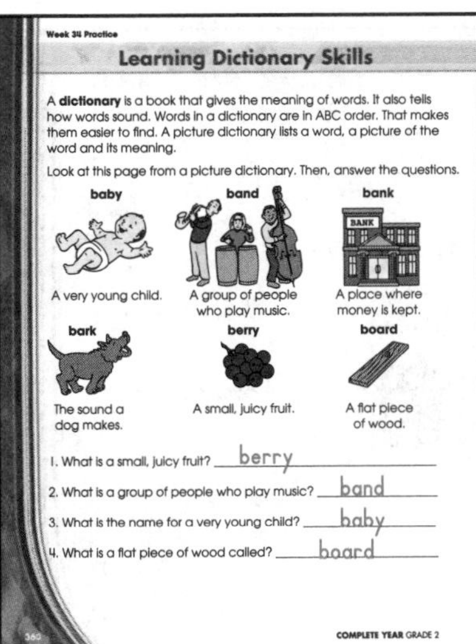
Week 34 Practice

Learning Dictionary Skills

A **dictionary** is a book that gives the meaning of words. It also tells how words sound. Words in a dictionary are in ABC order. That makes them easier to find. A picture dictionary lists a word, a picture of the word and its meaning.

Look at this page from a picture dictionary. Then, answer the questions.

baby — A very young child.
band — A group of people who play music.
bank — A place where money is kept.
bark — The sound a dog makes.
berry — A small, juicy fruit.
board — A flat piece of wood.

1. What is a small, juicy fruit? berry
2. What is a group of people who play music? band
3. What is the name for a very young child? baby
4. What is a flat piece of wood called? board

360 COMPLETE YEAR GRADE 2

360

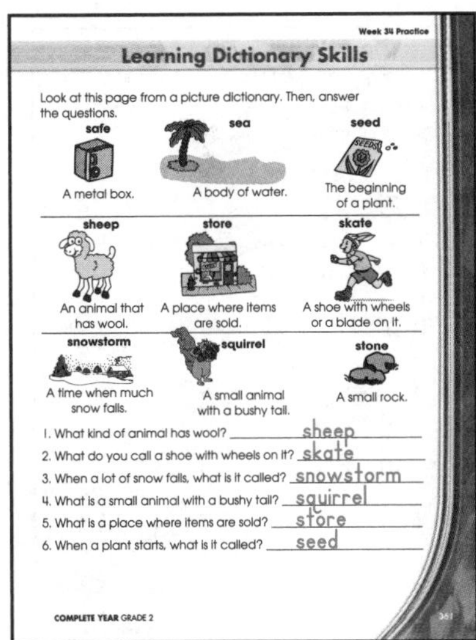
Week 34 Practice

Learning Dictionary Skills

Look at this page from a picture dictionary. Then, answer the questions.

safe — A metal box.
sea — A body of water.
seed — The beginning of a plant.
sheep — An animal that has wool.
store — A place where items are sold.
skate — A shoe with wheels or a blade on it.
snowstorm — A time when much snow falls.
squirrel — A small animal with a bushy tail.
stone — A small rock.

1. What kind of animal has wool? sheep
2. What do you call a shoe with wheels on it? skate
3. When a lot of snow falls, what is it called? snowstorm
4. What is a small animal with a bushy tail? squirrel
5. What is a place where items are sold? store
6. When a plant starts, what is it called? seed

COMPLETE YEAR GRADE 2 361

361

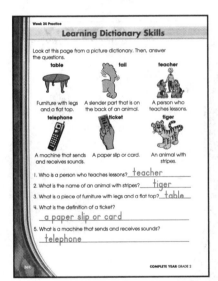

Week 34 Practice

Learning Dictionary Skills

Look at this page from a picture dictionary. Then, answer the questions.

table — Furniture with legs and a flat top.
tail — A slender part that is on the back of an animal.
teacher — A person who teaches lessons.
telephone — A machine that sends and receives sounds.
ticket — A paper slip or card.
tiger — An animal with stripes.

1. Who is a person who teaches lessons? teacher
2. What is the name of an animal with stripes? tiger
3. What is a piece of furniture with legs and a flat top? table
4. What is the definition of a ticket? a paper slip or card
5. What is a machine that sends and receives sounds? telephone

362 COMPLETE YEAR GRADE 2

362

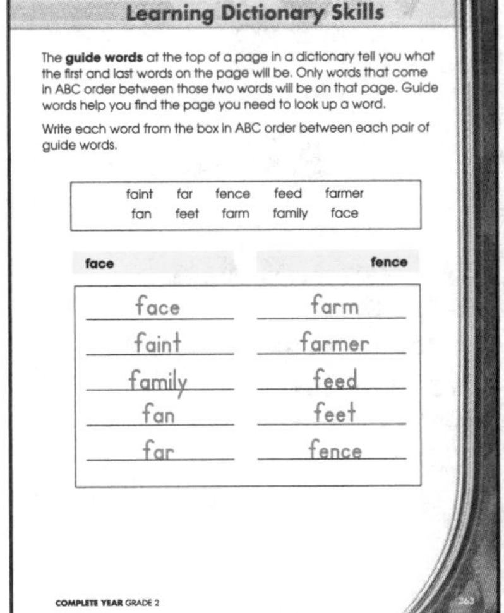
Week 34 Practice

Learning Dictionary Skills

The **guide words** at the top of a page in a dictionary tell you what the first and last words on the page will be. Only words that come in ABC order between those two words will be on that page. Guide words help you find the page you need to look up a word.

Write each word from the box in ABC order between each pair of guide words.

faint far fence feed farmer
fan feet farm family face

face — fence

face	farm
faint	farmer
family	feed
fan	feet
far	fence

COMPLETE YEAR GRADE 2 363

363

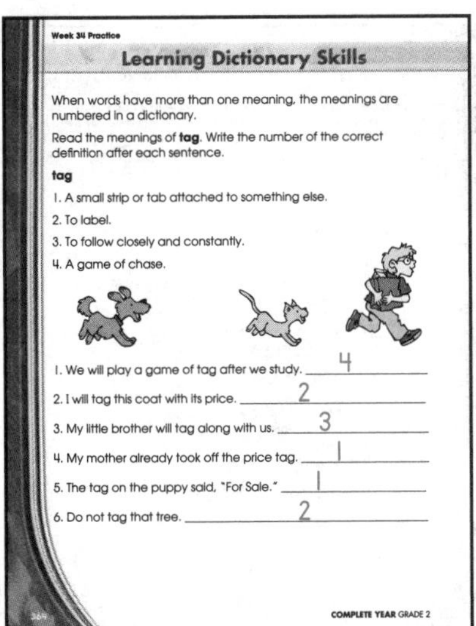
Week 34 Practice

Learning Dictionary Skills

When words have more than one meaning, the meanings are numbered in a dictionary.

Read the meanings of **tag**. Write the number of the correct definition after each sentence.

tag
1. A small strip or tab attached to something else.
2. To label.
3. To follow closely and constantly.
4. A game of chase.

1. We will play a game of tag after we study. 4
2. I will tag this coat with its price. 2
3. My little brother will tag along with us. 3
4. My mother already took off the price tag. 1
5. The tag on the puppy said, "For Sale." 1
6. Do not tag that tree. 2

364 COMPLETE YEAR GRADE 2

364

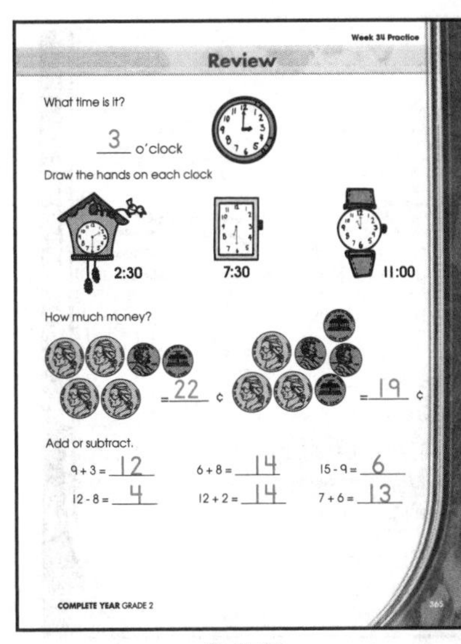
Week 34 Practice

Review

What time is it?

3 o'clock

Draw the hands on each clock.

2:30 7:30 11:00

How much money?

= 22 ¢ = 19 ¢

Add or subtract.

9 + 3 = 12 6 + 8 = 14 15 - 9 = 6
12 - 8 = 4 12 + 2 = 14 7 + 6 = 13

COMPLETE YEAR GRADE 2 365

365

Answer Key

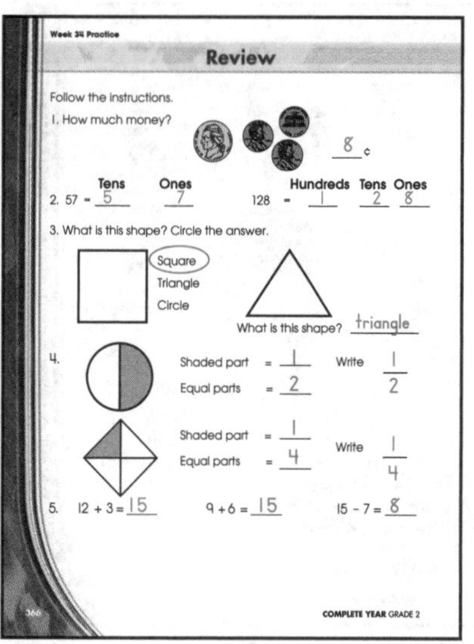
Week 34 Practice

Review

Follow the instructions.

1. How much money? 8 ¢

2. 57 = Tens 5 Ones 7 128 = Hundreds 1 Tens 2 Ones 8

3. What is this shape? Circle the answer.

Square (circled)
Triangle
Circle

What is this shape? triangle

4. Shaded part = 1 Equal parts = 2 Write $\frac{1}{2}$

Shaded part = 1 Equal parts = 4 Write $\frac{1}{4}$

5. 12 + 3 = 15 9 + 6 = 15 15 - 7 = 8

366 COMPLETE YEAR GRADE 2

366

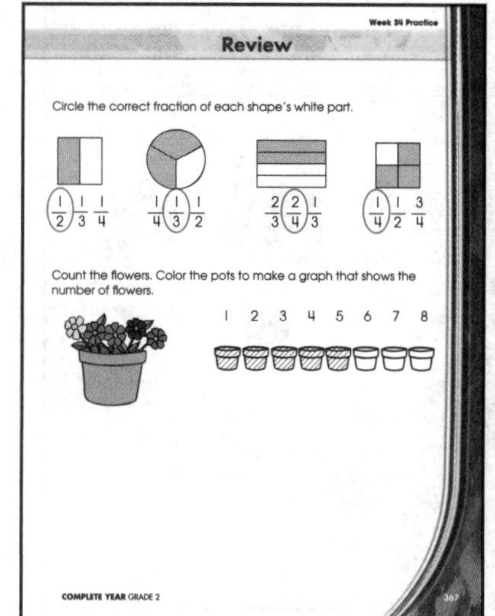
Week 34 Practice

Review

Circle the correct fraction of each shape's white part.

$\frac{1}{2}$ (circled) $\frac{1}{3}$ $\frac{1}{4}$ — $\frac{1}{4}$ $\frac{1}{3}$ (circled) $\frac{1}{2}$ — $\frac{2}{3}$ $\frac{2}{4}$ (circled) $\frac{1}{3}$ — $\frac{1}{4}$ (circled) $\frac{1}{2}$ $\frac{3}{4}$

Count the flowers. Color the pots to make a graph that shows the number of flowers.

1 2 3 4 5 6 7 8

COMPLETE YEAR GRADE 2 367

367

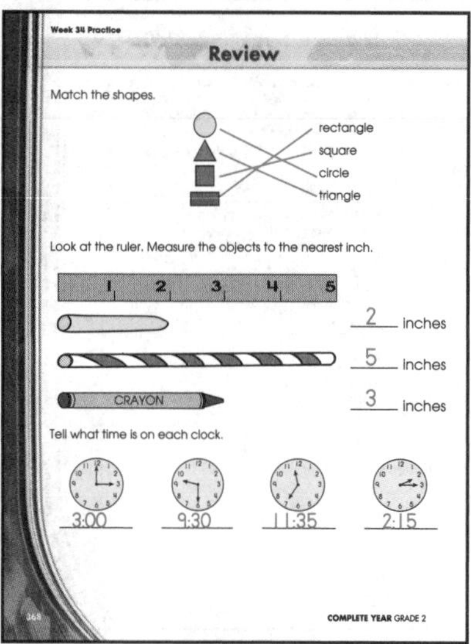
Week 34 Practice

Review

Match the shapes.

rectangle
square
circle
triangle

Look at the ruler. Measure the objects to the nearest inch.

1 2 3 4 5

2 inches

5 inches

CRAYON 3 inches

Tell what time is on each clock.

3:00 9:30 11:35 2:15

368 COMPLETE YEAR GRADE 2

368

Week 35 Practice

Following Directions: How to Treat a Ladybug

Read about how to treat ladybugs. Then, follow the instructions.

Ladybugs are shy. If you see a ladybug, sit very still. Hold out your arm. Maybe the ladybug will fly to you. If it does, talk softly. Do not touch it. It will fly away when it is ready.

1. Complete the directions on how to treat a ladybug.

a. Sit very still.

b. Hold out your arm.

c. Talk softly.

d. Do not touch it.

2. Ladybugs are red. They have black spots. Color the ladybug.

370 COMPLETE YEAR GRADE 2

370

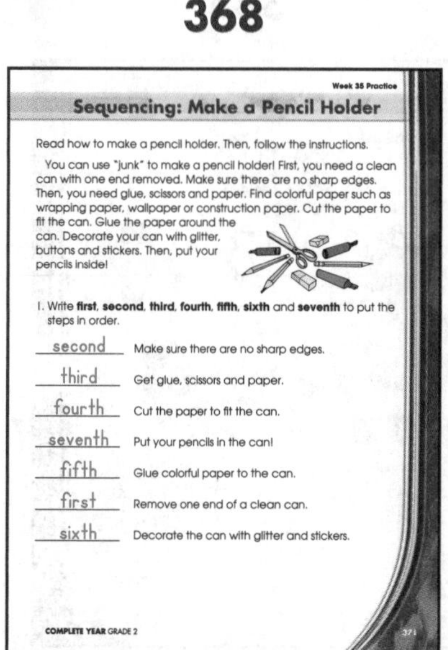
Week 35 Practice

Sequencing: Make a Pencil Holder

Read how to make a pencil holder. Then, follow the instructions.

You can use "junk" to make a pencil holder! First, you need a clean can with one end removed. Make sure there are no sharp edges. Then, you need glue, scissors and paper. Find colorful paper such as wrapping paper, wallpaper or construction paper. Cut the paper to fit the can. Glue the paper around the can. Decorate your can with glitter, buttons and stickers. Then, put your pencils inside!

1. Write **first**, **second**, **third**, **fourth**, **fifth**, **sixth** and **seventh** to put the steps in order.

second Make sure there are no sharp edges.

third Get glue, scissors and paper.

fourth Cut the paper to fit the can.

seventh Put your pencils in the can!

fifth Glue colorful paper to the can.

first Remove one end of a clean can.

sixth Decorate the can with glitter and stickers.

COMPLETE YEAR GRADE 2 371

371

Week 35 Practice

Sequencing: Follow a Recipe

Here is a recipe for chocolate peanut butter cookies. When you use a recipe, you must follow the directions carefully. The sentences below are not in the correct order.

Write the number **1** to show what you would do first. Then, number each step to show the correct sequence.

1 Melt the chocolate almond bark in a microsafe bowl.

6 Eat!

2 While the chocolate is melting, spread peanut butter on a cracker and place another cracker on top.

4 Let the melted candy drip off the cracker into the bowl before you place it on wax paper.

5 Let it cool!

3 Carefully use a fork or spoon to dip the crackers into the melted chocolate.

Try the recipe with an adult.

Do you like to cook? Answers will vary.

372 COMPLETE YEAR GRADE 2

372

Answer Key

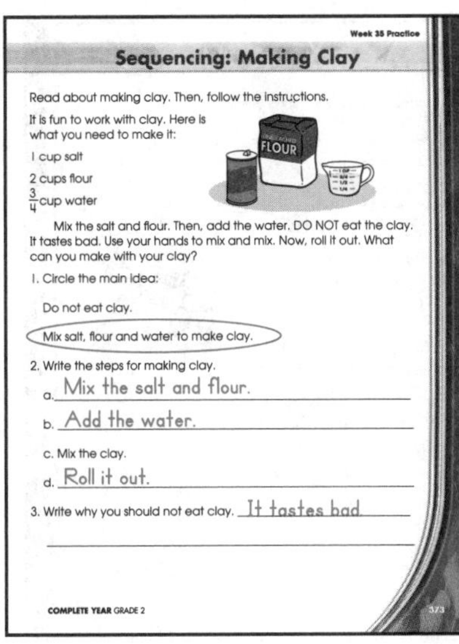

Week 35 Practice

Sequencing: Making Clay

Read about making clay. Then, follow the instructions.

It is fun to work with clay. Here is what you need to make it:

1 cup salt

2 cups flour

$\frac{3}{4}$ cup water

Mix the salt and flour. Then, add the water. DO NOT eat the clay. It tastes bad. Use your hands to mix and mix. Now, roll it out. What can you make with your clay?

1. Circle the main idea:

Do not eat clay.

Mix salt, flour and water to make clay. (circled)

2. Write the steps for making clay.

a. Mix the salt and flour.

b. Add the water.

c. Mix the clay.

d. Roll it out.

3. Write why you should not eat clay. It tastes bad

373

Week 35 Practice

Sequencing: Follow a Recipe

Alana and Marcus are hungry for a snack. They want to make nacho chips and cheese. The steps they need to follow are all mixed up.

Read the steps. Number them in 1, 2, 3 order. Then, color the picture.

5 Bake the chips in the oven for 2 minutes.

1 or 2 Get a cookie sheet to bake on.

1 or 2 Get out the nacho chips and cheese.

6 Eat the nachos and chips.

3 Put the chips on the cookie sheet.

4 Put grated cheese on the chips.

374

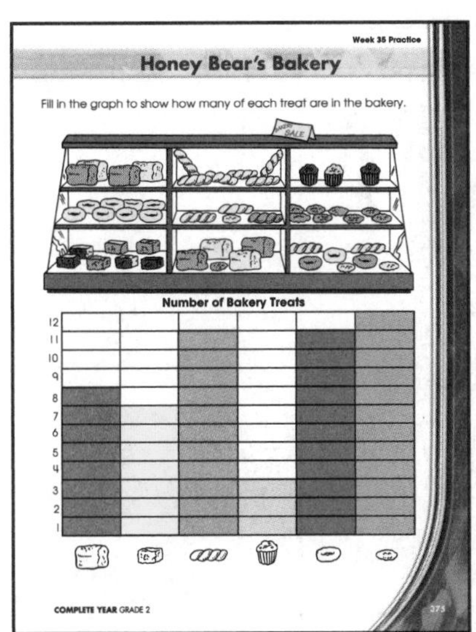

Week 35 Practice

Honey Bear's Bakery

Fill in the graph to show how many of each treat are in the bakery.

375

Week 35 Practice

Turtle Spots

Color the boxes to show how many spots are on each turtle's shell.

376

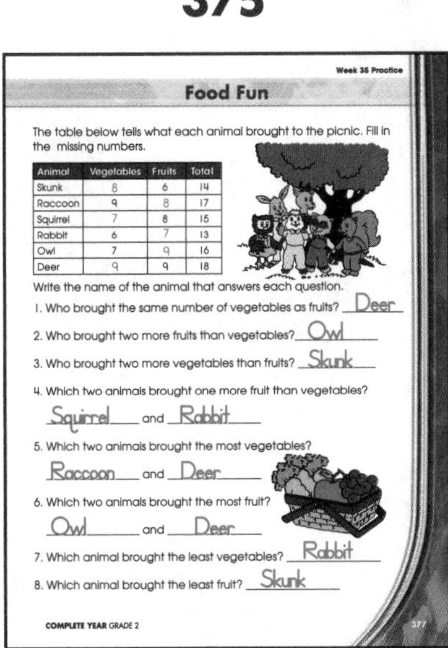

Week 35 Practice

Food Fun

The table below tells what each animal brought to the picnic. Fill in the missing numbers.

Animal	Vegetables	Fruits	Total
Skunk	8	6	14
Raccoon	9	8	17
Squirrel	7	8	15
Rabbit	6	7	13
Owl	7	9	16
Deer	9	9	18

Write the name of the animal that answers each question.

1. Who brought the same number of vegetables as fruits? Deer
2. Who brought two more fruits than vegetables? Owl
3. Who brought two more vegetables than fruits? Skunk
4. Which two animals brought one more fruit than vegetables? Squirrel and Rabbit
5. Which two animals brought the most vegetables? Raccoon and Deer
6. Which two animals brought the most fruit? Owl and Deer
7. Which animal brought the least vegetables? Rabbit
8. Which animal brought the least fruit? Skunk

377

Week 35 Practice

Television Survey

Ask five people h... they watch each day. ...ph. Refer to your graph t...

Answers will vary.

1. Which person watches the least TV? Sue
2. Which person watches the most TV? John
3. Did any people watch TV the same number of hours? No
4. What is the greatest number of hours that anyone watches? 5
5. About how many hours of TV do you watch each day? 3

378

Answer Key

Week 36 Practice

Fiction: Hercules

The **setting** is where a story takes place. The characters are the people in a story or play.

Read about Hercules. Then, answer the questions.

Hercules was born in the warm Atlantic Ocean. He was a very small and weak baby. He wanted to be the strongest hurricane in the world. But he had one problem. He couldn't blow 75-mile-per-hour winds. Hercules blew and blew in the ocean, until one day, his sister, Hola, told him it would be more fun to be a breeze than a hurricane. Hercules agreed. It was a breeze to be a breeze!

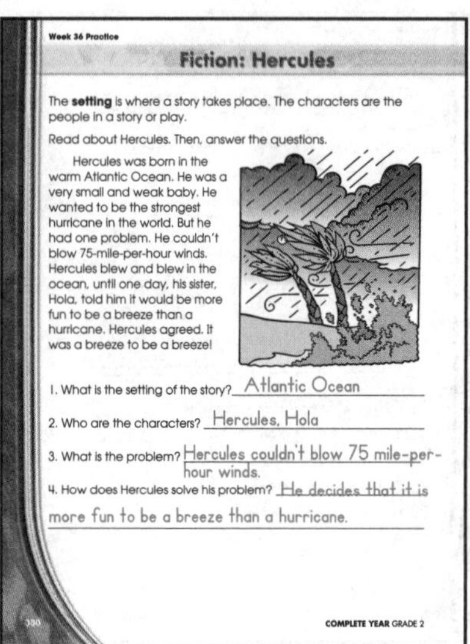

1. What is the setting of the story? Atlantic Ocean
2. Who are the characters? Hercules, Hola
3. What is the problem? Hercules couldn't blow 75 mile-per-hour winds.
4. How does Hercules solve his problem? He decides that it is more fun to be a breeze than a hurricane.

380 COMPLETE YEAR GRADE 2

380

Week 36 Practice

Comprehension: The Puppet Play

Read the play out loud with a friend. Then, answer the questions.

Pip: Hey, Pep. What kind of turkey eats very fast?

Pep: Uh, I don't know.

Pip: A gobbler!

Pep: I have a good joke for you, Pip. What kind of burger does a polar bear eat?

Pip: Uh, a cold burger?

Pep: No, an iceberg-er!

Pip: Hey, that was a great joke!

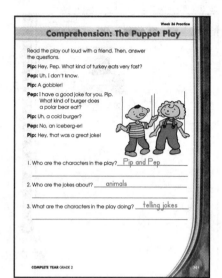

1. Who are the characters in the play? Pip and Pep
2. Who are the jokes about? animals
3. What are the characters in the play doing? telling jokes

COMPLETE YEAR GRADE 2 381

381

Week 36 Practice

Comprehension: Sean's Basketball Game

Read about Sean's basketball game. Then, answer the questions.

Sean really likes to play basketball. One sunny day, he decided to ask his friends to play basketball at the park, but there were six people—Sean, Aki, Lance, Kate, Zac and Oralia. A basketball team only allows five to play at a time. So, Sean decided to be the coach. Sean and his friends had fun.

1. How many kids wanted to play basketball? six
2. Write their names in ABC order:

   Aki Lance Sean
   Kate Oralia Zac

3. How many players can play on a basketball team at a time? five
4. Where did they play basketball? at the park
5. Who decided to be the coach? Sean

382 COMPLETE YEAR GRADE 2

382

Answer Key

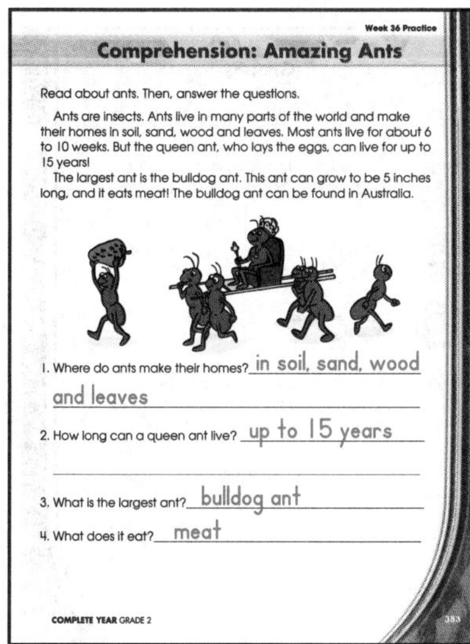

Week 36 Practice

Comprehension: Amazing Ants

Read about ants. Then, answer the questions.

Ants are insects. Ants live in many parts of the world and make their homes in soil, sand, wood and leaves. Most ants live for about 6 to 10 weeks. But the queen ant, who lays the eggs, can live for up to 15 years!

The largest ant is the bulldog ant. This ant can grow to be 5 inches long, and it eats meat! The bulldog ant can be found in Australia.

1. Where do ants make their homes? in soil, sand, wood and leaves
2. How long can a queen ant live? up to 15 years
3. What is the largest ant? bulldog ant
4. What does it eat? meat

COMPLETE YEAR GRADE 2 383

383

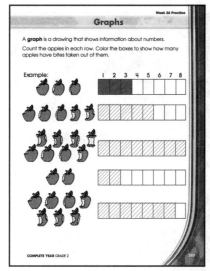

Week 36 Practice

Comprehension: Dirty Dogs

Read about dogs. Then, answer the questions.

Like people, dogs get dirty. Some dogs get a bath once a month. Baby soap is a good soap for cleaning dogs. Fill a tub with warm water. Get someone to hold the dog still in the tub. Then, wash the dog fast.

1. How often do some dogs get a bath? once a month
2. What is a good soap to use on dogs? baby soap
3. Do you think most dogs like to take baths? no

384 COMPLETE YEAR GRADE 2

384

Week 36 Practice

Graphs

A **graph** is a drawing that shows information about numbers.

Count the apples in each row. Color the boxes to show how many apples have bites taken out of them.

Example: 1 2 3 4 5 6 7 8

COMPLETE YEAR GRADE 2 385

385

Answer Key

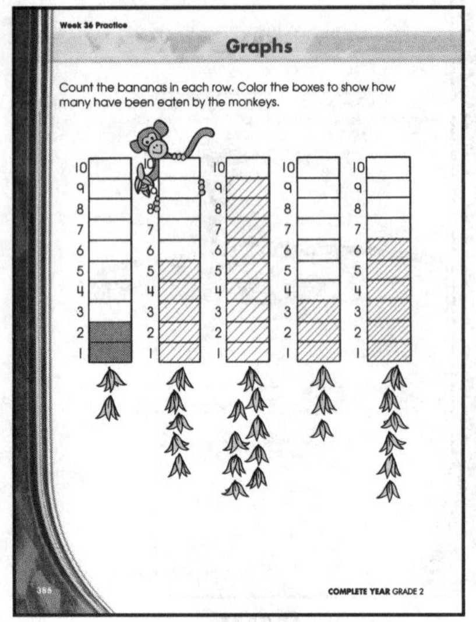
Week 36 Practice

Graphs

Count the bananas in each row. Color the boxes to show how many have been eaten by the monkeys.

COMPLETE YEAR GRADE 2

386

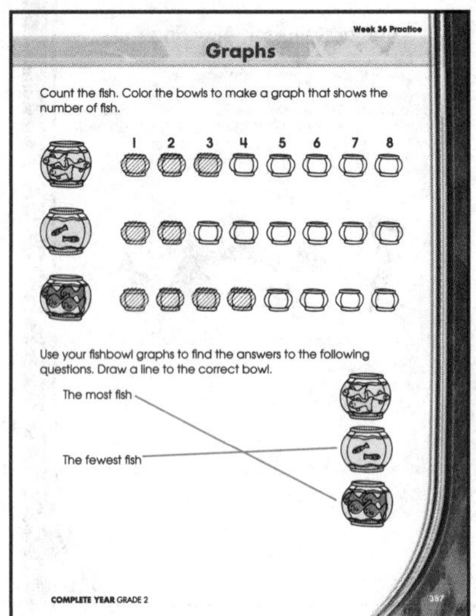
Week 36 Practice

Graphs

Count the fish. Color the bowls to make a graph that shows the number of fish.

1 2 3 4 5 6 7 8

Use your fishbowl graphs to find the answers to the following questions. Draw a line to the correct bowl.

The most fish

The fewest fish

COMPLETE YEAR GRADE 2

387

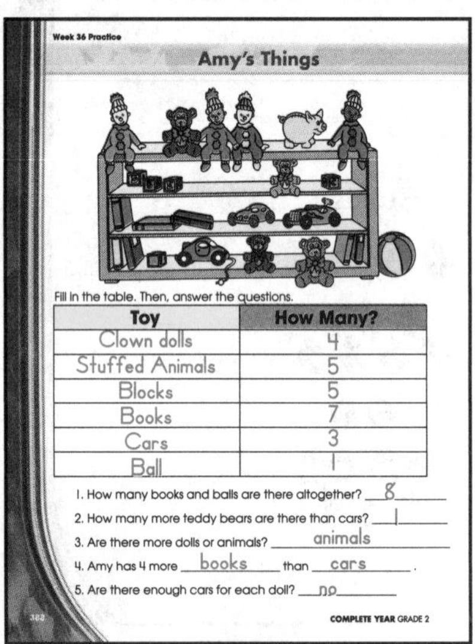
Week 36 Practice

Amy's Things

Fill in the table. Then, answer the questions.

Toy	How Many?
Clown dolls	4
Stuffed Animals	5
Blocks	5
Books	7
Cars	3
Ball	1

1. How many books and balls are there altogether? 8
2. How many more teddy bears are there than cars? 1
3. Are there more dolls or animals? animals
4. Amy has 4 more books than cars.
5. Are there enough cars for each doll? no

COMPLETE YEAR GRADE 2

388